JOURNALISM TODAY!

FOURTH EDITION

JOURNALISM TODAY!

DONALD L. FERGUSON
JIM PATTEN

National Textbook Company
a division of *NTC Publishing Group* • Lincolnwood, Illinois USA

Cover and interior design
Ophelia M. Chambliss-Jones

Cover photo credits
Front cover
Left: The Bettman Archive
Top right: Jeff Ellis
Middle right: Jeff Ellis, with permission of the *Chicago Sun-Times*
Bottom right: ©1993, *Chicago Tribune*

Back cover
Top left: Bradley Wilson
Bottom left: Jeff Ellis, with permission of the *Chicago Sun-Times*
Top right: Taylor Publishing, Dallas, Texas
Bottom right: Brent Jones/Marilyn Gartman Agency, Chicago

1994 Printing

Published by National Textbook Company, a division of NTC Publishing Group.
©1993 by NTC Publishing Group, 4255 West Touhy Avenue.
Lincolnwood (Chicago), Illinois 60646-1975 U.S.A.
Library of Congress Catalog Card Number: 91-60644
Manufactured in the United States of America.

3 4 5 6 7 8 9 AG 9 8 7 6 5 4 3

CONTENTS

Section 2   Gathering the News   55

Section 4   Writing Features, Sports, and Editorials   161

Section 5   Producing the School Newspaper 237

Section 6   Beyond the Newspaper   317

Section 7   Understanding the Technology   359

Acknowledgments

The authors wish to thank the following advisers, journalism instructors and school newspaper staffs for their generous help in preparing this edition of *Journalism Today!*

Reviewers— Advisers and Instructors

Betty Bell, Skyline High School, Dallas, Texas

Phyllis Forehand, Arlington (Texas) High School

Jack Harkrider, L. C. Anderson Publications, Anderson High School, Austin, Texas

Bernard Hupperts, Kaukauna (Wis.) High School

Patrick McCarthy, Lake Braddock Secondary School, Burke, Va.

Shirley Moravec, Clearwater (Fla.) High School

Leslie J. Nicholas, Wyoming Valley West High School, Plymouth, Pa.

Student Publications

The Arlingtonian, Upper Arlington (Ohio) High School

The Bear Facts, Hastings High School, Alief, Texas

Big Stick, Roosevelt High School, San Antonio, Texas

Blue Jay Free Flyer, Worthington (Minn.) Community College

Bugle Call, R. E. Lee High School, San Antonio, Texas

The Devil's Advocate, Hinsdale (Ill.) Central High School

The Epitaph, Homestead High School, Cupertino, Calif.

The Evanstonian, Evanston (Ill.) Township High School

The Fourth Write, San Antonio (Texas) College

Gateway Medallion, Gateway High School, Aurora, Colo.

Hi-Spot, Waverly (Neb.) High School

The Hobachi, Redlands (Calif.) Senior High School

The Journal, Parkersburg (W. Va.) High School

Leaves Yearbook, Sherwood High School, Sandy Spring, Md.

The Lion, Lyons (Ill.) Township High School

The Mirror, Monterey High School, Lubbock, Texas

The Oracle, East High School, Lincoln, Neb.

The Palantir, Canyon del Oro High School, Tucson, Ariz.

The Railsplitter, Lincoln High School, Des Moines, Iowa

The Skyline Oracle, Skyline High School, Oakland, Calif.

The Rustler, Fremont (Neb.) Senior High School

The Texan Times, Wimberley (Texas) High School

Tiger Tales, Joliet (Ill.) Township High School, West Campus

The Tower, Grosse Pointe South (Mich.) High School

The Viking Vanguard, Puyallup (Wash.) High School

The X-Ray, St. Charles (Ill.) High School

University Journalism Workshops/ Publication

Marquette University (Wis.) Summer Journalism Workshop (*Teen Perspective*)
University of Nebraska Journalism Workshop (*The All-Stater*)
University of Texas at Austin Summer Journalism Workshop (*Texas Achiever*)
Western Kentucky University, Bowling Green, Minority Journalism Workshop (*Limited Edition*)

Grateful acknowledgment is also made to the following professional journalists, publications and associations:

American Society of Newspaper
 Editors
The Arizona Daily Star (Tucson)
Associated Collegiate Press
Associated Press
Chicago Sun-Times
Chicago Tribune
The Denver Post

Intercollegiate Broadcast System
National Scholastic Press Association
The New York Times
Public Relations Society of America
Seattle Times
Society of Professional Journalists
United Press International
USA Today

And thanks to the following people who assisted in important ways to make this book possible: Terry Anderson; Jody Beck; Jack Botts; Linda Butler; Dr. Loyal N. Gould and B. C. Raffety, Baylor University; Prof. C. Bickford Lucas, University of Arizona; Susan Bridges Patten; Thomas L. Pendleton; Laura Plachecki; Mary Kay Quinlan; Jacqueline Sharkey; Stephen A. Smith; and Holly Spence.

Photographs

The authors wish to thank the students and staff of Evanston (Ill.) Township High School, Maine West Township High School, Des Plaines, Ill.; Wimberley (Texas) High School; and De Paul University, Chicago, Ill., for their cooperation in photographic illustration of this book.

Jeff Ellis, Photographer, pages 6, 7, 22, 23, 33, 54, 55, 64, 68, 78, 81, 86, 99, 100, 111, 122, 128, 146, 160, 161, 166, 175, 187, 199, 202, 204, 205, 214, 218, 223, 236, 237, 239, 245, 255, 267, 269, 271, 272, 277, 279, 285, 289, 297, 300, 306, 308, 316, 317, 322, 325, 339, 349, 358, 359, 365, 367, 371, 379, 384
Root Photographers, Chicago, Ill., pages 196, 276
Bradley Wilson, Photographer, pages 156, 157, 158, 159

Acknowledgment is also made to the following:
Aldus Corporation, page 380; AP/Wide World Photos, pages 37, 47, 57, 62, 125, 165; The Bettman Archive, pages 20, 46, 151; The Boeing Company, pages 171, 172; Delta Queen Steamboat Company, page 133; Ed Fischer, page 226; National Aeronautics and Space Administration, pages 19, 29, 108; North Central College (Naperville, Ill.) WONC-FM, page 337; Roosevelt University Multicultural Journalism Center, page 186; Mike Royko, *Chicago Tribune*, page 225; David Samson, Levi Strauss & Co., Foote, Cone & Belding, San Francisco, Calif., pages 301, 302, 303, 304, 305; The Taylor Publishing Company, pages 319, 330, 331; Telephoto, page 88; United States Information Agency, page 18; WGN-TV, Chicago, page 343.

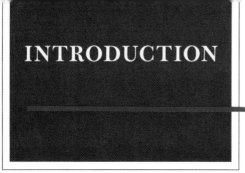

INTRODUCTION

When this book first appeared, about the time today's scholastic journalists had just started walking, Richard Nixon was president of the United States and Spiro Agnew was vice president. No one had ever heard of AIDS. Or of glasnost. Or of the Space Shuttle. Or of *USA Today*. Or of the Hazelwood decision. The Iran hostage crisis was in the future. So was the Iran-Contra affair. Network television dominated living rooms because satellite TV dishes, VCRs, and personal computers had not yet made their appearance. The Vietnam War was on, and Watergate was yet to come. The feminist movement's impact was just beginning to be felt, and no one yet worried that *Journalism for Today!*, as it was titled then, was written as though all journalists and all journalism students were men.

So much has changed. And yet so much remains the same. The following is from the 1972 introduction to this book. The thoughts are as valid now as they were then:

> The authors believe there is no subject that needs understanding more than journalism. The mass media today wield an enormous influence over daily life in this country. While they do not mold men's minds in the fashion once suspected, they do provide the information upon which persons in a democratic society can base their decisions, both in the polling place and the marketplace. It is essential that this information be as pure and untainted as human beings can make it. When the press errs, all of society lives with the mistake.

Massive technological developments have done little to change the job facing journalists as the twenty-first century approaches. The rules are the same: Journalists have to provide high-fidelity information to busy people. The information has to be concise and objective, attractively packaged, honest, fair, and worthwhile. The job was difficult two hundred years ago, and it is difficult now. What we used to do with creaky typewriters, we now do with computers and desktop publishing tools. But it would not matter if we were still using quill pens. The fundamental job is unchanged.

Journalism Today! explores the developments and reflects the new technology, but not at the expense of the basics. Writing remains at the core of everything journalists do, and writing remains a major emphasis of the book.

Print journalism, and basically that means newspapers, continues to dominate the book. Although it is true that the newspaper business has shrunk, it remains one of the most profitable industries in the country—and one of the biggest employers.

Although many newspapers (mostly afternoon papers) have died, many others have been born. And TV, radio, magazines, public relations, advertising, design, photography, and other information-gathering and -distributing careers are alive and well. The new technologies in many cases made news gathering, editing, and production in all media less costly and more efficient. There is no need for pessimism about the future of journalism.

There is a need to understand change. For whatever reason—and most scholars cite *USA Today*—newspapers are different now than they were at the first edition of this book. Newspaper stories are shorter. There is new reliance on the charts, graphics, maps, and design elements produced so easily with good desktop and computer equipment. Newspapers use more color, and they are easier to read. Progress is even being made in developing ink that does not rub off and get your hands dirty while you read!

Somewhat overlooked among all these positive changes is one that alarms some people. Traditionally, journalists have devoted their greatest attention to covering government. This book has asserted in the past, and does so again in this edition, that covering government is the foremost responsibility of journalism. This responsibility is imposed by the special freedom journalists enjoy under the First Amendment to the Constitution. Today there is evidence that the obligation to cover government is being followed less than in the past. More newspaper space and radio and TV time is devoted to so-called soft news: stories about health, changing lifestyles and relationships, consumer stories, features of all kinds. Such stories, in and of themselves, represent no problem. They are valuable for transmitting information—and for interesting hard-to-attract readers, especially those of the younger generation. But no nation can do well unless its citizens understand and monitor the activities of government.

Perhaps nowhere has change been more evident than in scholastic journalism. There was a time when student journalists were less sophisticated than they are now. Sports, homecoming royalty, cheerleader selections, and an occasional interview with the year's international exchange student were the usual fare. Although these stories are still covered, as they should be, most student journalists exhibit a more sophisticated approach to the news, covering issues of real concern to a real audience. Like commercial newspapers, a school newspaper ultimately will reflect the environment in which it is produced. Today this means school papers address the issues most important to their readers. It also means that school newspapers, like their commercial counterparts, are more ethical, more conscientious, more thorough, and more responsible than in the past.

No discussion of scholastic journalism today would be complete without an examination of the Hazelwood decision. The impact of this 1988 U.S. Supreme Court ruling is still being felt. Some scholars feel it will change the nature of scholastic journalism and, ultimately, of commercial journalism. Others doubt the ruling will have much impact at all. One effect is certain: At no other time in the history of scholastic journalism have so many students been aware of the issues that face them. Self-examination is under way everywhere as students, advisers, and school administrators grapple with the new situation.

On Hazelwood as well as all other journalistic questions, we believe *Journalism Today!* can be a valuable resource for scholastic journalists of the waning days of this century. Journalists now in school will be in charge in the studios and newsrooms of the next century. The time for preparation is now. The future looks exciting.

Other changes are occurring in modern journalism. More and more opportunities are developing for members of minorities, and for women. The profession is strongly emphasizing minority recruitment, including recruitment in secondary schools. Qualified women, African Americans, Hispanics, Native Americans, Puerto Ricans, Asians, and other minority people are finding doors opening to them that used to be closed.

Salaries for journalists are rising. This has been a true revolution. Where once journalists almost took pride in their low salaries, today a professional journalist usually earns a respectable salary. The best publishers and station owners know they must pay well to attract top talent, and they are beginning to do it. As a result, more and more of the most talented young men and women in colleges and universities are choosing journalism as a major. University journalism education is maturing as well, recognizing and reemphasizing the importance of a liberal education.

Journalism Today! is no substitute for an enthusiastic adviser and a committed student. The burden remains theirs. Our activities are designed to start students writing real stories about real people almost at once. We are short on formulas, long on pushing students to think and experiment. We ask students to work hard, but we think the results will be worth it.

Donald L. Ferguson
Jim Patten

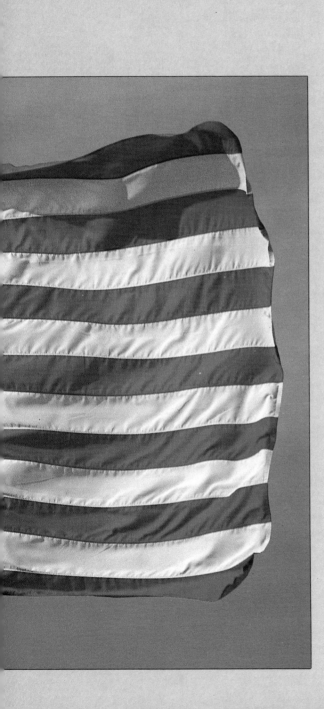

Journalism in a Democracy

THE HISTORY
OF AMERICAN
MEDIA

At this moment, you have within your reach any number of books, magazines, radio and television programs, musical recordings, and movies to show on a videocassette recorder. You may have information stored in a personal computer or in one of thousands of databases available to subscribers—not to mention newspapers of many kinds. You may even have a satellite dish in your backyard or on your roof, pulling television signals from the sky—including the sky over neighboring Canada and Mexico.

If you had lived in colonial America—indeed, if you had lived only fifty years ago—you would see how far we have come in journalism and in information processing.

Today, the whole world knows within minutes when a world leader dies or when the major powers on earth look up and see peace and democracy breaking out almost everywhere. But the colonists and the North American Indians of the seventeenth century were information paupers who rarely saw a newspaper. Communication was by letter and word of mouth.

America's history is inseparable from the history of its journalism. Early newspapers printed essays that stirred the revolutionaries and that chronicled the historic break from England. Today, journalists still help set the agenda. It has been said, in fact, that although journalists don't tell us *what* to think, they do tell us what to think *about*. They help a democratic nation make historic decisions by providing the facts and opinions needed to elect the leaders who decide national policy.

America's First Newspapers

The first American newspapers didn't look like the colorful, thick papers you see today. Often they were only one sheet long and contained little of what you think of as news. Letters, essays, material borrowed from whatever source an editor could find—

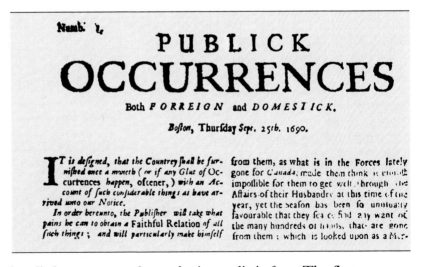

but little news—made up the journalistic fare. The first newspaper, *Publick Occurrences*, was published in Boston in 1690 by Benjamin Harris. After only one issue, the British colonial authorities suppressed the paper because they didn't like what Harris printed.

Fourteen years later the colonies had their first continuously published newspaper: the *Boston News-Letter*, started by John

Campbell in 1704. It was published "by authority," meaning it had the government's approval. Soon, though, as pioneers moved south and west, more newspapers cropped up. Most carried the "by authority" tag and were closely supervised by the British government.

Freedom of the Press

In those days, newspapers that attempted to criticize the government were guilty of sedition, the stirring of rebellion. The truth of their statements was no defense. In fact, the principle then was, "The greater the truth, the greater the libel." The government figured that false criticism was easier to turn aside than well-founded criticism.

A case in 1735 established truth as a defense against libel charges. In the *New York Weekly Journal*, John Peter Zenger printed articles critical of Governor William Cosby. The newspaper acted as a voice for the rising Whig (commercial) party. Zenger did not write most of the articles himself, but as the publisher he was arrested on a charge of seditious libel. Zenger was jailed on November 17, 1734, but did not come to trial until August 4, 1735. (The right to a speedy trial had not yet been secured.)

The case was considered open-and-shut. If Zenger printed attacks on the British crown, he was guilty of libel, even if his statements were true.

Andrew Hamilton of Philadelphia, considered by many the finest attorney of the period, defended Zenger. Then in his eighties, Hamilton was still brilliant and forceful. He stunned the crowd

In the Zenger case, lawyer Andrew Hamilton defended his client against libel charges, establishing truth as a defense.

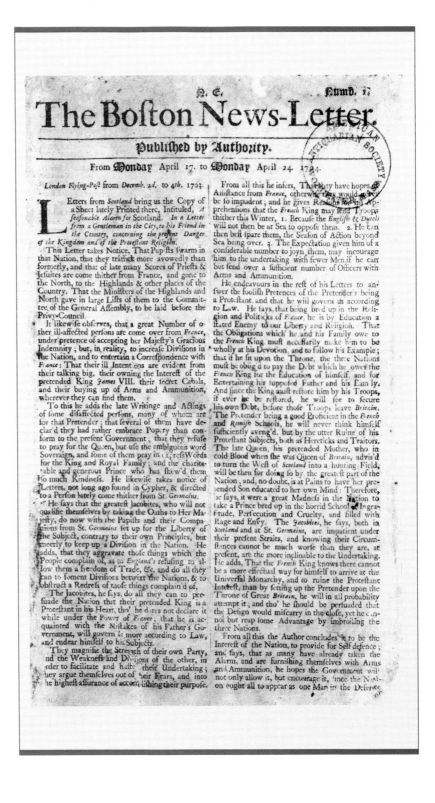

The *Boston News-Letter* was the first continuously-published newspaper in the New World.

when he said: "I do confess (for my client) that he both printed and published the two newspapers set forth in the information. I hope in so doing he has committed no crime."

To the court this seemed in effect a guilty plea, since its only concern was to prove that Zenger was responsible for publishing the articles in question. But Hamilton continued, "I hope it is not our bare printing or publishing a paper that will make it a libel. For the words themselves must be libelous—that is, false, malicious, and seditious—or else we are not guilty."

The judge denied Hamilton the right to prove the facts in the papers, so he appealed to the jury: "Every man who prefers freedom to a life of slavery will bless and honor you as men who have baffled the attempt of tyranny; and by an impartial and uncorrupt verdict, have laid a noble foundation for securing to ourselves, our posterity and our neighbors, that to which nature and the laws of our country have given us a right—the liberty both of exposing and opposing arbitrary power (in these parts of the world, at least) by speaking and writing—Truth."

The Crown had not counted on the will of people struggling to be free, in this case represented by the jurors. They deliberated only briefly before shouting "not guilty," and the celebrations began.

> *"Were it left to me to decide*
> *whether we should have a*
> *government without newspapers*
> *or newspapers without a government,*
> *I should not hesitate*
> *to prefer the latter."*
>
> *Thomas Jefferson*

The Birth of the Nation

The Zenger trial fanned the flames of freedom that were beginning to burn in the colonies. The colonial press of the day played a vital role in the birth of the nation. By 1775, when the Revolution began, thirty-seven newspapers were being published. These newspapers generally allied themselves with the patriots, at least partly because of their anger over the Stamp Act. They backed the Revolution and printed the cries to battle that rallied the rebels. In fact, some historians believe there would not have been a Revolution without the support of the press.

Newspapers then, and for the next century, lined up deliberately with political parties. This was the era of the partisan press. Readers who supported the fight for independence bought a Whig newspaper; those who were loyal to the British Crown bought a Tory paper. (Most papers today try to report political news objectively, although some ally themselves with a particular party on the editorial page.)

When the war ended and the Constitutional Convention met in Philadelphia, the framers did not, as many people believe, spend much time on the question of freedom of the press. The Constitution made no mention of a free press, because most state constitutions already covered the matter. But the Bill of Rights—the first ten amendments to the Constitution—was ratified in 1791. The First Amendment guarantees a free press with the words, ''Congress shall make no law . . . abridging the freedom of speech, or of the press.''

After the Revolution, the young nation grew rapidly, and so did the newspaper industry. Hundreds of newspapers opened all over the land. The first daily, the *Pennsylvania Evening Post*, was founded in 1783. Even small towns had papers, put out by printers who had to set the type one letter at a time by hand. The presses were clumsy, but the Industrial Revolution was at hand, and soon newspapers joined in a race for better technology, a race that continues in this century.

The Penny Press

The early newspapers carried little actual news. They were filled largely with essays, letters, editorials, and a few advertisements. Then in 1833 Benjamin Day founded the *New York Sun*, filled it with news, and sold it for only a penny. Day's staff covered the police beat, wrote about tragedies and natural disasters, and toned down the opinions. Thus was born the ''penny press,'' probably more truly the forerunner of today's newspapers than either *Publick Occurrences* or the *Boston News-Letter*.

Because it was so inexpensive and distributed by street sales rather than subscription, the penny press achieved a mass audience, made up primarily of the new working class of the Industrial Revolution. For the first time, too, advertising took on a major role. (To this day, it is advertising that pays the cost of producing newspapers and getting newscasts on the air.)

Two years later James Gordon Bennett started the *New York Morning Herald*. Although it sold for two cents, it continued the newsy ways of the *Sun*. Similar papers were soon founded in Boston, Baltimore, Philadelphia, and other cities.

One of the most influential penny presses was the *New York Tribune*, founded in 1841 by Horace Greeley. The *Tribune's* daily circulation never matched that of the *Sun* or the *Herald*, but its weekly edition had 200,000 subscribers—more readers than any other publication of that time.

Women had contributed to the growth and development of American journalism since Colonial times, operating newspapers and print shops. As the nation changed, so did the role of women. Cornelia Walter was editor of the *Boston Transcript* in the 1840s, and Jane Grey Swisshelm became the first woman to cover Congress, in 1850, working for Greeley's *Tribune*.

The *New York Times*, which today is usually considered the best newspaper in the country by professional journalists, was founded in 1851 by Henry Raymond. Until Adolph Ochs bought it in 1896, the *Times* was always in a precarious financial position. From the beginning, however, it set a standard for fairness and accuracy in reporting, a standard that has been widely imitated but rarely equaled.

In cities like Pittsburgh, Chicago, New Orleans, Atlanta, St. Louis, and Louisville, the penny press grew and prospered. Headlines grew larger and designs better as newspapers competed for street sales. It was not at all unusual for a major city to have eight or nine competing newspapers. (Today, few cities have more than one paper.)

Effect of the Telegraph

Although the telegraph was invented in 1844, its most widespread impact on newswriting was not felt until 17 years later, when the Civil War began. Reporters at battle sites had to transmit their stories by telegraph. To get the outcome into the story in case the telegraph broke down, reporters became more concise and began to develop inverted-pyramid writing.

Newspapers spread to Kansas City, Denver, Los Angeles, San Francisco, and points in between as the westward movement continued.

Shortly after the telegraph began to speed the reporting of news, the first news-gathering service was formed. This service, a forerunner of the Associated Press, began selling news to client papers in 1849. Over the next few decades competing wire services, including United Press, sprang up. By 1910 there were 2,600 daily newspapers in the United States; some of them had bureaus in the nation's capital and around the world. The information explosion was beginning.

Yellow Journalism

The late nineteenth century saw an era most journalists would rather forget, the age of "yellow journalism." The term refers to an unethical, irresponsible brand of journalism given to hoaxes, altered photographs, screaming headlines, "scoops," frauds, and endless promotions of the newspapers themselves. "Yellow journalism" derives from the name of the Yellow Kid, a cartoon character that appeared in the *Sunday World* during the 1890s.

The most notable of the yellow journalists were William Randolph Hearst, publisher of the New York *Journal*, and Joseph Pulitzer, publisher of the New York *World*. Their newspapers attracted huge audiences, and their competition for readers, advertisers, and each others' most talented writers was fierce. Color supplements, more illustrations, cartoon strips, and dramatic coverage of wars and sporting events sent the papers' circulations soaring.

The period was perfect for the circulation-building exploits of Nellie Bly, the name used by Elizabeth Cockrane, the most famous of the women journalists beginning to make names for themselves. Bly worked for Pulitzer's *World* and was noted for her "stunts," stories in which she made the news herself. Once she pretended to be mentally ill and was committed to New York's Blackwell Island Asylum. When she was released after ten days, she wrote a story exposing the asylum's poor conditions. The story sparked reform around the country.

Her most famous story was about her trip around the world. A book of that period, Jules Verne's *Around the World in Eighty Days*, was very popular. Bly set out to circle the globe in less than 80 days, and as readers everywhere followed her adventures, she did it—in 72 days.

Spanish-American War

During this period, a movement began in Cuba to seek independence from Spain. Beginning in 1895, the *World* and the *Journal* whipped up a war climate in support of the Cuban nationalists and tried to lure the United States into the conflict. One famous story of the time was about a *Journal* artist in Cuba who cabled Hearst that there was no war and he was coming home. Hearst is said to have wired back, ''Please remain. You furnish the pictures, and I'll furnish the war.''

When the battleship USS *Maine* blew up in Havana harbor in 1898, the Hearst paper featured a huge drawing and the headline: DESTRUCTION OF THE WAR SHIP *MAINE* WAS THE WORK OF AN ENEMY. Congress demanded that Spain leave the island, and war resulted.

This headline is an example of yellow journalism. W. R. Hearst, newspaper publisher, exploited the sinking of the *Maine* and whipped up public sentiment to go to war.

While the press is not solely to blame for the Spanish-American War, the yellow journalism of the time certainly contributed to an unhealthy atmosphere.

The vestiges of yellow journalism remain in the sort of newspaper sold at supermarket checkout stands, but for the most part it has been consigned to the journalistic graveyard.

The Pulitzer name lives on through the Pulitzer Prize and some distinguished newspapers. Today the Hearst chain of newspapers is much smaller than it was at its peak, when it included forty-two dailies. The Hearst Foundation has made a valuable contribution to journalism education through its newswriting, broadcasting, and photography contests for journalism school undergraduates.

Muckraking

The end of yellow journalism ushered in a period when American newspapers developed a significant social consciousness. Many papers crusaded for child labor laws, promoted hospitals and tuberculosis sanitariums, collected money for the needy, and exposed public graft.

A new medium came into its own during the late nineteenth and early twentieth centuries: the magazine. Such publications as *McClure's, Collier's, Munsey's,* and *The Saturday Evening Post* joined the fight for social justice that the newspapers had kicked off. They had circulations in the hundreds of thousands, and they battled corruption in all its forms. Patent medicine companies, child labor, the status of blacks, and the meat-packing industry all came under scrutiny. The Pure Food and Drugs Act of 1906 grew out of the crusades, as did many other reforms. Ida Tarbell's series on ''The History of the Standard Oil Company'' in *McClure's* was one of the first attacks on big business. Her investigative reporting put John D. Rockefeller, Standard Oil's president, on the defensive for years to come.

Critics of the crusading journalists labeled them muckrakers, which the reformers came to think of as a term of praise.

The Advent of Radio

At the turn of the century, a development was looming that would change the nature of the news—and of the world—forever. In 1906, Dr. Lee De Forest made improvements in the vacuum tube that made possible the new medium of radio. Although no one person invented radio, De Forest's vacuum tube was the key breakthrough.

De Forest made the first newscast in 1916 when he broadcast over a limited area the returns of the Wilson-Hughes presidential election. Regular daily programs started in Detroit in 1920, broadcast from experimental station 8MK, which became WWJ the following year. Station KDKA in Pittsburgh, Pennsylvania, broadcast the Harding-Cox presidential election returns of 1920, considered a milestone in radio journalism.

The National Broadcasting Company (NBC) was formed in 1926 and the Columbia Broadcasting System (CBS) in 1927. The Mutual Broadcasting System went on the air in 1934, and when

Edward R. Murrow, one of the most respected people in broadcasting, provided dramatic and accurate reports from London during World War II. He is shown here during a Voice of America radio broadcast.

part of NBC's network was sold, it was renamed the American Broadcasting Company (ABC) in 1945.

Soon a problem developed. In law, the airwaves are owned collectively by the public. In practice, stations saturated the airwaves and interfered with each other's broadcasts. A way had to be found to regulate radio to make sure frequencies were used properly. In 1912 a law was passed that empowered the Department of Commerce to assign wavelengths to license applicants. The Radio Act of 1927 broadened this power and created the Federal Radio Commission. This was the forerunner of today's Federal Communications Commission (FCC), which has jurisdiction over both radio and television. Although the FCC has jurisdiction, it does not have censorship power.

Radio fascinated the American public in the 1920s, '30s, and '40s. Great comedians like Jack Benny, Bob Hope, and Fred Allen drew huge audiences, and sporting events like football and baseball became accessible to everyone. Although it was primarily an entertainment medium, radio also drained advertising from newspapers.

Today, more than 500 million radios are in use, beaming words and music from 4,948 AM stations and 4,174 FM stations around the country. Radio still occupies an important place among the media. Most stations play music mixed with news, and millions of Americans get their first word of major news events from radio as they drive to or from work and school. In emergencies, radio broadcasts warnings and information to aid people.

The Impact of Television

The first television newscast took place in 1940. By the mid-1960s, 60 million TV sets were in use.

TV dramatically changed radio and newspapers. It took much of the entertainment role away from radio and the spot, or breaking, news role away from newspapers. Today, newspapers put less emphasis on breaking news; it makes no sense for a newspaper to announce breathlessly that an event occurred, when most of its

Direct broadcast satellites like this one make it possible to see news as it happens from around the world.

readers probably saw an account of it hours earlier on television. Modern newspapers put more emphasis on examining the background of current news events and covering trends and lifestyles in depth.

Early TV pictures were snowy, and transmission facilities were erratic. Today, both color and sound have improved. During a major news event—such as the first people landing on the moon—the nation stops to watch television. Some events, such as the Olympic Games, are viewed simultaneously around the world. Communications philosopher Marshall McLuhan called this phenomenon the "global village."

In the 1930s, President Franklin Roosevelt reached the American people through radio with his fireside chats. Today's presidents come to us in color through live news conferences, and presidential candidates debate each other as the voters watch. Press conferences also give the public a close-up look at news reporters in action.

Cable TV has magnified the influence of television in our lives. No longer do viewers have to depend on the national networks' judgment of what they should watch. Now there are alternatives that can afford to appeal to smaller audiences. More than 1,400 TV stations are on the air.

Television is a powerful medium. Its influence was brought home to many Americans during the Vietnam War.

The Vietnam War was the first war covered on television. TV brought the conflict into the livingrooms of American homes.

In World Wars I and II, the images transmitted from the battlefield to the audience were carefully censored. Most noncombatants remained unaware of the brutality and horror of war. But the Vietnam War was different. For the first time, battlefield images came to us nightly—in full color—and left millions of Americans horrified.

Protests against the war became common. Scenes of protesters clashing with police entered our living rooms. Critics of TV accused the medium of deliberately seeking out inflammatory material because it makes dramatic pictures. Whether that was true we do not know, but we do know how graphic the medium is and how hard it is to ignore. We also know that no one can be fully informed only through television news; the informed citizen still needs a daily newspaper.

Journalism Today

Our introduction discussed the current state of the newspaper business, including its apparent shrinkage and emphasis on so-called soft news.

While these trends are cause for alarm, other major problems face the newspaper industry specifically and journalism generally. Newspapers have lost in huge numbers their young readers, those aged eighteen to twenty-four. This mobile generation does not have the same relationship with newspapers that its parents had. Only a little more than a generation ago, it was common for families to subscribe to two newspapers a day, one in the morning and one in the evening. Whole families spent large parts of their day reading newspapers. The present generation, however, does not buy and read newspapers in the same numbers as its parents did, a development that has leaders in journalism alarmed. They are responding with special youth pages, a program called ''Newspaper in Education,'' and more stories and features that appeal to this audience.

The results of these efforts are mixed. There is some indication that young people are reading more than they were a few years ago. But this is a tentative finding and is overshadowed by others. According to a 1990 poll sponsored by the *Times Mirror* Center for the People and the Press, the current generation is less informed about world and national news than any generation in the past half century. No one was particularly surprised by the finding that newspaper readership was down (24 percent of the young people polled said they read a newspaper yesterday; 25 years ago, 67 percent said they read a newspaper yesterday). But it appears that even television news-watching is down. As the Associated Press

Tomorrow's professional journalists are being trained today.

reported, "In 1965, 52 percent of people under 35 said they watched the TV news 'yesterday'; this year, 42 percent of those under 30 said they caught the TV news 'yesterday'."

If you add a less-informed electorate to a trend in the mass media away from reporting on government and toward soft news, you can get a result that alarms some people. Good citizens should keep abreast of the news . . . and good journalism students *must* do so.

In fact, young people are flocking in record numbers to the schools and departments of journalism on college and university campuses. Some of the very best minds are being educated for journalism careers. The job market is crowded but not impossible, and journalism educators remain confident that jobs will always be there for well-educated, enthusiastic young people. These young people—possibly you—will create the future of American journalism.

The country's information needs continue to grow, as they have done steadily since the days of *Publick Occurrences* and the *Boston News-Letter*.

Wrap-up

Over the past fifty years, the processing of information has speeded up to the point that important events are known around the world within minutes of their happening. By comparison, the people who lived in colonial America were information paupers.

The history of journalism in America cannot be separated from the history of the country. The first American newspaper, *Publick Occurrences*, was suppressed after only a single issue in 1690 because the British authorities disapproved of it. In 1735, the authorities tried to suppress John Peter Zenger's *New York Weekly Journal* because of its criticism of the government. A jury acquitted Zenger, finding that truth, not government approval, was the standard for publication.

The press was instrumental in the colonial drive for independence from England, and the First Amendment to the Constitution of the new country guaranteed freedom of the press.

In the 1800s newspapers began to devote more space to events and less to opinion and, because they cost only a penny each, newspapers became immensely popular.

Technology, in the form of the telegraph, accelerated the transmission of news during the Civil War and led eventually to the establishment of news wire services like the Associated Press.

The close of the nineteenth century saw the era of "yellow journalism," sensational stories and screaming headlines aimed at boosting circulation. Joseph Pulitzer's New York *World* and William Randolph Hearst's New York *Journal* helped incite the Spanish-American War and prompt the U.S. invasion of Cuba.

Gradually, sensationalism gave way to reform. Magazines like *Collier's* and *The Saturday Evening Post* tried, often successfully, to better society and its institutions.

The improvement of the vacuum tube in 1906 led to the development of radio, the founding of the networks, and the creation of an instant news source for the American public. Television added pictures to sound, and a new medium was born. The realities of war, conveyed nightly on TV screens during the Vietnam War, turned a large segment of the public against involvement there.

Because of television, newspapers figure less prominently in the lives of young people than they once did. But the responsibilities of citizenship, of keeping fully informed, require a deeper understanding of events than television alone can provide.

On Assignment

Teamwork

1. Identify an editor (newspaper, magazine, or one of each), an attorney, and a radio or television executive knowledgeable about the First Amendment. Each team is to interview one of these people and exchange the information in class. How do the views of those interviewed agree or disagree on the First Amendment guarantee of a free press? How do they rate today's press and its use or abuse of this right?

   Do the same interview with the mayor, local politicians, one of your neighbors, a teacher, and two students.

Practice

1. From this list of the journalists most closely associated with the history of colonial newspapers in America, select two. Write brief biographies of each and discuss his role.

Benjamin Harris	Andrew Bradford
John Campbell	William Bradford
James Franklin	Hugh Gaine
Benjamin Franklin	William Hunter
John Peter Zenger	James Rivington

2. Take either side of the following question and write an essay: Should the American press be restricted by the government? Consider the following questions:

   a. If so, who would decide what the restrictions would be?

   b. What would the penalty be for violating the restrictions?

   c. Would such restrictions change the nature of American life? How?

   d. Is that good or bad?

   e. TV is to some extent a controlled industry. Is that good or bad?

Your Turn

1. Research the history of your local newspaper or newspapers. Find out who founded the paper and when. Was it ever affiliated with a political party? Who owns the paper?

2. Do the same with radio and television stations in your town.

THE RESPONSIBILITIES OF THE MEDIA

Journalists in the closing days of the twentieth century find them-selves in a tough, but not altogether new, position. They have gone from asking questions ("How much will the program cost, Governor?" "What's the starting lineup, Coach?") to a new role of *answering* questions. Just as the public is questioning its other institutions—Congress, the courts, the presidency, business, edu-cation, and industry—so, too, is it questioning the mass media.

Surveys indicate that public confidence in the press has de-clined. Journalists are viewed by many people as rude, arrogant, uncaring people who think only about "getting the story." In-creasingly, people object to intrusive behavior by journalists—for example, shoving a microphone into the face of someone whose house has just burned down and demanding, "How do you feel?"

Reading the newspaper is the way many people start their day.

Such behavior probably doesn't happen as often as people believe—but it *does* happen more often than journalists like to talk about. Inaccuracies, preoccupation with the trivial or the bizarre, insensitivity to minority groups or issues . . . the criticism is widespread.

The media are also criticized for their *bigness*, especially the largest newspapers and the major networks. People seem to be suspicious of giant organizations, although they eat at McDonald's and shop at Sears without any problems. The media, however, are seen as pervasive and powerful. No one doubts their pervasiveness. How much real power they have, however, is open to question.

People say the media are inaccurate. The media respond, "There's so much pressure on us, for time and space, it's a wonder there aren't more errors." That's an excuse you wouldn't accept from your dry cleaner—and certainly not from your doctor. And it shouldn't be accepted from the media, either. Sure, it's tough. But that's no excuse.

Then there is the charge of bias. Often, journalists are portrayed as left-leaning people who want to remake the country in their image. The truth is, most journalists are pretty middle-of-the-road, in all ways.

Some criticism is well deserved—and taken seriously by journalists. Some criticism is misplaced. Scandal, assassination, frightening and ever-more-rapid social change, unpopular wars, unpopular politicians—this turbulance is the daily fare of consumers of the mass media. Journalists are at the center of these events; they carry the message and often bear the brunt of the frustrations such messages arouse in readers, viewers, and listeners.

Often, hostility toward journalists is based on feelings instead of facts. This chapter will examine the media from two angles. First, it will describe what you can do to become a more discerning consumer of news. Second, it will look at what the media are doing to ensure that they properly use the power entrusted to them in a free society.

A Journalist's Job

There are ways to determine how well journalists do their jobs. Traditionally, journalists are charged with the following responsibilities in a culture that guarantees a free press. These are the functions of a journalist:

The political function

The press (by which we mean radio, television, newspapers, magazines, and all other news gathering and disseminating agencies) is the watchdog of government. Freedom always carries with it certain responsibilities. The guarantee of a free press carries the obligation of providing to the audience information upon which to base political decisions. Thus, the news organization doing its job properly will cover in detail the activities of government. It will fight attempts by the government to do the public's business behind closed doors. It will watch for scandal and wrongdoing. It will scrutinize budgets and programs to see if the public's tax money is being spent properly. This is the foremost of the press' responsibilities, whether in New York, Washington, and Ottawa or in Des Moines, Sacramento, and Dallas. This responsibility exists at the scholastic level too.

The economic function

The public needs information about products, goods, and services in addition to events. Through advertising, the press informs the public of such items. Business, industrial, and agriculture news performs the same function. (Advertising, it should be noted, although much maligned by consumers, is what pays the bills. Without it, there would be no newspapers or broadcasts as we now know them.)

Advertising sells goods, which helps the economy grow, which creates jobs. Advertising often is criticized for being in bad taste, and some of it is. You might, for example, find a commercial for a laxative offensive, but the presentation probably is not. The big question about advertising is this: Can advertising techniques be used to sell ideas as well as automobiles? Or, to put it another way, "Can advertising cause us to buy something we don't need and to vote for one candidate rather than another?" There is disagreement, but most people subscribe to the "limited effects" notion of the mass media. That is, consumers have psychological defenses by which they resist and mold messages from the mass media, including political advertising and product advertising, to fit their own needs. Consumers are neither children, unable to understand a commercial, nor zombies, powerless to resist. Advertisers seek brand-name recognition, not control over minds. If you buy an automobile, your decision about which make to buy might be influenced by advertising. But you weren't forced to buy that make.

The sentry function

The press watches society's horizons. What is peeking over the horizon to challenge us tomorrow? Technological change, the youth culture, new lifestyles, patterns of change in criminal justice, and the impact of changing habits of energy use all evolved after prediction in the mass media. In other words, the press must report not only what is happening today but also what is likely to happen tomorrow. When the United States became involved in the revolutions and social and economic difficulties of Central America in the 1980s, many experts thought the press had failed in its duties as a sentry. Those experts believe that journalists who lacked understanding of the region's culture, history, politics, and economics had not alerted the nation to the true extent of the problems there. On the other hand, the press is doing a good job in the 1990s alerting us to threats to the environment.

The record-keeping function

The mass media should reflect an accurate record of local, national, and world news. Who was elected to the school board? What bills passed Congress? What happened to the price of oil? Who died? Who won and who lost in sports? Who filed for bankruptcy? Who filed to run for public office? This function, too, is basic. The journalism of big headlines and splashy news programs

The reporting of important events, such as the launching of a space shuttle, is part of the journalist's record-keeping function.

depends on the underpinning of record-keeping. Consumers also need to know many things, including the data often found tucked away in the back of the paper.

The entertainment function

Mass media consumers need diversion as well as information. The comics, entertaining feature stories, and pictures help meet this need. The business of the press is serious, of course, but the audience is made up of people of all ages and interests. Few newscasts or newspapers should be without an entertaining or light element.

The social function

In times long past, people got their news from their neighbors on a person-to-person basis. Today, the mass media perform this function. "Did you watch the 'Tonight Show' last night?" is a reflection of the social function. The media substitute for simpler relationships of the past.

The marketplace function

The press provides the forum in which all sorts of ideas are presented; it becomes the marketplace of ideas. If the audience is concerned about the environment and conveys this concern through the press, then perhaps something will be done. If citizens don't want their trees to be cut down for a street-widening project, they turn to the forum of the mass media to generate support. Thus, a city's agenda is reviewed: Do we want wider streets for more efficient moving of traffic, or do we want the trees to remain and the automobiles' dominance of our lives to be curtailed?

The agenda-setting function

Scholars of the media recently added another function to the list, the agenda-setting function. This function is summarized by the comment noted earlier, ''While journalists don't tell us what to think, they do tell us what to think about.'' This new concept suggests that far from dictating our thoughts—a power once believed available to the mass media—the media have the power to determine what we talk about as individuals and address as a nation. If the media place saving the environment on the agenda, then the people will begin to pay more attention to improving the environment.

It is almost impossible ever to isolate the effects of the mass media, because certain causes are too complex to trace. Certainly, the media play a role in setting the agenda. In a drought, the media emphasize that responsible citizens conserve water. And water usage drops. But what, exactly, is cause and what, exactly, is effect no one knows. And here is a large question: Who sets the agenda for the mass media? Can the government place an item on the media's agenda (the war on drugs, perhaps) and then have the media place it before the public?

A few years ago, *Time* magazine listed its choices for the best ten large newspapers in the country. The list, in alphabetical order:

Boston Globe	New York Times
Chicago Tribune	Philadelphia Inquirer
Des Moines Register	St. Petersburg (Fla.) Times
Los Angeles Times	Wall Street Journal
Miami Herald	Washington Post

Time also mentioned what it considered some of the better smaller newspapers:

Georgia Gazette (Savannah)	Los Angeles Daily News
Akron (Ohio) Beacon-Journal	Bergen County (N.J.) Record
Wichita (Kan.) Eagle-Beacon	Raleigh (N.C.) News and Observer
Eugene (Ore.) Register-Guard	Anchorage (Alaska) Daily News
Fayetteville (N.C.) Times and Observer	Jackson (Miss.) Clarion-Ledger
Quincy (Mass.) Patriot-Ledger	

Evaluating the Media

How well is the press performing its agreed-upon functions? No one can read all the newspapers and all the magazines. No one can listen to all the radio newscasts and watch all the television newscasts. But you can monitor your own news agencies. To evaluate the media you use, try this system.

Newspapers

Study your local newspaper. Is it choked with self-seeking publicity releases? Are local issues and problems ignored in favor of Associated Press or United Press International stories from afar? Is government on the local level covered thoroughly? Does the editorial page contain a lively and readable forum through a letters-to-the-editor column? Is an occasional longer and more thoughtful letter published with special prominence? Do the editorials treat local issues, candidates, and problems, or do they comment only on national and international issues? Do the sportswriters really cover the sports scene, with probing stories and questions, or are they cheerleaders for the athletic programs? Are ''minor'' sports covered? Are the same people in the paper every day, with little coverage of minority or low-income groups? Does the paper have in-depth or investigative stories? How much space is devoted to stories of crime and violence? How much space is devoted to trivia: bridge columns, advice-to-the-lovelorn columns, and the like?

Radio

Is the news on your local radio stations mostly noisy bulletins and yesterday's stories culled from a newspaper? If the city faces a storm emergency or national disaster, does the station remain on the air extra hours with up-to-the-minute information? Are the news reporters disc jockeys who read wire service reports or are they real journalists? Are there special programs centered on critical *local* issues? Are any in-depth interviews ever heard? Is there a forum for opposing viewpoints?

Television

How much of a 30-minute local newscast is devoted to commercials? How much local news is presented? How much sports? How much weather? Does the station use its newscast to entertain you or to inform you? Do the anchors and reporters devote precious minutes to inane chatter? Are there ever any in-depth or investigative stories? How much time is devoted to such trivia as shopping center promotions, key-to-the-city presentations, and parades?

Magazines

The general-interest magazine with a huge circulation is a thing of the past. *Life, Collier's, Redbook, Look*—names out of journalism history—folded or changed so as to be unrecognizable. Except for *Time, Newsweek*, and *U.S. News & World Report*, today's magazine is apt to appeal to a narrow, special interest. There are magazines for every hobby and line of work, from baseball-card collecting to, yes, journalism (*Quill*, for example). Judging their performance requires special expertise, but some observations can be made. For example, is the magazine fair even when it has a preconceived position? A magazine promoting gun control should be fair to opponents of gun control, and vice versa. Are the articles varied in nature—some light, some serious—or is every story just fluff? What about graphics—are they up-to-date or old? Does the writing fit the overall tone of the publication? As for the three major news magazines, they are prime targets for study. Identify one important issue and read the coverage it receives in each publication. What can you conclude about the magazine from what you read, especially on the question of fairness? Does it seem to have a political bias? What differences in tone can you identify among the three magazines?

Other Performance Criteria

As you begin your study of journalism, it is worth your time— as a possible future journalist and as a citizen and consumer of the mass media—to ponder the performance of your news agencies.

The news is presented differently on TV than in print media, but the responsibilities of
the journalists are the same.

Here are some other questions you might consider. Better yet,
invite local news executives to class and ask them to comment:

1. Is it true the press is preoccupied with "bad news"?
2. Who owns the news outlets in your communities? Are they locally
   owned? If not, what does that imply?
3. Does your local daily paper have competition? Most do not. In more
   than 90 percent of American cities with daily newspapers, there is only
   one daily. Is that good or bad? You can get an argument on either
   side. Competition, some say, leads to screaming headlines that lure
   newsstand buyers. It also weakens newspapers economically, they say.
   The counter argument, of course, is that competition is good for newspapers just as it is for all businesses.
4. Do the same people who own the newspaper also own the radio and
   television stations? What does that imply? Is that good or bad?
5. What dilemmas do editors and news executives face because of lack of
   time and space? Are there any solutions?

6. What dilemmas do they face trying to balance news that the audience wants as opposed to news that it *needs*?

7. Do editors and news executives receive enough feedback from the audience? Do they want more? What would they do with it?

8. How good is the talent pool from which editors and news executives draw their employees? Are potential employees as skilled in the use of the language as they once were? What does that imply for them? For you, as a consumer?

9. Whose fault is it when the facts come out wrong in a story? Is it always the newspaper or station's fault? Might it be the fault of the news *source*? Might the "error" be in the minds of the audience?

10. If editors and news executives had unlimited money to work with, what would they change? Would the editor buy a new press or hire more good reporters?

Consider the issues raised in this chapter. As you work on your school newspaper, yearbook, news bureau, or broadcast, give some thought to how these issues pertain to the scholastic journalist.

The Ethics of Journalism

Fair play is a cherished idea in our lives. We expect justice to be blind. We demand honesty from public officials. We require all of our institutions—schools, churches, courts, Congress, the presidency—to set high standards. Throughout society, value is placed on right over wrong. Journalists are no exception to these expectations, nor should they be. Just as we expect the Sunday afternoon football game to be an honest contest, we also expect honesty from the press.

Many people, however, are alarmed about the state of journalism. More and more, polls indicate the audience is wondering just how fair and honest journalists are.

The 1980s brought to journalism an outbreak of unusual violations. Several reporters were caught making up stories or parts of stories. One had to give back a Pulitzer Prize, journalism's highest honor, when it was discovered that the main character in her prize-winning story, an 8-year-old heroin addict, didn't exist.

Cases of plagiarism came to public attention. There were incidents of "composite characters," fictional characters a writer had created by using characteristics of several real people. In some cases, quotations were found to be made up. These problems eroded public confidence in the press to the point where some citizens want to pass laws regulating journalists' behavior.

It is a nation's deepest customs and commitments, not merely its laws, that shape the nature of its society. Consider the following excerpts from the constitutions of China and the United States. Both provide for freedom of the press. We know, however, that only the United States truly provides such freedom.

"Citizens enjoy freedom of the press . . . The state guarantees the necessary material facilities."

Constitution of the People's Republic of China

"Congress shall make no law . . . abridging the freedom of speech or of the press."

Constitution of the United States of America

Credibility

Thoughtful journalists are alarmed, too. They know the value to society of a free press. They also know how valuable the credibility of the press is. To protect (or restore) that credibility, journalists today are putting more emphasis than ever on their ethical standards. Erring journalists find their colleagues in no mood to tolerate or forgive unprofessional conduct.

Many things govern journalists: time, space, economics, competition, geography, and the law. But it is the journalist's ethics, above all else, that provide the daily working guidelines to decide what gets into print or onto the airwaves. The responsible journalist tries to serve the audience's best interest.

Various codes of ethics, one of which is reprinted in this chapter, have been written and agreed upon by journalists. These codes all suffer from one fact: They are not enforceable by law. The Constitution's First Amendment states: "Congress shall make no law . . . abridging the freedom of speech, or of the press." It would be unconstitutional to jail a journalist who violated the ethical codes. A journalist who violates the *law*, of course, faces the same penalties as any other citizen.

Nor is it possible to require licensing or exams for journalists like those doctors and lawyers must pass. Licensing laws also run afoul of the Constitution. You can stop buying an unethical newspaper or stop watching the unethical newscast, but you can't lock up a journalist for a violation of ethics.

The framers of the Constitution believed a free press, even though occasionally irresponsible, is vastly preferable to a government-controlled press. Does that mean that newspapers, for example, may print anything they please, without regard to consequences? No. The law does play a role. If a newspaper prints libel (false defamation), it may be required to pay money to the libeled person. But note that this penalty comes *after* publication, not before. Prior restraint—the halting or forbidding of publication—is not permitted in the United States except under the rarest of circumstances, usually pertaining to national security in wartime. Government censorship is against the law.

With the protection of the Constitution and our customs supporting the right to publish, what keeps journalists honest? The answer is ethics: devotion to journalists' cherished idea of fair play.

Accuracy

Ethical journalists—by far the majority—subscribe to the previously mentioned codes, enforceable or not. Journalism attracts high-minded people who are devoted to serving their audience. Their principles are many, and the highest of these is accuracy.

To the ethical journalist, accuracy has a special meaning. Close doesn't count. Names must be spelled exactly right, down to the middle initial. A journalist cannot say a person lives at 1010 Sycamore St. if the address really is 1010 Sycamore Drive. There is no such thing as a small error. No one lacking a sense of detail should go into journalism. It is not sufficient to bat .300 or even .400, averages that would get a baseball player into the Hall of Fame. For journalists, the batting average must be 1.000. They must be accurate, in every detail, all the time.

How often does the press achieve this super-accuracy? Not often enough, of course. If you have ever been the subject of a news story, you may have observed an error. Maybe your name was misspelled, or your year in school was wrong. What was the effect, for you, the next time you read a story in the newspaper that had spelled your name wrong? Of course, you doubted what you read. Even the smallest mistake reduces credibility. Check. Double-check. Ask the source another question. Never, ever guess about anything. And never forget the importance of fair play.

Objectivity

Another of the journalist's highest principles is objectivity, the state of mind that journalists acquire to make them fair, neutral observers of events and issues. Journalists do not permit their personal feelings, their likes or dislikes, to color news stories. (Opinion, of course, is to be desired in columns and editorials.)

You may not like a speaker or what is said, but you report it straight, without any hint of your own feelings. You may think Kiwanians or Ku Klux Klan members or any other group are wrong, but you report what they do and let the audience decide.

Some people say that objectivity is impossible, that it is impossible to have opinions and not let them show. Even if this is true, which we doubt, the journalist still must strive for that ideal.

If you find the idea of objectivity hard to grasp, think in terms of neutrality, fairness, impartiality, balance (i.e., telling all sides of a story), and honesty. Whatever you call it, the fact is that journalists must set aside personal feelings. Always seek to provide the audience with unbiased accounts of the news. The journalist who vows to do this has taken a long first step on the road to professionalism.

Other Ethical Principles

Accuracy and objectivity are perhaps the two most important ethical principles journalists try to live by. But they are by no means the only ones. Some important precepts follow.

Although Ariel Sharon, former Israeli defense minister, proved during a libel suit that *Time* magazine's published statements about him were false, he lost the case because he could not prove actual malice on the part of *Time*; the jury decided the magazine did not know the material was untrue.

Good taste
Avoid sensationalism, and stay away from racy material. Sex and crime are subjects that require extreme caution in reporting and editing. Seek understatement, not overstatement. Never glorify bad behavior. Do not invade the privacy of others. Avoid profanity.

Simultaneous rebuttal, or right of reply
If you must print or air criticism of someone, permit that person to respond to the criticism *in the same story*. It is not enough to run the criticism this week and the response next week. The response may never catch up with the original criticism.

Fairness to all
Everyone in your audience—regardless of race, color, philosophy, religion, gender, age, or economic status—has an equal right to expect to be treated fairly. Do not apply different standards to different people or groups.

Plagiarism
Do not pass off the work of others as your own. No matter how much you like someone else's lead or phrase or story, you may not publish it as if you had written it. This is an absolute. You may quote from others' work, but you must give credit. In most classrooms, students are failed for this offense; in the newsroom, reporters are fired for it.

Attribution
Identify where the information came from ("the President said today. . . .") so the audience can judge for itself the value of the information. Do not use anonymous sources.

The truth
Never fake anything—your identity as a journalist, a quote, a photograph, a detail. Report only what you know beyond a doubt. Never speculate or guess.

This list is incomplete and is, in some ways, abstract. It is, however, sufficient to make the point: Journalists must play fair.

Before turning to a discussion of legal issues, read the ethical code that follows. It is the code of the Society of Professional Journalists, expressing in forceful language what most ethical journalists believe.

CODE OF ETHICS

Society of Professional Journalists

The Society of Professional Journalists believes the duty of journalists is to serve the truth.

We believe the agencies of mass communication are carriers of public discussion and information, acting on their Constitutional mandate and freedom to learn and report the facts.

We believe in public enlightenment as the forerunner of justice, and in our Constitutional role to seek the truth as part of the public's right to know the truth.

We believe those responsibilities carry obligations that require journalists to perform with intelligence, objectivity, accuracy, and fairness.

To these ends, we declare acceptance of the standards of practice here set forth:

Responsibility: The public's right to know of events of public importance and interest is the overriding mission of the mass media. The purpose of distributing news and enlightened opinion is to serve the general welfare. Journalists who use their professional status as representatives of the public for selfish or other unworthy motives violate a high trust.

Freedom of the Press: Freedom of the press is to be guarded as an inalienable right of people in a free society. It carries with it the freedom and the responsibility to discuss, question, and challenge actions and utterances of our government and of our public and private institutions. Journalists uphold the right to speak unpopular opinions and the privilege to agree with the majority.

Ethics: Journalists must be free of obligation to any interest other than the public's right to know the truth.

1. Gifts, favors, free travel, special treatment or privileges can compromise the integrity of journalists and their employers. Nothing of value should be accepted.
2. Secondary employment, political involvement, holding public office, and service in community organizations should be avoided if it compromises the integrity of journalists and their employers. Journalists and their employers should conduct their personal lives in a manner which protects them from conflict of interest, real or apparent. Their responsibilities to the public are paramount. That is the nature of their profession.

3. So-called news communications from private sources should not be published or broadcast without substantiation of their claims to news value.
4. Journalists will seek news that serves the public interest, despite the obstacles. They will make constant efforts to assure that the public's business is conducted in public and that public records are open to public inspection.
5. Journalists acknowledge the newsman's ethic of protecting confidential sources of information.
6. Plagiarism is dishonest and unacceptable.

Accuracy and Objectivity: Good faith with the public is the foundation of all worthy journalism.

1. Truth is our ultimate goal.
2. Objectivity in reporting the news is another goal that serves as the mark of an experienced professional. It is a standard of performance toward which we strive. We honor those who achieve it.
3. There is no excuse for inaccuracies or lack of thoroughness.
4. Newspaper headlines should be fully warranted by the contents of the articles they accompany. Photographs and telecasts should give an accurate picture of an event and not highlight a minor incident out of context.
5. Sound practice makes clear distinction between news reports and expressions of opinions. News reports should be free of opinion or bias and represent all sides of an issue.
6. Partisanship in editorial comment that knowingly departs from the truth violates the spirit of American journalism.
7. Journalists recognize their responsibility for offering informed analysis, comment, and editorial opinion on public events and issues. They accept the obligation to present such material by individuals whose competence, experience, and judgment qualify them for it.
8. Special articles or presentations devoted to advocacy or the writer's own conclusions and interpretations should be labeled as such.

Fair Play: Journalists at all times will show respect for the dignity, privacy, rights, and well-being of people encountered in the course of gathering and presenting the news.

(continued)

1. The news media should not communicate unofficial charges affecting reputation or moral character without giving the accused a chance to reply.
2. The news media must guard against invading a person's right to privacy.
3. The media should not pander to morbid curiosity about details of vice and crime.
4. It is the duty of news media to make prompt and complete correction of their errors.
5. Journalists should be accountable to the public for their reports and the public should be encouraged to voice its grievances against the media. Open dialogue with our readers, viewers, and listeners should be fostered.

Mutual Trust: Adherence to this code is intended to preserve and strengthen the bond of mutual trust and respect between American journalists and the American people.

The Society shall—by programs of education and other means—encourage individual journalists to adhere to the tenets, and shall encourage journalistic publications and broadcasters to recognize their responsibility to frame codes of ethics in concert with their employees to serve as guidelines in furthering these goals.

Libel Law

"If you print that I'll sue you for everything you own!"

Gulp.

Hearing someone threaten to sue you is an unpleasant experience. Stay in journalism long enough, however, and chances are fair that it will happen eventually. And if you go to court, the case will likely involve libel—or at least an accusation of libel.

Although ethical questions come up much more often than legal ones, the latter cannot be overlooked. Should an accusation of libel arise, the journalist needs to be prepared. And that includes the scholastic journalist. The student press is not exempt from libel law.

Libel laws are complex and changeable. Each court ruling provides subtle shifts in the law. One year it seems the press can print almost anything; the next year the law seems very restrictive. Libel laws vary from state to state. They vary widely depending on whether the person libeled is a private person, a public figure, or an elected official. What follows is a general overview.

First, libel is seldom considered a crime. It is usually a civil action, heard in a civil court. Commit burglary and you go to a criminal court, where the docket says: "State vs. John Smith." Libel cases are actions between citizens; the docket says: "Johnson vs. Jones." The person asserting that libel has occurred is the plaintiff. The person accused is the defendant. The penalty involves a money judgment, which can run into millions of dollars, awarded to the plaintiff.

Briefly, libel is printed false defamation of character. (Spoken defamation is slander, which we include under the general heading

Carol Burnett was the first celebrity to win a libel suit against the *National Enquirer*. Burnett claimed that an item in the *Enquirer* falsely portrayed her as a drunk. Shown here after her victory in court, Burnett answered questions from the press.

of libel.) To defame someone is to reduce that person's reputation. For libel to have occurred, you must have written something false.

What can reduce a person's reputation? "She cheats on exams." "He is immoral." "She is a liar." "He falsified his academic record." The possibilities are endless. Certainly, the gravest libels occur when one's basic morality, decency, or wholesomeness is questioned. Any publication of information that harms a person requires the greatest of care. In scholastic situations it should be avoided virtually all the time.

Assertions that someone is dishonest, associates with criminals, committed a crime, has a loathsome disease, or has general low character are dangerous. Proceed with special care. Remember that even if you *may* print or air such a story, you may decide *not* to for ethical reasons. Be aware that there is often a distinction between what you can get away with and what is right.

Defenses Against Libel

The best defense against a successful libel suit is good reporting. Check all facts. Get the other side. Let the accused person respond to any charge. Run corrections quickly and prominently.

Other defenses exist should you be sued.

Truth

At this point in the development of libel law, the courts have made it clear that no publication will be held responsible for libel if the story in question is true.

For example, you learn that 30 years ago the mayor of your city was convicted of burglary. He spent one year in prison for it. If you decide to run that story, and there is proof (that is, if the story is true in the eyes of the jury), you are almost certainly safe from successful libel action.

But that's only part of the story. You may *not* be safe from an invasion-of-privacy suit. That's a suit in which the plaintiff in the example says, "Yes, that's true about the burglary charge. But since that case I have had no further trouble with the law. In fact, I went to college, earned two degrees and have been a successful banker and civic leader since then. I have a family and attend church regularly. To dredge up that old case invades my right to be left alone and to live in peace."

You probably would lose a privacy suit.

Legal questions aside, however, be aware that in such cases as these the responsible journalists do the right thing: They serve the audience as a whole and its members as individuals. What good is served by bringing up the old case? If you are fair, honest, and ethical, legal questions usually take care of themselves.

Another possible trap is the misconception that attribution is a defense in libel cases.

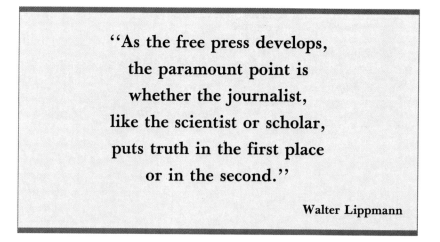

"As the free press develops,
the paramount point is
whether the journalist,
like the scientist or scholar,
puts truth in the first place
or in the second."

Walter Lippmann

Suppose Eric Sutton accuses Jill Keaton of being a criminal and you report it this way: "Sutton said Keaton had been convicted of burglary." Your sentence is *true*; that is, Sutton *did* say that about Keaton. Since truth is a defense, can you be sued success-fully?

The answer is yes, if the charge is false, because you spread the libel. You published it, and the damaged person can recover damages from you. You plead that you did, after all, attribute the information to Sutton. You lose. The principle is, "The one who publishes pays." You cannot duck a libel charge merely by saying that all you did was report accurately what someone else said. Attribution is no defense.

There are some exceptions. You may report whatever is said in an *official* legislative or judicial session without fear of a successful libel suit, provided your account is accurate and fair.

What is said on the floor of Congress or the state legislature or in a courtroom is *privileged*, meaning publication of such statements is immune from libel suit. If Eric Sutton accuses Jill Keaton in an open courtroom or on the floor of the state senate, you may print it without fear of a successful libel suit. If one senator says another is a liar, you may print that statement (with attribution, of course). The principle is that the public has a large stake in knowing what goes on in a courtroom or in the legislature. The press, therefore, may report such activities without the chilling effect that the fear of a suit can have.

And that suggests a major point. It may seem to you that the laws are in favor of the journalist. But this country has a deep, fervent commitment to open public debate. Our courts have a general fear of anything that restricts the information needed for that debate to be successful. Remember that a free press is one of the foundations granted in our Constitution. That freedom, properly handled, protects all of us, not just the person who owns the medium.

One last note about truth as a defense: To win a suit, the jury must believe you. What you know to be true may not seem so to the jury. Your witness may not be believed or may refuse to testify. Your documents may not be admitted into evidence. Be careful.

Fair comment

Another defense against successful libel suits is known as fair comment and criticism.

You are free to venture any opinion in reviewing books or records, theatrical events, movies, and the like. This is because a person who, for example, writes a book is thrusting himself or herself onto the stage and virtually asking for comment. If you review this book and say it's bad, we won't sue. If you say it's bad because it doesn't have a chapter on the responsibilities of the media, however, we may sue. You may express a negative opinion, but the facts you state must be true. For your defense of fair comment to convince a judge, you must explain the facts upon which your opinion is based. If your *facts* are right, your *opinion* is protected. Remember also that you must limit your comment to the public part of a performance or creative work. You cannot claim the defense of fair comment if you say a singer's record album is bad and he is also a thief.

Admit errors

A prompt correction if a published article has been shown to be false is both a legal and an ethical principle. It is only right that you admit it if you're shown to be wrong and run a correction to set the record straight. To do so in a libel case can help if you go to court. In effect, you are saying to the judge, "Yes, there may be libel here but it wasn't malicious. As soon as we found out we were wrong, we ran a correction." This may reduce the money judgment against you. In some states, special statutes make it a more complete defense.

Don't overlook the dangers presented by careless layout. For example, you would be in trouble if you have a photograph of the homecoming queen above a story on drug use or drunken driving. The implications would be read by all. Incidentally, a large libel suit in New Mexico recently involved just this issue: a headline over a photo and the implications it created. Here, too, if such a mistake slips through, you should run a correction as soon as possible.

Other Points of Libel Law

This general overview cannot touch on all the minute details of the law of libel, which fill whole libraries and have broad constitutional implications. But a few more points need to be made.

Our examples usually refer to newspapers, but the laws and principles apply to broadcasts, yearbooks, and magazines as well.

Also, when it comes to libel, some plaintiffs have a tougher time in court against the press than others. Elected public officials—for example, the President, a U.S. senator, or the mayor—must show a greater degree of *fault* by the press in order to win a libel suit. The senator who thinks he or she has been libeled must not only show the damage (as all plaintiffs must) but also must show that the press either knew it was printing a falsehood or exercised reckless disregard for the truth.

Both of these are rare, for the press generally does not knowingly print lies or *recklessly* disregard the truth. The idea here is, again, the country's commitment to open debate. The courts have said that for such debate to occur, the man or woman who has *sought* office must accept the criticism and attention that come with it.

In addition to the obviously public person, the courts are busily defining others who must show a high level of fault by the press in order to win libel suits. The police chief is a public figure even if not elected. But what about the beat patrol officer? The custodian in the police station? Such distinctions are difficult and should never be decided without the aid of counsel. The best thing is never to get into libel trouble. The worst is to try to handle it without expert help.

"Successful" Libel Suits

The alert reader may have noticed that virtually every time we have referred to a libel suit, we have qualified it by saying a *successful* libel suit. If you have an absolutely airtight defense, you won't lose the suit. But that doesn't mean you won't be sued in the first place. Anyone can sue anyone, and lawsuits are financially and emotionally draining.

Wise editors avoid lawsuits even if they think they can win. Exercise extreme care as reporters, editors, and photographers. (Yes, pictures can be libelous, and they can invade privacy.) Avoiding suits and being ethical are better than counting on legal technicalities. Also, get the other side in the initial story. People who see their side in print seldom sue.

Finally, who can sue? Anyone, as we have said. And who can be sued? The editor? The publisher? The answer is that anyone involved in producing the libelous material may be sued—the reporter who wrote the story, the editor who assigned the story, the editor who drew the layout, even the copy editor who wrote the headline or caption. All these people can be sued—"for everything they own."

Limits on Scholastic Journalism

On January 13, 1988, the U.S. Supreme Court handed down a decision involving the censorship of a school publication. The Associated Press covered the case, known as *Hazelwood School District* v. *Cathy Kuhlmeier*; an excerpt of AP's report appears on the next page.

Supreme Court Justice Byron White wrote the majority opinion for the Hazelwood ruling, a landmark decision that involves censorship on school newspapers.

The Supreme Court on Wednesday gave public school officials broad new authority to censor student newspapers and other forms of student expression.

The court, by a 5–3 vote, ruled that a Hazelwood, Mo., high school principal did not violate students' free-speech rights by ordering two pages deleted from an issue of a student-produced, school-sponsored newspaper.

"A school need not tolerate student speech that is inconsistent with its basic educational mission even though the government could not censor similar speech outside the school," Justice Byron R. White wrote for the court.

He said judicial intervention to protect students' free-speech rights is warranted "only when the decision to censor a school-sponsored publication, theatrical production, or other vehicle of student expression has no valid educational purpose."

The dissenting justices accused the court of condoning "thought control," adding "such unthinking contempt for individual rights is intolerable."

This cool and carefully worded report gave no hint of the debate, heat, and confusion that the court's decision would create in the ensuing years. Generally referred to today as "Hazelwood," the case and the ruling remain at the center of debate over student expression in secondary schools. The arguments on both sides of the issue are fervent and genuinely felt by their partisans.

One side says, "The First Amendment of the Constitution applies to all citizens, including high school students, and therefore school administrators have no right to interfere with what's published in a school newspaper.''

The other side says, ''The school newspaper is a school-sponsored activity, and the principal is the publisher of the paper, acting on behalf of the citizens of the school district, and therefore has the ultimate, legal control over what's published in the paper.''

Between these two positions, of course, are many people who believe that reasonable compromises can be found to protect everyone's rights and assure that legal responsibilities are met.

The Hazelwood Decision

Here are the facts of the case.

In 1983, staff members of *The Spectrum*, the student newspaper of Hazelwood, Mo., East High School, prepared a series of stories about student pregnancy and the effects of divorce on students. The principal, Robert Reynolds, deleted the two pages of the paper on which the stories were to have appeared. Reynolds said he blocked the stories because they invaded the privacy of the students involved, even though they were unnamed. He feared they could be identified anyway.

''He also believed,'' the Supreme Court said in its ruling, ''that the article's references to sexual activity and birth control were inappropriate for some of the younger students at the school.''

Reynolds took the position that he was publisher of the newspaper and as such could determine its contents.

The students sued. A federal trial judge ruled in favor of the

Reaction came swiftly when the Supreme Court ruled in favor of the Hazelwood School District.

school district. But the Eighth U.S. Circuit Court of Appeals ruled for the students.

When the U.S. Supreme Court came down on the side of school authorities, it said: "A school may in its capacity as publisher of a school newspaper or producer of a school play 'disassociate itself' not only from speech that would 'substantially interfere with its work . . . or impinge upon the rights of other students' but also from speech that is, for example, ungrammatical, poorly written, inadequately researched, biased or prejudiced, vulgar or profane, or unsuitable for immature audiences." The court said only that censorship must be "reasonably related" to educational goals.

The language was too broad for some people, and reaction came swiftly.

Mark Goodman, executive director of the Washington, D.C.-based Student Press Law Center, an organization that provides legal help to students in censorship cases, said that within hours of the decision, he received two calls from students complaining of censorship where none had existed before. Both cases involved stories about AIDS.

Many, but by no means all, school administrators responded favorably. So did many commercial newspapers, which appeared to favor the argument that the principal of a school has the same power to control content as the publisher of a commercial newspaper. Others argued that this is a bad analogy. They argued that what a publisher does is his or her business because the newspaper is part of private enterprise. But, they say, what a principal does is society's business and cannot be capricious or arbitrary, just as police officers and judges cannot be capricious or arbitrary. The difference between a commercial and a student newspaper, this reasoning goes, is that in a school, the publisher is the government—and the United States has never permitted government control of the press.

Reaction to the Decision

Thus the argument was joined.

The National School Boards Association and the National Association of Secondary School Principals had told the Supreme Court:

> School districts which provide the educational opportunity for students to write and prepare a school newspaper must be allowed to set their own standards of propriety in determining what to publish so that they may protect themselves from tort liability. When a school district sponsors a newspaper in this manner it, like any other publisher, cannot be expected to give its writers free rein to decide what should appear in print.

Editorials in the nation's press displayed journalism's diversity of thought. The *Arizona Republic*, the largest newspaper in Arizona, liked the decision: "Despite [Justice William J. Brennan Jr.'s] excited alarms and the TV reporting, which was almost universally lopsided in favor of the defendant children, the court's ruling leaves (a) the public schools more serene and thus better able to perform their legitimate functions and (b) the First Amendment intact."

The *New York Times*, perhaps the country's most respected paper, saw two sides: "The 5–3 majority is basically correct in upholding the authority of educators over students of this age. But the court's affirmation puts heavy responsibility on how educators will use that authority. It's a pity that the justices, who did not hesitate to sustain school officials beyond the strict needs of the case before them, could not find space to admonish school systems to wield their power with wisdom, care, and restraint."

Columnist James Kilpatrick took on student press freedom advocates, calling their arguments "horsefeathers." He wrote, "The real world is different. In a grown-up world, an editor is subject to a publisher. If the publisher says, 'Kill the piece,' that's it, sweetheart, the piece is killed."

The *Buffalo Evening News* said: "Freedom of the press is vital to our democratic freedoms, and that is why the Founding Fathers entrenched it in the Constitution. In the Missouri high school case, however, it is hard to fault the Supreme Court for refusing to inject a constitutional issue into what seems basically an educational matter."

In the *Saginaw* (Mich.) *News*, the comment was: "Good 'publishers' should respect the efforts of the student press, despite the inevitable errors. Nor have they been given free rein: Justice White said the courts may intervene when censorship serves no 'valid educational purpose.' If this decision brings gross abuses, then student journalists will be back in court with justice on their side."

The *Roanoke* (Va.) *Times & World-News* declared: "The Hazelwood case, and other situations like it, involve two separate and very distinct issues. One is a constitutional question, the right of a public school to control its own publications. The other is an educational question, the wisdom of exerting such control in hamhanded fashion."

The *Portland* (Maine) *Evening Express* said: "[I]t is important—vital, really—that school authorities practice restraint in exercising ultimate editorial judgment. The power to censor ought not to be used as an excuse to stifle dissent, eliminate controversial expression, or discourage investigative enterprise."

The *Gary* (Ind.) *Post-Tribune* saw it this way: "Those who see themselves as real educators will continue to support school newspapers as learning places for journalists—they will expect vigorous journalism and accountability."

College and university journalism professors observed, through a statement by the Secondary Education Division of the Association for Education in Journalism and Mass Communication: "The Hazelwood ruling has accented the need for effective high school journalism programs. We heartily endorse this goal. By allowing school officials to regulate student publications that reflect shortcomings in style and content, the Supreme Court has issued a challenge. Recent research has shown that work on student publications is related to success on college entrance exams and in freshman composition. School officials should recognize the value of nurturing excellence in scholastic journalism as well. The result should be stronger high school journalism programs headed by qualified teachers and advisers."

Forum Theory

If a publication is exclusively a class project and used only for training and practice by student journalists, it is difficult to argue for student control. But not even this issue is totally black or white.

The Spectrum, the student newspaper at the center of the Hazelwood case, was determined by the Supreme Court not to be an open forum. Had it been ruled a forum, the court's decision might very well have gone the other way. Under Forum Theory, once the government creates a forum, it cannot control the ideas expressed there. A forum is a place where ideas are exchanged. A city park, where people climb on soapboxes and tell what they think, is a forum. Many universities have a mall or a "speaker's corner" where people may speak. These areas are protected by society, and the ideas expressed there are protected as well. If a school newspaper is a forum, Hazelwood probably does not apply.

A school newspaper that has been declared a place where members of the school community exchange ideas—through columns, letters to the editor, guest columns—may be in a different legal position than a pure lab newspaper produced by students for practice and training. This in no way should affect student conduct or judgment, of course. Again, it is not the law that governs student journalists. It is their sense of ethics, of right and wrong.

Hazelwood has caused other controversies. How, ask critics of the decision, is it possible to teach First Amendment values in a school where students are censored? What of the educational value of good journalism classes? Aren't journalism classes meant to be learning experiences and doesn't Hazelwood undermine them? These questions worry not only journalism advisers and students but school administrators as well.

Some states are questioning Hazelwood itself. The Iowa, Colorado, and Massachusetts legislatures have passed bills that, in effect, sidestep Hazelwood. These states, along with California, which already had a statute protecting students from censorship, are immune from Hazelwood. Many local districts also have reaffirmed their belief in free student expression and, in essence, negated Hazelwood locally. Other states and local districts are certain to follow.

Others remain unconvinced about Hazelwood's effect. Although many advisers expressed dismay over the decision, others said, "This case is no big deal."

Just how big a deal it is remains to be seen, of course. Many experts described the legal situation as "confused." Administrators, no less than students and advisers, also are grappling with the impact. Has Hazelwood imposed new obligations on them? Many believe it has, and are keeping a closer watch on the journalism classroom. Others say they put their faith in the students and the advisers and will support responsible journalism.

There is the key: *responsible journalism*. No Supreme Court ruling, no law, no policy, or school guideline, can change the basic elements of good journalism. Press pioneer Joseph Pulitzer used to say the press had three rules to follow: "Accuracy, accuracy, and accuracy." We would add fairness, objectivity, and balance. We would add as well good taste, good judgment, and good sense.

Journalists who practice their craft with these principles in mind bring honor to themselves and to journalism itself.

Wrap-up

Public confidence in the press has fallen. Journalists are often seen as rude and insensitive, at least in part because they are the bearers of unavoidable bad news.

Journalists have many roles assigned to them by society. Their coverage of government fulfills the political function expected of a constitutionally protected free press. Advertising helps move products and thus benefits the economy. As the press surveys the horizon and alerts the public to what's "out there," it fulfills the sentry function. Sports scores, birth announcements, and the like keep society's records. Comics, feature stories, and other light fare entertain us. Information in the mass media provides daily material for conversation and thus enhances our social lives. And the media help set society's agenda, which can lead to solutions.

Wrap-up continued

Various ways exist to evaluate the media. Interested citizens can compare newspapers, radio, television, and magazines with professional standards.

Journalists try to meet the ethical standards that, more than the law, guide their work. Journalists are expected to be accurate and objective. Their standards emphasize good taste, fairness, care with attribution, and a devotion to truth.

A large problem for journalists is libel. Published material that is both false and damaging to someone's reputation can lead to a lawsuit with heavy financial penalties for erring journalists. Truth is the best defense for journalists. There is no libel without falsity.

The legal situation for scholastic journalists changed greatly in 1988 with the U.S. Supreme Court's ruling in the Hazelwood case. In that case, the court said school officials can legally censor student newspapers and other forms of student expression if the censorship is related to educational needs.

Educators and even journalists are divided over whether this decision was good or bad and there is disagreement over what effect it will have on scholastic journalism.

The decision permits a school principal to assume the role of publisher of the student newspaper. In that position, the principal can control the paper's content. Nothing in the decision requires censorship and many school districts continue to grant students and advisers final say over the paper. Some states have passed legislation reaffirming this freedom.

School newspapers that are open forums for the exchange of ideas are generally considered exempt from the Hazelwood ruling.

People on both sides of the Hazelwood controversy agree that the responsibility of student journalists is unchanged. The emphasis must remain on accuracy, fairness, objectivity, balance, good taste, good judgment, and good sense.

On Assignment

Teamwork

1. Working in teams, prepare a code of standards for the publications in your school. Compare your code to the First Amendment standards of a free press and to the code of ethics of the Society of Professional Journalists reprinted in this chapter. Review the codes prepared by the class teams. Working as a class, prepare a code for your school.
2. Invite your principal to discuss with your class the issues raised by the Hazelwood case. Also, ask school board members for their opinions.

Practice

1. Write a brief essay on each of the following situations. Be prepared to discuss your position in class.
   a. You're a reporter for your school paper. You're covering a meeting of the board of education. In the middle of

the meeting, the president of the board turns to you and says, "I'm sorry, but this part of the meeting is off the record. Please stop taking notes and do not report any of this in the paper." What do you do? Why?
   b. You are in the school cafeteria and you overhear two school administrators discussing "the massive number of students who cheat." Do you have a story or not? How would you proceed? Why?
2. If there is a law library in your area, find the complete text of the U.S. Supreme Court opinion in the Hazelwood case and write a news story about it.
3. Research the editorial pages of commercial newspapers in your area and compare their reactions to the Hazelwood decision. About two-thirds of the press supported the court's opinion. What did the papers in your area say?

Your Turn

1. Interview one or more reporters for a commercial newspaper on the question of using anonymous sources. Does the reporter use such sources? Why or why not? Report your findings.
2. Assume that you are the principal of a high school and you have learned that your school's newspaper intends to publish the following stories. In each case, tell what you would do and why you would do it.
   a. A student has created a disturbance in the cafeteria, turning over tables, throwing food, and upsetting an urn of hot coffee. He was subdued and taken to a local hospital for psychiatric observation. The school newspaper wants to run a story about the incident, using the student's name and photographs of the damage.
   b. An editorial is planned criticizing the football coach for pressuring the parents of the students he coaches into buying kitchen appliances from him.
   c. Newspaper staff members investigating the all-school activities fund, money intended to support all the school's clubs and organizations, have discovered that school administrators have spent the entire fund to support the basketball team. The staffers want to run a story.
   d. Members of the student council have circulated a petition in the school to have the council's faculty adviser replaced. The school paper wants to run a story.
3. Assume that you are the editor of the school newspaper for which these articles are planned. In each case, tell what you would do and why.

SECTION TWO

Gathering the News

CHAPTER THREE

WHAT IS NEWS?

The three chapters in this section are about gathering the news. And that's a more elusive activity than it once was.

We used to think of news in relatively simple terms. News equaled events. News was automobile accidents, airplane crashes, violent weather, earthquakes, fires, slayings. News was meetings, press conferences, speeches, births, marriages, deaths. The boundaries were not hard to define.

Then life in the twentieth century became more complex and sophisticated. And the nature of news changed. The press moved away from events and concentrated on trends, on in-depth coverage of major issues. News was intricacies of government, damage to the environment, changing lifestyles and relationships, population control, educational reform, automobile safety, political reform, the women's movement, the changing family.

Then another change took place. The news began shifting away from government, social issues, and "where are we going in this society?" Several factors account for this recent shift: declining literacy, loss of young readers, decline of circulation generally, the mobile society ("Everybody just moved here. They don't care about the city council."), television's need for ratings, and the consequent emphasis on the upbeat or the spectacular, a feeling that people were tired of "bad news." As someone said, "People are tired of reading about famines in Ethiopia."

USA Today pioneered the new attitude. Colorful, upbeat, optimistic, unconcerned with covering City Hall, *USA Today* is a tremendous hit with the audience. Many journalists, eager to find the solution to the problem of a declining audience, have followed *USA Today's* lead. These journalists believe the audience is bored with government news, with endless stories about squabbles over cable television companies, sewage plants, urban development, and which neighborhoods to zone to accommodate new shopping malls.

Other journalists argue that the press has a role to play and society needs the same kind of news it always did, *with emphasis on government*. The authors of this book share the latter view, but acknowledge that the changes that have taken place are based on economic realities. Perhaps it comes down to a choice like this: a newspaper that compromises its definition of news or no newspaper at all.

So what is news in the latter days of the twentieth century? It is "all of the above." Events, of course, are still covered. So are trends. But to these add lifestyles of the rich and famous, fashion,

Stories and photos about the weather are of perennial interest to newspaper readers.

health, the arts, leisure, exercise, sex, parenting, recreation, nutrition, film, video, music. The list is endless, because it encompasses all of modern life.

Definitions change. But one thing remains constant: Anyone who wants to know what news is should buy a newspaper and read it. Not that everything in a newspaper is news. But we do urge you to subscribe to a good newspaper and read it regularly. There is no better textbook for a student than a good newspaper. Your daily newspaper should provide you with a ready source of ideas. By reading it with an eye toward your own writing style, you will learn how news stories are put together. Compare your efforts with those of the professionals. Ask yourself how they differ. Ask yourself how you can improve.

Right now, presumably, you are a beginner. At any rate, you wouldn't be studying this book if you weren't interested in improving and developing your skills. The authors hope to smooth the path for you.

News Judgment

It is the reporter's job to evaluate events and to select from a variety of occurrences those that will interest readers, that will entertain, inform, or educate them. How do reporters do this? They use news judgment, their own good sense in determining which of a dozen items should be included in a story, and, further, which of the five or six chosen should go into that all-important first paragraph, the lead. You aren't born with news judgment; it is something you must absorb through experience, through reading newspapers (including your own), and through hard work. And while we cannot define "news," we can provide some guidelines for sound news judgment.

Historically, journalism teachers and texts have gone into some detail about the so-called elements of news or news values. These include such things as timeliness, proximity, and prominence, and we will look at these elements in some detail shortly.

Right now, let us look at the way one professor tries to teach students news judgment. The method is far from scientific, but it seems to work. When students hand in stories containing statements or paragraphs that are not news, he jogs their news judgment by making red marks across the offending sections and scrawling "Who cares?" all over the margins. He could write, "Use better news judgment. You should know that what you have written is not newsworthy because there is no proximity (or prominence or timeliness) here. In the future please be more careful. You are going to have to develop your news sense.'' If the professor did that, however, he would never get all the papers corrected. So he writes ''Who cares?'' and the students get the idea.

The ''Who Cares?'' Method

Thus, we come to a concrete way to measure, in a sense, the value of a news event. It is simply this: Ask yourself, ''Who cares?'' Who cares about this? How many people will be interested? Nearly everyone? Or nearly no one? If you are able to answer your own question by saying, ''A great many of my newspaper's readers will want to know about this,'' or ''Most of the readers need to know about this,'' or some similar positive statement, then you have news on your hands. If not, toss it out.

Let's try the ''Who cares?'' method of news judgment. Here are two simple events; one is news, one is not.

A. The mayor signs a proclamation designating next week as Clean-up, Paint-up, Fix-up Week.
B. The mayor announces an investigation into the disappearance of $75,000 from the city's general fund.

Now, who cares about each event? (This is childishly simple, but it makes a point.) Who cares about Clean-up, Paint-up, Fix-up Week? Practically no one. Politicians constantly issue such proclamations, mostly at the urging of special-interest groups. In this case, the special week is a lure for newspaper advertising from lumber yards, nurseries, seed stores, and paint stores. The media pay scant attention to such weeks. They are routine and of little or no interest to the audience, which has long since become bored by special ''weeks.'' Remember, news is the unique, the different, the departure from the normal course of events.

Who cares about event B? The answer is nearly everyone in the community. For taxpayers, and that includes practically every citizen, the handling of public money is a critical issue. The conduct of public officials draws intense concern in a democratic society. So, yes, event B is news. As you know, few news decisions in a journalist's life present such a clear-cut choice as those in this example. However, as a starter, think ''Who cares?'' and you'll be on your way to developing good news judgment.

Not all events are subject to such treatment. If your instructor had a fight with a neighbor, you might get a positive answer to the ''Who cares?'' question, but you wouldn't have news. Why?

Because some things are no one's business. Regardless of the readers' interest in gossip, a newspaper's duty is to rise above the level of spreading ugly stories that invade the privacy and upset the lives of innocent people. Like so many things in journalism, it is a matter of taste. One of your jobs as a journalist is to cull from the columns of your newspaper and your yearbook those items that would offend the readers' taste. This, too, is part of news judgment.

The constant variety of putting together the front page

By David Hall
Editor of The *Denver Post*

In the news business, we talk a lot about "front-page journalism."

One of the treasures of the profession, in fact, is a play (later made twice into a movie) called *The Front Page*, which is about the uproarious high jinks of hard-sell journalism in Chicago during the 1920s.

Editors pay a lot of attention to Page One, for it serves several important functions:

Most important, the front page should give readers a perspective on the day's news. Here you are, just awake and showered, coffee cup in hand: Your morning paper should help you start the day by making some sense of the world and your community.

We also use Page One to sell the newspaper. In a competitive market like Denver, sales of newspapers from vending machines and across counters are an increasingly important part of circulation. That accounts for our use of the colorful boxes across the top of Page One to attract the potential buyer's eye. Single-copy sales considerations also affect how boldly we display a good story. We're not embarrassed about competing for your attention.

Page One also is a guide to material inside the paper—not just daily news reports, but also features on entertainment, gardening, sporting events, and the like. Our front page lets you window-shop.

Editors choose stories for Page One after considerable thought. We try during the day to stay on top of news developments, and each afternoon at 4:30 *Post* editors meet around a large conference table and go over detailed lists (we call them "budgets") of what each department has planned for the next morning's paper.

I stuck last week's front pages on the wall and reflected on what variety they held.

The single event that dominated Page One from day to day was the Olympics. Who says newspapers ignore good news?

We touched on such varied other topics as the tax-increase debate, the mining of Red Sea shipping lanes, the changing demographics of Denver, the death of Richard Burton, the results of petitioning for changes in Colorado's laws, and a fascinating story out of Chicago on a rash of brick thievery from abandoned buildings.

My favorite front page was Thursday's. Why the six stories were chosen indicates some ways that *Post* editors think about news.

In six columns at the top we have a major piece of explanatory reporting on the legal tangle at Fort Logan Mental Health Center. A judge has sentenced three hospital administrators to jail for violating an order to confine two teenagers in secure areas; the administrators plead lack of space and money to follow the law. We chose Thursday (and devoted considerable space to reporter Bill Walker's story) because that was the day of a legislative hearing on the matter. We felt the *Post's* reporting could contribute to better public understanding of this controversy, and ultimately to a solution.

Also high on the page, and under a dark headline, was a story marking congressional passage of a bill that should help thousands of single parents collect child-support payments to which they are legally entitled. The story related importantly to the rising overall concern about the economic status of women.

The page carried a large photo of Air Force Academy graduate Alonzo Babers winning an Olympic gold medal in the 400-meter race.

It carried two controversial but significant local stories: One on a Denver commission asking for extra money to investigate complaints of misconduct against Judge Larry Lopez-Alexander; the other on an investigation into the financial position of Colorado's largest life insurer, Capitol Life.

The page contained a political story centered around the continuing controversy over whether a tax increase is needed to reduce the federal deficit. The Vice President was visiting Denver, and he reflected on the tax questions and other matters in a wide-ranging interview with political reporter Patrick Yack.

The sixth story on the page dealt with troubles the General Services Administration is having in installing new phone systems in Denver-area federal offices. This was more than a story about bureaucratic foul-ups; most important, it was a story affecting nearly 34,000 men and women who work here for the federal government. Denver is a major center of government employment, and the *Post* recognizes that stories about the federal workplace are just as important as stories about politics.

Page One is a small part of a newspaper, but day in and day out it is the most important part.

It's the place where every day the *Denver Post* must get itself and its readers off to the right start. It's your daily window to the world, and we try to make that view as clear and as meaningful as possible.

This article appeared in a weekly feature called Letter from the Editor. *David Hall invites readers to send questions about the* Denver Post *for possible future columns.*

The Elements of News

A little warning bell should go off in your head when you come across an item in bad taste. On the other hand, a bell should also ring when an item is legitimate news. This is just another way of saying that news judgment is, to a great extent, intuitive. Seasoned journalists do not need such guidelines as timeliness, proximity, or prominence. Instead, they rely on the bells in their heads. This is no help, you say, because you do not have bells yet. You have not acquired the intuitive judgment, a sort of sixth sense that allows you to weigh, often in a split second, the news value of an event. For this reason, we will discuss briefly the classic elements of news.

Depending on which authors you read, there are anywhere from five to twelve elements of news. We will look at those most generally recognized.

Timeliness

Timeliness relates to the newness of the facts. It is this element that makes a story about football more timely in November than in June. A story lacks timeliness for the school newspaper if the daily newspaper downtown already covered the story at great length two weeks earlier. Instead, the paper should concentrate on advance items, stories about coming events.

Proximity

Proximity refers to the nearness of a given event to your place of publication. Events occurring in your school generally have more news value than those occurring on the other side of the world. People like to read about things they are familiar with, and they are more likely to be familiar with those things closest to home.

This explains the reliance of most newspapers on local news, about which a great editor once said, "A tomcat on the steps of City Hall is more important than a crisis in the Balkans." This is no longer true, of course, because today that crisis in the Balkans could have far-reaching consequences that would dramatically affect the lives of your readers. What the editor said still makes a good deal of sense, however. To paraphrase him, "A minor dropout problem in our school is more important than a major problem in a school 500 miles away."

Prominence

Prominence refers to the "newsworthiness" of an individual. It is true that names make news, but some names make more news than others. Why? Because they are more prominent. Thus, if the star quarterback flunks a math exam and is ineligible for the big game, his troubles are newsworthy. Suppose you flunk the same exam. Is that news? Not unless there's some other factor involved. The quarterback, like it or not, is more prominent than you, and

Movie stars—celebrities—are newsworthy, especially when they win an Oscar. Here Whoopi Goldberg reacts to winning one for Best Supporting Actress in *Ghost* at the 63rd Annual Academy Awards.

his failure is more far-reaching. "There goes the ball game," will be the reaction to the news of his failure. When people learn that you flunked, they'll shrug, mutter "How about that?" and go on about their business.

The element of prominence explains a great deal about how news is handled. It explains, at least partly, why the press follows movie stars, why it interviews the governor, and why it runs story after story about well-known persons.

Consequence

The element of consequence refers simply to the importance of an event. Let's use our star quarterback again as an example. It is more important to more people that he flunked the math exam than that you flunked it, because of the consequences. The team may lose the big game. Hundreds, maybe thousands, of football fans may be disappointed—or they may be thrilled at the performance of the substitute who gets his big chance and makes good.

The element of consequence, incidentally, offers many opportunities for stories in your newspaper that do not, on the surface, seem to have any news value. For example, if the state legislature passes a bill providing state financial aid to local school districts, you should recognize that this action, even though it took place in the state capital, has important consequences for your school. Ask school officials how much money will come to your school and what will be done with it. This is an example of localization, the act of bringing out the local angle in a story. Another example would be the effect on construction plans for a new school in your town if steel or railroad workers went on strike. It is important to keep up with the news outside your school; you never know when an item in a daily newspaper or a periodical will lend itself to localization.

Human Interest

What are you, as a human being, most interested in? Chances are you are most interested in other people and how they behave. Human interest stories cause readers to laugh or cry, to feel emotion. If a little girl is trapped for days in an abandoned well, that's a human interest story. If a dog mourns at his master's grave, that's a human interest story. If that substitute quarterback we were talking about throws five touchdown passes, that's a human interest story. In other words, human interest stories are unusual. They are about the shortest basketball player, the fastest track runner, the youngest teacher, or the oldest custodian. They tickle the funny bone or cause feelings of sorrow, pity, or amazement.

The element of human interest explains why newspapers run a story when a 15-year-old genius graduates from college, or when

There is an almost uni-
versal interest in animals
and children. A dramatic
photo like this one can
draw readers' attention
to the page.

a bride on her way to the wedding gets lost and ends up at the wrong church. The fact that the world has one more college graduate is of no particular significance in itself, nor is the fact that someone got married. But wouldn't you want to read a story about a 15-year-old college graduate or a lost bride? Yes, and so would everyone else. It's human interest.

Conflict

An element of news that enters into many stories is conflict. Why do so many people attend sports events? Conflict. Why are so many people interested in elections? Conflict, at least partly. Why are strikes and labor disputes news? Conflict. Why are wars, to take the most extreme case, news? Conflict. Conflict involves tension, surprise, and suspense. (Who will win the football game? Who will win the election?) People are in an almost constant state of conflict with their environment. Husbands and wives fight over who will win custody of their children; homeowners fight to keep taverns from opening in their quiet neighborhoods; doctors fight to discover cures for diseases that kill their patients; and countries fight for supremacy in the world arena.

Other Factors   There are many other elements of news, including progress, money, disaster, novelty, oddity, emotions, drama, animals, and children. It would serve little purpose to discuss these at length. Let us just repeat that news judgment rarely involves a simple matching of an event with a list of elements to determine whether the event is news. Professional journalists may not be able to define news, but they know it when they see it. Students just have to develop a system of warning bells. Determining news value is not an exact science. You can't expect to rely on formulas. You're not a physicist, you're a journalist. While there are no shortcuts, we will show you an attempt to create "news arithmetic." This idea comes from *Editing the Day's News* by George Bastian and Leland Case. It may be helpful in developing those bells.

News Arithmetic

1 ordinary man + 1 ordinary life = 0
1 ordinary woman + 1 extraordinary adventure = NEWS
1 husband + 1 wife = 0
1 husband + 3 wives = NEWS
1 bank cashier + 1 spouse + 7 children = 0
1 bank cashier − $20,000 = NEWS
1 child + 1 lost dog = 0
1 child of Prince Charles and Princess Diana + 1 lost dog = NEWS
1 person + 1 achievement = NEWS
1 ordinary person + 1 ordinary life of 79 years = 0
1 ordinary person + 1 ordinary life of 100 years = NEWS

This little formula points up one thing. Curiosity is a human characteristic. Look for news items that will satisfy readers' curiosity, and remember, there are no shortcuts. Telling you that "it isn't news if a dog bites a man, but it is if a man bites a dog" is of little help. If a dog bites the President of the United States, that's news. If a dog with rabies bites a child, that's news. Nor does it help to talk about having a "nose for news." There is no such thing. While it is true that some reporters seem to make a career out of being in the right place at the right time, it's because they have trained themselves to know where the right place is. Their noses have little to do with it.

Generating News Story Ideas

Before you can even begin to judge whether a story idea contains enough news elements, you need to come up with the idea. One way to generate ideas for good news stories is for the newspaper staff to hold a brainstorming session. Our definition for this term is the fine art of obtaining numerous ideas within a short span of time.

It is important that staff time be used as efficiently as possible. Most newspaper and yearbook staffs meet for an hour a day; some meet only once or twice a week. There are stories to write, advertisements to sell, and pages to lay out. There is not a lot of time for discussions that end in long arguments without resolving the problems at hand. So use the brainstorming technique as a fast method of getting a lot of solutions, ideas, or alternatives for action in a very short amount of staff time. You can do it with large groups or you can do it with only two or three participants.

This section is included early in the book because you will find many activities, some for teams, that require that you plan how you will cover a specific subject, illustrate a photo series, or develop special information for your class discussions.

Brainstorming Sessions

Brainstorming, used effectively, will help you move from ideas into action quickly. This is our proposal for operating a typical, productive session. You will need to adapt it to your own needs and situations.

First, have the group leader—editor, business manager, or adviser—explain the problem to be considered. (Example: We are planning a special issue of the paper on problems facing today's graduate. What stories should be assigned?)

Give people a few minutes of "think time" in which to consider the idea. They might jot down two or three ideas.

Now have the group leader call on each participant, one at a time, to state a proposal for action in one short and complete sentence. Participants should not need to explain their thoughts or elaborate on them. There should be no discussion or criticism of any idea presented. (To continue the example: How does one hunt for a job? What are the additional opportunities for education? Does the government offer various types of employment? How about military opportunities? How do I establish residency for voting, in-state tuition fees, and other benefits? You can come up with quite a list of issues or questions that the new graduate will face. Each idea is briefly stated; each can be the basis for a story.)

As each idea is given, have it written down by a group recorder. You might want to put the ideas on the chalkboard or an overhead projector transparency.

Go around the group two or three times. Don't let people get by with stating what has already been said. Tell participants always to have more than one idea in mind, and urge them to let their imaginations run wild. Generally, the wilder the ideas the more totally productive the final results. No idea is a bad one unless it is not expressed. Participants can use ideas as springboards for expanding or building on suggestions of others. (Example: The original idea might have been, How does a recent graduate hunt for a job? Follow-up ideas might be, How important is the résumé? How do you arrange for and act during an interview? How do you know if the employer is really interested in you? Should you go to a placement company? Are job placement services available at our school? What references do you need?)

After you seem to have exhausted the input from the group, begin to narrow your list to one of top priorities. Here is where you can lose control, unless you are careful about procedure.

First of all, there is still to be no discussion of the list.

Have the group look over the suggestions. (If meeting time is a problem, have the recorder type the list and make each member a copy.) Have each participant select the five *best* ideas from the list or, if the list is small, the best two or three. Have participants write their choices down on a piece of paper *in order of priority*, with the best idea first. Don't let people try to influence each other; each person must evaluate the list for himself or herself.

Now compile the answers. You will see some common preferences rather quickly. Take the best choices as determined by "secret ballot" and put them into action.

The editors may need a brainstorming session on each of the best ideas to think them through to their final conclusions.

Advantages of Brainstorming

By now the advantages of this system should be obvious: (1) Participation comes from every staff member on an equal basis. No one person can dominate the discussion; every idea is important and equal for purposes of group evaluation. (2) A large number of ideas can be generated in less than five minutes. The more you use the system, the better you get at it. One of the authors participated in a group that came up with 112 ideas in less than one hour on the question of how to restore public confidence in public education. (3) Valuable time, often wasted by lengthy discussion dominated by a few, can be conserved for more vital functions.

Now, how many ways can you use this system? Why not brainstorm that question through for a starter? You will surely include:

1. Topics for editorials this week.
2. Topics for in-depth stories.
3. Topics for editorial page columns and cartoons.
4. Sources of advertising for a special issue.
5. Ways to sell the paper or yearbook more effectively.
6. Ideas for photo essays.
7. Locations for taking pictures of school leaders for the yearbook.

Brainstorming, sharing opinions, is an excellent way to insure quality in selecting photos for the school newspaper.

8. Theme topics for the yearbook.

9. Ways to raise funds to support publication "extras."

10. Ways to take more interesting photos of meetings, classroom activities, or concerts and sporting events.

11. Methods for increasing readership.

12. Items to include in a survey.

The process is easy, and it keeps getting easier with practice. Naturally, you will modify it to your advantage and to each situation. You can even do it all in writing.

The Brainstorming Technique

Brainstorming is the fine art of obtaining numerous ideas within a short span of time. The steps in a typical brainstorming session are as follows:

1. The topic, problem, or goal for the session is announced and explained as briefly as possible.

2. Participants have two or three minutes to consider the question.

3. One at a time, in rotation, each participant offers—in one short and complete sentence—a solution to the problem, or an idea for a project or action.

4. All ideas are written down by the group recorder.

5. There can be no criticism or discussion of any idea by any participant.

6. Participants may use previously mentioned ideas as springboards for additional ideas.

7. All participants should have a second or third idea ready in case their first one has already been mentioned.

8. After the group has been canvassed at least once, take ideas randomly from any participants. The ideas may now be typed and reproduced for all members, who indicate their top three to five choices for "best" ideas in order of importance.

9. The "votes" are counted and the ideas ranked.

10. Discussion, or additional brainstorming, can then center on each of the top ideas.

Wrap-up

Once-easy ideas of what constitutes news— mostly events and government—have been revised in view of changes in society and people's interests.

Busy modern readers appear to want shorter stories, often in list form, more color, and less "bad news." Because of *USA Today* and its colorful and upbeat approach, newspapers are changing.

As literacy as well as circulation decline, newspapers seek ways to capture a greater share of the mobile audience. Stories about local government do not have the same appeal to the city's newcomers.

These changes concern some people who believe newspapers have a constitutional role to play that mandates coverage of government. But newspapers apparently must decide whether to compromise or fade.

Therefore, where once newspapers concentrated on government news, they now deliver information on all aspects of modern life, including fashion, health, the arts, leisure, exercise, sex, parenting, recreation, nutrition, film, video, and music.

Despite these changes, students are urged to read newspapers for knowledge of what editors consider news. Serious journalism students certainly need to be users of the news. Reading newspapers is a good way to hone one's news judgment.

Some people decide what is news and what is not by applying the "Who cares?" technique. This means assessing how much reader interest a story has. The more people who care about the information in the story, the greater its news value. Of course, there is reader interest in mere gossip but ethical journalists avoid tasteless items.

Other journalists rely on more formal elements of news to determine a story's importance. Among many, the most-often cited are timeliness, proximity, prominence, consequence, human interest, and conflict.

Once a journalist is trained and experienced, news judgment becomes a matter of instinct, of course. Professional journalists make judgments without reference to techniques beginners often rely on.

Beginners are advised to make use of the technique of brainstorming, the art of obtaining numerous ideas within a short time. By carefully organizing and controlling brainstorming sessions, the staff can develop new ideas quickly and efficiently.

On Assignment

Teamwork

1. Working in teams, clip all the stories from your most recent local newspaper that contain the news element of conflict. Mount them on sheets of paper, underlining the conflict.

   Next, examine the front page of today's local newspaper and identify all of the news elements in it. Discuss what you have found out about the news judgment of the paper.

2. On separate cards, write a brief summary of each story on the front page you have been studying. Ask 20 students to rate the stories in order of importance. Is there a general agreement? Why or why not? What does this represent? How do the elements of news affect the raters' decisions? Write a report on your group's findings. Compare your results with those of the other teams.

3. Brainstorm five purposes for your school newspaper. Under each purpose you identify, brainstorm a list showing:
   a. how the paper is now meeting each purpose; and
   b. how the paper can improve its efforts to better meet each purpose.

Compare your lists with those of other groups in your class. Where do you agree? Where do you disagree? Why? Combine all of your lists into one.

Practice

1. Identify three possible school news story ideas for each news element mentioned in this chapter. State the story idea in a single sentence. For example, ''Grade averages are rising and causing concern over grade inflation.'' Then identify the audiences to whom the story will appeal. Ask ''Who cares?'' What element(s) are present?

2. Discuss in class or write an essay on this situation: Assume that a 15-year-old student has been involved in a serious crime. As a journalist, what do you report? What, if anything, do you leave out about the person? First answer in terms of ''Who cares?'' Then consider how your code of ethics affects your decision.

3. Brainstorm on these subjects to understand how the process works:
   a. How many ways can you use a cup half-full of cold coffee, assuming that you want to conserve either cup or liquid or both and use it effectively?
   b. What will life be like in the year 2010?

c. What might your school be like in the year 2010?

d. How many ways can you describe a banana?

e. What are some excellent ideas for school yearbook themes?

f. How many photo ideas can you develop in five minutes that will illustrate your school's athletic program?

g. How many photo ideas can you develop to illustrate your school's science program?

h. What topics would make interesting editorials for your school newspaper?

Your Turn

1. Identify one person on the faculty or staff or among the students who would be a good subject for a human interest story. Write one page explaining who and why. How would you approach the story?

2. Look through your local newspaper and identify one story you can localize for your school publication. Clip the article and mount it. Write one page explaining how you would localize it and why your student readers will want to read it.

3. Write a paragraph identifying one school-related story idea to demonstrate each element of news discussed in this chapter.

4. Assume you are totally free to identify a topic for a special issue of your school newspaper. Brainstorm a list of topics, then use the complete process to identify the 10 best ideas. Remember your audience. For each idea, brainstorm a list of articles you would assign to cover the topic adequately. Narrow that list to the best ten subjects for articles. (Keep these lists in your notebook for use later in the term.)

Eric Sevareid

Elucidation by Eric Sevareid at the close of a distinguished career as a journalist.

By my time of life, one has accumulated more allegiances and moral debts than the mind can remember or the heart contain.

So I cannot enumerate my betters, my mentors and sustainers during so many years of trying to use, with sense, this communications instrument, as unperfected as the persons who use it. But they know that I know who they are.

Many are gone, including the man who invented me, Ed Murrow. Some died in the wars we were reporting. I have gone the normal span of a man's working life, so abnormal in this calling—it is a happy surprise.

We were like a young band of brothers in those early days with Murrow. If my affections are not easily given, neither are they easily withdrawn. I have remained through it all with CBS News, and if it is regarded as old-fashioned to feel loyalty to an organization, so be it.

Mine has been, here, an unelected, unlicensed, uncodified office and function. The rules are self-imposed. These were a few:

Not to underestimate the intelligence of the audience and not to overestimate its information.

To elucidate, when one can, more than to advocate.

To remember always that the public is only people, and people only persons, no two alike.

To retain the courage of one's doubts as well as one's convictions in this world of dangerously passionate certainties.

To comfort oneself, in times of error, with the knowledge that the saving grace of the press, print or broadcast, is its self-correcting nature. And to remember that ignorant or biased reporting has its counterpart in ignorant and biased reading and listening. We do not speak into an intellectual or emotional void.

One's influence cannot be measured. History provides, for the journalist, no markers or milestones. But he is allowed to take his memories.

And one can understand as he looks back, the purpose of the effort and why it must be done.

A friend and teacher, the late Walter Lippmann, described the role of the professional reporter and observer of the news in this manner:

"We make it our business," he said, "to find out what is going on, under the surface and beyond the horizon; to infer, to deduce, to imagine and to guess what is going on inside—and what this meant yesterday and what it could mean tomorrow. In this way we do what every sovereign citizen is supposed to do but has not the time or the interest to do it for himself. This is our job. It is no mean calling, and we have a right to be proud of it and to be glad that it is our work."

In the end, of course, it is not one's employers or colleagues who sustain one quite so much as the listening public when it be so minded.

I have found that it applies only one consistent test—not agreement with one on substance, but the perception of honesty and fair intent.

There is, in the American people, a tough, undiminished instinct for what is fair. Rightly or wrongly. I have a feeling I have passed the test. I shall wear this like a medal.

Millions have listened, intently and indifferently, in agreement and in powerful disagreement. Tens of thousands have written their thoughts to me.

I will feel, always, that I stand in their midst.

This was Eric Sevareid in Washington. Thank you and goodby. ∎

CHAPTER FOUR

NEWS ORGANIZATIONS AND SOURCES

The first requirement for an efficient news gathering operation is a well-organized staff. Many ways have been devised to organize a staff, and this discussion may serve as a guideline.

The Newspaper Staff

The organization of a school newspaper closely parallels that of a commercial newspaper. At the top is the publisher. In theory, the taxpayers of your school district are the ''publisher'' of your newspaper and yearbook. In practice, the taxpayers can't perform that function, so they elect a board of education to oversee the school district, including your publications. But not even the board can be publisher and still perform its many other duties, so it appoints a superintendent who in turn appoints a principal of your school. And the principal functions as publisher.

Just as the publisher of a commercial newspaper is rarely concerned with the minute-to-minute operation of the paper, neither is the principal in most cases. Instead, the principal, usually working closely with the journalism adviser and the students, sets certain broad guidelines—general policies within which the newspaper staff, like everyone else associated with the school, must function.

Students who grumble that they are not free to print whatever they please should remember that the editor of the *New York Times* has the same problem. This is a fact of newspaper life, and only rarely does a publisher issue an order with which the honest, ethical journalist cannot live. It does happen, though, at commercial newspapers and at scholastic newspapers. When it happens, then the journalist—professional or student—has to decide what to do.

Serving as liaison to the publisher, the public, the faculty, the students, possibly the printer, and everyone else who wants to talk about the newspaper is the journalism adviser. He or she has a difficult job, sometimes caught between conflicting aims of students and administrators. The best advisers walk a tightrope and keep all their various publics happy. It is not an easy job.

Next in command are the heads of the various departments. These include the managing editor, or editor in chief, who has the overall responsibility for the editorial department—that is, the news operation. Other department heads are in charge of advertising, circulation, business, and, depending on how your newspaper is printed, the printing department. This chapter is concerned primarily with the editorial, or news, department.

Under the managing editor are various subeditors. Sometimes these are organized by "page," with each subeditor in charge of a particular section. This is usually unsatisfactory, because the news can seldom be categorized by page. There are some sports stories that rate page-one treatment and some so-called hard news stories that may belong on an inside page.

These subeditors carry various titles. The sports editor, obviously, has charge of the newspaper's sports coverage. There may be a news editor, who is, in fact, the chief copy editor and headline writer. There may be an editorial page editor, who works closely with the managing editor and most likely writes the editorials that express the newspaper's opinion.

By whatever names the subeditors go, they form the link between the top person, the managing editor, and the reporters. Under the sports editor, there may be two or three sports reporters, depending on the size of the newspaper. Under the news editor, there is usually a staff of reporters who carry out the assignments that have been determined by the news editor in conference with the managing editor and the publication's adviser.

Newspaper Staff Organization

Publisher

Managing Editor

| Layout Editor | Art/Designers |

| Photo Editor | Photographers |

News Editor
Feature Editor
Sports Editor
Other Dept.
Editors

| Copy Editors | Reporters |

Production Department

Composing Room

Platemaking

Press Room

Service Dept.

Mailing Dept.

Business Manager

Circulation Manager

Advertising Manager

Sales Depts.

The Production of a Newspaper

Newswriting and Production	Managing editor or other editor assigns story *or* Reporter finds story	Compositor sets type
	Reporter writes story	Proofreader corrects errors
	Reporter passes story back to editor	Layout editor and staff size photos, design pages
	Copy editor corrects copy, verifies facts	Production manager and staff print pages, assemble newspaper
	Managing editor approves story and photos	Business-circulation staff distributes, sells newspapers
	Editor writes headline	
	Managing editor approves layout	
Advertising	Advertising manager assigns ad responsibilities	Finished ads ready for layout
	Advertising staff sells space, creates ads	
Photography	Photography editor assigns photos	Photographer makes prints, provides caption material or writes caption
	Photographer takes picture	Prints are sent to editor

Types of Reporters

Reporters are of two types. (Some people say "good and bad," but that's not the point here.) There are beat reporters and general assignment reporters. The beat reporter checks the same news sources for each edition of the paper. If the beat (or run) is the fine arts department, the reporter will visit each of the art, music, and speech teachers as often as possible, cover the school plays and concerts, write the story about the soloists being selected for the annual spring music festival, report on the new band uniforms, interview the new speech teacher, and get stories about the debate team studying for its state competition. Similarly, the beat reporter who covers the school administrators' offices makes a point of seeing his or her news sources as frequently as possible. Beat reporters become specialists; they may not know everything that goes on throughout the school, but they'd better know everything that happens on their beat.

The general assignment reporter, on the other hand, goes wherever necessary. He or she may be covering the convocation speaker today and writing a piece about the lack of parking space tomorrow. Such a reporter is a jack-of-all-trades, doing the work passed out as the news editor sees fit.

A well-organized newspaper keeps a file of back issues, photos, and
story-related news items. Reporters often use these files for research.

Some people would include a third classification of reporter, the
"cub." This is the novice, who may be assigned to pick up brief
items from fairly regular sources or to check weekly with three or
four teachers to see if they have any news to offer. The cub who
does this work willingly and well, and who shows enterprise by
coming up with an important story on his or her own initiative,
will not remain a cub for long.

News Sources

Both reporters and editors must know where to go to get the news.
They cannot sit back with their feet on their desks waiting for
someone to walk in and hand them their stories. They must *go* to
the source—and dig, dig, dig, if necessary.

Who are the sources and where are they? Let's start with the
commercial newspaper and illustrate one major difference between it and the scholastic newspaper. Commercial newspapers
receive a considerable amount of their news from wire services,
organizations such as the Associated Press, United Press Interna-

tional, Reuters, and the *New York Times* News Service. Wire services provide news around the clock from around the world. No newspaper is fully equipped to cover the world by itself, so newspapers subscribe to services that provide this news for them. Except for these wire services, there is little difference between the types of news sources scholastic journalists use and those the professionals use.

Public Relations

There is, for instance, the public relations representative, whose job is to provide newspapers—including yours—with news about certain firms or organizations. Perhaps your school system has one; if so, introduce yourself and make sure your newspaper is on the mailing list. Public relations people see that any time the organization they work for makes news, the newspapers are informed of it. Often, the news releases they send will provide the incentive for your newspaper to dig deeper, to get a more complete story. Never assume that a news release is the whole story; always attempt to find out if something is missing. Remember that public relations people, by definition, are trying to present their employers in the best possible light. They have the welfare of their organization uppermost in their minds. Journalists, by contrast, must consider the welfare of the community they serve.

News Tips

Many news stories come in the form of tips. No newspaper staff, no matter how large, can be everywhere at once. Often, someone who is not a member of the staff will inform you of an event you may want to cover. Let it be known that you are on the lookout for tips, and you will be surprised at how many people will volunteer valuable information.

Sometimes material for a school newspaper comes from school administrators, teachers, or students who are not on the newspaper staff. These persons may come to the newspaper with ideas for stories or essays. Sometimes they have already written a story or essay; often these contributions can be valuable additions to the paper.

Incidentally, the solicitation of stories, essays, or "think pieces" dates back to 1721 when James Franklin announced in his *New-England Courant* that he "earnestly desires his friends may favor him from time to time with some short Piece, Serious, Sarcastick, Ludicrous, or other ways Amusing."

"Some short Piece, Serious, Sarcastick, Ludicrous, or other ways Amusing"

The Future Book

Another valuable source of news comes with the creation of a complete future book. A future book is a listing, by date, of events coming up that you might want to cover. If you hear in December that the board of education is going to consider a school bond issue in May, enter that fact in the future book under "May." The future book is simply a long-range calendar of events and ideas. If you run a story this week that mentions an event that will take place next semester or even next year, clip the story and put it in the future book. Then, as you plan coverage for the next semester or the next year, the clip will be there to help you.

Reporters and Staff Persons

Public relations people, tips, standard reference works, future books—all are available. But in the end, how well you cover the news will depend on what you know about the processes of gathering it. In this area, the reporter is the boss. He or she is on the front lines of journalism, where the action is. No newspaper, radio, or television news department is any better than its reporters.

Reporters are the eyes and ears of the news staff, constantly on the watch for story ideas. But they cannot do the job alone. The entire staff—each person described in this chapter—has an obligation to watch alertly for material. Reporters on all beats should turn in items for other areas and should share ideas for stories. No matter what formal organization is in effect, all must work together if the group is to succeed.

The people at the top of the organization—the editors—have an obligation to maintain good communication with the whole news organization staff. Editors need to be in constant communication with reporters and photographers to avoid duplicating assignments and to settle disputes over beats. Memos, bulletin boards, and staff mailboxes all provide ways for staff members to keep in touch with what others are doing. Frequent staff meetings are helpful. Such meetings are also one way for editors to publicly praise the work of the staff.

In an efficient news gathering operation, all members of the group work together creatively and smoothly to produce accurate, high-quality material.

Members of a newspaper staff work together as a team to keep their readers informed, as shown in this photo of the Chicago *Sun-Times* city newsroom.

Wrap-up

The first requirement for an efficient news gathering operation is a well-organized staff.

The organization of school publications parallels that of commercial publications. At the top is the publisher. The board of education, elected by the public, appoints a superintendent who in turn appoints a principal of your school. The principal functions as publisher.

The principal, usually working closely with the journalism adviser and the students, sets guidelines—general policies within which the publication staff must function.

Serving as liaison to the publisher, the public, the faculty, the students, and possibly the printer, is the journalism adviser. He or she has a difficult job and is sometimes caught between conflicting aims of students and administrators.

In the organization of a publication staff, the managing editor is at the top of the pyramid, determining policies and developing story ideas. Subeditors, sometimes organized by the page for which they are responsible, work under the managing editor's direction. Sports editors, chief copy editors, and editorial page editors are in this group. All help supervise reporters.

Reporters can either cover a beat, returning always to the same sources and subjects, or do general assignment work. General assignment reporters cover whatever is necessary.

Where does the news come from? At commercial publications, the wire services provide a great deal of copy. Student publications have no wire services and have to be staffed by people willing to dig for stories.

Public relations people try to keep publications, including school publications, informed. They are advocates of their employers, however, and the material they generate must be viewed accordingly. Tips from readers and a carefully kept future book help keep the news flowing.

The real eyes and ears of any publication are its reporters. They are on the front lines. How good a publication becomes depends on its reporters and how well they are supported. Helpful editors who maintain good communication are great contributors to any publication. Teamwork is essential to a smooth journalistic operation.

On Assignment

Teamwork

1. As a class, interview your school newspaper editor to learn how the paper is organized. Who does what? In teams, meet with staff members of other school publications in your town or vicinity, including college and university publications. Find out how they are organized. See if they have ideas you could borrow or adapt to your special needs.

2. Devise new approaches to the organization of your school newspaper. Develop an organization chart. Write short job descriptions for every person on the staff organization chart. What regular beats will you have? Write a summary of the adviser's role.

   Compare your organization plan with that of a local commercial newspaper. How are they alike? How are they different? Why?

   List ten improvements your team would make to your current school newspaper. Explain the reasons for them.

Practice

1. Research the effects of technology on the media. Consider computer data base searches, satellite transmission, cable, and other technological advances. Write a short report on your findings.

2. Discuss salaries with the personnel managers at local newspapers and TV and radio stations. There is a popular belief that people in the newspaper business are very much underpaid. Is that true? Has the advent of computers had any effect on salaries? Are enough talented people available to fill local staff needs?

Your Turn

Make a list of the stories in today's (or this week's) edition of your local newspaper. Do the same with today's local and national television newscasts. How do they compare? Which uses the most local stories? Which relies most heavily on the wire services mentioned in this chapter? Which provides the better service for your town? Why? Write a short report on your conclusion, and attach your lists.

Joe Murray

Life on the *Lufkin* (Texas) *News*, circulation 14,500, isn't trenchcoats and midnight meetings in underground garages, editor Joe Murray is quick to say.

It's the courthouse beat and school board meetings. It's a feature about the local pecan crop and the service group that does eye tests in schools. . . . Or maybe it's an investigation of a local boy's death—a boy, somewhat retarded, who joined the Marines and was beaten to death during recruit training. An investigation done entirely by telephone, it won the *Lufkin News* a Pulitzer Prize.

Murray, who became editor of the *Lufkin News* in 1969 when he was 28, considers himself part of the generation of news reporters who saw journalism as an avenue to writing short stories or novels.

"Now I look around at some of the young people going into journalism and they see the world sinking in a sea of corruption and they want to save it," he said. "Well, I say don't jump in without knowing how to swim."

To Murray, you don't belong in the newspaper business unless you really want to write. That means working at it. He says it takes "the five Ws and an R: That's writing, writing, writing, writing, writing, and rewriting."

Murray considers small-town journalism "much more rewarding" than a job on a big-city paper. "Almost everybody on the paper does a little of everything," he said.

"Everybody" in the *Lufkin News* newsroom consists of Murray, a city editor, an assistant city editor (who also writes and does page layouts, a courthouse reporter, a city hall reporter, a general assignment and feature writer, a sports editor, and a part-time college student. They put out a paper of from 12 to 36 pages on weekdays, more on Sundays.

In addition to daily news and feature assignments, each staff member is responsible for writing at least one editorial page column a week, a page-one feature, and a Sunday feature.

"Perhaps we're trying to do too much," said Murray. "But we're doing the things that need to be done."

Small-town newspapers are like their urban counterparts in many ways. All newspapers, Murray says, inform, entertain, and influence their readers.

"In Lufkin and most any other community, the people are complacent; they're apathetic," Murray said. They expect a newspaper reporter to attend the school board meetings for them and let them know what's going on.

But there are some differences. Someone who has always read a big-city paper "would be surprised at the local news on the front page" of a small-town paper, Murray said. "They might even find it laughable."

But as they became acquainted with the community they would

"find it very interesting to read about their neighbors and themselves," he said.

Critics of small-town papers often scorn them as gutless, afraid to offend advertisers, unwilling to rock the boat of the local establishment.

"That stereotype is certainly justified in some places," Murray said. He has heard all about editors who say, "Our advertisers have got us over a barrel."

On the *Lufkin News*, that doesn't happen. "We won't be intimidated; we won't be blackmailed," Murray said. "We do the thing that's right.

"There's a lot of good anyone can do in journalism, and it isn't necessarily on a national story, a Pulitzer Prize-winning story," the small-town editor says.

Often, Murray says, it's a minor story that presents an opportunity "to help other people who don't have power or influence or money, people who don't have anybody to turn to but their newspaper." ∎

MAKING THE INTERVIEW WORK

Being assigned to conduct an interview can be terrifying, because chances are good that your instructor will not ask you to interview a peer (that's too easy). Instead, you will likely be asked to talk with a newspaper editor, teacher, public official, or someone similar. This places you in a one-on-one situation with someone who may seem intimidating to you.

What you need is some help.

There are those who believe that the best way to learn how to conduct an interview is, well, to conduct an interview. While this sink-or-swim theory has its advantages, many students simply sink. So think of what follows as a swimming lesson.

On the late-late TV show, the reporter crashes into the police chief's office and threatens, "Either I get the full story—now—

A student journalist on a special assignment, notebook in hand, interviews a firefighter.

or I'll expose you as the incompetent political hack that you are!'' The chief pleads for time. ''Give me until midnight. If we don't have the killer by then, you can go ahead and print the story.''

Reporters rarely threaten news sources during interviews. That old movie scene between the chief and the reporter *is* an interview, however. An interview takes place any time a reporter asks a question. It may be during a quick telephone call, or it may be in an intimate two-hour chat. The type of interview will be determined by what the reporter wants to know: information, facts, opinions, or personal details.

Don't ever threaten your news source or use coercion. Don't challenge what the source says except for clarification (and then don't fail to do so). Don't argue; listen. That's important. You can't hear if you're talking. So be quiet and listen, even when the source seems to be wandering from the subject. Sometimes the digression is more interesting than what you asked about.

Preparing for the Interview

With that in mind, let's get you started interviewing. The first step is knowing what it is you want to find out. The second step is deciding whom to ask. This, of course, means knowing who can be expected to know what. The rule is to go to the primary source of information, the person whose business it is to know what you want to find out. This seems painfully obvious, but it apparently is not. An instructor was startled when two of his students, sent to get information about a power failure, quoted him in their stories. He had said, "I understand it was caused by construction workers who cut a power line." It turned out, however, that that was not the cause—and the stories looked pretty silly. Ask only what someone is likely to know (unless, of course, you simply want an opinion).

Once you know what it is you want to find out and whom to ask about it, you can decide what sort of interview is involved. If you want information about plans for a new building, make an appointment to talk to the appropriate administrator. If you want 15 opinions about the grading system in your school, ask 15 instructors. Always identify yourself as a reporter before asking questions. (There are exceptions to this on the professional level, but they need not concern us.) A simple statement such as "I'm _____ of the paper, and I'd like to ask . . . ." will usually suffice.

You must be comfortable with people and be able to meet and talk with them without being overly nervous. Reporters run the risk of distracting their subject if they are uptight. If you're nervous, try to hide it. Remember that most people enjoy being interviewed. They enjoy talking about themselves and expressing opinions to interested people. This works in your favor.

Asking Questions

Prepare your questions *before* the interview. Know what you're going to ask. Be straightforward. Don't make a speech every time you want to ask a question. Ask it clearly and simply. Avoid questions that can be answered with a simple yes or no. When you give subjects that choice, too often they will take it. And "no" is not the liveliest quote in the history of journalism. You want to ask questions that will get a quotable response. "What do you think about . . ." is a better way to start a question than "Do you think . . .?" In other words, ask good questions. Don't ask an administrator what the family dog's name is. (Who cares?) If your questions are superficial, the answers will be, too. Instead, ask if the citizens of your community are adequately supporting the school financially. Ask what the administrator would do to upgrade the school if unlimited funds were available. Ask about grading policies: Are they fair? Ask if the student government is too powerful or too weak.

Reporters at a press conference must be well prepared with straightforward, clear questions.

The questions you ask are your key to the success of any interview story. Student journalists often are advised to avoid asking embarrassing questions. This is bad advice. As a journalist, you *must* ask embarrassing questions. But keep good taste in mind. Then ask what you must ask. Don't pry; don't snoop. Don't ask hostile or leading or loaded questions. But you do have to get the truth if you can; that's almost a definition of journalism. Ask what you have to, as politely as possible. If you don't get an answer, ask again.

Pay attention to *how* the question is answered. Does the subject answer calmly and easily, as if the question has been asked a thousand times before? Or does he or she grope a bit? Does the subject, perhaps, pay you the finest compliment? ''That's a good question.'' Note also what questions the source does *not* answer. Sometimes a ''No comment'' can be very revealing. Above all, if you don't understand what is said, stop and ask for clarification.

Just before the interview ends, ask if there is anything else you should know. Many a routine story has been turned into a good one simply because the reporter had the good sense to leave time for the source to volunteer information.

The Formal Interview

Much of what we have been talking about so far in this chapter applies to all interviews—that is, all the times when you as a reporter ask questions. But there is another kind of interview that involves all of the above and more. This is the formal interview, in which the reporter tries to paint with words the portrait of a human being. Properly done, such a story reveals the subject's personality to your readers. They come to *know* the person through your story.

The formal interview requires more preparation than the informal variety. You must be fully informed about your subject before you even call to make an appointment. Dig through old copies of your newspaper or your city's paper. Talk to the subject's spouse or old friends. Remember, you are trying to portray a complete human being. Know the subject as intimately as possible before you start the interview. There can't be any "dead air" while you think of your next question.

Your choice of language can work in your favor. The very word "interview" can scare off a subject, so perhaps "talk" or "meeting" would be better when you call for that appointment. And when the interview is over, don't say "Bye-bye." Say "Thank you."

You've made the appointment, done your research, and arrived on time at the person's house or office. To start the interview, to get yourself and the subject warmed up to each other, try asking the relatively trivial but necessary questions. Get down the basic data: exact name (including middle initial), age, address, family status (for example, number of children).

Look ahead to the inverted pyramid discussion in Chapter 6. Imagine a pyramid with the small part at the top. Why not ask questions in that order? Start with the small, unimportant things first and then, as you and your subject become comfortable and the tension fades, get to the bigger, more important questions. Avoid the mistake of a student whose first question to the instructor was, "Do you think your contract will be renewed next year?" The question was blurted out as a result of nervousness, and it certainly got the interview off to a rocky start.

Observing Actions

In formal interviews, the reporter tries to make the reader "see" the subject. This is best accomplished with a description of the subject's actions and surroundings through his or her own words.

Look for the quotes that convey personality to the reader. When the star of a Rose Bowl game of 50 years ago says, "I'm always glad to talk about that game, because it gets better every year," you get a certain insight into his personality.

Actions are important. Does the subject sit on the edge of the chair or pound the desk for emphasis? Does he or she tell a particularly revealing joke? (If so, don't just laugh and go on; put it in the story.)

Being Friendly

How do you get subjects to give you personal details? How do you get them to open up to you and enjoy talking to you? You already know the answers intuitively from your personal life. Nobody likes a grinch. Let your personality come through. Smile. Laugh at your subject's jokes. Maintain good eye contact. Express interest in the subject and in what he or she has to say. Be flexible; the subject's departures from your agenda may be very revealing. Relax. Listen carefully. And always be on the alert for concrete, descriptive details.

Taking Notes

What about taking notes? Develop your own system, something you can rely on and will be able to translate after the interview. Skill in shorthand can be helpful. Lacking that, invent a system of speedwriting. Then fill in the details after you've left the interview.

If the source agrees, a tape recorder can be valuable in the interview. It helps you get exact quotes, quotes that sound precisely the way the source talks, as opposed to the way he or she sounds when the quotes are *almost* exact. Small tape recorders are inexpensive, and they can add a great deal of realism to an interview.

Writing the Interview Story

When writing up the interview, try to avoid general descriptions of your subject. Don't, for example, say that the store owner is short; tell the reader he's 5'2". Don't say the executive is lively; say she moves about the office during an interview, juggling project after project even as you talk. Don't just say the author is intelligent; point out that he's written six books (you might have asked him if he ever looks himself up in the catalog of books at the library). Don't say the volleyball coach is athletic; say she has won four championships and displays the trophies in her office. In other words, be specific in your detail.

Using Details

Here are some examples of detail by Gay Talese, a fine American journalist, writer, and researcher:

> [He was] fifty years old, a lean and well-tailored man with gray hair, alert blue eyes, wrinkles in the right places. . . .
>
> He had an angular face that suggested no special vitality; wavy gray-black hair combed tightly back from his high forehead, and soft, timidly inquiring eyes behind steel-rimmed glasses. His voice was not strong; it was, in fact, almost high-pitched, wavering and imploring when he spoke normally.

And this description of an office:

> Traditional English, thirty-five feet long and eighteen feet wide, trimmed in draperies of a white linen stripe, it is lined with a blue-black tweed rug that conceals the inky footprints of editors who have been up to the composing room. Toward the front of the room is an oval walnut conference table surrounded by eighteen Bank of England chairs. . . . In the rear of the room, a long walk for visitors, is Daniel's big desk and his black leather chair which, according to the decorator, was selected because it produces a minimum of wrinkles in Daniel's suits.

Using Quotes

Use as many direct quotes as possible when you write the interview story. Quotes, the person's own words, bring him or her to life. It is through these that we come to know the subject best, especially if you've asked the right questions. Probably the single most important question is Why? Others are Who? What? When? Where? How? (That's six questions right there.) As you write, remember to stay out of the story. Don't say, "I asked . . ."; just give the answer.

> *Not this*: When asked how it felt to be the first man on the moon, he replied, "It was exciting and exhilarating."
>
> *This*: He said being the first man on the moon was "exciting and exhilarating."

Q and A Technique

One effective story technique that has won acceptance from readers is what journalists call "Q and A." In this system, the reporter's exact questions are reproduced, followed by the source's exact answers. Instead of a story, in the usual sense, the newspaper presents virtually a verbatim transcript of the interview.

This means, of course, that the journalist has no way of signaling to the reader the most important statements in the interview. But that might not be a bad thing. The Q and A technique allows the reader to determine, without interference, what is or is not important.

It's a good technique, approved by many sources. Don't try it without a tape recorder, though.

An Ethical Question

To conclude, let us pose an ethical question. What if the person you interview wants to read the story before you print it? At one time, this was considered an open-and-shut case: Tell the source no. It's an intrusion on the journalist's right to print whatever he or she decides. Besides, there's no time. Those are still good arguments and plenty of journalists operate that way. But there is a distinct trend away from this. More and more journalists are reading back stories to their sources. In at least one course in the School of Journalism at the University of Missouri, students are *required* to do so. Many other journalists have decided to abandon the old way. The first rule if you decide to do this, however, is to make clear to the source that you don't *have* to do this and that you don't *have* to accept his or her suggestions about your story. In other words, you have to keep control of the story.

There are reasons a reporter might want to read back a story to a source. First, it's good human relations. It shows the source that you care about accuracy. Second, it helps eliminate mistakes. There's a story about a reporter who asked an official in a telephone interview how many people had been killed by a tornado that struck a town. The source answered, "Three to five." The reporter heard and reported "thirty-five." Major error! Had the reporter read back the story, this error would have been eliminated. (In fairness, of course, reading back a story to a source is probably impossible when working on deadline on a breaking story.) The small errors that irritate sources will be caught in a readback. If the source says he graduated from Arizona State University and you write down University of Arizona, the readback will reveal the mistake.

Finally, it would be very difficult for a source who sues you for libel to prove actual malice if you have read the story to him or her. As you know, for public figures to win a libel suit against a journalist, they must show actual malice—that is, the story was published with reckless disregard for the truth or with a known falsehood. If you read the story to the source, you certainly cut off libel suits based on actual malice.

Advisers and staff members should discuss this issue and adopt a policy that applies to all staff members. It would not be good for some staffers to read back stories and others not to.

The story on page 94 illustrates the effective use of quotes. This was a difficult story to do—it's about the school budget—and would be difficult to read if it were not for all the good quotes.

Interviewing Guidelines

The first rule of newswriting is this: *Go to the primary source*. If you want to know about the physical condition of your school building, don't ask a teacher, ask an administrator. Furthermore, don't ask the principal's secretary or assistant. *Go to the person whose business it is to know*. If you want to know why there are so many dropouts, talk to the guidance counselors, the administrators, the superintendent, and, finally, the dropouts themselves.

In gathering the news you will be, in one form or another, interviewing people. To get you started, here are some basic rules of interviewing:

1. *Be prepared*. Don't go to an interview cold. Have some information (from your files or your future book) in your head before you start.

2. *Have your questions ready*. Don't go to an interview expecting your news source to tell you voluntarily what you want to know. You're going to have to ask, and it can be embarrassing to admit that you don't know what your next question should be.

3. *Whenever possible, make an appointment*. You can't expect to waltz into a busy official's office and get 30 minutes of his or her time unless you first set up an appointment. Then make sure you *arrive on time*.

4. *Dress properly*. A good guideline is to dress the way you expect your interview subject to be dressed. The manner in which you dress will affect the way you are received and the cooperation you get from your source. You are a beginning *professional*, and no professional would think of conducting an interview unless properly dressed for the occasion.

5. *Look your subject in the eye*. Don't be so busy taking notes that all the source sees are your flying fingers and the top of your head. It makes some people nervous to see every word being written down. Rely on your memory, jotting down key words and transcribing your notes thoroughly as soon as possible after the interview.

6. *Don't ask negative questions*. That is, don't say, "No news yet?" Don't make it easy for your subject to say no.

7. *Have a note-taking system*. For example, write "rr" for "railroad." (By the way, keep your notes even after you have written the story. Sometimes sources deny ever having said what you attribute to them, and it will help you prove your case if you can produce the original notes.)

8. *Leave the door open for another talk*. Even with the most careful preparation, you may forget to ask an important question. Ask the subject if he or she would mind if you made contact later, personally or by phone, for a follow-up.

9. *Take three things with you on every assignment: a pencil, a piece of paper, and a grain of salt*. Be skeptical. Don't believe everything you're told.

10. *Verify your facts*. This means making sure names, dates, and all other facts are correct. Even a common name like Smith can be spelled several different ways (for example, Smythe, Smithe). Always check. Don't ever be afraid to ask what you might fear is a silly question. The only stupid question is the one not asked. Being courteous to your news source is important, but it is not discourteous to interrupt and ask, "Would you mind spelling that?" Accuracy in the news columns begins with accuracy in the reporter's notes.

Board axes budget
District saves money by sending report cards home with students

By Patrick Grimaldo

When seniors paid $30 for parking spaces, they were the first to feel the effects of a reduced budget adopted by the school board August 27. Still more students will realize the board's cutbacks when they carry progress reports and report cards home instead of the mailman.

The budget, prepared by the superintendent and four assistant superintendents and the budget and planning office, cut over $4.6 million from the previous one, leaving $10.6 million for the district to function, according to school board documents.

Lubbock Independent School District has dipped into its reserve fund the last two years earlier each year to force the school board to hold the line or to raise taxes, school board member Linda DeLeon said.

The board voted 5–2 not to raise taxes.

As instructed, Principal Waylon Carroll made 9.04 percent cuts in each department's instructional budgets. "We're not getting enough now," Rheba Johnson, librarian, said. The library lost over $1,400 from the book fund, and the income of $300 now goes to the district's general fund, Johnson said.

The new cuts will not affect the drama department as a majority of its funding comes from the plays put on by the students, drama teacher Harlan Reddell said. But the foreign language department is a different story.

Foreign language teachers will have to slow down in buying more VCR tapes for its library. "The instructional quality will not go down," French teacher Michele Wade said. "It's the things that make the class more interesting that we'll have to do without." This includes charts and Spanish board games.

Major cuts include a loss of $1.2 million in capital outlay, meaning there will be no new major projects, no new furniture and no new fixtures. That means if a chair or table should break, that item will not be replaced if it is not in stock, DeLeon said.

All capital outlay requests, such as new band equipment and audio visual equipment, have been cut, Carroll said.

The million cut from the building maintenance fund leaves nothing to keep Lubbock schools in good condition. DeLeon said that includes not painting classrooms or fixing such items as broken doors or tiles.

School board records indicate that five high school positions were cut from the budget, one from each high school, saving $115,000. Other personnel reductions include three administrative positions, executive information systems director, staff development coordinator and elementary computer consultant. These personnel reductions, made through attrition, saved $141,000.

In a memo to the school board assistant superintendent of finance Ronald Gooch said $150,000 would

be cut from the substitute budget.

"There will be enough for teachers' illnesses," Velma Ruth Shambeck, assistant superintendent of elementary education, said. "We'll have to do closer monitoring for other absences."

Another major loser in the budget cut was the athletic department, which lost $161,000.

"I haven't been able to notice anything different," head coach Bob Brown said. Except for a cut in insurance funding, the cuts have not seemed to affect the department, he said.

The budget will hack $200,000 from the summer school fund, but the effects are not known since the summer school program has not been planned out yet, Gooch said.

Equipment repair lost $150,000, but LISD's maintenance contract with the Marriott will help take up some of the slack, DeLeon said.

Libraries lost $30,000 as did professional travel.

Despite all the cost-cutting, salaries, which make up two-thirds of the budget, went up. With the 3.2 percent raise a teacher who made $30,000 last year will now make $30,460, DeLeon said. Administrative salaries went up in varying degrees.

Eight percent of the budget for LISD comes from federal funding, 52 percent from the state and 40 percent from local sources.

The majority of the local funding comes from land taxes. The district gets 90 cents per $100 evaluation and two cents of that goes to the reserve. If a piece of land is worth $10,000, then the school gets $90 from the taxes, and $2 of that goes into the reserve fund, DeLeon said.

Should the district need more money, it borrows the money using the reserve as collateral and pays it back later with the reserve fund.

The district has always had to borrow money late in the school year, DeLeon said, but because of previous budget cuts the district has run out of money earlier.

Tuesday the school board dipped into the reserve when by a 5–2 vote they voted to spend more than $250,000 on 16 new teachers for overcrowded elementary classrooms.

The borrowing has reduced the reserve in the past seven years to $1.3 million. The declining reserve and earlier requests for loans is making bank officials term the district's financial situation "questionable," according to DeLeon.

School board member Leota Matthews along with DeLeon suggested a 1.9 percent raise in the tax base from 90 cents to 91.9 cents per $100 evaluation.

The average value of a home in the district is $48,271; therefore a 1 cent increase would have given the district $400,000 and a 1.9 cent raise $760,000, DeLeon said.

The average school tax levy for a taxpayer is $434.44, Gooch said. A 1.9 percent increase, then, would

have raised the tax to $443.62, $9.18 more.

The four Lubbock teacher organizations, Lubbock Educators Association, Lubbock Classroom Teachers Association, Association of Texas Professional Educators and Lubbock Federation of Teachers, backed DeLeon and Matthews.

"We're going to make it," Carroll said. "We've got pretty good equipment throughout the school." The quality of education should not suffer, he said.

But DeLeon is not so optimistic. "We're in for a world of hurt," DeLeon said.

The Mirror,
Monterey High School,
Lubbock, Texas

LISD Budget for Last Seven Years

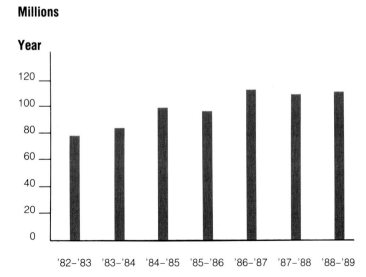

Millions

Year

Wrap-up

Interviewing is an essential journalistic skill. Good techniques can be learned and should be understood before students begin interviewing.

Good reporters neither threaten nor (generally) contradict their sources. They do not argue. They listen. They realize they cannot learn anything while doing the talking themselves. They select their sources carefully and prepare well for each interview, making up a list of questions and deciding in what order those questions will be asked.

Good questions are clear and understandable, short and to the point. Open-ended questions (''What do you think about . . .?'') usually are better than yes-no questions (''Do you think . . .?'') because quotable responses are needed. Journalists sometimes have to ask difficult or embarrassing questions to do their jobs well but this should always be done with care and concern.

Formal interviews require more preparation. Reporters need to research the subject in advance and set up an appointment in a comfortable place to talk. The opening minutes of the interview should permit the source and the reporter to warm up to one another. The reporter should use this time to determine basic data (exact name, age, and so forth).

Reporters often write word portraits of people in longer formal interviews and profile stories. Such word pictures require a keen sense of detail of the subject's words and actions.

Reporters who are friendly and relaxed with their sources often do better than those who are nervous or artificially tough. It does not hurt to smile or to laugh at a source's jokes.

Reporters need a system of capturing their source's words, whether through careful note-taking, speedwriting, or using a small tape recorder.

Good quotes and concrete detail are emphasized in stories based on formal interviews. Descriptions of people and their surroundings help bring those people to life. The quotes should illustrate the source's personality.

One effective story technique, called ''Q and A,'' reproduces in question-and-answer form the reporter's exact questions and the source's exact answers. It is a transcript of an interview rather than a story. The Q and A technique allows readers to determine what is important.

Journalists generally do not permit their sources to read stories before publication. Sometimes prepublication checking does take place, but only if the journalist wants it to and only if the journalist maintains control of the story. Prepublication checking can eliminate inaccurate names, dates, and figures.

On Assignment

Teamwork

1. Devise ten questions you would like to ask the President of the United States. What news elements did you include? Will each question be of interest to your student readers? Teams should compare their lists. What accounts for agreements and disagreements?

Practice

1. Watch one of the Sunday morning news-interview shows and write a critique. What research went into the reporters' questions? How did the journalists react to vague answers from the guests? Did they follow up? Did they follow up on each others' questions? See if you can find a newspaper account of the interview the next day. Does the story reflect what you saw happening? Why or why not? How would you have handled the interview? How would you have written the story? Compare your perceptions with those of classmates who saw the same program.

2. Prepare all the questions you want to ask of a high-ranking school official or local official, in the order you want to ask them. Exchange your list with another student and critique each other's approach. What was missed? Did you include follow-up questions? Keep your refined list handy for writing an interview story later.

3. Record an interview with a classmate, taking notes as you interview. Using only your notes, write a story of the interview, with plenty of quotes. Then listen to the tape of the interview. Are your quotes accurate? If not, what do you think is wrong with your note-taking techniques?

4. As a class, listen to and analyze a recorded radio or television interview. Were the questions soft or hard? Were the answers predictable? Do newspaper reporters tend to be tougher interviewers than broadcast journalists? How could the interviewers have done a better job?

5. Discuss this question: Do the reporters on ''60 Minutes'' have an advantage over local reporters? What is the difference between the techniques available to a network reporter who comes to town for one story and those available to a local reporter, who must deal with the same sources over and over? Write a short essay on your thoughts.

Your Turn

Conduct a telephone interview with a classmate in or out of the journalism class. Observe how your note-taking changes when there is no need for eye contact. Also note that because you cannot encourage answers by nodding or smiling, you must use your voice. Are telephone interviews more or less accurate than face-to-face interviews? Why? Write a short report on your observations.

Writing the News

WRITING
NEWS STORY
LEADS

The proper study of journalism begins not in the journalism class but in the English class. This is because there is one skill so basic to journalism that anyone who doesn't have it, or the willingness to work to acquire it, might as well look elsewhere for a career.

That skill is writing.

Before you are able to write a news story, an editorial, a column, or even a headline, you must be able to write. This doesn't mean you have to be Ernest Hemingway or Virginia Woolf. But it does mean that you must be comfortable with words, that you can grasp the fundamentals of spelling, grammar, and punctuation, that you know a good sentence from a bad sentence. It implies that you read a lot, and not just newspapers, either. All writers are readers.

So pay attention in English class, because unless you first become a writer, the chances are great that you will never become a journalist.

Writing is not, as many people believe, an inherent talent that some have and some don't. Writing *can* be taught. It can't be taught the way physics is taught; there is no 1-2-3 formula that will lead you to good writing. Perhaps we should say writing can be *self*-taught through trial and error. By writing, and by having your writing criticized, you learn to avoid certain errors. We hope your instructor challenges every word you write, questions every comma, and examines every sentence for flaws. There is nothing quite so educating as real criticism. But again, the burden is the student's. The teacher can help by preparing you and making you write and rewrite. But the writing is up to you.

Getting Started

Now let's take you out of that English class and put you into journalism; that is, let's take you out of the theory of writing and put you into the practice of writing.

There is nothing awesome about writing news stories. Your basic writing skills and some specialized information—because, after all, journalistic writing is specialized writing—are all you need. Let's start with the beginning of the news story: the lead.

The lead (pronounced to rhyme with *seed*) is the first paragraph of the news story. It usually, but not always, consists of just one sentence. (There are few rules of writing that use the word "always." There are no unbreakable rules.) More than that, it is the do-or-die paragraph, the place where you win or lose your reader. Therefore, your lead must have *impact*. The lead must not waste words; it must come to the point quickly.

The Inverted Pyramid

Why must the lead come to the point quickly? What about the story that unfolds chronologically, with the punchline at the end? Well, we're discussing *inverted pyramid* writing.

Imagine a pyramid upside down. The broad part at the top is where the main facts go. That's the lead. As the pyramid narrows, the facts become less significant until, as you reach the pointed bottom, the facts may be dispensable. The story that springs a surprise at the end doesn't follow this pattern.

There are many reasons for using the inverted pyramid style

The Inverted Pyramid

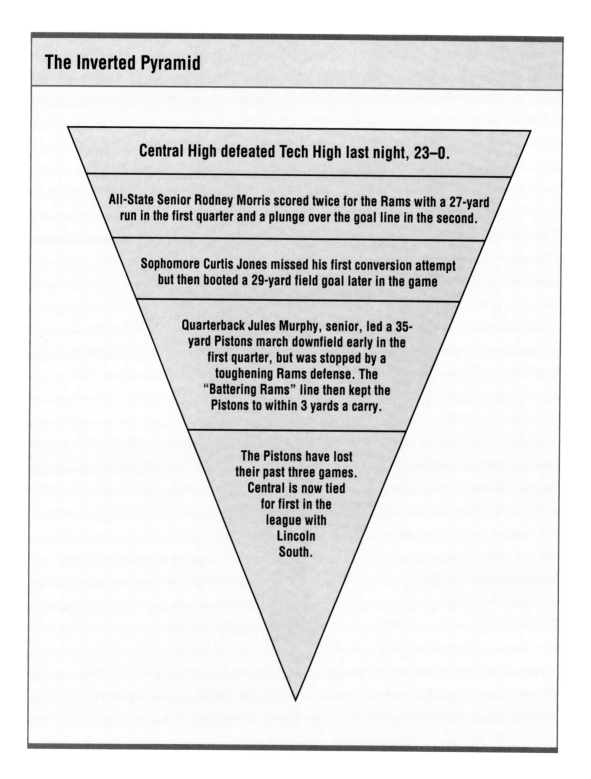

Central High defeated Tech High last night, 23–0.

All-State Senior Rodney Morris scored twice for the Rams with a 27-yard run in the first quarter and a plunge over the goal line in the second.

Sophomore Curtis Jones missed his first conversion attempt but then booted a 29-yard field goal later in the game

Quarterback Jules Murphy, senior, led a 35-yard Pistons march downfield early in the first quarter, but was stopped by a toughening Rams defense. The "Battering Rams" line then kept the Pistons to within 3 yards a carry.

The Pistons have lost their past three games. Central is now tied for first in the league with Lincoln South.

in newswriting. First of all, it's a natural way to tell a story. If you want to tell a friend about the football game, you begin by telling who won; you don't start with the kickoff. The final score, then, goes into the broad part of the top.

Second, the inverted pyramid style enables a reader in a hurry to get the essential information without reading the entire story. Suppose the lead says:

Central High defeated Tech High last night, 23-0.

Readers who have time to read only the first paragraph may not know who scored the touchdowns, or how or when, but they know the essential fact. They know who won.

Third, the inverted pyramid is an aid for the headline writer. Most headlines are based on information contained in the first paragraph, so *the most important facts should be in the first paragraph.* Finally, the inverted pyramid makes it easy to trim a story that won't fit into its alloted space. A properly organized inverted pyramid story can usually be cut from the bottom up without too much damage.

Sounds easy, doesn't it? Just arrange the facts in descending order of importance and write them down. A computer could do it. And what's worse, there's nothing creative about it.

But how do you decide which facts go first? This decision is made on the basis of your news judgment, and by now you know how sticky that can get. After you've written the lead, how do you make it flow into the second paragraph, and the second into the third, and so on? Writers using inverted pyramid style juxtapose *related* facts in descending order. They must make judgments. They must decide when to weave in some background, when to break the steady flow of the story with some colorful or explanatory material. All this requires practice—and creativity.

Writing the Lead

Let's return to the lead. It must get the reader's attention honestly and quickly, while telling something about the story. The lead is the hardest part of the story, because it is the most important. Every lead you write must be an example of the very best writing you can achieve.

How do you write a lead? Picture a reader looking over your shoulder. You know what you want to say. Now make that reader understand you. Don't bore readers with a lead they have read a thousand times before. Don't just fill in the blanks, substituting the name of this year's class president for last year's. *Write*. Suppose the story is about the appointment of a new principal. You could write this:

Arthur Learned, 42, has been named principal of Central High School.

That lead comes to the point quickly and certainly conveys the essential information to the reader. But let's face it—it's dull. It's a formula lead, and it lacks luster. Suppose you dig into Mr. Learned's biography—you might be able to write a lead like this:

An Air Force flier with a closetful of medals is the new principal of Central High School.

Better? Sure, but the objection could be raised that the second lead used more interesting information than the first. Exactly! The best material goes into the lead, provided it doesn't distort the story or emphasize the wrong angle.

Be Objective

Let's try it again. The citizens of your town vote to build a new high school. You know that this is big news and you want to write a good story. You sharpen your imagination and write:

At long last, the citizens of Smithville opened their pocketbooks in recognition of the value of education. Yesterday they demonstrated their faith in the youth of America by approving a $5-million bond issue for a new high school.

Your news editor tosses the story back at you with a curt order: "Rewrite it." Puzzled? Here's the point: The lead is full of clichés ("at long last," "value of education," "demonstrated their faith," "youth of America"), and it's full of opinion. *Your opinion has no place in a news story*, in the lead or anywhere else. The reporter must be *objective*. Clearly, the example shows the writer's own feelings of elation over the new high school.

Here's one way the story could be handled:

Smiling and relaxed after hearing that a $5-million bond issue for a new high school has been approved, Principal Arthur Learned today commended Smithville citizens for what he called their progressive attitude toward education.

All the facts are there, and instead of the reporter's opinion the reader learns the principal's viewpoint.

Some journalism texts teach leads by category; that is, the student is told there are summary leads, staccato leads, parody leads, punch leads, cartridge leads, astonisher leads, and so on. Or they say there is a type of lead for each of the parts of speech, and six more for the five W's and the H (Who, What, Where, When,

The Five W's and One H

WHAT?	Second Place in the National Secondary School Drama Festival
WHO?	Lucy Fields and Wendel Thurston
WHERE?	The Barrington Center for the Performing Arts, New York City
WHEN?	May 17
WHY?	Best Duet Acting
HOW?	Competed against students at the regional, state, and national levels

Seniors Lucy Fields and Wendel Thurston won Second Place at the National Secondary School Drama Festival held at New York City's Barrington Center for the Performing Arts on May 17. The two competed in the Best Duet Acting category against high school students in regional, state, and national run-offs.

Why, and How). Perhaps these methods serve a purpose. If they encourage students to use imagination and creativity, then they are worthwhile. But such categories may only cloud the issue. Can you imagine a reporter for the *New York Times* hurrying back from a meeting of the United Nations Security Council thinking, "Should I write a summary lead or a cartridge lead? Or maybe I ought to try an astonisher." It doesn't work that way. What the *Times* reporter is thinking is, "I need a lead that will pull my reader into the story. It must be smooth, concise, readable, and interesting." Before the reporter gets back to the office to write the story, he or she may have mentally constructed and discarded a dozen leads before deciding on the one to use. Not once do the categories come to mind.

Students should make their lead work for them. They should write it as well as they possibly can and then rewrite it. Writing, someone once said, is *re*-writing; this is particularly true of leads. Seldom is the first lead that pops into your head the best one.

We mentioned the five W's and the H. These are elements that properly belong in nearly every story. There was a time when editors felt all six belonged in the lead, but this is no longer true. The best lead is the one that tells the story best. To repeat one of the main themes of this book: There are no shortcuts, there are no formulas. Writing is a creative process, and journalistic writing is as creative as any other.

Summary Leads

One category of lead, however, is worth defining because it is the most widely used. The *summary lead* provides in the first sentence the briefest possible summary of the facts. The following are summary leads:

> The president today announced a 90-day wage–price freeze.
>
> Principal Arthur Learned has resigned.
>
> A powerful earthquake rocked central Peru today.
>
> The City Council voted 4–2 to increase Smithville's sales tax to 5 percent.

Here are three strong summary leads—packed with clear, solid information—from an edition of *Tiger Tales*, the school paper of Joliet (Ill.) Township High School, West Campus:

> With a key win against Lockport, the varsity girls' team snapped a three-way tie for the SCIA title two weeks ago, then claimed sole possession of it when Romeoville defeated Joliet Central last week.
>
> With an undefeated 3-0 record, the Scholastic Bowl Team is heading toward another flawless season, following last year's 9-0 record and SCIA championship.
>
> Promoted as the last dance before the Prom, the girls-ask-guys Valentine's Dance will be held February 17 from 8–11 P.M. in the cafeteria.

Summary leads work best in inverted pyramid stories. They can be bright and attractive, but they can also be a crutch for the lazy journalist because they are relatively easy to write.

As newspapers shift their emphasis from hard news to soft and as TV continues to beat newspapers to the punch on breaking stories, the inverted pyramid and summary lead are waning in importance. Still, every journalist should be able to construct a quick, clean lead under deadline pressure. Everything else builds on that skill.

Good Leads

Here are some examples of good leads that appeared in the *New York Times*. Why are they good? For one simple reason: They make the reader want to read the rest of the story.

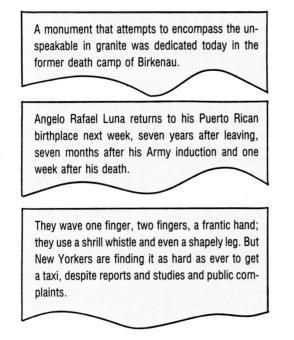

A monument that attempts to encompass the unspeakable in granite was dedicated today in the former death camp of Birkenau.

Angelo Rafael Luna returns to his Puerto Rican birthplace next week, seven years after leaving, seven months after his Army induction and one week after his death.

They wave one finger, two fingers, a frantic hand; they use a shrill whistle and even a shapely leg. But New Yorkers are finding it as hard as ever to get a taxi, despite reports and studies and public complaints.

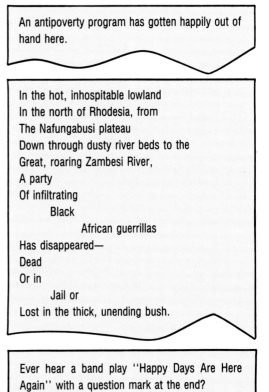

An antipoverty program has gotten happily out of hand here.

In the hot, inhospitable lowland
In the north of Rhodesia, from
The Nafungabusi plateau
Down through dusty river beds to the
Great, roaring Zambesi River,
A party
Of infiltrating
    Black
        African guerrillas
Has disappeared—
Dead
Or in
    Jail or
Lost in the thick, unending bush.

Ever hear a band play "Happy Days Are Here Again" with a question mark at the end?

What lead sentence would you write for a story about Sally Ride, the first American woman astronaut?

Creativity

Note particularly the lead beginning, "In the hot, inhospitable lowland . . ." It is virtually poetry. It is evidence that the journalist can be creative, and that the writer who wants to may attempt any device, as long as it works. There's no rule against writing a news story in iambic pentameter, *if it works*. Don't be afraid to try, though be prepared to work far harder than you would have to for a more conventional lead.

These inventive leads all moved over the wires of United Press International:

> SAMARKAND, USSR—The conductor wore white tie and tails and the orchestra wore sweatshirts. The audience wore gumboots and the heroine fanned herself with a copy of *Pravda*.

> CAPE TOWN, South Africa—A dead woman's heart pumped life Monday through the body of a 55-year-old grocer who gambled on medical history's first human heart transplant even though he is a diabetic.

> LONDON—Psst . . . wanna buy London Bridge?

Leads from School Papers

The excellent leads that follow come from high school and college newspapers.

He walked with a *Palantir* reporter, along the dusty roads, crisscrossing the hills that will soon be plowed under to make way for the AiResearch building. ''This is an ugly mess,'' ecology-cult author Edward Abbey hissed, twirling a sprig of grass between his teeth.
—*The Palantir*, Canyon del Oro High School, Tucson, Ariz.

It may be chicken feed to some, but for the Schreiber family of Carol, Ken and Pat, it's a serious business. Part of a prizewinning clan of chicken raisers, they've accumulated two grand champions and one reserve champion.
—*Bugle Call*, R. E. Lee High School, San Antonio, Texas

On the day after Thanksgiving, the entire world was Christmas shopping in Houston.
—*The Bear Facts*, Hastings High School, Alief, Texas

Sue's hands were sweating and she ''felt funny.'' Pulling her car quickly off the St. Paul street, she told her friend, ''Something's happening to my twin sister Sheri in Chicago.''

Then it came to her. Sheri, who was about seven months pregnant, was having her baby prematurely. She drove home, called Chicago and confirmed her ''awareness.'' Sheri had indeed just had a baby.

Steve and Shawn, Bev and Brenda, Dave and Dan . . . ''A lot of twins think they have a mystical communion—an unusual awareness of one another,'' observes Prof. David Lykken of the departments of psychiatry and psychology at the University of Minnesota.
—*Blue Jay Free Flyer*, Worthington (Minn.) Community College

''You wouldn't believe the stereotypes we have to put up with,'' claimed junior varsity cheerleader Sylvia Morin. ''Supposedly we are all snobs, we only date jock boys, we don't drink, smoke or toke. We're just All-American young ladies with our noses up in the air.''
—*The Tower*, Grosse Pointe, South (Mich.) High School

I heard loneliness today and I heard courage. I talked to Bill Biggs.

After his Dec. 30 auto accident Bill was in the hospital for three months. Then for three months he was at the Gonzales Rehabilitation Center. Now he's home, learning to cope with paralyzed legs and damaged eyesight.
—*Big Stick*, Roosevelt High School, San Antonio, Texas

Mrs. Lillian McCutcheon was sitting in the housemother's room on the tenth floor with her feet up on the air conditioner giving herself a manicure.
—*The All-Stater*, University of Nebraska journalism workshop

Norman Williams gets paid to do unto others what he would not want others to do unto him.

—*Teen Perspective*, publication of the
Marquette University Summer Journalism workshop

While dressed in protective white suits with respirators that looked like something out of a science fiction novel, four trained professionals from ALAMO Incorporated spent the summer removing asbestos from West's pipework.

—*Tiger Tales*, Joliet (Ill.) Township High School, West Campus

Under an almost full Friday the 13th moon, the Red Devils suffered an 18–13 defeat to the second-place York Dukes as York scored the game-winning touchdown with 30 seconds remaining on the clock.

—*The Devils' Advocate*, Hinsdale (Ill.) Central High School

What was once a flourishing, green, spider plant of Kathy McKown, business teacher, in room 222 is now a mere stub in the soil, on the edge of its death bed.

—*The Rustler*, Fremont (Neb.) Senior High School

As he inched his way around the corner of the mountain, he found himself suddenly staring up at a huge expanse of rock directly in front of him. Looking over his shoulder, he could see the tiny dotted trees of the Colorado landscape thousands of feet below him; the river had become nothing more than a thin, blue line.

—*The Arlingtonian*, Upper Arlington (Ohio) High School

Jim is 16 years old. He is a straight ''A'' student who rarely gets in trouble and never breaks the law. However, when Jim gets his driver's license, his father's insurance will nearly double.

—*X-Ray*, St. Charles (Ill.) High School

He's friendly, understanding, caring and loving. He's also easy to talk to and very likable. But that's not all. He has a good sense of humor. He's confident, loyal, fair and supportive. And he's diplomatic and gentlemanly. He's Dale Mitched, retiring principal of Puyallup High School.

—*The Viking Vanguard*, Puyallup (Wash.) High School

When Judy Schwank walks into the village hospital, hundreds of dying children will be there to meet her. Word has spread that she is coming, and as many as 125 homeless, limbless, or sightless children will be waiting for help and waiting to die.

—*Limited Edition*,* newspaper of the minority journalism workshop at Western
Kentucky University

See complete news story, ''Local woman gives children chance to live,'' on pages 136–37.

From peaceful protest to bloody massacre, the American dream in China is dying along with many of its activists. Still, the message broadcast by those in Tiananmen Square is reaching the world and the University of Texas is not exempt from hearing it.

—*Texas Achiever*, publication of the summer journalism
workshop at the
University of Texas at Austin

The word "rodeo" often conjures up visions of worn-down arenas draped with red, white and blue cloth and . . . young males covered with dust, grime, sweat and who walk with a distinct limp.

Women win blue ribbons in fruit preserve contests, become rodeo queens or watch from the grandstands.

However, the stereotypes do not apply to freshman Nancy Donica. When rodeo time comes, Donica can be found in the middle of the competition.

—*The Fourth Write*, San Antonio (Texas) College

Writing effective leads requires concentration, critical thinking, and imagination.

The following leads, all from *The Lion*, the top-notch paper of Lyons (Ill.) Township High School, were atop various types of stories. But they meet the main rule: Every one of them captures the reader's interest and lures the reader into the story. Enjoy them.

Meet Mike Warnke. He's a short man of about 30 with wire-rimmed glasses resting on chubby red cheeks.

The sun creeps up over Stone Ave. Railroad Station. Briefcased urban cowboys cluster around chipping green radiators and iron-grilled ticket windows. There they wait, in the sweet-stale aroma of years past, for their silver stallion.

The scene is a boutique, overflowing with American Indian trinkets and exotically shaped jewelry. Neon signs flash ''Gyros'' above the multitude of people filling the streets.

New Town, composed of gift and craft shops, artists' studios, coffee houses, galleries, pubs and casual eating places, has recently experienced a surge of development that has brought mixed feelings about New Town's future.

High over the roofs of faded stores filled with Saturday sale shoppers, a newspaper, caught on a bitter March wind, slipped past a beige marble gargoyle. Chipped into the edifice of the LaGrange Theatre, the gargoyle counted the small line of anxious children waiting below for the doors to open on the matinee.

When the soft swift winds blow and the earth is cool dark mud, it is April and a time for kites.

If you're wondering why some of these leads are two or more paragraphs long, it's because a lead can be any length. Remember, a good lead is one that works, and sometimes a longer introduction works well.

Leads to Avoid

Now here are some bad leads.

In the school auditorium last Friday afternoon, Principal Arthur Learned introduced convocation speaker Lt. Gov. Charles Smith, who announced that he is in favor of raising the driving age to 18.

This lead is a flop because it wastes the reader's time. The main fact here is that the lieutenant governor endorsed raising the driving age. But before the writer says so, the reader is told where the convocation was held, when it was held, and who introduced the speaker. It is not enough to get the main fact in the lead. *It must come in the first few words of the lead*, unless some special effect is achieved by withholding the information.

Length

Seniors would be given the last Friday of May for final examinations, the school colors would be changed from red and blue to crimson and blue, retiring teachers would be given plaques of appreciation from the student body, and the editor of the school newspaper would be elected from the student body under bills introduced in the regular weekly meeting of the Central High School Student Council Friday.

This lead is too long. Leads should be short, because they are easier to read and because long paragraphs, both in the lead and in the body of the story, are unacceptable for typographical reasons. Since most newspaper columns are narrow—just over two inches wide—paragraphs must be kept short, usually about three or four typewritten lines. People do not want to read paragraphs that are too long, and even a paragraph that appears short when typewritten or on the screen will seem long when it is squeezed into a narrow printed column. The preceding lead could be rewritten as follows:

Bills introduced at the Friday meeting of the Student Council would:

—Give seniors the last Friday in May for final examinations.

—Change the school colors from red and blue to crimson and blue.

—Provide for plaques to be given by the students to retiring teachers.

—Provide for election of the editor of the school paper by vote of the student body.

This is a common way of dealing with stories that have more than one "main fact."

Here is how the *College Clamor* at Mott Community College in Flint, Mich., handled a similar problem.

The MCC Board of Trustees voted Jan. 26 to:

—pink-slip the entire faculty and staff, with the exception of President Charles N. Pappas.

—approve a budget of $11,905,009 for this year.

—transfer $208,500 from auxiliary enterprise income and student fees to an emergency operating fund.

—change the rules on registration and tuition payment for next fall.

Content

Your Student Council is considering several new projects.

The trouble with this lead is that it doesn't say enough. What projects? The lead must provide information. Another problem is the use of "your," which should be reserved for direct quotes and editorials, because it puts the writer into the story. Use "the" as a substitute.

Grammar   Here's another problem lead:

> A reminder to those who enjoy good new records. The library has 22 new records which it is willing to loan out! All students are invited to come and look them over!

In the first place, the opening sentence isn't even a sentence. There are times when sentence fragments are acceptable, if you use them effectively, but that first sentence isn't one of them. Is it news that the library is willing to "loan out" its materials? That's what libraries are for. (The word "out" is unnecessary. And "loan" is an adjective or noun, not a verb. Make it "lend.") Inviting the students to the library, or anywhere else, is not the function of the newspaper. Quote someone as saying that students are invited, if that is appropriate information. In the case of the library, however, it goes without saying that the students are invited. Further, exclamation points should be avoided in newswriting; they are seldom necessary. A better way to express the thoughts in this lead would be:

> Twenty-two new records have been placed in the school's lending library, the head librarian announced.

Consider the grammar of this lead:

> Alumni and friends of Iowa State University in the northern California and Nevada area will meet for their annual dinner meeting Friday in Las Vegas, Nev.

This creates the problem of the misplaced modifier. Where is Iowa State University, in Iowa or spread over northern California and Nevada? It is the alumni, obviously, who are in California and Nevada, but that's not what the lead says. Careful rereading of your stories will eliminate many such problems. The solution is simple. Keep modifiers and what they modify close together in the sentence.

Remember to keep the time element clear:

> The lawyer for three persons convicted of contributing to the delinquency of a minor today remained certain he would win their freedom from jail terms.

When did the three contribute to the delinquency of a minor? Today? That's what the lead says, but common sense tells us otherwise. This lead illustrates the general need to *keep the principal verb and the time element together*. Make it:

> The lawyer for three persons convicted today of contributing to the delinquency of a minor remained certain he would win their freedom from jail terms.

Be sure your lead contains meaningful information:

Principal Arthur Learned discussed some of the problems of our school at the Science Club meeting Monday afternoon.

Why not tell your readers which problems were discussed and what was said about them? In stories about speeches, panel discussions, and the like, the emphasis should not be on the fact that someone spoke or that a panel discussion was held. Instead, the lead should emphasize *what* was said. This lead could have been written *before* Mr. Learned spoke to the Science Club, in contrast to a successful lead, which provides fresh, real information.

Wrap-up

Journalism students should pay attention in English class because good writing is essential to all journalism. Students need to be comfortable with words and have a good grasp of spelling, grammar, and punctuation. They should read a lot, too. All writers are readers.

Writing can be self-taught if there is an instructor challenging the student's work and if rewriting is done.

Getting started specifically in newswriting means working on leads, or first paragraphs. If the lead fails, no reader will read on. So leads come to the point quickly and in few words.

Most news stories are written in inverted pyramid style. The main facts go at the top of the pyramid. As the pyramid gets smaller toward the bottom, the facts become less important. The inverted pyramid style is fading somewhat in the face of changing news values—more soft news, less hard news—and because television almost always has fast-breaking hard news before newspapers.

The inverted pyramid is used because it gets to the point quickly and is a natural way to tell a story. The pyramid also makes it easy to trim a story from the bottom up if it's too long for its allotted space.

The inverted pyramid sounds easier than it is. Knowing about it does not mean a beginning journalist will automatically know how to make stories flow or pick the right news angle.

Leads need to get the reader's attention honestly and quickly. They should be creative and interesting and make use of the best material the writer has.

The lead should be objective and not convey the writer's attitudes or beliefs.

Labels on leads (summary, staccato, parody, cartridge, and so on) contribute little to learning. Leads need to be smooth, concise, readable, and interesting—no matter what label they carry.

All stories should include the five W's and the H (who, what, where, when, why, and how) but not in the lead. The best lead summarizes the entire story but uses the best elements—not all of them.

Good leads are creative and make use of various techniques but share one characteristic: They make readers want to continue. Bad leads are slow getting to the point, are too long or contain too many peripheral points (unnecessary times and places, for example), express the writer's opinion, or confuse readers through misplacement of the time element.

On Assignment

Teamwork

1. Working in teams, visit the library and examine old newspapers. Copy the leads of several stories for each of the eras mentioned in the history chapter: the partisan press era, the yellow journalism era, and the Civil War era. Also look at old magazines. Make a short presentation on your findings to your class.
2. At the library or local newsstand, find copies of English-language newspapers published outside the United States. Contrast them to U.S. papers. How do the writing styles differ? Do foreign newspapers seem to look at the news differently? Why or why not? Prepare a presentation on your findings for your class.

Practice

1. Secure copies of a morning and an afternoon paper, and study their accounts of the same news event. What are the news elements? How do the papers differ in their selection of lead elements? Why? Which approach is more effective? How could either have done a better job? Rewrite the leads to demonstrate your ideas. Write a two-page essay on your findings, and attach the articles.
2. Clip and mount five stories from your local paper that are written in inverted pyramid structure. Identify the elements of the lead—the five W's and the H. What kind of news judgment do you think the reporter used in writing the lead? What news elements are present? How could the lead have been improved? Rewrite the leads to make them better, and be prepared to defend in class the changes you made.
3. Compare the leads on radio and television accounts of news with those in a newspaper. How do they differ? Why? Which approach is better? Why? Write about your findings.
4. Do the writers of short stories or novels have problems with leads? Read the first five paragraphs of a successful book and see if you find any similarities between newspaper leads and book leads. Write a short essay on your findings. Write a lead based on the beginning of the book.

Your Turn

1. Write a lead—*only* a lead—based on the following facts.
   The Board of Education met Monday night.

The board accepted the resignation of Harry Smith, who has been the janitor at East Side Elementary School for five years.

The board approved a budget for the next fiscal year of $6.5 million. That will mean a tax increase of six percent for all homeowners in the school district.

The board went into executive (closed) session to discuss a sensitive matter. (There is a rumor around the school that the discussion concerned extending the school year.)

The board accepted a gift from a 1927 graduate of Central High School. The gift was a copy of her unpublished autobiography for the school library.

The board passed a resolution praising the work of long-time School Board Secretary Jane Magee.

The board approved an appropriation of $3,500 to repair the furnace at Taylor Junior High School.

The board learned that its president, Deborah Morre, is moving from the city and will resign, effective at once.

2. Write a lead based on the following information.

A special convocation or assembly (use local terminology) was held at your school Friday afternoon.

The speaker was Herbert F. Maximillian.

Mr. Maximillian is a city architect.

His title is assistant city planner.

This is the text of his short speech.
      Thank you, Mr. Principal. I enjoyed that introduction very much.
      Now, if I may, I would like to tell you of a plan I have been working on for several years.
      My plan is to build a space station on the moon. I figure the federal government could finance this little project for, oh, around $56 million, give or take a few million.
      What we want to do, see, is get a space station up there before anyone else. We want to be first. And it could be an easy thing, too.

We have the technology to do it right now. We have sent men to the moon. Surely we can build houses up there too!

In one year—just one short year—we could have enough housing up there to accommodate 10 astronauts. Each would have his or her own sleeping quarters and there would be a recreation room with video games, television, the whole shooting match.

The reason they would be up there, of course, is to do research. Without the glare of city lights or the distortion of our atmosphere, the astronauts could get a much better view of deep space through their telescopes. A much better view.

And, you know, someday we've got to start looking into interplanetary travel, and we sure could launch a rocket from the moon with less effort than from the earth.

Not only that, but the presence of a space station on the moon would give our people a great psychological boost. And we sure need that in these awful times.

Space research would also help us solve problems of overpopulation, too, because someday there are going to be too many of us down here for the old earth to support. We will have to live out there, in space. And we need to get going on this right now.

Thank you very much.

About 500 students attended the speech. They applauded politely at the end of the speech.

3. Ask the city council, board of education, or zoning commission to provide you with the minutes of its last meeting and the agenda for the next meeting. Write a lead based on the minutes. Write a lead based on the agenda.

4. Write a lead based on the following information.

The new phone book for your town has been published.

It contains 18,573 names of individuals and 675 names of business organizations.

It contains 453 white pages and 87 yellow pages.

It includes listings of 654 federal, state, county, and city governmental offices.

Last year's book had 432 white pages and 54 yellow pages.

Last year's book had 16,342 names of individuals and 534 names of business organizations.

Last year's government listings added up to 578.

The first individual listed in the book is Marion L. Aardvarque. The last is Shirley P. Zgbniewski.

The first business is Acme Motors, Inc. The last is Zart's Bicycle Co.

In a press release, the telephone company (United Phones of Anytown) announces, "This is the most complete, most thorough, most accurate telephone book in Anytown history. We are extremely proud of it."

You reach Ms. Aardvarque and ask her about being first. She says, "Who cares? My phone bill is out of sight no matter where I'm listed."

Ms. Zgbniewski says, "I'm always last. It was even that way in grade school. Always last to recess, last in the lunch line. I guess I'm just destined to be last, no matter what I do."

5. Remember the questions you developed in Chapter 5 (Practice, 2) for interviewing a ranking school official or other local official? Conduct the interview. Write three different styles of leads, and attach your questions. In the next chapter you will complete the story.

CHAPTER SEVEN

WRITING NEWS STORIES

A thorough reading of the lead-writing chapter is a good start to learning how newswriting works. But it's only a start. The process continues, step-by-step.

Let's say you've written a good lead and you have readers interested in your story. You have them on the hook; now you want to reel them in. If the first paragraph is the most important in the story, the second certainly is the next. You don't want your reader losing interest, not after all the effort you put into writing the lead.

One way to hold interest is to use a quote—the sound of a human voice—immediately. Quotes add a personal touch to a story.

Here's a lead:

The library will remain open two hours longer than usual as students prepare for final exams, Principal Elizabeth Anderson announced Friday.

Now here's what some people call a back-up quote, one designed to support the lead:

> "We need to make it as easy as possible for our students to learn," Dr. Anderson said. "It's important to everyone on the faculty and to all the students."

What you're doing is linking the lead to the second paragraph, making your story unfold logically and coherently. You're using transitions.

A noted American publisher once said, "There is nothing wrong with the newspaper business that a little more talent in writing and editing won't cure."

One of the keys to this writing talent, one of the indispensable skills, is the *transition*. Transitions are words, phrases, even whole paragraphs that hold a story together. News stories without adequate transitions fall apart. Transitions take your readers from subject to subject, fact to fact, time to time, and place to place without losing or confusing them along the way.

Using Transitions

Transitions come in many forms. For instance, are you able to recognize the transition between these two paragraphs?

> President Bush today signed into law a new tax reform bill, expected to raise an additional $10 billion a year for the federal treasury.
>
> Bush signed the bill in a White House ceremony and then handed out two dozen souvenir pens to the Republican senators who steered the bill to passage.

The transition there is the repetition of the word "Bush." Because the word appears in both paragraphs, the reader knows the subject hasn't changed. It is still President Bush we're talking about; our reader has not been lost.

Let's try another example.

> "There is no reason why the people of this country cannot unite in a common purpose.
>
> "Those who would tear us apart have no place in an orderly society," Jones added.

In this example, the quotation marks at the beginning of each paragraph serve as a signal that the person who was speaking in the first paragraph is still speaking in the second.

Here are some transitional words that come in handy for the newswriter:

for example	finally
besides	then
consequently	later
furthermore	and
however	but
likewise	or
moreover	meanwhile
nevertheless	also
therefore	in addition
thus	in general

Once you know what transitions are, however, you are only halfway home. You must still master their use. Generally speaking, the transition should be unobtrusive. That is, it shouldn't stick out; it should accomplish its job with a minimum of attention. While this is desirable, it is not always possible. The first duty is to the readers, and if it takes an obvious, blatant transition to help guide them through the story, so be it.

Read the excerpt on the next page and note the transition, set in italics. The transition is necessary because the author is signaling a complete change of subject.

Journalists today often rely on microcomputers to write their news stories. Word processing programs make it easy to rewrite, edit, move copy around, and insert transitions where needed.

The battle eventually led to the establishment of the Interstate Commerce Commission for regulation of rates.

But that was later. Turn now to the Populist Revolt, a fascinating chapter in the state's history.

The entire paragraph is a transition; there's nothing subtle about it. See if you can spot the problem in these two paragraphs:

A Democrat, *Smith* was more important in the inner workings of the administration of former Gov. John P. Jones than his administrative title indicated.

A native of Central City and holder of business administration and law degrees from State University, *Anderson* is a jet pilot veteran of the U.S. Air Force and presently is a captain in the Air National Guard.

Anderson? Who's he? Readers will assume the subject is Smith, and the writer gives no clue to indicate a change.

On the other hand, notice how the following story hangs together, even though it deals with topics in sharp contrast with one another.

Media, police, officials prevent trouble at state fair

[1]The state's major news media, law enforcement officials and State Fair authorities revealed a plan that officials said may have prevented political riots at the State Fair, which closed Thursday.

[2]Repeated and widespread *rumors* had it that paid troublemakers, supposedly from Omaha; Wichita, Kan.; Sioux City, Iowa; and Kansas City, were to be in Lincoln to create trouble.

[3]Reporters, in cooperation with fair authorities and police officials, refused to print the *rumors*. Law enforcement groups including the State Safety Patrol, the Lincoln Police Department and the Lancaster County Sheriff's office made extensive *preparations* for possible trouble. The National Guard was notified.

[4]Officials believe the *preparations* may have been responsible for the lack of any *violence* at the fair.

[5]*Another act of violence*, of a different nature, also was avoided; the grand champion lamb, usually swiftly turned into *lamb* chops after the fair, was granted a reprieve.

[6]Its buyer, John DeCamp of Neligh, donated the *lamb* to the Lincoln Association of Retarded Children (LARC) School as a pet for the children.

[7]It was the first time in fair history that a grand champion has been spared from the slaughterhouse.

[8]Vickie Jorgensen, from whom DeCamp bought the lamb, said she was "oh, so very happy at the news. I can't believe it, it's so wonderful."

[9]"Chub," grand champion 4-H market steer, sold for $2 a pound to Cooper Feeds of Humboldt, bringing $2,272 for its owner, Jackie Dobesh. *She wept when she parted from the champion.*

[10]*But there was no weeping among fair officials.* Manager Henry Brandt announced that Thursday's 15,000 attendance established a record. This year's fair drew *418,000 compared to last year's 415,000.*

[11]*Most of the thousands* who jammed the fairgrounds were unaware of the rumors of trouble and the behind-the-scenes preparations that were going on.

[12]Tear gas, riot sticks and riot helmets were obtained. Various law enforcement agencies held special training sessions. Lincoln police

were *prepared* to use more than a third of their total *force* should trouble develop.

[13]A so-called tactical platoon of officers under the command of Inspector Robert Sawdon was alerted and *prepared* to respond rapidly. All members of the *forces* maintained round-the-clock contact with the department.

[14]State Safety Patrol officers circulated through the fairgrounds with portable two-way radios. National Guard units and authorities were available.

[15]Reporters, who faced a barrage of questions about the riot rumors, worked closely with law enforcement officials and fair authorities. It was agreed that only reports that were "extremely reliable and could be proved" would be printed. Not a line appeared in any metropolitan newspaper.

[16]The most persistent rumor was that trouble was planned for Labor Day, always a day of huge attendance. When that day ended, fair officials *sighed with relief.*

[17]*An even bigger sigh* was issued when the fair closed Thursday at midnight.

Tying Paragraphs Together

Notice how repetition of the word "rumors" holds together paragraphs 2 and 3. The same is true of the word "preparation," which glues together paragraphs 3 and 4. Then there is a major shift, from possible serious violence to the "violence" of turning the grand champion lamb into lamb chops. This shift is accomplished with the phrase "another act of violence," which ties together paragraphs 4 and 5. The story shifts again between paragraphs 9 and 10; the transition is accomplished smoothly by repeating the idea of weeping. Moving from paragraph 10 to paragraph 11 presents another problem for the writer: how to get from figures on fair attendance back to the rumors of trouble. The writer overcomes the problem with the phrase "most of the thousands" at the opening of paragraph 11, which repeats an idea included in the preceding paragraph. The "sigh of relief" ties together the final two paragraphs.

Notice, also, that although the story is written in inverted pyramid style, it doesn't just taper off at the end. There is a closing paragraph that is obviously meant to be just that. The newswriter owes as much to the reader in the last paragraph as in the first.

The Body of the Story

Now that you've written the lead and hooked it to the second paragraph, it's time to write the body—the rest of the story. If you've written a traditional inverted pyramid lead, you have probably summarized the story in your first sentence. Now you must elaborate on that.

A story about an event like this fire ought to unfold in inverted-pyramid style, with the main facts first and the rest of the story told in descending order of importance.

Simply retell the story in more detail in the next few paragraphs, making sure you bring in all the background necessary to give the reader full understanding. This involves the tie-back, which means bringing into the story last week's, last month's, or last year's developments. If the story is a simple one with just one main fact to convey, the task is not too difficult. If it's an announcement of the results of the French Club's election, for example, name the new president in the lead, then go into secondary details as your pyramid narrows. The second paragraph might name the other officers, the third might tell more about the new president, the fourth might describe the election, the fifth the outgoing president, and the sixth what the group is going to do next. An example of such a story is on the next page.

French club elects president

Michelle Kelly Baker, senior, has been elected president of the Central High School French Club.

Other officers elected are Duane Beck, vice president; Lawrence Kubek, secretary; and Jane Smith, treasurer.

Baker previously served as vice president of the club. She also is a member of the Student Council and last year studied in France as an exchange student. She plans to major in French at State University.

She and the other officers were elected in balloting Thursday by club members under the supervision of French instructor Barclay Faris.

Baker replaces outgoing president Tom Pelley.

The French Club's annual art show is being planned for early next semester, Baker said.

Notice how this story fits the classic inverted pyramid pattern, with each successive paragraph just a bit less important than the preceding one.

If the story is more complex—that is, if it has more than one main fact—your job is harder. You must summarize, giving all three or four main facts in the lead, if possible. In the next section of the story, give the most important detail of each main fact; after that, provide additional but not quite so important information on each fact.

We could draw charts for you, with big boxes becoming smaller and smaller as the pyramid gets narrower. But as in so many areas of writing, it is more effective to develop your instincts than to rely on a formula. With practice, you will learn how to place facts in *meaningful* descending order.

Organizational Patterns

Not all stories can be written in inverted pyramid style. In fact, fewer and fewer are being written that way because of the evolution of the American newspaper. The inverted pyramid puts the most important facts at or near the top of the story. But with the influence of television and radio, all this is changing. It makes little sense for a newspaper to announce something that everyone saw on television 10 hours earlier. So newswriters have modified the inverted pyramid. Newspaper writing reads more and more like magazine writing; it is becoming more creative.

Different Patterns

There are still traditional story types that do not lend themselves to inverted pyramid style. For instance, there is the story with the surprise ending. Compare these two treatments of the same facts:

Inverted pyramid	Surprise ending
The 18-month-old son of East High School Principal Arthur Learned was unhurt Friday when he crawled into his father's car, pulled it out of gear and rode it down a hill where it struck another car.	Police Friday decided not to book a young ''driver'' involved in an accident on 12th Street.
Learned said he had put the boy, Gerald, in the car and was trying to get in himself when the boy pulled the gearshift.	The youngster was behind the wheel of a car that careened backward down a hill and struck a parked car.
The car, parked in front of the Learned residence at 222 S. 12th St., rolled backward about 50 feet and struck a parked car.	The driver was Gerald Learned, son of East High Principal Arthur Learned.
	The car was parked in front of the Learned home at 222 S. 12th St. when Gerald, who had been put in the car by his father, pulled it out of gear.
	Gerald is 18 months old.

The story also illustrates one way an event can be given reader appeal through novel treatment. Such treatment often means the difference between a story that appears on page one with a box around it and a story that ends up on page 27, buried near the want ads. Never be afraid to try an unusual approach.

Personality interview

The personality interview, in which the writer sketches with words the portrait of one human being, is another type of story that cannot be handled with the inverted pyramid. Here the writer may back into the story, perhaps with an anecdote from the subject's life. On rare occasions, writers may use a quote from the person as the lead.

Action stories

Still another type of story that requires a different approach is the action story. This is most effectively handled by unfolding chronologically. For instance, if a dog wanders into your school,

An action story can always be enhanced with a photo, if your photographer happens to be in the right place at the right time.

your story will be more interesting if you don't simply state the facts that the dog appeared, sniffed around for a while, and was finally chased out. You may want to begin with the dog entering the building, then give a minute-by-minute account of the activities that followed, telling how the dog stopped first in the journalism classroom and was chased from there to the chemistry lab, where he upset some test tubes, and so on. The last paragraph might be about the dog scurrying out the door and heading home.

Combination style

An increasingly popular way of writing news stories combines the summary lead and the chronological style. The writer summarizes in the first paragraph and then tells the rest of the story in the order in which it occurred. Thus, the story of the dog might begin:

A dog with a cold nose for news Thursday strolled into the journalism class, saw that his help wasn't needed, and then took the grand tour of the building, upsetting test tubes, disrupting gym classes, and disturbing study halls before being expelled.

After that summary, the next paragraph would start the chronological unfolding of the story:

The dog's presence became known during fifth period when he stuck his nose in the offices of the *Oracle*. . . .

Color sidebar

The "color sidebar" requires some approach other than the inverted pyramid style. It is a story related to but kept separate from another on the same subject. In the case of a major storm, the main story tells about the number of deaths and amount of damage. The sidebar might be the eyewitness account of a survivor or an interview with an official of the National Weather Service describing how the storm developed. A sidebar supplements the main story, providing extra detail or "color."

Newspaper Style

No matter what sort of story you are writing, you must follow certain well-established guidelines. You must follow newspaper style for capitalization, abbreviation, spelling, and the like. Behind this style, set forth in the individual newspaper's stylebook, is the necessity for a newspaper to be consistent. It doesn't make much sense for one reporter to spell "basketball" as two words while another spells it as one, or for one reporter to write "Mr. Learned" and another "Learned." (Of course, full names are always used in the first reference to someone in a story.) The stylebook should address whether males and females will be treated the same way in the second reference. Opinions differ on this, and on the use of the title "Ms." Consistency counts. If a newspaper is sloppy on details of style, readers believe, then it probably is sloppy on more important things, such as accuracy. So learn the stylebook and follow it.

Sexist Language

Make sure you eliminate sexist language from your publications. The time when writers routinely used male pronouns to describe everyone is past. It is not acceptable to write, "For a student to receive credit for the course, he must pass the final exam." Some writers say, "For a student to receive credit for the course, he or

These two stories illustrate the use of the color sidebar. Here, the news story about the flood includes the facts of the disaster. The color sidebar highlights the personal plight of individuals caught in the event.

Sonora flood damage at $100 million

Continued from Page One

meters of water per second into the river, where the water had been receding.

Some officials and the townspeople are fearful that next month and in March the runoff of mounting snow in the Sierra Madre may cause the river to spill over again.

But Solano said that from Jan. 15 to Feb. 15, the remaining water in the dam will be used to irrigate dry farmland in the valley.

Some 98,280 acres of planted or cultivated fields here were destroyed, said Victor Manuel Vega Ibarra, secretary of the municipality.

"The land was either ready to plant or harvest," he said. "The loss is great, and it is going to effect the town's economy greatly."

Crops that were destroyed included tomatoes, chilies, cucumbers, squash and wheat. Ibarra said about 2,000 pigs and 2,000 cows are in danger of dying because there is no way to get food to them in the surrounding ranges.

Many Red Cross volunteers and soldiers have worked around the clock for the past eight days distributing clothing, blankets and about 360,000 pounds of food.

Dr. Victor Alberto Aragon Sanchez said sickness has begun to spread among the children and elderly in the town, but he added that it is under control. The common illnesses include bronchitis, colds, influenzas, tonsillitis and laryngitis.

"Emotionally it is bad," Sanchez

said. "Many of the people are very nervous and depressed because they have lost everything."

Doctor Adolfo Leon Velasquez, director of the city's health department, said all the townspeople have been vaccinated for typhoid fever, tetanus and polio.

"We are ordering everyone to boil their water where there is no running water, and we are putting chlorinated tablets into the drums

Prison guard Mario Alvarez carries a box of tortillas across a canal to the prison

that hold water," Velasquez said.

He said latrines are also being built.

Velasquez said it is certain that underground water has become contaminated since the disaster because raw sewage is being pumped into the flooded areas.

The sewage usually drains into canals that carry it to the river. But city officials are pumping it into the flooded areas so that it doesn't back

up into homes.

According to Ibarra, Sonora Gov. Samuel Ocaña promised city officials he will have workers assess the damage once the water recedes and will set aside aid for houses to be constructed.

Ibarra said the city will receive about $187,500 for the construction of about 750 houses.

He said the houses would be temporary shelters built out of wood, treated laminated board and tin.

'We will start over because it is our land'

Water submerges fields; sadness fills hearts

By Carmen Duarte
The Arizona Daily Star

HUATABAMPO, Sonora — The woman sat on the small bed and stared at her sleeping baby boy.

He entered the world on New Year's Day after his parents and relatives scrambled from their *campo* because of a threatening flood.

He was born healthy to Berta Alicia Maldonado Huipas, 20, a Mayo Indian. She is worried, now, about what she will be able to offer her firstborn.

Like three other women who gave birth under similar circumstances, Berta is living in a classroom at the Gen. Fausto Topete Elementary School here.

The classroom was cold. People were wrapped in blankets, sleeping on a cement floor.

One woman sat in a corner sur-

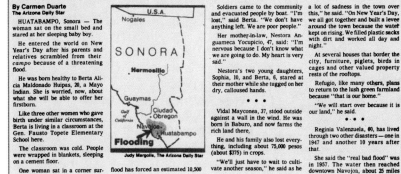

Judy Margolis, The Arizona Daily Star

flood has forced an estimated 10,500

Soldiers came to the community and evacuated people by boat. "I'm lost," said Berta. "We don't have anything left. We are poor people."

Her mother-in-law, Nestora Anguameca Yocupicio, 47, said: "I'm nervous because I don't know what we are going to do. My heart is very sad."

Nestora's two young daughters, Sophia, 10, and Berta, 6, stared at their mother while she tugged on her dry, calloused hands.

• • •

Vidal Mayconea, 37, stood outside against a wall in the wind. He was born in Baburo, and now farms the rich land there.

He and his family also lost everything, including about 75,000 pesos (about $375) in crops.

"We'll just have to wait to cultivate another season," he said as he

a lot of sadness in the town over this," he said. "On New Year's Day, we all got together and built a levee around the town because the water kept on rising. We filled plastic sacks with dirt and worked all day and night."

At several houses that border the city, furniture, piglets, birds in cages and other valued property rests on the rooftops.

Refugio, like many others, plans to return to the lush green farmland because "that is our home."

"We will start over because it is our land," he said.

• • •

Reginia Valenzuela, 60, has lived through two other disasters — one in 1947 and another 10 years after that.

She said the "real bad flood" was in 1957. The water then reached downtown Navojoa, about 25 miles

she must pass the final exam." That solves the problem of sexist language, but it is wordy and awkward. This is better: "For students to receive credit for the course, they must pass the final exam." In other words, use plural nouns and pronouns. Rules against sexist language should become part of your stylebook.

Below are some sexist "traps" and expressions you can use to avoid them.

mankind	*use* humanity
man-made	*use* synthetic, machine-made
mailman	*use* lettercarrier
businessman	*use* business executive, manager
fireman	*use* firefighter
policeman	*use* police officer

Clarity

The style we are concerned with here is a more general writing style. Because newspaper writers are never certain who will read their stories or under what circumstances, they must select words with the utmost care in order to eliminate as much confusion as possible. They must develop a clear, simple, concise way of expressing themselves. *This does not mean that they should write for someone with a sixth-grade mentality.* This is a myth that has been repeated so often that a lot of people believe it. With public education free and required by law, where would all these sixth-grade minds come from? The answer is that they are in the sixth grade.

That implies, to repeat, a clear, concise, simple writing style. It means that all excess wordage must be culled from every sentence. Don't write: "The Association of the Bar of the City of New York." Write: "The New York City Bar Association." Don't write: "He was wearing a shirt that was made of cotton and that had been borrowed from a friend of his." Write: "He was wearing a borrowed cotton shirt."

Go over every sentence you write looking for words to cut. Don't expect the copy editor to do this for you; the editing process *begins* with the reporter.

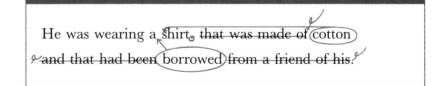

Sentence Style

The good newswriter selects short words and sentences as well as short paragraphs, not because the audience is ignorant but because such elements are easier to read. Writing in short sentences doesn't mean adopting a "Dick-and-Jane" style. (The flag is red. It is white. It is blue.) But it does mean writing most of the time in *simple, declarative sentences* rather than complex ones. It means avoiding the semicolon and relying on the period. In this way the newswriter not only limits the length of the sentence (and makes it more readable) but also reduces the amount of information the reader has to swallow in one gulp.

Don't get the idea that all good writing comes in short words and short sentences; there is no ideal sentence length. Certainly writers who decide never to write a sentence of more than, say, 15 words are in trouble. Not only will they have a series of choppy, jerky sentences but they will never finish a single story because they'll be too busy counting words.

Just for fun, we counted the words in this bit of writing by Mark Twain from *Life on the Mississippi*, chapter 4.

[1]Once a day a cheap, gaudy packet arrived upward from St. Louis, and another downward from Keokuk.

[2]Before these events, the day was glorious with expectancy; after them, the day was a dead and empty thing.

[3]Not only the boys, but the whole village, felt this.

[4]After all these years I can picture that old time to myself now, just as it was then: the white town drowsing in the sunshine of a summer's morning; the streets empty, or pretty nearly so; one or two clerks sitting in front of the Water Street stores, with their splint-bottomed chairs tilted back against the walls, chins on breasts, hats slouched over their faces, asleep—with shingle-shavings enough around to show what broke them down; a sow and a litter of pigs loafing along the sidewalk, doing a good business in watermelon rinds and seeds; two or three lonely little freight piles scattered around the ''levee''; a pile of ''skids'' on the slope of the stone-paved wharf, and the fragrant town drunkard asleep in the shadow of them; two or three wood flats at the head of the wharf, but nobody to listen to the peaceful lapping of the wavelets against them; the great Mississippi, the majestic, the magnificent Mississippi, rolling its mile-wide tide along, shining in the sun; the dense forest away on the other side; the ''point'' above the town, and the ''point'' below, bounding the river-glimpse and turning it into a sort of sea, and withal a very still and brilliant and lonely one.

Sentence 1 has 17 words, sentence 2 has 19, sentence 3 just 10. Sentence 4 totals 208 words, a word counter's nightmare. Can it be said, then, that good writing comes only in short sentences? Not unless you think Mark Twain was a bad writer. Thus, while it is a general guideline to stick to short sentences, long sentences can be effective, too, if used correctly. Keep in mind that there is little relationship between length of sentence and beauty.

"Before these events, the day was glorious with expectancy; after them the day was a dead and empty thing."

Photo courtesy of the Delta Queen Steamboat Company.

Wordiness

We are not all Mark Twains, of course. But we can write well if we pay attention to the words we choose. The reason we write is to communicate, not to show off our vocabulary. Here are some examples of pretentious words, with shorter, clearer synonyms in parentheses:

assuage (ease)
corpulent (fat)
circuitous (roundabout)
appellation (name)
identical (same)
erudite (learned)
conflagration (fire)
inundated (flooded)
edifice (building)
precipitation (rain, snow)

fallacious (wrong)
endeavor (try)
indisposed (ill)
purchase (buy)
proceed (go)
inebriated (drunk)
terminate (end)
constituency (voters)
demeanor (behavior)
location (site)

Such "show-off" words can trip up a potentially good writer. Such a writer may feel stifled at first but should recognize that journalism is "controlled creativity"—that is, because journalists must, above all, communicate, they are not free to sling words around with abandon. They have to watch their language. Besides, it's as easy to be creative with small words as it is with big ones.

Slang and Jargon

Another pitfall for the student is overuse of slang. Call a football a football, not a pigskin. Jargon is another trap. Can you translate this?

> Objective consideration of contemporary phenomena compels the conclusion that success or failure in competitive activities exhibits no tendency to be commensurate with innate capacity, but that a considerable element of the unpredictable must invariably be taken into account.

You might recognize this paragraph if we restore it to its original condition as it appeared in Ecclesiastes:

> I returned, and saw under the sun, that the race is not to the swift, nor the battle to the strong, neither yet bread to the wise, nor yet riches to men of understanding, nor yet favor to men of skill; but time and chance happeneth to them all.

People addicted to jargon never say "no." They say, "The answer is in the negative." Bad weather is "unfavorable climatic conditions," and marriage is "entering a state of blessed matrimony."

Redundancy

Still another trap is redundancy. Such expressions as "2 A.M. in the morning" and "the globe is spherical in shape" are redundant. You may write "2 A.M." or "2 in the morning," but there's no sense saying it twice. And it is sufficient to say the globe is spherical. "In shape" isn't needed because the word "spherical" contains the concept of shape.

Clichés

Beginning writers can get into trouble with clichés, too. The cliché is an overworked, overused, old, and trite expression. Here are some examples:

acid test	hands across the sea	little white lie
at long last	heated argument	milk of human kindness
avoid like the plague	hit the nail on the head	raining cats and dogs
beat around the bush	dead as a doornail	right as rain
blunt instrument	in the limelight	sadder but wiser
calm before the storm	kicked off the event	selling like hotcakes
dull thud	Lady Luck	smart as a whip
get down to brass tacks	last but not least	take off the gloves
grateful nations	light as a feather	white as a sheet
		with bated breath

You could make your own list. Clichés reveal to the alert reader that the writer is too lazy to invent bright new figures of speech. A good guideline is: *Never use a figure of speech that you're used to seeing in print.* Journalism instructors usually take great delight in spotting clichés in their students' stories. Write "high noon" in a story and you may get a sarcastic note asking, "When is low noon?"

A Special Problem

A master of the English language, Theodore Bernstein of the *New York Times*, coined a word to describe the next writing hazard. The word is *monologophobia*, and it means, roughly, the fear of repeating a word. As Bernstein points out, the ailment leads to such paragraphs as "Sugar Ray flattened Bobo in 12 rounds in 1950, outpointed him in 15 sessions in 1952, and knocked him out in two heats last December 9." This leaves the reader wondering if a round, a session, and a heat are the same thing (they are). Have no fear of repeating a word, because if you do you may end up with such silly synonyms as "yellow metal" for "gold," "grapplers" for "wrestlers," and "thinclads" for "members of the track team."

Some people call this the "elongated yellow fruit" school of writing. The following article explains why.

Four Bananas Aren't Three Bananas and One Elongated Yellow Fruit

By James L. Kilpatrick

HOLLINS COLLEGE, VA.—The student editors had come from a dozen Southeastern colleges to swap suggestions and receive awards; and now we were assembled on a white veranda, with a spring rain drenching the boxwoods, and the talk turned easily to shop talk.

All of the young writers had read E.B. White's *Elements of Style*, and most of them had browsed in Fowler's *Modern English Usage*. They had profited from Ernest Gowers and Ivor Brown and from courses redundantly styled "creative writing." They put the question to me, as a visiting newspaperman: Would I give them my own set of rules with a few random examples thrown in, for writing newspaper copy? It was a temptation not to be resisted.

I pass these rules along here, for whatever value they may have to fellow workers in the carpentry of words. Every editor in the land could add some admonitions of his own.

1. *Be clear.* This is the first and greatest commandment. In a large sense, nothing else matters. For clarity embraceth all things; the clear thought to begin with; the right words for conveying that thought; the orderly arrangement of the words. It is a fine thing, now and then, to be colorful, to be vivid, to be bold. First be clear.

2. *Love words*, and treat them with respect. For words are the edged tools of your trade; you must keep them honed. Do not infer when you mean to imply, do not write fewer than, when you mean less than. Do not use among, when you mean between. Observe that continually and continuously have different meanings. Do not write alternately when you mean alternatively. Tints are light, shades are dark. The blob on the gallery wall is not an abstract. Beware the use

of literally, virtually, fulsome, replica, many-faceted, and the lion's share. Pinch-hitters are something more than substitutes. Learn the rules of that and which. When you fall into the pit of "and which," climb out of your swampy sentence and begin anew.

3. As a general proposition, *use familiar words*. Be precise; but first be understood. Search for the solid nouns that bear the weight of thought. Use active verbs that hit an object and do not glance off. When you find an especially gaudy word, possessed of a gorgeous rhinestone glitter, lock it firmly away. Such words are costume jewels. They are sham.

4. *Edit your copy*; then edit it again; then edit it once more. This is the hand-rubbing process. No rough sandpapering can replace it.

5. *Strike the redundant word*. Emergencies are inherently acute; crises are grave; consideration is serious. When you exhort your read-

ers to get down to basic fundamentals, you are dog-paddling about in a pool of ideas and do not know where to touch bottom. Beware the little qualifying words: rather, somewhat, pretty, very. As White says, these are the leeches that suck the meaning out of language. Pluck them from your copy.

6. *Have no fear of repetition*. It is better to repeat a word than to send an orphaned antecedent in its place. Do not write horsehide, white pellet, or the old apple when you mean baseball. Members of City Council are not solons; they are members of City Council. If you must write banana four times, then write banana four times; nothing is gained by three bananas and one elongated yellow fruit.

7. If you cannot be obviously profound, *try not to be profoundly obvious*. Therefore, do not inform your reader that something remains to be seen. The thought will have occurred to him already.

8. *Strive for a reasoned perspective*. True crises come infrequently; few actions are outrageous; cities and economies are seldom paralyzed for long. A two-alarm fire is not a holocaust. Not much is imperative or urgent; still less is vital. To get at the size of a crowd, divide the cops' estimate by 3.1416.

9. *Style depends in part upon the cadence of your prose*. Therefore listen to your copy with a fine-tuned ear. In the prose that truly pleases, you will find that every sentence has an unobtrusive rhythm that propels it on its way. With a little re-arranging, you can keep the rhythm going. But do not do this always; you may sound like Hiawatha.

10. *Beware of long sentences*; they spread roots that tend to trip the reader up. The period key lies nicely on the bottom row of your machine, down toward the right-hand end. Use it. Use it often.

The Whole Story

Now here's an example of a well-written news story. It was written by Tiffany Anderson for the Western Kentucky University (Bowling Green) minority workshop, directed by James Highland. You read the lead to the story in the preceding chapter. Now let's take a look at the whole story.

Local woman gives children chance to live

By Tiffany Anderson, Stratford High School

When Judy Schwank walks into the village hospital, hundreds of dying children will be there to meet her. Word has spread that she is coming, and as many as 125 homeless, limbless, or sightless children will be waiting for help and waiting to die.

Schwank is trying to help those who can't help themselves. She's on a mission to protect Central and South American children from un-necessary death.

It may sound like a fairy tale, but it's real and happening in Bowling Green.

Schwank has made 35 trips to Guatemala to get sick children and bring them to Bowling Green to heal, and she plans to return in July. She and her husband, William, who is from Guatemala, have kept more than 100 children in their home.

"Most (children) only stay two to three months," Mrs. Schwank said.

The children—ages three weeks to 19 years—come from the poverty-stricken countries of Guatemala, Equador, Brazil, Haiti and Honduras.

Four out of 10 Guatemalan children had a disease which can be cured, and it is these children who will gain a chance for life. Families will be left behind, but a new one in America will be made while they heal.

After surgery and bones mend, most of the children will be sent back to live happier lives.

"In these countries poor people are treated just as blacks were treated during slavery," Schwank said. "Everyone in Guatemala isn't poor."

Children rummage through junkyards searching for food.

"One out of three children are severely malnourished," said Schwank, who is also a nurse in Bowling Green. And "babies die because their countries don't have ventilator machines."

All heart machines are unplugged because there is no money to support them. And it isn't uncommon for children to be killed on nearby railroad tracks.

With the assistance of Pam Goff, president of the Kentucky/Tennessee chapter of Heal the Children, Schwank has placed children in 40 homes across Kentucky and Tennessee. Heal the Children is a volunteer organization designed to help sick children in countries around the world.

"Fifty-five to 60 kids stay in Kentucky. They are in Liberty, Lexington, Louisville and Bowling Green. There are also some in Nashville," Schwank said.

About 200 children are on a waiting list to come to homes in Kentucky and Tennessee. Most of the children chosen to participate have polio.

The children's surgeries are paid for as a donation by hospitals, a cost of $2.5 million dollars in the last two years.

Schwank donates more than her time. She said it's not unusual for her to spend $15,000 of her own family income each year.

Besides her own four children, Schwank has four others living with her.

"Most of the children do not have problems" adjusting to life in America, Schwank said, but ironically, the younger children are afraid of Schwank unless they live with her.

Most of the young children burst into tears when they see her.

That's because Schwank is the one that takes them from their village to the doctor for painful medical treatment.

However, most problems occur with the teenagers. They may run away because—once they've lived in the United States—they don't want to go home.

"One child could not cope," she said. "Her treatment was stopped, and she went home and will die."

Schwank said she's drained emotionally, physically and financially, but plans to "pass on the torch" to her children. Schwank feels that if out of 200 kids she can reach 10 and in turn those 10 kids each help 200 kids, Heal the Children could help 2,000 children.

"Everything is worth it just to see that one moment when they go home to their families."

Notice how the repetition of Schwank's name ties the lead and the second paragraph together. So does repetition of the word *help* and the notion of death. The story also is helped by the good quotations scattered throughout. And the contractions lend a feeling of informality. But what is perhaps most impressive about this story is its heavy emphasis on facts. For example, we know Schwank has made thirty-five trips to Guatemala and she and her husband have kept more than one hundred children in their home. The ages of the children are reported. We also learn how many children in Guatemala are diseased, how many are malnourished, who in the

United States is helping, how many children are placed in which care agency, how many are waiting, how much it all costs, where the money comes from, and much more. The story's ending obviously is planned; it didn't just happen.

Too many scholastic journalists round up a couple of quick quotes, toss in some opinion and a clever opening, and call it a story. This story, on the other hand, is colorful, well-organized, and full of facts.

Here is another well-done inverted pyramid story. It is from the *Epitaph*, a remarkable and much-honored newspaper produced at Homestead High School in Cupertino, Calif. Notice how this story could be trimmed after virtually any paragraph and would still make sense and convey information.

Also, the story is properly attributed (and the verb used is "said"), balanced (people for and against the new policy are quoted), and tight and concise (it would be hard to eliminate any "fat" from this story).

A sidebar headlined "Official tardy policy" sets out the penalties. The *Epitaph* makes good use of a quick, clear list instead of burying the penalties in the body of the story. Today's students should always look for ways to pull important information from a story and highlight it as an easy-to-read list or a graphic.

New Tardiness Policy Announced

In response to teacher complaints about student tardiness and cutting, the administration plans to institute random tardy sweeps next semester to catch students out on campus during class, said Ethel Kopal, assistant principal in charge of discipline.

Administrators and campus supervisors will conduct unannounced campuswide searches after the start of selected periods, noting names of students found out of class without identification tags. Students caught will receive unexcused absences and may not attend class, Kopal said.

Although the administration can hold tardy sweeps any time, Assistant Principal Bill Richter said target periods will be third and fifth periods.

The most tardies occur during first period and the periods following brunch and lunch, said Imperia Murtha, attendance clerk.

The policy will go into effect soon after second semester starts, Kopal said, adding that the administration will announce exactly when the crackdown will begin.

Richter, who proposed the measure, said a similar policy proved successful at Monta Vista High

School, where he worked before coming to Homestead this year.

Math teacher Elwin Stocking also said the measure will prove beneficial. "In the long run, it will aid in the learning process for those students who were tardy the first couple of times," he said.

But English teacher Nelson Pereira said the measure was unnecessary. He said he does not consider students entering class late a significant disturbance, noting that the administrative summons during class causes equal disruption.

He added that teachers, not administrators, should handle the problem of student tardiness.

Junior Dave Bundgard said he thinks forcing tardy students to miss all of class would be counterproductive. "It's better to be in class for 45 minutes than to sit in the cafeteria," he said.

Many questioned the measure's fairness. Junior Bonnie McCluskey said the school should not punish students for tardiness, since "(being tardy) means the student tried to get to class on time."

Official tardy policy

Tardy sweeps next semester will supplement the current tardy policy, which is enforced mainly by teachers.
1st tardy: Teacher warning
2nd-3rd: Teacher detention
4th: Teacher detention and letter home

5th-6th: Administrative detention
7th: Administrative detention and possible student contract
8th-10th: Administrative detentions and possible parent conference
Habitual tardiness: Possible removal from class with F grade

Wrap-up

The lead-writing chapter is a good start to learning how newswriting works. The process continues step-by-step.

If the first paragraph is the most important in the story, the second paragraph certainly is the next. One way to hold the interest built up in the lead is to use a quotation, the sound of a human voice, immediately. Some people call this a back-up quote, one designed to support the lead. Such a quote links the lead to the second paragraph, helping the story unfold logically and coherently. This is one type of transition.

Transitions can be entire sentences but usually they are one word: *but, also, therefore, however*. To aid the reader, sentences and paragraphs should be tied together logically.

After the lead and transitional quote, the story—told in skeletal fashion in the lead—is then simply re-told in greater detail.

The preceding describes the inverted pyramid style of writing. Many other techniques are used, including the rare surprise ending.

One increasingly popular style uses a summary lead followed by a chronological account. This is especially effective in describing action.

Stories that amplify or are related to other stories are called *sidebars*.

Details of style should be kept in mind. A publication needs to be consistent, always spelling words the same way (''adviser,'' not ''advisor''). The stylebook dictates these decisions and everyone should follow it.

Modern writers avoid sexist language and avoid using the pronoun ''he'' to describe the entire human race. Words that are inappropriately male (''mailman'') should be eliminated (use ''lettercarrier'' instead).

Short words (''rich,'' not ''opulent''; ''marriage,'' not ''matrimony'') and short sentences aid busy readers. So does tight writing. Elim-

inate such usages as ''Easter Sunday'' and ''Jewish rabbi.'' Redundancy is an enemy of clarity. It is 2 in the morning or 2 A.M. but never 2 A.M. in the morning. There is no need to say it twice.

Jargon also can interfere with communication. Don't use ''unfavorable climatic conditions'' when you really mean ''bad weather.'' Clichés also should be avoided.

Writers should not use worn-out figures of speech, such as ''acid test,'' ''last but not least,'' ''dead as a doornail,'' or ''avoid like the plague.'' Use of clichés exposes lazy, uninventive writers.

Fear of repeating a word (''monologophobia'') can lead to inelegant expressions, such as ''elongated yellow fruit'' for ''banana.'' Have no fear of repeating words.

Look for ways to pull important information from a story and highlight it as a list or graphic.

On Assignment

Teamwork

1. Working in teams, scour the sports and news pages of your local newspaper to find examples of the clichés and other overworked figures of speech mentioned in this chapter. Clip the articles and compare what you find with the other teams' articles. Rewrite what you find.

2. Develop a stylebook for your school newspaper, determining style for anything not covered in the AP-UPI stylebook and making any necessary adaptations. For example, how will you refer to women on the second reference in a story? To instructors on second reference? Is it the Industrial Arts Building on first reference, or is IAB sufficient? Does the word *the* in the name of your paper take a capital T? These are the sorts of things the AP-UPI stylebook does not settle. Compare your stylebook to those created by other teams and the one being used by your newspaper. Adopt an official class stylebook to use in future assignments.

3. Brainstorm with your team a list of stories that could run in the next edition of the school paper. Compare your list with the other teams' lists and select the top story ideas. Each team will then determine different ways to write the story (for example, straight news, feature, chronological). Each team member should use a different approach. Attend the event or interview the sources as a team. Write your story in the style assigned.

Practice

1. Find plain, simple words for each of the complex ones here.

approximately	assist	ascertain
liable	locate	terminate
difficult	insufficient	presently
conflagration	encounter	initiate
municipality	utilize	lacerations
corpulent	resides	matrimony
propensity	purchase	declared
vehicle	forward	observed
provide	personnel	maintained
employment	prohibit	complained
inconvenience	paramount	implement

2. Edit the following sentences to remove all excess words:

The two will enter into a state of holy matrimony next week.

The fire broke out at 2 a.m. in the morning.

They were completely surrounded on all sides.

New freshmen often find it hard to adjust.

Her future plans include attending college at State University.

The accident occurred at the intersection of Broadway and Pantano.

The bell rang, indicating it was the hour of noon.

She received the bouquet of flowers as the day drew to a close.

Your Turn

1. Complete the stories for which you wrote leads in the exercises in Chapter 6.

2. Complete your interview story from Chapter 5.

3. Clip examples in your local newspaper of color sidebars, surprise endings, inverted pyramid writing, personality interviews, summary leads, transitions, and combination summary-chronological stories.

Katti Gray

Like many successful journalists, Katti Gray started small. Now a reporter for *Newsday* in New York City, she began her professional journey in Wichita Falls, Texas.

Highway 287 stretches northwest from Fort Worth, Texas, through miles of flatness and blink-away towns. Armed with a journalism degree, experience at her college daily, and internships at the *Dallas Times Herald* and the *Fort Worth Star-Telegram*'s Washington bureau, Gray set out on Highway 287 for her first job, as a reporter for the *Wichita Falls Record News*.

Gray graduated from Texas Christian University with majors in journalism and political science, an education she feels is a good combination for a journalist. Like many new journalism graduates, she took a job at a mid-sized daily in a mid-sized town, hoping to get practical experience reporting a variety of stories.

Covering the social services beat, she learned how to establish and maintain rapport with her contacts on a day-to-day basis. And she has learned how to dig out underlying issues from daily news.

Through her more general assignments, she said, she has learned how to be enterprising.

"I learned quickly that you can't come back from an assignment and tell the editor there was no story. They won't listen to that," she said.

With some professional experience under her belt, Gray left the *Record News* and joined the Fort Worth *Star-Telegram* in June 1985. For four years she worked there as a business reporter before moving on to *Newsday* in August 1989. Gray is one of two reporters covering Islip, Long Island.

New York City journalism has proved to be dramatically different from her work in Texas.

"It's far more sensational," she said. "New York is real different. I did some far more substantial work in Fort Worth."

But, she said, big city journalism has given her opportunities unavailable at her previous jobs and has taught her to be "a whole lot more sensitive to how the media exploit people's tragedies."

"We do not respect people's privacy," she said. "There are times when I want to jump up and say I don't want to do this."

The new experiences haven't changed Gray.

"I'm still very much the same person," she said. "I still believe the media have the potential to make a difference in people's lives."

But newspapers have a long way to go to give a voice to people who have none, she added. "We need to make the media a fairer craft."

Her New York City bosses, she said, would benefit from visiting smaller newspapers to see the bril-

liance and mediocrity there. "Good journalism goes on all over the country.

"Kids need to realize that to be important you don't have to be a *New York Times, Washington Post, Chicago Tribune*, or *Newsday* reporter," she said.

College fueled her idealism, pointing out the great powers and potentials of the media, but she also had to learn to deal with practical realities.

"Not everyone can win a Pulitzer. Every story you write will not liberate or emancipate somebody. You sometimes do things you are intellectually opposed to."

But something, something undefinable and ideal, she said, keeps journalists on their beats and at their video terminals. ∎

HANDLING QUOTES FAIRLY AND ACCURATELY

One of the basic journalistic functions is reproducing what people say. An announcement by the President, a ruling from a judge, a speech by a visitor to the town, an interview—stories about such events amount to one thing: The accurate and fair reporting of what was uttered—or, in some cases, what was not uttered.

Roger Tatarian, former vice president of United Press International, told one of the authors of this text about his dismay the first time a speech of his became the subject of a news account. Until he read the story, Tatarian had believed that speakers' complaints about being quoted out of context were just excuses—excuses that usually meant the stories were accurate but the speakers now wish they could retract their words. Tatarian's own experience showed otherwise. The local newspaper account of his speech was garbled and inaccurate, and the point of what he was saying got lost entirely.

One of the authors of this text had a similar experience. He was stopped by a reporter who asked three questions, and a verbatim account of the responses would have read: "Nixon. Yes. No." Instead, the reporter fabricated complete sentences, and the quote was completely unlike anything that had been said. The reporter in this case was more unethical than inaccurate, but the story illustrates the point. Too often, there are great differences between what is said and what is subsequently published or aired.

One of the authors of this text frequently asks students in his university survey course on journalism if they have had their names in the paper in the past year or two. Typically, one hundred hands go into the air. Then he asks, "Were the stories completely, totally accurate?" Virtually all the hands go down. Upon discussion, it turns out that the students feel they were misquoted or their words distorted. In fairness, of course, sometimes—frequently—it *is* a case of "boy, I wish I hadn't said that!" But too often words are misquoted or twisted, and that can lead to hard feelings, canceled subscriptions—even lawsuits.

Direct Quotation

Beginning journalists should pay a great deal of attention to the skills involved in handling quoted material.

Ideally, when you enclose a sentence or part of a sentence in quotation marks (quotes), you are telling your readers that that is *exactly* what the speaker said. You're not saying it's close or almost. You're saying "these are the exact words." Well, that's where the discussion of quotes always begins, at least. Anyone who's ever spent any time reporting knows that this ideal is seldom, if ever, reached. It can only be a starting point for discussion.

How is it possible to reproduce exactly what people say? People start sentences they never finish, they back up and start again, they say "ya know," "like I said," "ummmm," "ahhhh," and so on. We expect precision and logic in written communications

PEANUTS

© 1964 United Feature Syndicate, Inc.

or in a prepared spoken presentation. But extemporaneous human speech doesn't work that way. People think out loud, expressing half-formed thoughts and working out what they want to say as they go. It is virtually impossible to reproduce this speech exactly, and *why would you want to?* The job is to convey information . . . and there's no information in "ya know."

The journalistic ideal of reproducing speech *exactly* as it was uttered needs to be reexamined with an eye toward slight and very careful change. Studies indicate sources care about this issue a great deal less than do journalists. Sources want their thoughts and ideas conveyed accurately to the public. They care less about their exact words. So does this mean journalists can just come close, be almost perfect? Of course not. Regardless of everything that's been written here, most quotes must be 100 percent, absolutely word-for-word perfect. These would include important remarks by politicians (What *exactly* did the President say about the nation's economy), remarks certain to touch off controversy (a business executive's remarks that could be interpreted as racist), or historic words. In 1969, for example, there was discussion by journalists over what Neil Armstrong had said as he took the first steps on the moon. Was it "one small step for man . . ." or "one small step for *a* man . . .?" No one was inclined that day to just come close.

You can invent your own scenarios in which the exact language is crucial. Most of the time, journalists simply take out the "ya knows" and the "hmmms" and no harm is done. Faced with a tangled, unclear sentence, most journalists decide not to use a direct quote but to try and convey the source's ideas in clearer words. No one (at least no one with a commitment to ethics) alters quotes a great deal. A bit of sanitizing goes on, of course. But that's about the extent of it.

Tape recorders can be a great aid to a reporter. For important interview assignments, or any assignment in which capturing someone's words is important, we suggest using a tape recorder. Buy a small recorder, the size you can hold comfortably in your hand. Some people are intimidated by recorders so you don't want to show up with a big one. If the source agrees, turn on the recorder at the beginning, set it aside, and just let it run. You can do this during speeches and meetings, too. In some cities at school board or city council meetings, the area near the speaker's podium is a forest of recorders placed there by print and broadcast journalists.

Always take good notes even if you're using a tape recorder. Sometimes the batteries go dead or the tape breaks or gets twisted in the mechanism. Don't rely completely on a tape recorder.

Ethically, you should never tape record someone without permission, either in person or on the telephone.

If you're not using a tape recorder and are still concerned about exact quotes, take very careful notes, in shorthand or speedwriting if you know how, and flesh them out from memory as soon as possible. You will be surprised at how well your memory works. In most cases, no one expects you to reproduce every single word, every "ah-hem," but your goal is to come as close as possible.

There are exceptions to this. What if, during a speech or interview, the subject uses a four-letter word, the kind many people find offensive? What do you do? The easy answer (and frequently the right one) is to simply take it out, ignore it. But there are times—rare times, to be sure—when profanity is exactly right, when it conveys the point in the best possible way. If that is the case, then quote it. But don't ever sprinkle in four-letter words just to prove your sophistication or your freedom; it is naïve and immature.

Another exception occurs when the subject uses poor grammar. There's no need to reproduce bad grammar exactly as it was spoken, especially if there is no reason to expect the speaker to be a grammarian. For example, if you are interviewing your elderly custodian who has only a few years' formal education, don't make him seem illiterate. On the other hand, it would be foolish for you to take a colorful character who uses a lot of quaint phrases and make her sound like an English professor.

One of the authors of this text once took a beginning college journalism class to hear a speech by comedian and civil rights activist Dick Gregory. The stories they wrote about the speech

After covering a speech, the thorough reporter verifies facts, figures, and the correct spelling of names, briefly interviews the speaker for more detail on facts, or for a quote on the speaker's personal feelings on the subject.

made Gregory sound like the university president, when in fact he made a point of using ghetto language and slang. In other words, their stories were inaccurate because they had lost the speaker's unique flavor and approach.

Paraphrasing

Often paraphrasing is helpful. It is perfectly proper, often even desirable, for a reporter to paraphrase a person's words: to put into the reporter's own words the speaker's ideas. Thus, if a direct quote is long or rambling or poorly stated, the writer may revise it, knock off the quote marks, and simply add "he said" or "she said" at the end of the sentence.

Suppose the speaker says, "We are doing everything in our power at police headquarters to see to it that there is a parking place for everyone who drives to school. We hope everyone involved will be patient. We'll work it out, I promise." There's little doubt that a journalist could say that more concisely by paraphrasing, in which case it could read like this: "Chief Jones said police are trying to find parking space for everyone at school. He urged patience and promised to find a solution for the crowded lots."

There is one hazard to paraphrasing: Certain words must be adjusted. For instance, if the direct quote is, "We decided to go to a movie," the paraphrase has to read, "They decided to go to the movies, he said." Notice the shift in pronouns. "We" is a word reserved for direct quotes and editorials; so are "us" and "our." It is *the* country, *the* school, *the* town, not our country, our school, our town. Writing in the first person injects the reporter into the story; it amounts to an editorial opinion.

Partial Quotation

There is a compromise between the overuse of paraphrased material and the overuse of long blocks of quoted material: the partial quote. The writer is free to directly quote part of a sentence while paraphrasing the rest. For example:

> The school needs a dress code, the principal said, because students are becoming "sloppy in dress and sloppy in thought."

> Jones said he was "walking on a cloud" after scoring the winning touchdown.

The material enclosed in quotes in the preceding sentences constitutes partial quotes.

Beware, however, that this is not carried to absurd extremes.

For example:

> Jones said he was ''happy'' after scoring the touchdown.
>
> She was in ''critical'' condition, the hospital spokesperson said.

What purpose do the quotation marks serve in these examples? None at all.

Here are some other instances where quotes are unnecessary:

> After three defeats, it appears the season is ''down the drain.''
>
> The course is ''a piece of cake.''
>
> The music is ''a killer.''

You get the point. If a slang word or phrase is exactly right, use it and skip the quotes; they will add nothing except confusion. The reader will either understand the slang or not. The quotes will not make any difference.

Attribution

Beginning writers often have trouble with attribution. What is meant by attribution is this: Since it is often not possible to really know what people mean or feel or believe, we report what they *say* they mean or feel or believe. We report what the person said and make a point of pinning it on that person. Attribution amounts to giving the reader the name of the source. For example:

> The superintendent *said* she will resign.
>
> The police chief *said* Jones had confessed.
>
> Taxes will go down, the governor *promised*.
>
> Police *said* the accident occurred because of slick streets.
>
> There is no way Tech can win, the coach *said*.

The verb you use to indicate your source is important: *stated, declared, noted, pointed out*, and so on. The best of all such words is *said*. It is a neutral word that contains no editorial overtones; it is unobtrusive and rarely becomes tiresome no matter how often it appears in a story.

Be very careful which word you select when you depart from *said. Stated* is very formal. *Pointed out* should be reserved for absolute facts (The sun rose, he pointed out). *Charge, demand, shout,* and the like have editorial connotations. Whatever you do, stay away from this kind of construction:

> ''I could care less,'' he frowned.
>
> ''It's no problem of mine,'' she shrugged.

"How bad this is," he grimaced.

"Wonderful idea," she smiled.

You can frown, shrug, grimace, or smile all you want, but no words will come out. The verb you use must indicate speech formations by lips, mouth, and tongue.

Here is an excerpt from "The Short Happy Life of Francis Macomber," a short story by Ernest Hemingway. Notice it did not bother him to keep repeating "said," nor does it get monotonous.

"We'll put on another show for you tomorrow," Francis Macomber *said*.

"You're not coming," Wilson *said*.

"You're very mistaken," she told him. "And I want *so* to see you perform again. You were lovely this morning. That is if blowing things' heads off is lovely."

"Here's the lunch," *said* Wilson. "You're very merry, aren't you?"

"Why not? I didn't come out here to be dull."

"Well, it hasn't been dull," Wilson *said*. . . .

"Oh, no," she *said*. "It's been charming. And tomorrow. You don't know how I look forward to tomorrow."

"That's eland he's offering you," Wilson *said*.

"They're the big cowy things that jump like hares, aren't they?"

"I suppose that describes them," Wilson *said*.

"It's very good meat," Macomber *said*.

"Did you shoot it, Francis?" she asked.

"Yes."

"They're not dangerous, are they?"

"Only if they fall on you," Wilson told her.

"I'm so glad."

"Why not let up on the bitchery just a little, Margot," Macomber *said*. . . .

"I suppose I could," she *said*, "since you put it so prettily."

"Tonight we'll have champagne for the lion," Wilson *said*. "It's a bit too hot at noon."

"Oh, the lion," Margot *said*. "I'd forgotten the lion."

Need for Attribution

When should you attribute? The need for attribution is in direct proportion to the amount of controversy attached to the statement. Thus, a story about a robbery and the arrest of two suspects would need heavy attribution. But a story saying a downtown street has been closed for repairs would need little attribution, because it is common knowledge and noncontroversial. The best approach is

When in doubt, attribute

The next question is where to attribute, where to place the "he saids" and "she pointed outs." In general, attribution works best at the end or in the middle of a sentence. Give the quote first and the source of the quote second. In a long quote, attribution should come at the first logical point in the first sentence. Try this lead:

> Professor Pat Braintower on Thursday told a group of law students that America's poor need free legal advice or they will lose their rights.

This version is smoother and easier to read and comes to the point more quickly:

> America's poor need free legal advice or they will lose their rights, Professor Pat Braintower told a group of law students Thursday.

It is also perfectly acceptable to interrupt a quotation in the middle for attribution. For example:

> "Our students are mature," Jones told teachers Tuesday, "but they do not always act like it."

On the other hand, this interruption for attribution is awkward:

> "Our students," Jones told teachers Tuesday, "are mature, but they do not always act like it."

It is especially helpful to interrupt in the middle if the quote is long and unwieldy; then the interruption serves as a breath pause for your reader.

Perhaps the most important point concerning attribution is this: Always make it absolutely clear *whose* opinion is being expressed. Given a choice, the reader may conclude that the opinion is the reporter's—and this is *not* the impression we want to leave. So don't let quotes float free of their source. This construction, for instance, is wrong:

> Jones was elated. "It was my first touchdown ever."

And so is this, because the reader has to wait too long to find out who is talking:

> "It was my best day. I got the ball on a dead run. It was a perfect pass, and I just outran the secondary. One guy dived at me near the goal, but he missed," Jones said.

In the latter example, the writer should have identified Jones as the speaker right after "It was my best day."

Lest anyone doubt the importance of attribution, consider the embarrassment on the part of the press and the confusion on the part of the audience when media across the country reported that prisoners, during a New York prison riot, had slashed the throats of their hostages. Almost without exception the press failed to attribute this "fact" to its source, and when it became evident later that no throats had been slashed, the press looked pretty bad. And the public must have wondered how many other statements in the story were false.

Speech Stories

A fruitful source of news is the speech. Speeches by newsworthy individuals are almost always covered by the press, because journalists know that public pronouncements of great importance are often made in speech format.

Corazon Aquino of the Philippines speaks to the House Foreign Affairs Committee at a reception held in her honor.

Covering a speech is, in a sense, one of the easiest of all assignments. On the surface, at least, it consists of one person speaking—and that is quite simple. But dangers are present. The reporter must be careful to get down exactly what the speaker says. Then the reporter must try to select the speaker's main points for inclusion in the story. There probably has never been a speech story that could have been written in the order the speech was given. The lead, the speaker's main point or points, often comes late in the speech, and the writer must tell the reader immediately what the main point was.

The best speech story is a well-designed mixture of direct quotes, paraphrasings, and partial quotes. The lead distills the essence of what the speaker said; it summarizes and explains. The lead gets to the point. It does not waste the reader's time with needless detail, such as where the speech took place. Save that for later, unless there are special circumstances. The lead emphasizes *what* was said, not the simple fact that a speech was made.

Leads

The lead that is a single direct quote is usually not the best. These are poor leads:

> ''America must solve its problems in this decade or face the loss of world leadership.''
>
> ''We are going to solve the parking problem because we have 500 new students and they deserve a place to park.''
>
> ''I do not choose to run for president.''

They are poor because they are dull. The reporter can paraphrase, such quotes into more readable journalistic style:

> The U.S. faces loss of world leadership unless it does something about its problems, Sen. Wright said Tuesday.
>
> The addition of 500 new students at Central High School is crowding its parking lots, but Police Chief Robert Jones pledged Tuesday that he would find a solution.
>
> Governor Smith Tuesday withdrew from the primary election race, leaving the statehouse open for what is expected to be a strong rush from Democrats.

The quote lead can also distort. The temptation is to take that one great quote and place it at the top of the story. But almost certainly the headline will be based on the lead, and unless the quote sums up the speaker's message, the distortion will be magnified in the headline.

The Audience   When you cover a speech, pay close attention to the audience. How many people were there? How many times was the speaker interrupted by applause? Which lines calculated to get applause stirred no one? Were there hecklers or protesters present? How many? What was the speaker's reaction?

Watch for the obvious omission, for what the speaker does *not* say. (She did *not* announce the new budget, she did *not* announce her candidacy, she did *not* say who would pay for the new programs she proposed, she did *not* say who would draw up the new policy or who would approve it.)

And finally, you must realize that the phrase "he (or she) concluded" can be used only once in each speech story. In the Dick Gregory assignment mentioned earlier, no fewer than nine different statements by Gregory were followed by the words "he concluded." What the students really meant, of course, was that their stories were concluding and they were going home.

Wrap-up

Reproducing accurately what people say is a basic journalistic function. Sometimes sources claim they were misquoted when they really were not, but journalists still need to emphasize accuracy in quoted material.

Too often, there are great differences between what is said and what is published or aired. Words can be misquoted or twisted, and that can lead to hard feelings, canceled subscriptions—even lawsuits.

Beginning journalists should pay a great deal of attention to the skills involved in handling quoted material. When journalists enclose a sentence or part of a sentence in quotation marks, they are telling readers that that is *exactly* what the speaker said. They are not saying it is close or almost what was said.

It is difficult to reproduce exactly what people say. People start sentences they never finish,

they back up and start again, they say "ya know," "like I said," "ummmm," "ahhhh," and so on.

The journalistic ideal of reproducing speech *exactly* as it was uttered needs to be reexamined with an eye toward slight and careful change. Studies indicate sources care about this issue a great deal less than do journalists. Sources want their thoughts and ideas conveyed accurately to the public. They care less about their exact words.

Most of the time, journalists take out the "ya knows" and the "hmmmms" and no harm is done. Faced with an unclear sentence, most journalists decide not to use a direct quote but to try to convey the source's ideas in the journalist's words.

Tape recorders can aid a reporter. Small, unobtrusive ones are best. Good notes are important, however, even when a tape recorder is used. Sometimes batteries die or the tape breaks. Journalists should never tape record someone without permission, either in person or on the telephone.

Generally speaking and depending on circumstances, most journalists clean up profanity and bad grammar. Often they simply paraphrase the source's words—that is, they express the source's words in their own way and take off the quotation marks.

Journalists carefully attribute quotes. It is important that readers know at all times where the information they are looking at came from. The verb most favored for attribution is *said* because it has no overtones.

Various rules and suggestions apply to handling quotes, including where to interrupt a sentence to insert attribution.

Quote leads (leads that are all quote) generally are avoided as lazy and uninteresting.

On Assignment

Teamwork

1. Invite members of a speech class to give speeches to teams of journalism students. Each team should hold a question-and-answer session with the speaker. Now write a news story covering the speech given to your team. Compare your story to those of others on your team. (They would be your competition at an event like this.) Analyze the differences. Have the speech students review the stories and compare the writers' coverage with the original text. Each speaker should note where he or she was misquoted or quoted out of context.

2. As you noted in the excerpt from ''The Short Happy Life of Francis Macomber'' on page 147, the attribution used by Hemingway is simple and short—mostly just ''said Wilson,'' ''she said,'' and ''Margot said.'' This practice is recommended for journalists; it helps keep the focus on the quote. To reinforce this point and have some fun at the same time, you might try writing some Tom Swifties.

   Tom Swift was the hero of a series of children's adventure books. Tom never simply ''said'' anything. Here's an example:

   ''Yes, it's an emergency,'' Tom returned slowly.

   Now, a Tom Swiftie is a humorous exaggeration of an elaborate method of attribution, often with a pun thrown in. Here are some Tom Swifties:

   ''I'll have a hot dog,'' said Tom frankly.

   ''Let's dig into it,'' said Tom gravely.

Some Tom Swifties involve allusions:

"We need a fielder who can hit sixty home runs," he said ruthlessly.

"I don't care for fairy tales," she said grimly.

Working in teams of three or four, try building an extended dialogue of Tom Swifties. Then, compare your team's dialogue with those of the other teams.

Practice

1. Write a story based on a presidential news conference or televised speech. Compare your story with that of a classmate. Did he or she choose to emphasize the same or different topics? Why?
2. Ask ten students you do not know well for their opinions on a school issue. Write a story suitable for publication, quoting them correctly.
3. Clip and mount a speech coverage story from your school or local newspaper. Did the writer use different types of attribution? Underline them. Was sufficient background included so that the reader had a clear knowledge of the subject and the speaker? Mark it. How well were quotes used? Rewrite the lead.

Your Turn

1. Find a speech being delivered off campus and cover it (with at least two classmates). Compare your coverage with that of your classmates and local media. Did you use the same key points? What news elements were used? Underline your transitions and attributions. Write a letter to your classmates commenting on their coverage of the speech. If possible, reach the speaker for reaction to any local media coverage. You might even ask the speaker to critique your story. Were the various stories accurate? Were they fair?
2. Find a story on a speech covered by a daily newspaper. Underline the verbs. Is "said" used most? What other words appear frequently? Study the use of attribution by professionals. Begin a log of verbs and keep it in your notebook. Which ones seem to be used most often? Which are rare? Mark all the verbs in your speech coverage story and add them to your log.

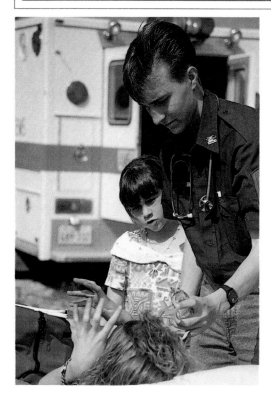

Covering accidents, fires and other emergencies is a tough job even under the best of circumstances. Like any other story, it is a process of pulling together many pieces. It involves identifying sources, gathering the necessary information and writing and editing the story. Design, layout and production make an account of the event available for the reader. The following series of photographs shows reporter Rachel Lee's story about an 18-year-old Emergency Medical Technician, a fellow student at Wimberley High School (Texas), who volunteered to save lives.

Emergency Medical Technician Gabe Harcrow goes through a training exercise involving a single car collision. Most emergency medical personnel go through these exercises regularly, giving reporters and photographers a chance to learn how to work with the medics, fire personnel and law enforcement officials. Reporters must always remember that, in any emergency, the job of the emergency personnel is public safety. Reporters must never interfere with this job.

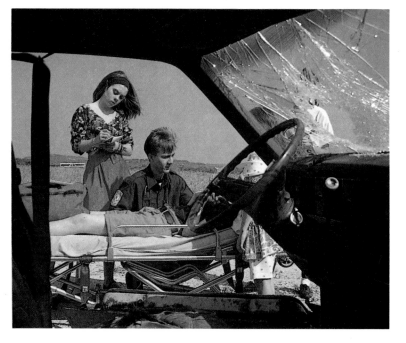

This training exercise gave high school reporters Shelley Whitten and Rachel Lee and photographer Chris Barnes a chance to learn the procedures of the local Emergency Medical Service. Even big-city emergency personnel will work with reporters to help foster mutual understanding of each other's job.

After the emergency or training exercise is over, Lee realized she needed more information. So, she scheduled a follow-up interview with Harcrow at school. Reporters should never hesitate to call a source back for more information or to clarify points of confusion.

Writing the story is the fun part. Lee said she spent most of her time writing the lead, which must grab the reader's attention. When writing her first draft, Lee concentrated on just getting coherent sentences down in a logical order. She spent time refining the sentences and making the story flow better once the basics were down on paper.

After Lee had rewritten her story a couple times and entered it into the computer, she turned it over to a copyeditor, Ty Pearson, who fixed errors, using a stylebook and any other references, and made sure the facts were correct and in the proper form.

While the writers were working on writing and editing, Barnes worked to get the film developed and the prints selected and printed so everything would be ready for production. Barnes spent time working with Lee to make sure the photographs he selected reflected the main points of the story.

After the story was completed and the final photographs were selected, layout artist Jonathan Allen formatted the stories and placed them on the page. Other writers wrote headlines and cutlines. Working with a computer helped the students realize the impact of their design.

The paper went to press at 5 p.m. on Tuesday, and staff members distributed it to students Wednesday morning. Staff members of the Wimberley High School *Texan Times* enjoy getting reactions from other students. Even when the feedback is not entirely positive, students learn how to become better communicators.

Photographs by Bradley Wilson
Special thanks to North Hays County Emergency Medical Service, the Wimberley Volunteer Fire Department, Kyle Gerdes and Ron Spangenberg.

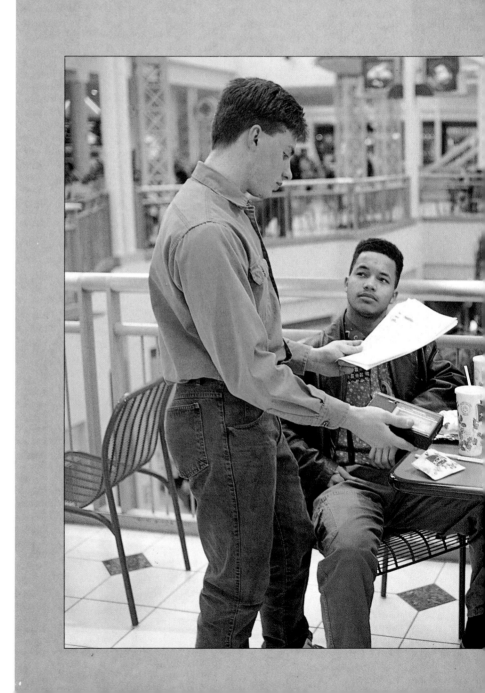

Writing
Features,
Sports, and
Editorials

In-Depth
Reporting

Tremendous change has come to high school journalism. Once monuments to trivia, most high school publications today are tributes to serious journalism, produced by talented young people committed to their task of serving a modern audience. Even the most casual inspection of the best of today's scholastic publications quickly reveals the extent of the change. If Rip Van Winkle had started his famous nap in the 1970s and awakened in the 1990s, he would be stunned. Where homecoming queens once reigned supreme and editorials went no further than urging school spirit, scholastic publications today are on top of the news. And the news is reported in depth.

Despite forces in society to the contrary, most notably *USA Today* and its imitators, high school journalists are producing long, thoughtful pieces on important subjects. The trend in the commercial press is evident. Since the public has a short attention span, give it superficial stories, lots of pictures, charts, graphs, maps, and "factoids"—isolated bits of information unconnected to anything.

TV stories are measured in seconds and newspaper stories grow shorter and shorter. Political campaigns are decided by the impact of sound bites and one-liners during face-to-face debates. Bucking this trend, while adopting its best innovations (notably in graphics), are the nation's scholastic journalists.

Modern scholastic publications, often making creative use of desktop publishing tools, consistently produce high-quality stories—even whole sections—on topics once considered out of bounds for students. These days, you're apt to see in-depth treatment by scholastic journalists on everything from school budgets to the environment; from censorship to family crises; from animal rights to standardized tests, teen stress, teen insurance rates, school security, and student rights.

And much more. The list is long. It represents the catalog of interests young people have today. It also represents, in many ways, a catalog of subjects that teens need to know about.

What these and similar subjects have in common is the need for sensitive, objective, *in-depth* treatment. Subjects such as these do not lend themselves to superficial treatment.

Though heard less these days than formerly, a frequent criticism of the press is that it is superficial. Critics argue that the lack of space or time forces the press to hit only the highlights—and too often the sensational highlights—of public issues and events. They claim that issues laced with subtleties cannot be explored properly under the constraints of speed and brevity.

The critics have a point. Not *all* stories need in-depth treatment, but some do. Unfortunately, too many journalists operate superficially even when covering the stories that need deeper treatment. This chapter explores the need for such treatment.

Stories with Substance

In too many newsrooms, the reporter who suggests an in-depth story that may require weeks of research and writing is told that there is no time for such a project and no space to run it. But it doesn't have to be that way. Here are some examples of in-depth reporting. Watergate is the most famous example, but stories with substance don't have to uncover wrongdoing. They may present information on important economic or social issues. Such stories can benefit readers' lives in many ways.

Development of the Boeing 757

At age 28, Peter Rinearson was a reporter for the *Seattle Times*, newly assigned as the paper's aerospace writer. He brought an outstanding record from the University of Washington, where he was inspired by Professor William Johnston.

Searching for an interesting in-depth project that would help him get a grip on his new beat, Rinearson hit upon the idea of preparing "a special report on the conception, design, manufacture, marketing, and delivery of a new jetliner—the Boeing 757."

"I discovered," Rinearson remarked later, "that just as I didn't really understand what Boeing does, the community didn't really understand. Even a lot of people at Boeing didn't know much beyond their direct area of responsibility."

So he went to work. For six months, Rinearson did little but work on the Boeing 757 story. He compiled about 1,200 single-spaced typewritten pages of interviews. He talked with fifty to sixty people. His project occupied almost every waking hour. "If I wasn't eating or sleeping, I was reporting or reading in libraries, involved with the story at one level or another," he said.

The *Seattle Times* ran his stories as a series spanning eight days. It was 25,000 words long, and when reprinted in a special package later, it occupied 16 full-size newspaper pages. Hardly superficial. You will find excerpts from "Making It Fly" on pages 171–174.

Rinearson received mail from all over the world, including this telegram from the president of Columbia University: "You were awarded Pulitzer Prize for feature writing today. Congratulations."

Fighting superficiality requires commitment from both reporters and editors. In Rinearson's case, reporting and editing came together in sparkling fashion. Not yet thirty at the time, Rinearson earned journalism's highest award.

This chapter also is about fighting superficiality.

Thorough, complete stories—stories with substance—are the goal. Some people call this in-depth reporting. Others argue that such reporting is investigative by nature, and in some quarters investigative reporting is unpopular. Was Rinearson's story investigative? He says no.

"I don't know what that is. Investigative reporting sort of suggests uncovering wrongdoing, and I have done some of that. It pleased me that I was able to win the prize with something other than an account of wrongdoing. Since Watergate and beyond, if you want to win a Pulitzer Prize, it seems you have to go out and topple a president, or find something wrong."

Investigative reporting team Woodward and Bernstein, shown here in 1973 at the *Washington Post*, won a Pulitzer prize for their story on the Watergate scandal. Bernstein is on the left.

Watergate

If ever there was an investigative story, it was the story of Watergate, the name applied to an array of deeds and events in the early 1970s that led to the resignation of President Richard Nixon.

The Watergate story began with a phone call to Bob Woodward of the *Washington Post*. Five men had been caught inside the Watergate Hotel offices of the Democratic Party. The young reporter, later teamed with Carl Bernstein, was launched on one of the biggest stories of the century—the story that did, indeed, help topple a president.

It did a lot more, too. It stirred a wave of infatuation on the part of the media with investigative reporting, a wave that continued virtually unabated into the 1980s.

Two schools of thought exist on such reporting. One says the media have no greater duty than to sniff out and expose wrongdoing and that it is impossible to overdo it. The other says the media definitely *are* overdoing it, that they are seeking evil rather than seeking news, and sniffing prizes rather than sniffing wrongdoing.

There is probably truth on both sides. Done right—repeat, done right—thorough, in-depth stories represent journalism at its finest. Sometimes there is wrongdoing.

Military Brutality

Consider Ken Herman. Barely out of college, he was a reporter for The *News*, a small paper in Lufkin, Texas. Covering a story

Student reporters today concern themselves with stories about government, political, and social issues.

about the death in training camp of a local Marine, Herman was dissatisfied with the official answers to his questions. He continued to dig until he uncovered a story of brutal training practices. His stories in The *News* won a Pulitzer Prize.

Criminal Courts

Or consider Donald L. Barlett and James B. Steele, two *Philadelphia Inquirer* reporters who spent hundreds of hours poring over official criminal courts' records and then pronounced the courts in sorry shape. Justice, they concluded, was far from blind to color, social status, age, and other factors. They, too won the Pulitzer Prize for feature writing.

Avoiding Superficiality

In each of these cases and many more, one theme stands out: Reporters must dig and dig and dig. They must ask and ask and ask. Such stories do not come easily.

So what does all this have to do with the scholastic press? You're not "Woodstein," as the two *Post* reporters came to be known, and chances are you could sniff around your school forever and not find scandal. But you can decide that superficiality and sensationalism are the enemy. You might not be able to undertake massive investigations (you might, too; lots of school papers have), but you certainly don't have to settle for shallow stories that contribute nothing to public understanding.

The scholastic press has changed. As students have become more sophisticated, better educated, and more involved, their newspapers have begun to recognize that they can no longer satisfy their audience with gossip columns, frothy features about the "in" crowd, and other trivial stories. They must explore the news in depth, dig beneath the surface, and report news that really counts. They must concentrate on causes as well as effects; they ask, "Why?" *Why* are teacher salaries so low? *Why* do so many students drop out of school? *Why* are so many students killed in traffic accidents? *Why* do some students cheat? *Why* do some of the best teachers leave the profession? They must, in other words, be ready to tackle any subject.

As the Commission on Freedom of the Press said in its historic 1947 report, "It is no longer enough to report the fact truthfully. It is now necessary to report the truth about the fact."

Saul J. Waldman of the American Newspaper Publishers Association also observed a changing scholastic journalism scene. He noted that around the country—places as diverse as White Plains, N.Y.; Salt Lake City, Utah; and El Paso, Texas—more "well-researched, well-documented, and well-written" stories are being produced by scholastic journalists. He cited stories on integration, school dropouts, and voting. Wrote Waldman:

What's so unusual about these? Perhaps nothing today. But I would guess that in my day—and that's not so long ago—these same newspapers were writing about "Guess what blonde with initials M.D. was seen holding hands with Freddie Football-player across the aisle in Wednesday afternoon study hall?"

All three of these newspapers are high school newspapers—and in case you haven't looked lately, they're not what they used to be. . . .

The most striking thing about today's school newspapers is the subjects they're writing about. Integration. Dropouts. Drug addiction. The quality of education. Censorship in the school library. . . .

There is far less concern with the class play, the basketball team, even the honor roll, than in the past. The gossip column, once the staple of the high school press, is virtually extinct.

—The Quill

Emphasizing in-depth reporting, or backgrounding, or complete reporting (or whatever you decide to call it), implies several things to the scholastic journalist. First, of course, it means better reporting. No longer can a student grab a couple of quick quotes from a school official, dash off six or seven paragraphs, and call it a good news story. On one assignment the reporter may speak with the same source four or five times, interview a dozen faculty members, attend city council and board of education meetings, and talk to scores of students. Reporters are becoming dedicated to the proposition that their publication can inform its readers about what they are most interested in—their school—better than any other newspaper in the world. Sure, the scholastic newspaper may get beaten by the paper downtown on the account of Friday night's football game. But there's no reason why the scholastic journalist has to play second fiddle when it comes to reporting through thorough research.

Finding Space

Another implication of such reporting in the school is this: Many (though by no means all) in-depth stories are quite long. Where are you going to get the space to run such stories? It is too scarce already. The first thing you do (if you haven't already) is eliminate trivia. You're dealing with a young adult audience; don't insult their intelligence.

Many of the small stories you run can be condensed into one "bulletin board" type of column. Instead of publishing three paragraphs on the coming meeting of the Spanish Club, three on the Science Club, and four or five on the class play that you've already devoted half a dozen stories to, combine them into a bulletin board or calendar. You may even want to set it in small type, so it would look something like this:

Thursday
Spanish Club, room 407, 3:45 P.M.
Science Club, physics lab, 3:50 P.M.
Repertory Theatre rehearsal, campus center, 6:30 P.M.

Friday
Pep rally, auditorium, 3:45 P.M.
Dress rehearsal, senior class play, auditorium, 8 P.M.

Instead of running five stories, which taken together might eat up an entire column of space, you have included all the information in just a couple of inches. (The Spanish Club, by the way, won't be upset about your new way of treating advance notice of their meetings if you explain that one day you intend to write a complete story about the club and all its activities.)

Another way to save space for in-depth stories is condensation of usually lengthy stories into a ''news brief'' format. Thus, a four-paragraph story about band tryouts can be condensed into just one paragraph:

Before	**After**
Do you like music, travel, flashy clothes? Students who can answer yes to these questions should contact John P. Jones, band director. Jones is seeking new talent to fill out the 100-piece organization that plays at all home games. Tryouts are scheduled for Sept. 1 at 3 P.M. in the music room.	Band tryouts will be Sept. 1 at 3 P.M. in the music room, Director John P. Jones announced.

The Quality of Writing

Let's return to Saul Waldman's comments regarding student journalism:

> Coupled with their concern and courage is a two-dimensional improvement in the quality of their journalism. One dimension is the trend to depth reporting. . . . The other dimension is the quality of the writing itself, which is evident right down to such basics as sentence structure and word usage.
>
> Professional observers of scholastic journalism have noted that the upgrading of subject matter and writing go hand in hand: As the student journalist tackles more difficult subjects, he tries harder and as a result writes better.

The *Seattle Times's* Rinearson received calls from people who told him they had not intended to read his stories but had glanced at the first three paragraphs and couldn't stop. People *will* read long stories if they are beautifully written.

Rinearson also found personal satisfaction in doing his Boeing 757 story. He called it "enthralling" and "very exciting intellectually." Satisfying the reporter's needs is secondary to informing the public, of course, but there is no reason to ignore that part of the work.

Rinearson's series, titled "Making It Fly," makes good reading. He paid attention to the writing, stepping back and taking a longer look, slowing his pace. The name you give to such enterprises doesn't matter much. Rinearson's story wasn't investigative in the usual sense of that word. But it certainly was in-depth and thorough—a story with substance.

Rinearson's series in the *Seattle Times* chronicled the birth of a new jetliner—the Boeing 757. A *Times* introduction to the series said, "This is the story of 30,000 people making 130,000 pounds of high technology fly. It is also a tale of world political and financial forces, risk, painstaking compromises, and the complexities and subtleties of the industrial process."

The series is that and more. It also is a demonstration of the heights journalists can reach when their publications make a commitment to excellence. And it is an example of clear, exciting writing, writing that makes a complex story clear to an average reader.

Rinearson, at the start, faced an awesome task. His decision to tell the whole story of the Boeing 757 took him to the plane's very conception. The series opens as the heads of Eastern Airlines and Boeing discuss the plane in a "four-minute automobile ride on a sun-drenched August day in 1978." The executives agree; the Boeing 757, a 175-passenger airplane, would be built. Rinearson described the multi-billion-dollar moment of decision:

"And so, with a handshake—just as the car jiggled over some railroad tracks—the Boeing 757 was born."

The decision ended months of negotiations and launched an amazing spurt of technological creativity—all of it described later by Rinearson.

In painstaking detail, "Making It Fly" explores the plane's development, including the incredible financial risk for everyone involved. Design and manufacture follow. Finally, the plane is ready for testing.

Here is Rinearson's account of the testing process.

Look for the following as you read "Making It Fly":

✔ A compelling opening, or lead

✔ Good use of detail ("Twenty-eight times the 757 dragged its tail down the Edwards runway.")

✔ Good use of quotes ("You just keep loading it until the thing finally goes 'kaboom.' ")

✔ Suspense (Unlike the inverted pyramid story, some depth stories can unfold almost chronologically, inviting the reader to read on.)

✔ Plain, simple language, enhancing readability

✔ A complete absence of clichés and worn-out figures of speech

✔ A good ending

Making It Fly

By Peter Rinearson

"WE ALMOST LOST ONE."

That was the urgent communique from one top federal aviation official to another last Nov. 16 after a particularly dramatic 2-hour, 17-minute flight by a Boeing 757.

Leroy Keith, who heads the Federal Aviation Administration's certification program for jetliners, was at FAA headquarters in Washington, D.C., when the phone call came.

Darrell Pederson, a Keith lieutenant, was on the line from Seattle. He was supervising Boeing's efforts to prove the 757 airworthy, and his call attracted attention because it interrupted an important meeting.

Keith recalls Pederson's message. "He said, 'Well, . . . we had . . . we almost lost one.' He was quite frank about it."

During a certification flight, a 757 had ingested ice in its huge Rolls Royce engines, setting off cockpit alerts and creating a roar

that one person on board said sounded disturbingly like a car without a muffler.

Keith said Pederson sounded shaken on the telephone. "He said it had an icing encounter and went back to Boeing Field drifting down on minimum-power setting, and got back and found the fan blades were damaged on both engines."

Later there would be differences of opinion about just how serious the problem had been, and whether the airplane really had been in any peril.

The crew intentionally had been seeking ice build-up on the airplane's wings to prove its performance under such conditions and had lingered in circumstances which any commercial pilot would have avoided. It was not a situation likely to be encountered by an airplane carrying passengers, because commercial pilots don't go looking for trouble.

The objective of flight testing is to uncover potential problems, even those that are extremely unlikely. Boeing and FAA officials agree that every new airplane design has unforseen snags that need to be discovered and corrected, and it's not fair to judge an aircraft until this process is complete. . . .

A Boeing flight engineer with significant responsibility for the program described the Nov. 16 flight this way: "They were descending into terrain and didn't have power to climb. It's very dangerous. You can lose a plane that way. We don't fly with parachutes because we expect to land in the middle of a runway every time."

The engine problem, coming so late in the 757's development, posed logistical difficulties for Boeing, Rolls Royce and the 757's first customer, Eastern Airlines. The airline wanted its first plane within a month, but the FAA wasn't about to certify it until there was conclusive proof that the problem had been solved.

For their part, neither Boeing nor Rolls wanted an airplane operating with any safety question lingering.

John Winch, who directs Boeing's flight-test and certification programs, said the company went to unprecedented lengths to ensure both the 757 and 767 were thoroughly tested.

The FAA's certification procedures for the Boeing 757 and 767 are said to be the most comprehen-

sive in history. After suffering the sting of criticism over difficulties experienced by the McDonnell Douglas DC-10 long after it was certified for flight, federal officials intensified their efforts to be certain the 757 and 767 certification programs were beyond reproach. . . .

The 757 and 767 have two-man crews and equipment for low-visibility landings, both of which required additional certification efforts, said Brian Wygle, Boeing vice president of flight operations.

The 757 carries more than 100 computers, and federal inspectors sought proof that both the airplane's hardware and the intricacies of the computer software were fail-safe.

Certification is a painstaking process—and an expensive one. "You spend $1.5 million to $2 million per airplane just to put the certification instrumentation parts in," a Boeing engineer said. It has been estimated that flying jetliners that are equipped for flight testing

and certification costs more than $50,000 an hour.

The task of certifying two airplanes simultaneously added to the challenge. At the peak of the certification effort, 17 aircraft (including models other than 757s and 767s) were involved in flight testing, said James Lincoln, manager of the data section of Boeing flight-test engineering. . . .

Flight testing has a splashy reputation, a lingering image of the do-or-die pilot tempting fate to prove his machine. But a Boeing flight-test engineer said "we don't do much of that 'white knuckles and silk scarves' stuff any more."

Still, in their more dramatic moments, flight tests aren't for the faint of heart.

Testing and certifying an airplane involves pushing it into what Phil Condit, general manager of the 757 program, calls "far corners"— performance situations one hopes an airplane will never have to encounter in actual service.

Far corners can be terrifying to the uninitiated.

A 757 cruises with maximum fuel efficiency at 80 percent of the speed of sound, or mach .8. Its maximum intended speed is mach .86. But Boeing pressed the airplane to mach .92 in flight testing. A far corner.

Such flights, said Rick Lentz, 757 flight-test aeroanalysis lead engineer, "can be frightening, because the plane responds with buffeting. The tail assembly is groaning and wings are flapping— and until you've been through this a few times, you're not sure it will hold together."

The fear is personal, not corporate, Lentz added. Anxiety is normal for a person who hasn't been through it before, although Boeing is confident the airplane will perform as intended, he said. . . .

Not every dramatic test takes place in the air. Boeing routinely destroys one airplane of each model to see what it takes, to see if it's really as tough as the engineers say it is.

The 757 test happened last July 16. Enormous pressures were applied to a 757 airframe inside a hangar. The wings were bent upwards . . . first two feet . . . then five . . . eight . . . 10 . . . At 11 feet, 6 inches of deflection, both wings snapped.

"It's like loading a bridge," Condit said. "You just keep loading it until the thing finally goes 'kaboom!' That's exactly the sound it makes. I felt it in my knees. I don't know if that was the excitement or the boom."

The results were pleasing, because the airplane proved 12 percent stronger than engineering esti-

mates, and because, in a tribute to Boeing engineering and quality control, both wings failed at the same place and at almost the same moment—just 14 thousandths of a second apart.

Imagine what must go through the mind of a test pilot about to take off in a jetliner which never has flown before.

Wind-tunnel tests say the aircraft will fly. Engineers say the design will soar like a dream. Mechanics and inspectors have looked over the huge machine.

But will it really fly?

John Armstrong, chief test pilot for the Boeing 757 program, said he felt little anxiety about taking off for the first time ever in a 757 on Feb. 19 of last year. . . .

Armstrong and Boeing called it a "perfect first flight" upon landing, although later they admitted that a design problem, later corrected, prompted them to temporarily shut down one of the 757's two engines during the flight. .

Armstrong, piloting the "No. 1" 757, had general good fortune throughout the 11-month flight-test program—a program which involved five different airplanes, each conducting separate tests specified years in advance.

Like the rest of the 757 project, the requirements of a 1,254-hour flight-test program were scheduled with precision back in late 1978 and 1979, before Boeing irrevocably committed itself to the financial and other risks of a new-airplane program.

A chart created at the end of 1978 shows Armstrong's 757 was to fly 375 hours of tests, between February and December 1982 when certification was to be com-

plete. The timetable was met. . . .

When local television viewers see news stories on the 757 or 767, they are sometimes treated to rather unusual footage of a Boeing airplane touching its tail to the runway during takeoff. It's an interesting sight—and not always explained by the newscaster, who may be reporting Boeing sales figures or some other issue unrelated to flight tests.

The tail dragging is known as "Vmu" testing, and it was one of the missions of 757 No. 1. It took place last June in southern California, at Edwards Air Force Base, the same place the Space Shuttles have landed.

Twenty-eight times the 757 dragged its tail down the Edwards runway. Each was a test of the characteristics of the 757 at minimum-speed takeoffs (Vmu stands for Velocity-minimum unstick, with "unstick" signifying the wheels departing the runway).

The object was to determine the lowest speed of safe takeoff under various conditions so that a schedule could be established to guide pilots in selecting appropriate take-off speeds.

Avoiding damage to the airplane during the tail scraping involved careful work by the pilots and the temporary addition of an oak skid to the bottom side of the rear of the airplane.

Pilots lifted the nose of the airplane off the ground rapidly, lowering the tail in what is called "rotation." When they sensed the tail was about to touch the ground, they would slow the rate of rotation. . . .

Though Armstrong's 757 was put through its paces relatively uneventfully, the opposite was true of

757 No. 3, flown by a fellow test pilot, Kenny Higgins.

Problems began the first time the airplane was flown: the landing gear would not retract fully.

The flight continued, with the wheels hanging out of the airplane at a strange angle, but it was cut short at 39 minutes. The basic airworthiness of the airplane was established, however. . . .

[Later, Higgins was to fly No. 3 on the "ice flight" of Nov. 16.]

For most of its 2 hours and 17 minutes, the Nov. 16 flight was uneventful. The pilots were intentionally building up two inches of ice on the 757's wings, then shedding it with anti-ice systems.

But the unexpected struck rudely toward the end of the flight when chunks of ice broke off the center hubs of the two Rolls Royce engines and damaged the fan blades.

Rather than heating the engine's "spinner cone"—the hub in the center of the outer fan blades—Rolls had elected to use a flexible tip it believed would flex to keep ice from building up.

The Nov. 16 flight proved dramatically that the flexible tip wouldn't always work.

Immediately upon ingestion of the ice, both engines began to rumble and cockpit instruments showed high levels of engine vibration. The vibration could be felt throughout the airplane, including the cockpit.

Higgins and Dick Paul, the FAA pilot on board, cut back the engine power, alternately idling one engine, then the other. They aborted the tests, retracted the flaps and raised the landing gear.

The left-side engine was vibrating particularly badly on the return to Boeing Field, and the pilots agreed to land with the engine idling rather than possibly push it too far by running it hard.

Finding ice hadn't been easy for Boeing. There had been a weeks-long search for the appropriate test conditions. Then, suddenly, there was an abundance of ice—and an unexpected problem.

Engineers in the back of the airplane, monitoring banks of instruments and watching the ice on the wings, were pleased with the amount of ice they finally had found.

But in the cockpit, where the engine performance was alarming the pilots, there was no elation. Upon landing, Higgins told the FAA: "I was not happy."

Rolls and Boeing solved the problem by substituting a heated spinner cone for the flexible tip. It was a rush job, with round-the-clock shifts in Rolls Royce's plant at Derby, England, producing the spinner on a few day's notice.

The airplane was certified and rushed into service by Eastern Airlines, which took delivery of its first two 757s at the end of December.

But the FAA made the certificate valid for only six months. The airplane was perfectly safe, the FAA said, but it wanted a seat in the cockpit repositioned so that FAA personnel who occasionally ride along on commercial flights could have a better view of pilot activities.

Boeing and the FAA dug in over the issue, and it looked for a time as if the matter would end up in court. But in late May, the FAA granted a permanent certificate after Boeing agreed to move the 757 seat just 7½ inches.

Hundreds of Boeing flight-test employees gathered at Longacres on Jan. 22 to celebrate the certification of the 757. The FAA came in for more than a little ribbing, including a skit in which an outlandish chair with a chicken attached to it was displayed and proclaimed to be, by a supposed FAA representative, a "damn good seat."

But the flight-test crews gave themselves a bad time, too. The test pilots and their airplanes were roasted in good humor.

When it was Higgins' turn, a top Boeing engineer named Pete Morton explained the astronomical odds against all the problems Higgins had encountered with 757 No. 3. He gave Higgins a T-shirt with the slogan "Extremely Improbable."

Higgins, having weathered a stormy certification filled with unlikely events, replied: "Extremely improbable to me means that it happened yesterday."

—from the *Seattle Times*

Introductions to In-Depth Stories

In Chapter 6 we discussed writing news story leads. Longer, thorough stories sometimes require more of an introduction than the quick, one-paragraph summary that often begins a more routine news story.

In-depth stories often lend themselves to unusual treatment in other respects, too. Here are some examples.

In the story that follows, the reporter sought insights into the life of the American trucker. Her technique was to ride a couple thousand miles across country with a trucker, soaking up the feeling of life on the road. She decided on a first-person approach. Following is the introduction to her story.

On the Road: A Reporter's Account

By Nancy Kehrli

If a reporter wants to learn about truckers—as I did—she climbs into a 16-ton truck loaded with 38,300 pounds of beef in Spencer, Iowa, and headed for Elizabeth, N.J.

She becomes a trucker for 2,659 miles through Iowa, Illinois, Indiana, Ohio, Pennsylvania and into New Jersey and back again.

During three days and seven hours of trucking, she talks to dozens of truckers. She learns to sleep for two or three hours at a time and to be wide awake and jostling down the Interstate before sunrise.

She learns to be ready to hop down from the truck when it stops so she can interview drivers while the truck is fueled.

Recently, I rode with Darrell and Jan Smidt of Milford, Iowa, who truck for J. & L. Trucking, Inc.

From Iowa to New Jersey and back, this is what the truckers talked about:

Truckers have problems. The speed limit's too low; fuel prices too high. Because of this, they say, their revenue is suffering. The government has done little since the last two shutdowns to alleviate their situation, truckers say. Consequently, a May 13 truck shutdown is being planned.

Many drivers have Citizen Band (CB) radios they rely on to communicate with each other on the road. However, some states want stricter regulations on CBs, and some would like to see them taken out of trucks. The truckers say "no way."

What they call high prices and poor service at truck stops also anger the truckers, as well as having to obtain licenses, registrations and in some cases authority to travel into each state. They want standard licensing that would cover them traveling cross-country and unification of all state and federal weight and length limitations.

Truckers say they also are plagued by lack of stability in freight rates, cars that pull out in front of them without realizing how hard it is to slow a loaded truck quickly and lost hours spent waiting to be loaded and unloaded.

All of these problems add fuel to an already tense situation for the trucking industry, and truckers say it's time they took action. They say they've waited long enough for outside help.

The rest of her story was a close-up examination of each of the issues raised in the introduction.

The first-person technique also was used effectively in the next example. In this story, the reporter decided to trace her family's roots in a small town in South Dakota. Here is her introduction:

Vitame Vas

By Lynn Silhasek

"Vitame Vas" reads one storewindow along the snow-packed main street in Tabor, S.D. The Czech greeting means "we welcome you."

The townspeople are Czech, too. A Petrik owns the Pheasant Bar. The name Cimpl is painted on the town's grain elevator. Vyborny owns the machine works and Koupal has the construction company.

The names peer at me from the storefronts, like old folks staring at a newcomer in town. They haunt me as I drive through town until I remember the distant cousins who go with them. And they offer their own "we welcome you."

For me, it's a welcome back. Back to my own first generation whose story begins in several southeastern South Dakota communities west of Yankton. Back to a time when the names on the shops, the stores and the bars were intertwined with those of Kocer and Base, the names of my mother's parents.

In the next story, the writer set out to explore the reasons for declines in certain college entrance test scores. When her research was finished, she decided the test format itself would work as an introduction. So this is what she wrote, emphasizing once again that a good journalist uses the devices of writing in whatever way works, not by rote or formula.

Testing, Testing

By Lynn Roberts

The following questions will test your knowledge of today's college-bound students and tests they take to measure their reasoning abilities.

For some questions there is no single correct answer. Select the answer that best fits the question and proceed to the next question. Begin when you are told and continue until you finish or are told to stop.

Go.

1. College-bound students today are: (a) smarter than students five years ago; (b) the same as students five years ago; (c) dumber than students five years ago; (d) none of the above.

Recent declines in scores on the Scholastic Aptitude Test (SAT) and the American College Test (ACT) might indicate (c) as the correct answer, but these scores alone probably do not show the complete picture.

The next example represents the essence of everything we've said about leads. The lead is dramatic, colorful, and compelling, and it pulls the reader into the story.

The story, by Jim Pratt, then a student at the University of Nebraska, was reprinted all over the county in newspapers with a combined circulation of about 5 million. It's about the little town in Kansas where four killings led to Truman Capote's book *In Cold Blood* (itself a gripping example of in-depth reporting). Pratt set out, thirteen years after the killings, to see what effect the book and a movie had on the town. This is the introduction of his prize-winning story:

A Kansas Town Remembers

By Jim Pratt

HOLCOMB, KAN.—A harsh north wind whips dust through Holcomb, battering a few worndown stucco dwellings before losing itself in the western Kansas plains. Ponies tied to fence posts shake their manes in the wind and a dog lopes down a deserted dirt street.

Holcomb is a quiet town. Discounting the Mobil gas station (3.2 beer, soda pop, a few groceries), the only gathering place with refreshments is El Rancho Cafe, and in an adjacent room, a bar named Something Else.

Holcomb's few streets, mostly unpaved, often are empty.

Thirteen years ago today, however, the streets were jammed with cars belonging to law enforcement people, ambulance attendants and the curious. For Holcomb had just been stunned by four murders.

Subsequent reverberations would make the town known to millions.

It was early Sunday morning, Nov. 15, 1959, when Herb Clutter, 48, his wife, Bonnie, 45, and their two youngest children, Nancy, 16, and Kenyon, 15, were blasted point-blank with a shotgun by two ex-convicts with no previous records of violence. The motive was robbery.

The murders shocked the town. Herb Clutter was a prominent farmer, and he and his family were well liked. But the murders probably would have been forgotten had author Truman Capote not read a *New York Times* story about the killings and decided to use them as a vehicle for his book *In Cold Blood*.

Capote went to Holcomb shortly after the slayings. He spent nearly a year and a half in the area doing research. He followed the hunt, capture, trial, and imprisonment of the two killers, Richard Hickock and Perry Smith, until they were executed April 14, 1965.

The book inspired a movie, also named *In Cold Blood*, which was filmed in the town.

For a while after the killings, Holcomb was gripped by fear, gossip, and controversy. But 13 years has allowed the town to relax and to grow, relatively unscarred by the experience. The population is up 25 percent, from about 270 at the time of the slayings to 340 today. The school has a new addition. There are new homes, a new water tower, a new post office.

Curiosity seekers still stop to view the house near town where the Clutters were slain. Once a showcase, the house now seems weatherbeaten.

Townspeople no longer discuss the murders or the aftermath. They would like to forget it.

''It was such a long time ago that it almost seems like it never happened,'' one woman said.

This final introduction sets up a contrast. After the first few paragraphs, the readers have one impression. But then the results of the research are brought in and the impression changes. The effect is stimulating to the readers, so they are liable to stay with the story to the end.

Cop on the Beat

By Gayle Smith

You see them every day—the police officers on patrol.

He's the man in the blue suit with the shiny buttons and funny hat who picks up the little boy crying—alone and lost in the Christmas crowd.

She's the woman in the car with the flashing red light who pulls you over for doing 50 in a 20-mile-an-hour zone.

He's the first man there when you call at 3 a.m. to report a prowler in your home.

But most often, the patrol officer is seen pacing through your neighborhood or driving slowly through the streets, alert to possible crime. You assume that because he or she is there and in uniform, your neighborhood is safer, that her or his very presence helps to discourage would-be criminals.

But that may not be so.

An experiment in Kansas City strongly indicated that the presence of a uniformed patrol officer does not prevent crime. If this is true, it would shake the foundations of police protection.

Thorough Reporting

Research, organization, time for reflection on what your research uncovers, and writing—these are the elements of thorough reporting.

Modern school newspapers are broadening their horizons to look at their readers' entire environment. That means getting out of the school building and into your city, for what takes place there affects students and should not be ignored.

If you're looking for further examples of the type of reporting we've been talking about, read the *Washington Post,* the *Philadelphia Inquirer,* the *Los Angeles Times*, the *Wall Street Journal*, the *Des Moines Register*, the *Miami Herald*, The *New York Times*, and similar newspapers. For top examples of writing, see *Sports Illustrated* and *Rolling Stone*, among other magazines. For a combination of good reporting and good writing, read Mike Royko, the *Chicago Tribune* columnist.

Most high school publications today are tributes to serious journalism, affected deeply by change in the last decade. Where homecoming queens once reigned and editorials merely urged school spirit, scholastic publications today are on top of the news and reporting it in depth.

Despite the forces of superficiality, high school journalists are producing long, thoughtful pieces on important subjects. Much of the commercial press has decided that because the public has a short attention span, it consumes only superficial stories, pictures, charts, graphs, maps, and "factoids." Television news stories are measured in seconds and newspaper stories grow shorter. High school journalists appear to be bucking this trend.

Often using desktop publishing tools, high school journalists produce high-quality stories and sections on topics once considered out of bounds for students. The list of stories now done by high school students represents the interests of young people. These subjects need sensitive, objective, thorough treatment.

Though heard less these days than formerly, a frequent criticism of the press is that it is superficial. Critics cite lack of space and time.

In-depth stories, stories with substance, can present important information that affects people's lives. Some in-depth stories are investigative—rare but not unheard of in high school newspapers. Perhaps the best-known such work was done by Bob Woodward and Carl Bernstein, *Washington Post* reporters widely credited with exposing the Watergate scandal during the Nixon presidency.

Whether stories are called investigative or in-depth, one theme stands out: Reporters dig. They decide that superficiality is the enemy. The changing high school press is putting more emphasis on the *why* of the five W's and the H.

In-depth stories often run longer than routine stories. This can create a space problem. Handling routine club notices and meetings in a list format can help solve this. Space saved this way can be used for in-depth stories.

Generally, the quality of writing for in-depth stories has to be better than the usual newspaper fare. Readers of long stories must be nursed through them by careful writing and organization. In-depth stories require introductions, not just leads. Scenes, anecdotes, a first-person approach—all can produce a high-quality introduction.

The elements of thorough reporting are research, organization, time, and good writing. Modern high school newspapers are broadening their horizons, looking wherever the news takes them for information that affects students.

Examples of excellent in-depth reporting in the commercial press can be found in many newspapers and magazines.

On Assignment

Teamwork

Brainstorm with your team for current ideas for an in-depth story for your student readers. Select five. Do the same for related sidebar stories for each of the five ideas. Brainstorm sources and coverage angles for each story. Brainstorm questions for each story. Select your best story topic. Select a project editor (who will write also). Assign stories to team members. Research and write the stories. Edit carefully for style. Keep all the finished stories to use in later assignments.

Practice

1. Go through your local newspaper. Find at least three stories treated superficially that should be expanded and given in-depth treatment. Interview editors and/or reporters on the paper. Do they agree? Why or why not? Write an interview story on your findings.
2. Identify a thorough story in any newspaper. Compare it to magazine articles. What similarities and differences appear? Which style do you like better? Why? Write an essay on your findings. Attach the story.
3. Clip and mount leads and the next four paragraphs from five in-depth stories. Write your comments on what is good or bad about each lead as it relates to the overall story and brings you into the story.

Your Turn

1. Go through several issues of your school paper. Where will you find the space for a thorough story? What can be eliminated? What can be condensed? What can be put in a bulletin board column? Could you find a page of space? Mark your ideas on the issues and write an essay on how you would find the space for an in-depth story.
2. As a class, conduct an interview with a local professional reporter who does in-depth or investigative reporting. Ask him or her to explain the techniques. Discuss the pros and cons of this type of reporting. Write a story about the interview.
3. Watch a local evening television newscast. Is the station news staff doing any in-depth work? Does that suggest anything about the role of newspapers as they relate to TV? Read a copy of *USA Today* with our observations about in-depth versus superficial reporting in mind. Write an analysis of the role and value of stories with substance as opposed to television news. How does *USA Today*'s approach fit?

James Risser

In Washington, D.C., where there are more reporters than in any other city in the United States, there are more stories than all those reporters could ever write. The problem for most reporters assigned to the capital is learning which stories to discard.

James Risser, formerly of the Des Moines (Iowa) *Register*, says that was the case for him.

Now the director of the John S. Knight Fellowship at Stanford University, Risser says that the most interesting story he ever worked on—one that won him a Pulitzer Prize for national reporting—could easily have ended up in the trash.

A "short and blandly worded" news release from the U.S. Department of Agriculture said that five grain inspectors in Houston, Texas, had been suspended from their jobs after being indicted for accepting bribes.

Presumably, that news release crossed the desks of scores of other reporters, but Risser, a journalist with a law degree who always kept his eyes open for possible conflicts of interest, noticed the five inspectors were not government employees. They worked for private companies that, he correctly guessed, were controlled by the very people whose grain the inspectors were supposed to be checking.

For nearly a year, Risser spent almost all his time writing stories about widespread scandal in the grain exporting business. His stories led to other indictments, a congres-

sional investigation, and legislation.

The results of an investigative reporting job aren't always as dramatic as those of Risser's look at the grain industry.

The work isn't dramatic either. Hours of poring over records and calling officials who didn't want to talk to him were as much a part of the investigation as the "cops and robbers" atmosphere "where you're chasing the crooks," Risser said.

In 1979 Risser won an almost unprecedented second Pulitzer Prize for reporting. His story was about the impact of modern farm practices on the environment.

Risser worked on the student newspaper in high school, but decided in college he wanted to be a lawyer. "I don't really know why," he said.

He practiced law for two years before deciding he would rather be a reporter. Working part-time, he took all the undergraduate journalism courses required for a degree.

He joined the *Register* in Des Moines and for five years covered city and state government. Covering the federal government is not much different, except that his readers are 1,000 miles away.

At the Iowa legislature, Risser said, "I would write a story and I would know that everybody in the legislature was reading it." He got "immediate feedback. Everybody would tell me it was a terrific story or it was a rotten story. The stories that I write [now] are basically not read in Washington."

"As a result," he said in an interview in his office two blocks from the White House, "some Washington bureaucrats don't feel the same compulsion to talk to you or to return your calls as they would if they knew your story was going to be read here."

The bureau, of which Risser was chief, covers the Iowa members of Congress and senators (who all read the *Register* daily), stories that other reporters aren't covering or aren't covering well, Risser said.

The reporters don't have specific beats, but Risser said he generally follows consumer and environmental issues.

He said his background as a state and local government reporter was the best preparation for reporting in Washington. He recommends against reporters taking the time to earn a law degree, though it does sometimes help in deciphering a bill or doing research.

And, he said he wouldn't hire anyone for the Washington bureau who hadn't spent several years as he did working for a local paper, learning about the paper and the state. ■

CHAPTER TEN

WRITING FEATURE STORIES

It was one of those slow days journalists dread. Most of the copy had gone to the composing room, and the few remaining reporters and copy editors were lounging around the newsroom, chatting or working the crossword puzzle. Nothing very newsworthy had happened that day; the paper was going to be dull. Then the news editor got an idea. It was March 16, and since it was a morning newspaper it would carry the date March 17. The editor knew St. Patrick's Day is usually an overworked subject, so a new angle was needed. The editor picked up the telephone and to the surprise of everyone within hearing distance asked for the overseas operator. When the operator came on the line, the editor placed a person-to-person call to the lord mayor of Dublin, Ireland. It was the middle of the night in Dublin, so the editor was unable to speak to the lord mayor (his personal assistant did come to the phone, however). Then the editor wrote a humorous story about the difficulties of transatlantic telephone hookups and the reaction of a Dublin official on St. Patrick's Day.

The article was a feature story (and so good that the management didn't even complain about the telephone bill).

On another night an enterprising young reporter was assigned to write a Halloween story. Not one to take the easy way out, he decided to walk through one of the local cemeteries at midnight, alone.

His feature story made chilling reading.

One of the authors of this text, when a beginning sportswriter for a daily newspaper, did something to make the sports editor angry. In retaliation the sports editor made the following assignment: "Get a feature story. I don't care what it's about or where you get it, but I want it on my desk before you go home tonight." Panicking, the reporter set out to find a feature story. He ended up going water skiing, even though he had never tried it before and couldn't even swim. Pictures taken from the shore clearly showed his fright.

The feature story he wrote about the experience was given special treatment in the Sunday edition of the paper and drew many favorable comments (as well as restoring him to the good graces of the sports editor).

Humanizing the News

Just what is a feature story? Would it help if we told you that a feature story is usually lighter, more human, possibly funnier than a regular news story? That most feature stories are not related to any current news event? That a feature story is usually not written in inverted pyramid style and that it may be about anything or anybody?

That description may give you an idea. By now you have guessed that, like news, feature stories are tough to define. Some people say there is no such thing; by that they mean that *all* stories should be readable (and a feature story that isn't easy to read isn't worth the effort). They fear that the only time a reporter will "write bright" is when the assignment specifies a feature story.

Timelessness

Some properties of the feature story can be isolated. The main characteristic of most features is that they are "evergreen." That is, they are just as acceptable for publication in next week's paper as in this week's. There is no time element involved. But even this is not always true. The news-feature, for example, is pegged to a specific item of news and is usually published the same day as the news story, or at least as soon as possible after it. Such stories as these are said to have a news peg, a reason for existence on their own.

Creative Style

Feature stories provide latitude but not license. While feature writers are a trifle more free with regard to the use of language, they certainly are *not* free to throw away the rule book entirely. Opinion and speculation are not allowed. The same ethical standards that apply to the straight news story apply to the feature story. But the good feature writer soon recognizes that such stories sometimes provide a better chance than straight news for literary ingenuity. It's hard to write a truly clever, bright story about the student council meeting, particularly if nothing out of the ordinary happens.

Truly clever or bright stories can be hazardous, too. The danger is that writers, especially (but not exclusively) beginners, will become carried away by the sound of their own words. They will try to be funny, or cute, or even overly somber. Such stories are very difficult to pull off, and will be miserable if they fail. The delightful thing about feature stories is that often the subject matter itself is funny or cute or somber. If the writer doesn't intrude too much, these elements will come through on their own. Sometimes a writer can kill a good story by being too expressive.

Subject Matter

Another characteristic of the feature story is that it is not limited in subject matter. It may be historical, throwing new light on an old subject or simply reviewing some event of years past. It may be about a remote place or an obscure person. (Remember the football team's water boy? He's feature material.) It may be about someone's unusual hobby, or someone's interesting relative. It may be written in the first person (as the waterskiing feature was). It may provide background to a developing or continuing news story. It may summarize or wrap up a story that has been told in small pieces over a long span of time. It may rely heavily on the use of anecdotes.

In many cases, a feature story concentrates on the mood of an event and therefore may be more accurate than the straight news story. (This is true of some sports stories.)

Above all, the feature story is about what people are interested in. That is close to the definition of the human interest story and trying to separate the two is difficult. Is an interview with the 15-year-old genius who graduated from college a feature story or a human interest story or both? The fact is that it doesn't make any difference how you label it as long as you are able to recognize and gather such stories. One of the problems of journalism is overlabeling. For example, these are some of the labels given to feature story leads: news summary, distinctive incident, quotation, question, analogy, picture. Many people believe that having a label for every lead and every story makes it easy for students. We think it only confuses them. Journalism students should be concentrating on reporting techniques and sentence structure—on *writing*—not on memorizing lists of labels.

Personality Features

To get you thinking in terms of publishable features, consider this: Every person on earth is worth a feature story. Somewhere in the background of every human being there is an incident, an idea, a problem, a thought, a relative, an opinion, a hobby, a hope that will make interesting reading. A journalism professor once decided to prove this notion to his students. On the first day of class he picked a name at random from the roster and called a student to the front of the class. The professor didn't know her; in fact, he had never seen her until that day. As the class watched, he interviewed her. The next time the class met, the students were amazed at the feature story he had written. Some even thought the whole thing was rigged. But the fact is, the result would have been about the same no matter which student had been chosen.

Interviewing a newsworthy individual who visits your school can often provide an idea for a personality feature. Here, high school journalists interview U.S. Senator Paul Simon.

Photo courtesy of the Multicultural Journalism Center, Roosevelt University, Chicago, Illinois.

A feature can be written about teachers and students at your school and their special accomplishments. Attending a school event such as a science fair can provide the journalist with ideas for personality features, as well as straight news stories.

All human beings are possible subjects for a feature story. Today, the student the professor chose is a feature writer for the *Miami Herald.*

Some people make better stories than others, however. Perhaps your school newspaper publishes many stories quoting the principal, but has never gotten around to doing a personality feature about him or her. While all the students know the principal's name, they probably don't really know anything about the person. This is a subject that is ripe for a personality feature.

When you do a personality feature, try to answer the question "Who is this person, anyway? What does the principal think of today's younger generation, specifically? What does he or she do on weekends? What are his or her opinions on politics? Ecology? Sports? Where would your principal like to spend a vacation? What are his or her goals for your school? If you ask enough questions, you're bound to get an answer that will lead you down the road to a feature story. In features, as in everything else in journalism, there is no substitute for the hard work of digging for the facts. While actually writing the story, however, the feature writer usually has a chance to exercise more imagination than the straight news writer.

Finding
Subjects

The feature story elevates routine news to page-one news. For instance, here is a feature story (or is it human interest?) about a lost dog. Lots of dogs get lost, and most of the time they don't rate mention in the newspaper. But this one is different—and perhaps that's part of the definition of the feature story:

Where are you, Dutch?

Her name's Dutch, and she's the floppy-eared, friendly pet of five children.

She's a German shorthaired pointer with nearly enough points to win her champion title.

She's an eager hunter with the true instincts of a thoroughbred.

But she's lost—and the frantic efforts of a Norfolk family to find her have failed. For Dutch is lost, fighting for her life, in downtown Kansas City, Mo.

In the early morning hours of Sept. 28, Dutch chewed and clawed her way out of her cage after a dog show in Kansas City.

Since then she's been seen repeatedly in the area. Apparently she hides out during the day and roams at night.

The dog's owners, Dr. James and Jane Dunlap, have spent many weary hours, nighttime hours, searching for Dutch.

Once, five days after she escaped, the couple saw Dutch staring at them in the darkness. They called her, but she fled.

Dutch's fresh tracks were seen last weekend.

The Norfolk physician has enlisted the aid of the Heart of America Kennel Club, Kansas City police, veterinarians, and business people in the area.

They set a food trap, but it was stolen.

This weekend they sent "wanted" bulletins to be posted in the area where Dutch hangs out. They've made several trips to Kansas City to search and to help organize the dragnet.

A Kansas Citian has offered to bring a rare tracking dog into the hunt, and a veterinarian is standing by with a tranquilizer gun should Dutch be tracked down and then bolt.

The Dunlaps figure Dutch is frightened and confused by her three weeks lost in the hubbub of a city. The Dunlap children, ranging from kindergarten to junior high age, refuse to give up hope.

Last Saturday the pheasant season opened in Nebraska. The Dunlaps spent the day searching Kansas City for Dutch.

Kansas City police helped. The Dunlaps lauded the K.C. police force as bright, alert, and helpful.

Dutch, officially "Doc's Duchess Grosshoax," is about 2 years old. She was a gift from Jane Dunlap to Dr. Dunlap, but has become (along with a cat, and the cat's frequent kittens) a much-loved, highly valued member of the family.

Dutch has 9 of 15 points needed to win her championship. More than likely she would have picked up the six points this fall.

In the meantime, the Dunlap family waits for news from Kansas City.

Tone

We have said that the feature story must be objective, just as the news story is. But do you detect a note of sympathy in the tone of the lost-dog story? This is part of the latitude allowed the feature writer. Feature writers may not come right out and express their opinions, but—and we almost hesitate to say this, for fear you'll misunderstand—they may, through the careful choice of words,

A feature story on a school play might be a personality interview of the star performer or a behind-the-scenes look at the actors' preparations.

write a story whose tone is emotional. The total effect of the story may appeal to the reader's emotions, but the writer is on thin ice if personal opinion is openly expressed.

Features and School Papers

Feature stories play a particularly important role in the scholastic press. Because most such newspapers come out only once a week or every two weeks or even once a month, they should rely heavily on features. The straight news has already been covered by the daily newspaper downtown; scholastic journalists, then, should be on the watch for feature stories and should featurize even straight news stories. Further, scholastic journalists should pay special attention and devote more space to events that are going to happen rather than to those that have already taken place (and been covered by commercial competition).

An unusual event can prompt special coverage and result in a feature. The *Chicago Tribune* ran the following feature about teen journalists on an Oakland, California, school newspaper and their coverage of the 1989 earthquake in northern California.

Quake throws teen journalists into the big-time

The Skyline Oracle is usually your typical high school newspaper, carrying articles by earnest if unpolished student-reporters on such teenage concerns as the senior prom or the state university system's latest admission requirements.

Tuesday, Oct. 17, however, was anything but normal for students at Skyline High School in Oakland, Calif. They, like so many other residents of northern California, were terrorized by the most powerful earthquake to strike the U.S. since the one that virtually destroyed San Francisco in 1906.

So the day after the quake the Oracle's staff decided to scrap their planned issue. As they met in Skyline's parking lot (the school was closed until it could be inspected for structural damage), they had already decided they would cover the hottest story going.

The earthquake special by students in Oakland, Calif.

This ambitious goal would catapult nearly 20 of the paper's reporters and photographers, most of whom are 17 years old or younger, into the world of big-time journaltism, if only temporarily. In fact, quite a few seasoned professional

journalists never have a chance to chase a story of such magnitude. The Oracle may be the first high-school newspaper ever to deploy its staff to cover a disaster the way a professional newspaper might.

Before they were through, the Skyline students would find themselves attending a presidential press conference, lucking into being only one of two news outfits to tour the Nimitz freeway with California's governor, conducting numerous interviews and capturing in compelling photos the drama of it all for a special earthquake issue of their paper distributed to 2,000 or so readers last Friday.

One of the problems in being a high-school journalist, as the students discovered, is that some people don't take you seriously. When Eric Gurowitz, the editor-in-chief, and Lucas Zahas, a photographer, went to cover President Bush's press conference at Moffet Naval Air Station outside Oakland, they were stopped by a Secret Service agent after they flashed high-school press passes.

"He said the high-school press is not officially recognized by the government as official press," said Gurowitz, a senior. "On the inside, I wanted to scream at him and say, 'We are official!' But on the outside, I said, 'Yes, sir. I can understand your concern for security.' "

Shortly afterwards, the young men encountered a naval officer who reiterated the Secret Service explanation but said he would check to see what could be done. Then, out of the blue, the officer told the high schoolers that while he was away they shouldn't "run down the hallway" even though they had no intention of doing so.

"It was kind of condescending, but they were nervous because they

hadn't had much time to organize [the President's] security," said Gurowitz.

The two eventually were allowed into the room before the President arrived but were told to stand apart from the professional press "so we wouldn't bother them," recalled Gurowitz. Once Bush appeared, however, they mounted the raised platform with the balance of the press corps.

"On one side of me there was a guy with a New York Times press pass and on the other side was a guy from the AP. Then I looked down at my high school pass. It was kind of funny," Gurowitz said.

"I felt kind of silly with my little Konica," said photographer Zahas, also a senior. "All the other photographers were carrying big expensive Nikons with lenses a foot and a half long," he said.

"We kept looking at each other and saying, 'This is really incredible, this is really incredible,' " says Gurowitz. "We were the only high school journalists there."

A lucky traffic jam

Another 17-year old senior and member of the newspaper staff, Shahla Amadyar, pulled off something of a journalistic coup when she found herself one of only two reporters to accompany Gov. George Deukmejian on his tour of the collapsed Cypress section of I-880, also known as the Nimitz freeway.

She talked her way into the governor's press conference at Alameda Naval Air Station. Then, after the governor answered the last question, he and his staff along with the police, military authorities and press people formed a convoy to travel across Oakland to visit the destroyed highway.

By Frank James

As fate would have it, just about all the other members of the fourth estate somehow wound up behind Amadyar's car, which was tagging the officials. A massive traffic jam caused the press cars behind hers to be blocked by congestion. Consequently, only her car and that of a San Francisco Examiner reporter in front of her made it all the way to the Nimitz with Deukmejian.

At the Nimitz, a security official moved a few orange traffic cones to allow the convoy past, but when he spotted the youthful Amadyar he began to replace the cones to block her.

"I just pointed and kept on going," said Amadyar. "He started running after me, but I just kept pointing and driving." The guard gave up the chase.

Her good fortune held even after she discovered she had only two exposures left before arriving at the Nimitz. She was able to bum some film from the governor's official photographer.

Amadya, who also reports for a community newspaper in Oakland, said people didn't seem reluctant to be interviewed by a 17-year old. "I

think it was the way I presented myself. It wasn't 'Hey, what happened? Oh, my God!' like a teenager. I was real professional."

A peek at the pros

Covering the biggest earthquake in the U.S. in nearly 100 years gave the students a chance to see real professionals up close and personal. They marveled as network anchors jumped out of limos to do their standups in the Marina district. "I was standing behind Peter Jennings' producer and could see the copy of the script Jennings was reading," said Gurowitz. "I didn't realize they had it all printed out like that."

Then there was a conversation Gurowitz had with a radio newsman. "He had been in the same clothes for three days, and he was trying to dissuade me from going into journalism. 'It's so much hard work. You don't want to do it,' " Gurowitz remembers the reporter saying.

Because the school was closed from the time of the earthquake until last Monday, the students composed their stories on the personal computers some had at home. The photographs, some of which were

good enough to appear in a big metropolitan newspaper, were developed in Zahas' home darkroom.

"They did a great job," said David McGibney, the Oracle's advisor and journalism teacher at Skyline. He said this is the first issue of the 28-year-old paper devoted entirely to one subject. "They muscled their way in, and let's face it, that's what you have to do if you want to get the story."

For the students, covering the earthquake left them feeling ambivalent. "There was the excitement and the pressure of getting [the newspaper] out. But there was incredible loss of life," said Chad Davidson, a production editor who also took some photos. "We have real mixed emotions."

"It's one of the best experiences I've had," said Zahas whose father took his photos of President Bush to work to show them off. We've never done anything like this before. This is real journalism."

How do you top an earthquake? "I don't know. That's what I'm worried about," said Zahas. "Everything else is going to seem boring."

Student coverage is tuned to the concerns of teens

A promotion box on page 1 of the special earthquake edition by students in Oakland, Calif., promised "stunning accounts of the biggest quake since 1906."

What followed in the Skyline High School Oracle were 17 stories and 34 photographs, encompassing many of the same subjects covered in the national press and a few distinctly high-school related themes:

Among the former were accounts of the quake itself ("Who would think such a rumpus would occur?"); aid for victims ("Oakland seemed to take good care of its residents"); an analysis of the freeway collapse ("This horrible tragedy, according to . . . structural engineers, could have been avoided"); the World Series ("It seems absurd to some that in the face of this harrowing ordeal the

World Series is being continued, but logical to others"); and an editorial-style consideration of the quake's social implications:

"It is important to realize that the Quake not only has the direct impact of destruction and death, but the effect of revealing and compounding the unsolved problems of the urban existence, as well."

A back page story noted that "six members of the football team and 10 members of the Titan Cheerleader Squad volunteered up to five days at the Martin Luther King Elementary School self-supported shelter. . . . Eric Albert '90 and Deon Strothers '90 cooked hamburgers and vegetables for the victims.''

Finally, a "Where were you?" survey might only have come from the teen milieu:

- "I was in my room jumping on my bed and listening to my stereo."—Shelly Hawkins '91.
- "I was in the middle of football practice . . . At first I just thought I was tired, but then I saw the goal posts swaying . . . and I thought the end of the world was here."—Lonnie Long '91.
- "I was on Skyline campus learning to drive stick in my Dad's car and I had just killed the engine. I thought I did something to cause it to explode when it started shaking."—Amber Niewold '91.
- "I was out front sitting in a car talking to my boyfriend. I was in total control of the whole situation, but he was paranoid."—Jamie Dotson '90.

Wrap-up

Feature stories are usually lighter in tone than regular news stories. They usually are timeless, or "evergreen," unless they are news features and are related to a specific timely news story. Features permit writers to exercise more creativity in language than regular news stories, but the rules about objectivity and opinion still apply. Writers have latitude but not license.

Features permit creativity in story ideas, too. Topics range from historical dates to interesting people and everything between. Features occasionally are written in first person. They may rely on anecdotes.

All people are possible subjects for a personality profile, a story that answers the question "Who is this person, anyway?" Personality profiles are thorough, in-depth stories about one person.

Many routine stories have been elevated to page-one status through feature treatment. This treatment does not permit opinion, but it permits a different tone, a different total effect.

Features are very important for scholastic publications. Often, the news available to a school paper has already been covered by the commercial press. So school newspapers often have to rely on features to hold the interest of their audience.

On Assignment

Teamwork

1. As a class, brainstorm ideas for feature stories that would be appropriate for a future issue of the school paper. Select the best ideas. Three students should research and write each story. Critique each other's stories in a two-page memorandum.
2. Stage an argument, play, skit, or some other three-minute activity. Require other journalism students to watch *but to not take notes*. Afterward, they are to write down what they saw, then write a straight news story about it. Discuss the stories as a class, then write a feature story based on the experience.

Practice

1. Write a feature story based on this information:

  A poet gives a speech.

  His name is Rasputin Roundy.

  He says he cuts dictionaries apart and randomly pastes the words on paper. He says this is poetry.

  "Because I am a poet, everything I do is poetry by definition," he says.

  He is dressed in a three-piece light-green suit and wears socks that do not match.

  He is from Princeton, New Jersey.

  The speech, first in a local university's series, was given Monday.

  After the speech, no one applauds and Roundy leaves the stage angrily.

2. Write a feature story from this information:

  Your school football coach, Knute Leahy, is a very superstitious man.

  He always wears the same hat during games—an old Navy cap he wore during World War II.

  He wore the hat during a naval battle in which five U.S. ships out of six were sunk by the enemy. He was aboard the one that didn't sink.

  He whistles "Dixie" throughout the game. Once he got bored and whistled "White Christmas," and the team lost 63–2.

  He has been coach here since 1955.

  He is 62 years old.

  His record as coach is 90–140–10.

  He also teaches history, and his favorite historical character is George S. Patton, a World War II general.

  Leahy was born Friday, Oct. 13.

  Asked about his superstitions, Coach Leahy said, "I am not superstitious. I just believe in covering all the bases."

Your Turn

1. Submit five ideas for feature stories to your instructor. Identify possible sources for each one. Your teacher will select one for you to write.

2. Imagine you are the feature editor of your newspaper. You need one story for each reporter on the paper, and you have twenty-five reporters—that means twenty-five ideas. When you go home from school today, keep your eyes and ears open, and listen to the news.

Jules Loh

If there's anyone who is the behind-the-scene reporter at a news event, it's the feature writer, according to one of the best-known such writers.

Jules Loh, author of "Elsewhere in America," a biweekly feature column carried by the Associated Press, said feature stories go beyond reporting the obvious facts to touch on the heart of the news.

"The feature story is the big uncovered news story in America," Loh said. "It tells not just what happened, but what it was like to be there."

Loh has been writing features since his high school days, when he would hang around the *Washington Post* newsroom. He worked as a cub reporter for the *Post* while attending George Washington University in Washington, D.C., where he earned a degree in English and history in 1952.

Without a doubt, feature writing is the best possible job, according to Loh.

"I know of no other job, including that of the traveling sales rep, that allows what I've done," Loh said. "I've done stories in every part of the nation."

Although traveling has made him appreciate the diversity of the U.S., Loh admitted his on-the-road job can get lonely.

But the rewards far outweigh the inconveniences. Loh said he finds satisfaction in telling his readers what it was like to be there rather than just to report the facts.

"All the time I was writing hard news, I was always interested in features," Loh said, recalling when he was a general assignment reporter for the *Waco* (Texas) *Tribune-Herald* and later for the Associated Press bureau in Louisville, Ky.

His feature-writing talents evolved from his efforts to give as much information as possible about the stories he was reporting.

"I tried to tell more, to make it unnecessary for another reporter to do the color story on a hard news assignment."

Loh was quick to praise straight newswriting, adding that the best feature writers he knows are reporters.

However, feature stories have an enduring quality that news stories sometimes do not, Loh said.

"When we get around to celebrating our [America's] Tricentennial, my stories will be more valuable to researchers because they tell about what it was like," he said. "I tell about the people, their dreams, worries, and daily life."

Inspiration for his features often originates in the hard news of the day. Loh said he spends a great deal of time reading newspapers from across the nation, looking for the seed for a good story.

Story idea in mind, Loh sets off to find his source, whether it be in the Pacific Northwest or the bayous of the South. Inevitably, by the time he reaches his destination, several more ideas have sprung into his mind, Loh said.

Preparing for the feature story interview requires as much time as writing the story, Loh said. He tries to find out as much as possible about his subject, which requires constant reading in many sources.

"The feature story can be almost anything—from a 600-word piece on a sheepherder in Montana to a 6,000-word piece retracing the trail of Lewis and Clark," Loh said.

"The stories can be very profound, multifaceted, or one-dimensional. The idea is to put the reader there."

Recommending reading constantly to improve writing, he advised, "Saturate yourself with poetry. It teaches a leanness of expression and a quality of rhythm."

Also important to developing a good flair for features is continual writing. "Just write," Loh urged, using whatever seems interesting for a subject.

Good feature writers take time to develop. "Like baseball pitchers, feature writers are made, not just born," Loh said. "It comes with practice." ■

WRITING SPORTS STORIES

> Outlined against a blue-gray October sky, the Four Horsemen rode again. In dramatic lore they are known as Famine, Pestilence, Destruction and Death. These are only aliases. Their real names are Stuhldreher, Miller, Crowley, and Layden. They formed the crest of the South Bend Cyclone before which another fighting Army football team was swept over the precipice at the Polo Grounds yesterday afternoon as 55,000 spectators peered down on the bewildering panorama spread on the green plain below.

That is perhaps the most famous lead ever written for a sports story. It was written by Grantland Rice, one of the finest sportswriters of all time. Such a lead would never get past the copy desk on today's streamlined newspaper. Heartless copy editors, trained that a lead should come to the point immediately and concisely, probably would rewrite it to read as follows:

NEW YORK—Led by an all-star backfield, Notre Dame yesterday defeated Army at the Polo Grounds before 55,000 fans, _____.

The blank is for the score. Did you notice that Rice did not include the score in his first paragraph? We can forgive him because he was writing in a different time and for an audience that had not seen the game on television. That audience had time to read on to the second paragraph—or the third or fourth—to get the score. Today's audience does not.

But Rice's lead still has a good deal of appeal despite the fact that it is outmoded today. It is colorful, original, and full of action. If all sports leads were colorful, original, and full of action there would not be such a split in the attitudes toward sportswriting. But there are two schools of thought on sportswriting.

One holds that sportswriting is the *worst* writing in American journalism today.

The other holds that sportswriting is the *best* writing in American journalism today.

The authors of this text agree with both schools. When sportswriting is bad, it's awful. When it's good, it's excellent.

When writing a sports story, the good reporter avoids trite expressions and gives the audience what it wants—colorful, lively writing. When thousands of people have watched a game, they expect more from the sportswriter than a play-by-play rehash.

The Sports Story

One of the reasons sportswriting is often bad is that sports reporters tend to be the worst overusers of trite expressions. This apparently stems from two things: the fact that sports has developed some perfectly acceptable semi-slang of its own and the fact that games are action events. The former tends to make writers believe that if some slang expressions are permissible (knockout, red-dog, bomb), then so are others. The trouble, however, is distinguishing between the vivid language of sports and the trite language of mediocre sportswriters. The second fact causes many sportswriters to believe that, because sports is so full of action, they must adopt a special kind of English to capture it. The truth is that action will be evident in the story if it is inherent in the event; special language, such as "toed the ball," "split the uprights," or "whacked a four-bagger" merely disguises the action.

Let us, for the moment, take the view that sportswriting is some of the best writing there is and see if we can find out why. One reason is that sportswriters, while they must be objective, are allowed more freedom to be partisan. They're for the hometown team, and everyone knows it. Thus they are able to do a bit more than simply describe an event. They can—indeed, they must—interpret it. If the coach rants and raves on the sidelines, or if the spectators boo the officials, sportswriters are free to pick words more descriptive than "angry" (the word most likely to be used by a reporter telling the mayor's reaction to some ordinance passed by the city council). Sportswriters are expected to convey a word picture of exactly what happened, and this inevitably leads to colorful language.

Lively Writing

Further, sportswriters are aware that the events they describe have been witnessed by hundreds, perhaps thousands (or even millions, if televised) of people. They do not turn to the sports page to read a play-by-play rehash. They want to know how the coaches and players reacted, what kind of pitch Ryne Sandberg hit for the winning home run, or what all the quarreling was about in the third quarter when the officials handed out a 15-yard penalty. Long before the rest of America's journalists had recognized the need for interpretive reporting, sportswriters were forced into it. This led them to be more aware of reporting (they had to have *something* to offer fans who had seen the game) and of writing.

Sports fans want the stories they read to reflect the tension, the color, the excitement, the joy or the sorrow of the game. The audience, in other words, demands colorful, lively writing; it is preconditioned to it. Let the city council reporter question the mayor's wisdom in vetoing the new city budget and readers will object that opinion belongs on the editorial page. But if the football coach decides to go for it on fourth down deep in the team's own territory and the strategy backfires, eager fans expect to find the writer's opinions about the coach's unwise decision in their coverage.

Fans tend to believe that they are just as knowledgeable as sportswriters. This is not a serious problem for sportswriters who know what they are doing. (For instance, the writer must know that the usual strategy on fourth down deep in your own territory is to punt!)

Avoiding Clichés

Now let's argue the side that views sportswriting as some of the worst writing there is. This judgment is due largely to one major blunder, the overuse of clichés. The lazy sportswriter never says ''baseball'' when ''the old apple'' will fit. That this is absurd should be obvious. Readers of the sports page appreciate plain English and lively verbs as much as anyone else. List after list of these trite phrases have been drawn up. Here are several that wise sportswriters avoid:

horsehide	under the arcs	triple threat
pigskin	greenclad warriors	run roughshod
paydirt	scoreless deadlock	pellet
gridders	tally	pilfered sacks
grapplers	counter	bingle
thinclads	canto	cagers
burn the nets	stanza	raised the curtain on the season
rip the nets	chapter	rang down the curtain on the season
sizzle the nets	coffin corner	functioned like a well-oiled machine
singe the nets	hot corner	local gridiron
capped the drive	lammed the pill	the tide shifted
snagged the aerial	banged the apple	the oval
crushed the opposition	booted the pigskin	mailcarriers
forms the nucleus	caged the	blanket the threat
knights of the maples	spheroid	

Many sportswriters defend such language on the grounds that it is colorful. They call it sports "slanguage" and say there is nothing wrong with it. What they are doing is confusing legitimate sports terminology (birdie, eagle, etc.) with the tired clichés of a past era. There is no reason for sportswriters to be any less conscious of good English than straight news reporters. Both need figures of speech, but these should be bright and inventive. For instance, this is how Jim Murray, syndicated columnist for the *Los Angeles Times*, once described the University of Southern California football team: "The USC varsity hits the field like a broken ketchup bottle. They're not a team; they're a horde. You can't beat them; you must dismember them."

Organizing Sports Coverage

The problems just discussed are equally applicable to the professional and the student sportswriter. Let's concentrate on the scholastic sports page.

Basically, sportswriters will be writing three types of stories: pre-game, game, and post-game. Before writing any of these, they must prepare. They must know as much about the game as possible: all the rules, all the various strategies and the reasons behind them. They must get to know the coaches and players, who are the source of information and interviews that brighten the

Interviewing coaches is an important part of the sportswriter's work. A coach's comments enhance the game story and cast light on the game, the players, and the opposing team.

coverage. Bare facts of the contest are seldom enough for the curious fans. They want to know how the coaches and players feel, what they think of their opposition, and how they view the big game. Beginning sportswriters should read the sports pages thoroughly, watch sports events on television, perhaps participate in sports. They should immerse themselves in the subject matter. (They should know that in some sports, *low* score wins.) This means watching practice sessions as well as games, to become as familiar as possible with how the players perform and how the coaches think. If permission can be obtained, they should travel with the teams. Once the writers thoroughly understand what they are going to write about, they can plan their coverage.

The Pre-game Story

The scholastic sports page must pay special attention to pre-game, or advance, stories. This is because your account of the game itself will be old news by the time it gets into print. Thus, the only way you can give your readers any information they can't read in the local daily newspaper is by emphasizing the pre-game story.

In order to get information for that crucial pre-game story, the sports staff is going to have to organize early, perhaps even before school starts for such sports as football.

The problem is not in getting information about your own team, but in finding out about the other team. Letters sent to the coaches of your school's opposing teams asking *specific questions* almost always will produce usable material. The opposing coach usually is glad to tell you how many returning letterholders there are, which of them were all-state or all-city last year, how many starters were lost from last year's team, the size, weight, position, and year in school of everyone on the team, last year's record, and similar information. The coach will likely cooperate if you ask for an assessment of the team's strengths and weaknesses, although this information will probably be of a general nature. More specific information may come from the sports editor of the school whose team your school is going to play. The coach may be a bit close-lipped about the team's chances; the sports editor probably will level with you.

Armed with information about the opposing team, you will turn to your own team to gather material for the pre-game story. This story should contain the following information:

1. The score of last year's game(s) between the two schools.
2. The team's physical condition (any injuries?).
3. The starting lineups.
4. Comparisons between the two teams' records so far this season, including how they came out against common opponents.
5. Comments on the styles of play. (Does one team emphasize offense, the other defense?)
6. Significance of the game. (Will the winner be the conference champion?)
7. Analysis of individual players. (Does each team have a quarterback competing for all-state recognition?)
8. Historical background of the rivalry. (Who leads in the series of games between the two schools?)

It will help the present staff and future staffs if you compile a complete record of your school's sports history. Old yearbooks and microfilmed copies of your local newspaper on file in the city library should provide the information. Fans will be interested to learn that since the rivalry began, Central High School has won 34 games, lost 22, and tied 4 against Tech.

Pre-game coverage should not overlook related spirit activities. The sports page is the proper place for stories about the band's plans for a halftime show, new cheerleaders, pep rallies, and the like. The conscientious sports editor does not ignore the so-called minor sports, such as tennis and golf, either. There is reader interest in these sports. Nor should the editor ignore the reserve or junior varsity teams. These are the varsity players of the future, and how they fare is highly important not only to the teams but to the fans. And certainly, sports activities by both sexes should be covered. The editor must not let sexism—from either angle—creep into the sports page.

The Game Story

Covering the game is the true test of sportswriters. They must keep detailed, accurate notes of an event that is happening too fast for the untrained observer to follow. The writers have more comfortable surroundings—the press box—than the fans, and must make good use of this working space. A note-taking system, a method of keeping a play-by-play record, and some system for recording statistics may be of the writer's own invention, but should be simple and easy to read. Nothing is more frustrating for the sports reporter than searching after the game for some missing fact that should have been written down when it happened. The sports reporter must watch for turning points in the game: the fumble that sets up the winning touchdown (and who recovered the fumble); the substitute who comes off the bench and leads the team to victory; the shift from zone defense to man-to-man defense that bottles up the opponent's top scorer.

The sports reporter is free to analyze the game. If it was a case of your school's offense overpowering the opponent's defense, say so (if you're sure). If the wet field or the wind played a part, say so. Reiterate the consequences. Tell the fans once more that the winner is the conference champion.

It should be obvious from all this that sports reporters are busy during the game. They must watch the game, the sidelines, the spectators, and the officials, all the while keeping careful, detailed notes. Therefore, *sports reporters cannot be cheerleaders*; they can be partisan, but they can't let this interfere with the job of reporting. They can't be on their feet shouting when they should be calmly recording the action. About the second time a student sports reporter jumps up and shouts "Kill the referee!," spilling the professional reporter's coffee, he or she will no longer be welcome in the press box. Student reporters have every right to cover the games

Your team's win–loss record or the record of wins over a particular rival may be the lead you need for your next sports story.

and should resist any attempts by professionals to eject them from the press box. The student will find little support, however, from a professional whose notes are soggy from the coffee spilled on them.

If sports editors are to function effectively within limited space, they will have to limit details on game stories; they're old news anyway. Brief accounts, crediting those who scored or who played well, will suffice most of the time. If the sports editor decides to run a complete game story even though the local daily newspaper has already done so, then a new angle must be found, perhaps combining the advance on tonight's game with accounts of past games. The editor must be able to offer something the daily newspaper did not. If he or she can't do that, then by all means the game story should be featurized. There would be little point in announcing the winner in a lead two weeks after the game has been played. If a feature angle is chosen, the sports reporter should remember not to make the same "mistake" Grantland Rice did. Include the score, somewhere, and if needed for clarity, tell the name of the game.

The Post-game Story

This type of story could just as easily be called a sports feature, sideline story, background story, sports interview, or locker-room story. Post-game stories include, among others, interviews of the players after the game, descriptions of the spectators' actions during the game, historical features on a sport or a rivalry, wrap-ups (or reviews) of the season after the last game, and discussions of rule changes.

The lead and the tone of such stories are usually somewhat different . . . those of game and pre-game stories. The latter are usually written with standard techniques, probably including a summary lead. (The exception would be a game story published two weeks after the game, when a feature angle would be needed.) Sports color stories, on the other hand, follow the same general pattern as feature stories; they should be vivid and colorful, but not overdone.

The post-game color story gives the sports reporter an opportunity to untangle confusing events that occurred during a game, by talking with the official who made the controversial ruling, for instance. It also gives the reporter a chance to update the reader on scoring records and individual statistics that he or she didn't

Fans at a sporting event—such as those at this basketball game—stand, applaud, and generally have a good time. Sportswriters, however, must keep their eyes on the game.

have time to compile immediately after the game—for example, the new team scoring standings in basketball or the number of yards per carry of the backs in football.

A last word of caution: Sportswriters mustn't carry partisanship to extremes. A sports columnist who invariably predicts his or her team will win, for instance, eventually loses all credibility.

Sportswriting Today

Sportswriting is fun, but it isn't easy. The sports reporter must be a keen observer and a good interviewer—and as good a writer as anyone on the staff. The late Red Smith, one of America's best sportswriters, said, "Sportswriting is the most pleasant way of making a living that man has yet devised."

The following article agrees, but points out some of the hazards involved in sportswriting.

The Best Seat in the House

By C. Bickford Lucas

Once upon a time, sportswriters wrote about athletic heroes and heroines and their exploits in grandiose style with the emphasis on adjectives, clichés, and adoration.

Every sport had its Cinderella team. And the clock usually struck midnight.

Sportswriters had favorite phrases, such as never-say-die, there's no tomorrow, heartbreaking defeat, and moral victory.

They relied on jargon, such as round-tripper, paydirt, portsider, cager, icer, gridder, and "genuine" superstar (as opposed to an imitation superstar).

Some veteran sportswriters look

back fondly on the "good old days" when men were men and women were women, and the women stayed out of the locker room and the press box.

Managing editors took a dim view of sports departments, frequently calling them toy shops peopled by undisciplined, unprofessional, beer-guzzling, poker-playing, illiterate journalistic misfits.

The sportswriters took pride in being mavericks, but that's about all they took pride in. Many were unabashed supporters for the schools, teams, or sports they covered. They were often flattered, frequently pampered, and sometimes paid by sports promoters.

And they were envied. Sportswriters were paid to watch events other folks paid to see, and the writers usually had the best seats in the house.

It was exciting and fun.

It still is and probably always will be. Sportswriters work where the action is. This country and many other countries are caught up in the joys of both spectator and participatory sports. That's the fun of it, and the writers are a vital part.

Without writers, there would be no record of the grand achievements, no chronicling of the victories and the defeats, no literature about the elation and the disappointment. The human side of sports would be lost forever.

The business has changed dramatically in recent years. Standards for sports departments are as high as or higher than the standards on the city and news desks of most newspapers, particularly the better newspapers.

The excitement of covering a Super Bowl or World Series has to

Sportswriters have the best seats in the house, in this case the scorers' table at a basketball game. To record the action accurately, they must keep good notes.

be experienced to be appreciated. For the most part, you are dealing with interesting people doing interesting things. And your audience is virtually guaranteed.

The jobs are there for talented men and women. The opportunities for good writers are endless.

Although style, spelling, and grammar are essential in sports writing, just as they are in any type of newspaper writing, the drama, humor, and thrills of sports events give the reporters more latitude.

Some of the best—and unfortunately, some of the worst—writing can be found on the sports page. Good sportswriters paint vivid, accurate pictures with their descriptions. They write about people. They give their readers insight into the events. They tell the story behind the story.

Because television can provide the score faster than a newspaper can, the writer must go beyond what happens on the field. A well-written story leaves the writer with the satisfaction of a difficult job well done.

Sometimes the sports reporter must be the bearer of bad tidings. If a writer's team is doing something it shouldn't, the writer must cover—not cover up—the story. The writer's responsibility is to the reader, not the team he or she is covering.

A homer means two things to a sportswriter. One is a four-base hit in baseball. That's okay. The other is a writer who believes in "my team right or wrong." That's not okay, even at the scholastic level. Among responsible journalists there is no reason for hometown bias and boosterism.

That's not to say a writer can or must be totally impersonal. Writers are not made of plastic. It's difficult not to have feelings about teams or individuals you deal with on a regular basis.

A sportswriter without emotions will write colorless, dull stories. But the writer's feelings should not be apparent to the reader. Cheering in the press box is unacceptable.

The positives of being a sportswriter far outweigh the negatives, but students considering this line of work should be aware of the pitfalls.

It is hard work, and the hours can be devastating. Forget weekends—that's when many sports events takes place. Forget nights—even baseball usually is played at night these days.

It puts a strain on family life, primarily because of the hours and travel time. Some sportswriters on larger newspapers spend almost as much time on the road as they spend at home. It's a nice way to see the country or the world (with your employer paying the way), but it can create havoc with your family or social life.

An increasing number of athletes are refusing interviews. Some coaches and players verbally, and sometimes physically, abuse writers.

In spite of the recognition and visibility, many sportswriters lead lonely lives. There are lots of parties and press conferences, and hobnobbing with celebrities can be fun, but it's tough to socialize with athletes who may earn more in a week than you earn in a year.

But there is camaraderie in the profession, and the majority of the athletes, coaches, and owners are decent, friendly people. The problem is getting too close. It is difficult to write a story that might cost a friend a job or cause embarrassment. But sometimes it must be done if the writer is to retain credibility.

On the other side of the coin, sportswriting is still basically more fun than heartache, more exciting than boring, more flexible than inflexible, and an outlet for the creative urges sometimes stifled in other types of newspaper work.

To be successful, a writer must be enthusiastic, dedicated, devoted, tireless, ethical, imaginative, resourceful, inquisitive, stubborn, flexible, fair-minded, thick-skinned, knowledgeable and, above all, accurate. Lazy people looking for an easy way into the stadium need not apply.

Mr. Lucas is a journalism instructor at the University of Arizona in Tucson. He was sports editor of the Denver Post *for 14 years.*

Wrap-up

Two schools of thought exist about sportswriting. One says sportswriting is the best writing in journalism. The other says it is the worst. It can be both. When it is bad, it is awful. When it is good, it is excellent.

Some sportswriters overuse trite expressions like "tally" for points and "cagers" for basketball players. The language of sports has color built into it so there is no need for clichés.

Sports stories often need interpretation and occasionally judgments can be made by writers to provide this interpretation. Readers want sports stories to reflect the tension, color, excitement, joy, or sorrow of the contests.

Careful planning is needed for effective sports coverage. Often schools exchange information from coaches or writers. Good records need to be kept to aid future staff members.

Scholastic journalists follow professional rules and do not cheer in the pressbox. They keep busy tracking the game, looking for key plays or turning points.

Scholastic journalists often are at a disadvantage in getting their stories printed because the commercial press publishes first. This means student journalists need to develop different angles and approaches, often emphasizing advance stories of contests.

Sports stories should be vivid and colorful but not overdone. Open partisanship for one team can damage credibility.

Sportswriting has been called "the most

pleasant way of making a living that man has yet devised.'' Without sportswriters, there would be no record of the grand achievements of athletes. But the work can be difficult and demanding, requiring odd work hours and a great deal of travel. Coaches and players are not always cooperative with the press, particularly after defeats.

On Assignment

Teamwork

1. Make a list of so-called minor sports. Each team should select one of the minor sports, and each member of the team should identify at least one story about that sport. Make sure the stories explain key parts of the game: scoring, rules, terminology. Interview the coaches and players. Write the stories. After they have been critiqued and evaluated, keep them for use in a later chapter.

2. Have each team member survey ten students on the importance of sports in a scholastic setting. Do sports cost too much? Are injuries a problem? What is the role of the sportswriter? How many students attend games? What reasons are given by those who don't? Are sports overemphasized? Do athletes' grades suffer because of the time spent at practice and traveling to games? Are boys' and girls' sports financed equally? Should they be? How do the students feel about minor sports? About the sport your journalism team is covering? Compile all the answers into one in-depth story to go along with the package of stories developed on your team's minor sport.

Practice

1. In the sports page of your local paper, identify and underline the trite, overused sports jargon. Underline in a different color of ink the legitimate, colorful language of the sport. Discuss your findings in class.

2. Watch a college or professional game on television. Make notes of the turning points of the game, the major strategies, the major errors, the star players. Clip an article about the event from the local paper. Compare your list of key elements to those that appear in the newspaper. Are they the same or different? Why? Who do you think is ''right''? Why? Write an essay on the findings.

3. Test your critical thinking. Did you know that sports commentators on radio and television often are paid, at least in part, by the teams they cover? What does that suggest? If you are in a town where that takes place, interview commentators and team officials about the situation. Can commentators be objective? Do team officials want them to be? What if they criticize the team's performance? How do your school coaches feel about this? How do you feel? Write an essay on this subject.

4. Compile a list of substitute words for the list of sports clichés in this chapter.

5. One criticism of many sportswriters is that they are virtual cheerleaders for the teams they cover. Invite local sportswriters to class to discuss the role the sportswriter should play.

6. Assume you know that a member of your school team is ineligible, perhaps for academic reasons or because he or she is too old. The player is a star whose loss would be critical to the team. Should you run a story? Ask the coaches what they think. Write an essay on your position. Does your code of ethics affect your position?

Your Turn

1. Attend your school's major sports event this week and write a feature story, or color sidebar, about all that happens at the game: the cheerleaders, the band, the crowd, the weather, the excitement, the halftime show, and so on. Do not write about the game itself.

2. Write a pre-game, game, and post-game story of a major athletic event in your school this week. Attach comparable stories from the local paper and compare them to your stories. Are the news elements different? Try to account for any differences.

3. Write a story about a school sport with which you are unfamiliar. Choose an upcoming event for your article, then in order to become more knowledgeable about the sport, interview the coach and players, observe a practice, and watch an actual game. Read others' stories covering the sport. Write yours and check it with the coach or one of the players for accuracy.

4. Exchange sports stories with another student. Your task is to edit the other's writing to make it more lively, exciting, and immediate. Try to make readers feel they were in the stands participating in the event.

Valerie Lynn Dorsey

Gender and ethnic changes in newsrooms across the country may be best reflected by the increasing number of women moving into the traditionally all-male bastion of sports news.

"More and more blacks and females are in the business," says Valerie Lynn Dorsey. "We're always going to be challenged. Women aren't supposed to know anything about sports. And racism is a part of society."

Dorsey, who joined the staff of USA Today in January 1988, says organizations such as the Association for Women in Sports Media and the National Association for Black Journalists make it easier for women and minorities to break into top jobs.

These supportive organizations, however, won't do all the work for you, Dorsey says, adding that success takes hard work. She says she had to work extra hard because she got a late start.

Journalism wasn't always her goal. She originally studied civil engineering at the University of Texas at El Paso.

"I flunked pre-calculus. That's when I realized I wasn't going to be an engineer," she said.

She began looking into public relations as a career until a professor read some of her work and convinced her to go into print journalism.

With no high school newspaper experience and only one semester on her college paper, Dorsey says she still has a lot of catching up to do.

"Most of what you need to know you learn on the job. You have to expect to start small and work your way up. There's nothing wrong with starting at a small paper."

Her chance to join USA Today came while she was at the Pensacola (Fla.) News Journal. Both publications belong to the Gannett Newspapers group, which brings up journalists from its local publications for four-month training programs with USA Today. Dorsey was one of those brought up.

Coming from a small paper and being a black, female sportswriter, Dorsey says she thought she would be "pigeonholed into doing little things."

"It was not as bad as I thought it would be. I was just surprised at how much freedom I was given," she says.

Talking to other writers and reading the newspaper helped her learn more about USA Today's terse writing style.

"I can see now a lot of excess stuff you really don't need. You can be informative in short space. It's a challenge."

She says she also has been challenged by the competition and needling she sometimes faces as a female sportswriter.

Her interest in sports started when she was a child. Dorsey is the oldest of six children. Because her father didn't get his first son for several years, she says she became his "surrogate son." She remembers going to many Atlanta Braves games with her father.

Even though that changed after her brother was born, the love of sports was ingrained in her. Now she is right where she wants to be.

"Don't give up," Dorsey advises women aspiring to be sportswriters. "Hang with it. This is not an easy profession."

The most important thing you can learn from school is ethics, Dorsey says. "You learn things like don't date the athletes you're covering. (You learn how to) carry yourself, the way to present yourself. You can't act like you're out there to snag a million-dollar husband. Don't go into interviews wearing a teeny, weeny leather miniskirt."

For experience outside school papers, Dorsey suggests that students string (serve as correspondents) for their community papers.

"Or when you go to watch a game, jot down some notes. Then when you write the story, see how it compares with what you read in the paper.

"I always think you can't learn too much," Dorsey says. "I think that at the same time though, you need to check out things on your own." ∎

CHAPTER TWELVE

WRITING EDITORIALS AND THE EDITORIAL PAGE

The newspaper editorial is often referred to as "the voice of the paper." It is up to the staff to make sure this description is accurate. It is not a simple task.

Everyone has opinions. The newspaper, when it expresses its opinions—or the radio or television station that offers opinion features and editorial voices—amplifies its voice by the number of readers or listeners. Therefore, when an editorialist speaks or writes, the responsibility weighing on his or her expression is extremely heavy.

In the past, student newspapers found little to editorialize about other than school spirit or the food in the cafeteria. Student editors were often told they should not editorialize on curriculum, athletics, administrative policy, school board decisions, or such issues outside the school as politics (local, state, or national), the environment, or the economy.

PEANUTS

Recent trends, however, are letting student journalists write about any issue of vital interest to their readers. And, if we are realistic, what issue should not be of importance to a real "student"? The very term implies the role of a seeker of knowledge, and that knowledge certainly is not limited by the walls of the classroom or the activity program. When student journalists are aware of their responsibilities as the voice of their school, the expression of viewpoints on whatever issue they select will be of high quality.

As a student journalist, you must never forget the need for research in developing an editorial. Too many student editors rush to their keyboards and pound out 200 words on a burning issue in the school or community, only to discover later that the inferno was really only a lighted match that quickly went out when the truth was known.

If the student is serious about taking on a major foreign policy issue, the positions of the President or candidates for any office, the dangers of pollution, or other meaty, worldly issues, he or she must do the homework necessary to express an informed, intelligent viewpoint.

As an editorialist, you should first become saturated with all the available information on the subject about which you will write. Then develop a strong conviction based on your research before writing an editorial viewpoint of about 200 to 500 words. (If the editorial is much longer you will be guilty of overkill and find readership dropping.) When the editorial has been completed, let it sit overnight. Take a look at it in the morning—you may see the need to start over.

Types of Editorials

There are many types of editorials. Any attempt to list them all will fail. However, following are ten major types or functions of the editorial.

Explain

A new policy on graduation requirements may have been issued over the summer. Your staff feels the system deserves clarification and an expression of support. Naturally, you probably will already have a news story on page one, but a writer is reporting the news, not commenting on it. You do this in an editorial. The following editorial explains and supports a new school policy.

Policy will sweep up truancies

By instituting the tardy policy last September, the RHS administration virtually eliminated tardiness to class and made significant progress in improving the attendance rate. But although this measure successfully fulfilled its basic intent, it did create excessive truancies, a problem compounded by the lack of an organized policy.

Discovering that tardiness results in harsh consequences whereas truancy bears no penalties, most students obviously found it easier to be truant rather than be tardy.

In the hope of countering this persistent problem, a committee of teachers representing various sections of the school met over the summer and formulated a plan to deal with the truancies. Diligently considering the input of counselors, administrators, and fellow teachers, it introduced a feasible and equitable policy which obtained unanimous support from the school board. The plan will take effect at the beginning of second quarter, Nov. 13.

Categorizing semester from quarter classes, this policy clearly demonstrates its liberality by having two separate provisions to deal with a student's failure to clear an absence within 24 hours of returning to school.

For semester classes, a student will receive parent notification on his second and fourth violations and will have to drop the class upon his fifth truant. Similarly, for a student taking quarter classes, the school will consult his parents after the first and second offenses, and he will have to drop the class on his third truant.

Once the student drops the class, the administration will send him to a counselor who will provide him with four options. These alternatives include a referral to Orangewood Continuation School, to the Redlands Independent Study Education (RISE), to Adult Education evening school, and to the new off-campus Alternative Study (for seniors) or to study hall (for juniors and sophomores).

Eliminating any extra hours a teacher may spend in keeping students after school, this policy also provides a more effective deterrent for truants than the lenient penalty of detention. Although seemingly severe to those continually absent from class, the policy is fair to all students by allowing them a number of chances before they have to drop a class.

By reducing the number of habitually truant students, RHS can improve its average daily atten-

dance and thus increase the amount of money it receives from the state for school purposes. Furthermore, by dissuading students from wandering off campus, this policy can lead to a decrease in vandalism, crime and disruptions and hopefully improve relations between the city and the school. Most importantly, it encourages higher education standards by insuring consistent student attendance. Teachers want their pupils in class, for truant students not only deprive themselves of the opportunity to learn but also impede the progress of the class as a whole.

No doubt, this supplement to the attendance policy will successfully prevent students from taking truancies lightly, discouraging them from opting for truants instead of tardies. With proper enforcement by the staff and cooperation from the students, the truant policy will surely improve the school through its beneficial results.

The above editorial reflects the opinion of the majority of the Hobachi staff.

Hobachi
Redlands Senior High School
Redlands, Calif.

Persuade

Maybe your school has just been forced to close the student lounge area because of the mess continually left by students using it. Your job might be to persuade the student council to appeal to the administration for a second chance, or to persuade the students to change their attitude toward the lounge if they want to keep it. Your editorial might take the leadership to spell out guidelines for reopening the lounge and supervising it through student service clubs. There are many issues within and outside the student world that require persuasive, responsible voices in order to help readers reach valid resolutions. The following editorial praises an action taken by the local city council and urges expansion of a summer jobs program.

Jobs on the ball

With the school year coming to a close and summer approaching, the City of Evanston must once again be alerted of the need to provide summer jobs for its youth. It is essential for the community to channel the energy of its kids into programs which will be positive and productive.

The City Council recently took a step in the right direction when a proposal was made to hire members of the ETHS basketball team to teach youngsters in a summer sports clinic.

The fact that the council is considering this proposal recognizes the fine effort that the basketball team members put forth this past season, and it is allowing them an opportunity to use their skills to benefit both themselves and the community.

One must realize, however, that the council's action can only be considered a first step. By awarding such a program to the team members, it is recognizing the outstanding achievements of only a small sector of the youth community in the city. If the council sees fit to acknowledge the accomplishments of a select few, then it has an obligation to expand this program in order to provide opportunities for youth who have excelled in many different areas.

Besides sports clinics and recreational jobs, ETHS students could be put to work in many other aspects of the community. The skills acquired by outstanding vocational students could be applied in different facets of city maintenance and office jobs. The artistically gifted student could be given work in city cultural programs and organizations, and those youth who excel academically could be given an opportunity to do work in city-run educational programs.

By hiring outstanding students, the city could save money on the cost of labor, curtail the problem of youth unemployment, give students an opportunity to train in an occupational situation, and perhaps even improve the quality of the work done by employing students who are motivated by their interests in these fields.

Consideration of giving employment to members of the basketball team shows that the city has already taken the first steps in providing more summer jobs for the youth of Evanston. Now the council must continue to move in the right direction.

The Evanstonian
Evanston Township
High School,
Evanston, Ill.

Answer

There has been criticism about your student delegation's conduct at a recent convention. Your job may be to answer that criticism in the form of a defense. Or, if the situations described are true, you may choose to answer the criticism with facts and admissions, along with an apology if appropriate.

Warn

An early warning might have kept the student lounge area open. An alert staff can see problems that lie ahead. Your reporters should know what is going on around the campus or school. They should be alert enough to pitfalls to predict difficulty for the educational community. The warning might be a strong one, or a mild one, more like a yellow light of caution.

Briefly comment

There are a number of situations about which opinion might be limited but in need of expression. Many editors will write an

Students reading an editorial recognize that the editorial is the voice of the newspaper, not just one person's opinion.

occasional potpourri editorial in which they comment briefly on a wide variety of subjects. They might commend the cheerleaders for the excellent rally, the team for its sportsmanship, the school board or trustees for the new school calendar or science facilities, or a scholarship winner.

Regularly comment

A regular editorial column written by one person with an interesting point of view can be an entertaining and educational addition to the editorial page. The writing is usually more personal, lively, and light. There is opportunity for satire. The writer should be capable of dealing with many topics and still project the same personality. A special skill of the editorial columnist is to convey, often lightly, a significant message through the treatment of a seemingly insignificant topic. For more on columns, see pages 222–225.

Criticize

If you look at some school papers as your weekly exchange comes in, it may appear that student editors think the word *editorial* is synonymous with criticism. They are not happy unless they have "really let 'em have it today." This is far far from the truth. A newspaper that continually finds only bad and evil in the world is doing a disservice to its readers. That paper is not helping to build a good community by constantly tearing at it. There is a place for criticism, but the editorial writer should know that place and use it wisely and correctly. When there is a need to criticize, do so. But be sure your criticism is constructive, or you will be guilty of the same thing of which you accuse others—an inability to do what is right or needed. Editorialists have a journalistic responsibility to balance criticism with suggestions and alternative courses of action. The paper that does not will find its readers no longer respecting its voice, if they continue to read it at all.

Praise

Student editors often forget that they can issue words of praise and congratulations through editorials. This may be due to a misunderstanding of the editorial role (traditionally interpreted as crusading fighter). People like to read praise for themselves and others they know. When a person or group does something worthy of praise, pass it on. Here again, don't overdo it and get sloppy in the process; we don't want to have to "break out the violins" while reading it. Sometimes, as in the following editorial, you can pass out roses for an outstanding performance.

Fee cuts aid clubs

By Lynn Gallagher

When students went through registration this year, they may have noticed the activity participation fee was changed from $20 per activity to a $20 fee covering all activities the student may wish to join.

This change was brought about by the School Board partly because the financial need of the school is not as great due to the passage of the referendum. "The Board really deserves credit for this," said Robert McBride, Student Activities Director and Assistant Principal.

McBride hopes that student involvement will be heightened. "I feel the one-time fee will help. It's an effort to engage more student activity," he said.

Some clubs that died after the $20-per-activity fee was instituted in 1984 may appear again.

McBride also feels the one-time fee will give an opportunity to begin new special interest clubs. McBride has made a recommendation to Associate Superintendent John Vanko for several new clubs including: French, Spanish, German,

Math Honor Society, Art Honor Society, Photography Club, and an academic team.

One of the new clubs students can choose from is the History Club, started by Diane Ring, history teacher. The club is a group of students who participate in history-related activities, such as going to museums, reading selected books, and watching historical movies.

With a current membership of 15 people, Ring said she doesn't know if the changing of the $20 fee had anything to do with membership.

She also said the extension of the fee was a great accomplishment. Ring said, "Having to make consecutive payments (for different clubs) could have obstructed some students' ability to join."

Three international activity clubs are underway. French teacher Sharon Soper is the French Club adviser. Spanish teacher Julie Harbecke is the Spanish Club coordinator. German teacher Mary Pold advises the German Club.

Becky Blaine, director of the

National Art Honor Society, opened the St. Charles chapter of the national organization this year.

Blaine "was aware of the honor society" and felt it would give people interested in art a group to belong to.

The $20 participation fee that covers all clubs and activities "has made it [enrollment] easier," Blaine said.

Although a national fee and a local chapter fee exist, Blaine hopes to use fundraisers to collect money for the fees.

The new activity fee is in accordance with the recommendation by the 1985 North Central Association Evaluation concerning the improvement of student activities.

Ginny Sebek, chairman, said, "The elimination of the $20 participation fee for all clubs and organizations will encourage more student participation, enable more special interest clubs to be established, and aid staff morale."

Junior Tina Mock and Kirin Kalia and Chris Lazarski, freshmen, also contributed to this story from X-Ray, *St. Charles, Illinois.*

Entertain

Your opinions on major issues may be a little forced from time to time. The alternative to forcing an issue might be to create a little humor through an entertaining editorial. Perhaps there was a humorous incident relating to a computer foul-up when your grade reports were issued; fifty student identification numbers got jumbled and a lot of failures appeared where there should have been pass grades or even A's. You can reconstruct the untangling, report other people's reactions, and comment lightly on the computer age. Entertaining editorials are not easy to write, but they are rewarding. You might find some good topics in fads and fashions, the weather at the last football game, or the mountain of forms needed to change classes or sections. Some entertaining editorials have clear morals and make a point more effectively than taking off the gloves and slugging away. Many editorial columns use this method.

Lead

A newspaper can create public reactions and build new programs. Many community newspapers have started the wheels turning to build freeways, recall local politicians, establish commissions or study committees, get schools built or streets beautified. Since a newspaper can magnify its voice and opinion greatly, it can become a force for change; it can provide community leadership. A newspaper has the obligation to seek to improve its community, and that is not accomplished through constructive criticism alone. Seek improvement and development. Granted, you will find obstacles, such as budget limitations. But student bodies have furnished their own lounges, built their own student centers, provided funds to build Peace Corps schools, landscaped their school properties, established minority or special scholarship funds, initiated laws, and done many other things without the leadership or financial assistance of the governing board. Many newspapers have brought together boards, parents, students, and community members to achieve goals. A newspaper that fulfills the leadership role wisely in its editorial policy will find itself widely respected.

Writing the Editorial

An editorial is only slightly different from a news story as far as the writing goes. Research your topic, then write a clear, concise, simply worded editorial. The idea is to reach your readers, to grab their attention with an important issue. After getting readers' attention, you want to carry them with you—smoothly, logically, and consistently—so they begin to think seriously about the issue you are presenting. Generally you can divide an editorial into three or four parts. Some will fit the general construction of a speech: introduction, body, and conclusion. The specific parts of an editorial are

1. *Introduction*—a brief statement of background concerning the editorial topic. Don't assume your readers already know the basis for your comment.
2. *Reaction*—the position of the editorial and your newspaper.
3. *Details*—support for the position you are taking.
4. *Conclusion*—comments on recommended solutions, alternatives, and direction, and a restatement of the paper's position.

Introduction

In the introduction you state, as briefly as possible, the background needed for the editorial:

> Last week the Student Council voted unanimously to close the student lounge areas because the students were not keeping them clean. Trash left from lunches or cleaned-out notebooks was found on tables, benches, floors, and in the hallways. Council members had placed warning signs and signs urging cleanliness throughout the areas for the past few weeks to no avail.

This introduction gives a brief history leading to an action. You and your readers are starting off together.

Reaction

Next comes the reaction. You set the reader up to receive your opinion. Continuing our example above:

> The Council action was justified and necessary. Not only do the lounges require costly time to clean, they are reflections on the school and the students' pride in it. A "who cares?" attitude toward maintaining the school's clean appearance could translate into a "who cares?" attitude toward scholastics, sports, and other activities that are sources of school pride.

Details

The reader knows your opinion, but you aren't finished. You now go into details that support your reaction and lead to a conclusion at the end of your editorial:

> The situation became evident several weeks ago when Council member Stephen Smith urged the Council to establish clean-up patrols to keep the lounge areas presentable and usable. The Council responded by appealing to the students' sense of pride, especially those who use the lounges. Signs were posted throughout the school in an effort to capitalize on this "spirit."
>
> Last month, Dr. Jane Roberson, student activities adviser, appeared before the Council and made an appeal at the honors convocation for students to clean up their mess in the lounges.
>
> All of these efforts and appeals evidently fell on deaf ears. The lounge areas are eyesores. We cannot take pride in such a situation. A picture appearing with a story on the lounge closing on page one of this issue gives the reader a view of the problem. We are sure you will agree—it is a mess.

Conclusion

You have established some background, expanding and repeating in some cases what you briefly mentioned in the introduction. Now conclude your editorial. You could end by saying, "Shame on you," or by applauding the Council's decision to take strong action. You could make an effort to lead, compromise, or appeal for a second chance. You may want to offer several alternatives and leave the options up to the Council or the student body:

> The paper urges the Council to conduct an open forum next week concerning the problem and to seek student suggestions on how the lounges might be reopened and kept clean. Among the issues students and Council members might consider are student clean-up patrols, as recommended several weeks ago by Council member Smith. It might be possible for several organizations to volunteer for a week of clean-up duty, spreading the job around and making more people aware of the need for cleanliness.
>
> While we agree with the decision to close the lounges, we cannot stand by and not urge the Council, the administration, and students to seek solutions for reopening the lounge areas as soon as possible.

Guidelines

In writing editorials you will find that not all subjects fit into this formula and you may find a better one, but it should give you an idea of the elements that help make an editorial a responsible voice of the paper. A newspaper must do more than just report the news and print advertising. It has the responsibility and obligation to print opinions that have been researched and are well thought out.

Keep these tips in mind as you write:

1. Be brief.
2. Be concise.
3. Come to the point quickly.
4. Be sincere.
5. Don't take yourself too seriously.
6. Don't preach—persuade.
7. Avoid all gossip or hearsay.
8. Admit errors—don't be afraid to change positions.
9. A little humor never hurt anyone.

If there is not enough time to do a good job of writing your editorial, wait until the next issue or don't write one. Remember, a newspaper editorial page is not a toy or a personal possession, and the student who has the title "editor" has no monopoly on good ideas for editorials.

In selecting your subjects, choose those important to your readers. Readers are not as likely to care about ecology in Australia and how pollution is plaguing Europe as about the smoke coming from the industry down the block or pollutants recently dumped into the local river. Just as in a news story, proximity and the other elements of news play an important role in determining editorial subjects.

If you select controversial subjects, don't write until you have done the necessary research; and don't be afraid to ask for outside opinions or criticism on your work before it is published.

No one likes to read a weak editorial or one that is unfair. Likewise, you should not ignore the existence of another viewpoint that may oppose yours, but you are not obliged to print it. Your letters-to-the-editor column offers the opposition a chance to reply. Be sure your editorial can withstand their arguments without engaging in a battle of "can you top this" with counter-letters and editorials. Let readers judge your editorial on its merits and the criticism it might get in light of those merits.

When you are through writing, ask yourself if you can summarize the entire point of your editorial in one or two sentences. If not, you had better start over or forget it, because you have missed the point—and your readers will miss it, too. Ask another staff member to read the editorial and write a one-sentence summary. Limit yourself to making just that one essential point. Don't try to save the world and solve all its problems in one editorial.

Remember, too, that editorials are not written in the first-person singular; never say "I." But do use "we" and "you." Develop an informal approach. An editorial should be read as a conversation between two people, the editor and the reader.

The Editorial Page

In addition to the editorial, there are a number of other components comprising the editorial page. These include columns, cartoons, letters to the editor, and opinion features.

Student journalists have broader options for developing editorial columns than their counterparts on the local newspaper. While people like Art Buchwald, William Safire, Ellen Goodman, Carl Rowan, and Jack Anderson are confined to editorial columns that usually deal with politics and government, the school columnist has an array of subjects available. Because of the limited space in your paper, columnists should be selected carefully and with variety in mind.

Opinion pages reprinted by permission of the *Journal*, the school newspaper of Parkersburg (W. Va.) High School.

Editorial Columns

A column differs from an editorial only slightly. It requires the same amount of hard work and research to develop your subject matter correctly. Give your readers enough background about the subject you select, and reason with them so they will accept your conclusions or opinions. Unlike the editorial, the column is not the voice of the newspaper; it is the voice of its writer only. Newspapers, however, seldom publish columnists who do not agree with the newspaper's editorial voice. For example, a newspaper that expounds on the Republican Party's virtues is not likely to hire a columnist who embraces the Democratic Party's line. In the student press this will probably not be a problem, especially since one of your newspaper's objectives is to express a diversity of viewpoints for your readers; you were not "hired" to express a viewpoint of a specific nature.

Avoiding gossip columns

Before going any farther, we should warn you that gossip columns, reporting all the latest rumors and who had the "wild" party last Saturday, are not responsible subjects for the school press. They are examples of the kind of writing that has been a major source of problems. In many schools they alone have been the reason for the paper's coming under tight supervision and limitations by the school's administration or journalism sponsor. And, as you already know, you are not immune to libel suits just because you are operating a school paper. All of your column's items should be in good taste and in keeping with the canons of responsible journalism.

Types of Columns

There are as many types of columns as there are prospective writers. Among some of the general types are:

Profile columns

A profile column centers on certain outstanding individuals—students, instructors, or people in the community. The writer discusses the individual's views on current topics and weaves into the column little bits about him or her: likes and dislikes, plans after finishing school, activities and community contributions. The column writer can take liberties in drawing conclusions or using phrases that would not appear in a news story or feature (such as "an outstanding sports record," or "a genuine concern for people").

There are some problems in this type of column, and you should have solutions to them. What criteria will you use to select the students you write about? In a large school the number of candidates for such an honor is considerable. You will get a lot of criticism unless you have firm standards. Do not use popularity as your standard.

You will also want to stay away from such details as the subject's favorite food, where he or she likes to go on dates, and whether he or she wears designer jeans. Unfortuntely, most profile columns resort to such trivia. Rather, ask about the subject's views on student activities, the value of being in sports, plans for the future, why he or she has made a particular career choice, how a teacher contributed to his or her success.

Fashion and fad columns

You may be really pushing it to try to write a good column on the changing world of styles very often during the year. An occasional fashion column might be refreshing if it is done with flair and some study of fashion trends. Some publications run columns like this with special issues containing several news features and advertising.

An occasional column about club activities in the school, such as a chess tournament, can add variety to the editorial page and give small, special interest clubs a little coverage.

(There is no rule that says a certain type of column has to appear in every issue you print. Some are seasonal and some should be occasional to prevent staleness. If the column isn't good, don't run it!)

In-the-clubs columns

A good way to give credit to clubs or student groups may be a "club" column. In it you wrap up a vast number of projects, urging attendance at a dance, speech, or other activity and inserting opinions about the projects being undertaken. An important note here: Don't ignore clubs that have only a few members, or the ones you aren't personally interested in. It is easy to write about the Letter Club, but it may take some work to come up with comments on the Computer or Chess Club. An occasional column of this nature might eliminate a lot of small stories that are of little value and weeks old.

Names-in-the-news columns

Another way to wrap up awards and pass out congratulations to officers, groups, or people who do nice things for your school or the student community might be through a column about people. Be sure this doesn't become a gossip column. Never make obscure comments; every reader should be able to understand what you're talking about.

Entertainment columns

Some school papers—when they can come out in time to be of value—write movie reviews or reviews of theater productions in the school or the community. The entertainment column could also review records. Often this type of column can be sold as paid advertising on a page other than the editorial page. However, be sure you don't get into a conflict of interest and lose objectivity because someone pays the bill or gives you records or movie passes.

Question-Answer columns

You are familiar with the Ann Landers and Dear Abby columns. Don't try them unless you are qualified to give advice of this type (and few people are). You might implement a question-line column, however; students do have concerns about which they would like answers. You naturally cannot do as comprehensive a job as the local paper can. But you can answer student-, career-, or community-related questions, such as "How do I enroll in a study skills program?"

Chicago Tribune columnist Mike Royko is known for his style—sometimes funny, sometimes slashing—always excellent.

Satirical or philosophical columns

These are probably the most common types of columns in the student paper. They take a lot of work and should not run unless there is a valid reason for writing the column. Like an editorial, it must be able to make its point to the reader; if it cannot, then it is probably of little value. Be careful to verify your facts.

Other ideas for columns

Look at other student papers and community newspapers for more ideas, such as hobby columns, sports columns (there is no law that says they have to be on the sports page), humorous columns, anecdotal or historical columns, or guest editorial columns—by famous people, other students, alumni, faculty, administrators, or parents.

We urge you to use the same approach toward writing any of these columns—research, develop your approach and position, write, think, rewrite if necessary, and then print—but only if it's good.

Letters to the Editor

The editorial page should always contain a place where readers can react to your opinions or comment on subjects that concern them. You would be guilty of monopolizing and stifling dissent if you did not allow space for letters to the editor.

A letter to the editor must be responsible, based on fact, and signed by the writer. You have an obligation to verify that the person whose name is on a letter actually wrote it. You may allow the use of pen names or initials but should keep on file for several weeks all letters you receive, whether you use them or not. If a letter is in bad taste or libelous, you are correct in turning it down. If you get several letters on the same topic, in order to save space, you may select one that is representative and add a note: ''We have received several similar letters from . . . .''

Editorial Cartoons

Just as a picture is worth a thousand words, one good editorial cartoon may be worth a thousand editorials. An editorial cartoon is usually simple in design, centered on one topic, *well* drawn (there is nothing worse than one poorly drawn), and timely. Usually it relates to a subject or event familiar to readers in their everyday life. It may tie in with the front-page news article or the lead editorial. In any event, an editorial cartoon is a valuable piece of journalism. The best advice we can give you is this: Be or find an artist, and be alert, like any good journalist.

Old toxic waste containers   New toxic waste containers

Opinion Features

An opinion feature is a feature story in which the writer expresses his or her opinions, makes interpretations, and draws conclusions for the reader. This type of article belongs on the editorial page rather than a news page and should be labeled ''Opinion Feature.''

Some people also interpret the opinion feature as a story wherein a number of people are asked to comment on a topic of current interest. An example of this is the roving reporter who asks five or six people, ''What do you think about the student right to conduct political rallies on campus?'' The views of the people interviewed are presented without further comment. *USA Today* uses this approach regularly.

Point-Counterpoint

If you study the editorial pages of leading newspapers, you will see a variety of editorial page elements. Many newspapers are adopting ways to broaden viewpoints beyond those of the staff and editorial writers. A popular technique is to use a point-counterpoint approach, inviting individuals with opposing views on a topic to express them in side-by-side opinion articles. Then, going a step farther, the paper may ask four or five people to give a one-paragraph opinion on the same issue, thus assuring that a variety of viewpoints have been expressed. Most often, the lead editorial of the newspaper—the newspaper's point of view—addresses the same topic. The reader is served through the variety of opinions expressed, and encouraged to look at more than one side of the issue.

Mini-torials

A mini-torial is a very, very brief editorial, usually one or two sentences. Like the editorial cartoon, it gets its point across quickly. It usually is written in a humorous manner but conveys a serious message. Readership is quite high, and several mini-torials in each issue accomplish much. It is also something to which all staff members can contribute on an equal basis.

Here is a series of mini-torials from *The Contact Lens*, a student workshop publication at the University of Nebraska:

Awakening Love

How do I love thee, All-State activities. Let me count the ways—one, two, threeee . . . . zzzzzzzzzzzzzzzz.

—Judy Thompson

Terse Verse
In all the world there's nothing worse
Than editorials set to verse.

—Michelle Grady

Oh Bring Back
To solve the poverty problem, the Federal funds must be brought back from outer space and used in the inner cities.

—Marcia French

Running, Riding
There's one thing wrong with the idea of people who jog. They are usually the ones who drive two blocks rather than walk them any other time.

—Joe Hermsen

Open Up
There is a serious problem confronting the world. Why do people lock up their minds and refuse to stimulate themselves with the ideas of others?

—Debbie Rosenwinkel

Responsible Editorials

The editorial page is a vital force in American journalism. In the student press, it can be a force for constructive development and opinion formation, or it can be a fun-and-games page people casually read and dismiss.

Most journalists think of themselves as editorialists. But not all journalists realize the tremendous degree of responsibility that goes with the right to express editorial viewpoints. You have the ability to make or break a project or program, to influence the degree of acceptance of a new policy, or to lead changes in existing policy. The choice will be yours and that of your fellow staff members. Most student publications do have responsible editorial pages. A statement of editorial policy, such as the one following, can set the tone of an editorial page.

Editorial policy named

Hi-Spot members will, at all times, be working under the code of ethics that has been set down as journalistic standards. Freedom of the press, honesty, accuracy, impartiality, decency, and equality will be used to benefit reporter and story subjects. Never will a statement be considered true just because an accusation is made.

All editorials will reflect views that are backed by research and fact. Questions on story content, editorial policy and controversial issues will be interpreted by the executive board which will consist of the editor, managing editor, photography editor, page editors, business manager, advertising manager, and adviser.

Hi-Spot editorials will never be by-lined because they represent the ideas of a part of the staff with whom others may disagree. The **Hi-Spot** will protect the rights of any person submitting editorials. The executive board will decide when editorials are suitable for publication.

All letters to the editor will require a signature (or signatures) of those who submitted them. The names may not be published but pen names will be substituted upon request of the writer. Again, signatures are required on the original for the protection of the **Hi-Spot**.

Speak-outs and letters to the editor are encouraged from staff and non-staff members alike. All letters must be signed and turned in to the mailbox provided in the journalism room (room 18S) or to a **Hi-Spot** staff member. The **Hi-Spot** reserves the right to edit all letters, with regard to libel, without changing the substance of the letter. The **Hi-Spot** also reserves the right not to publish any letter for incriminating reasons or that person will be given a chance to respond in the same issue. The **Hi-Spot** will not publish obscene or libelous material; rulings will be made by the executive board.

Money for the publication of the **Hi-Spot** will come from advertising sales. No ads are to appear on the cover page nor the editorial page.

In accordance with Nebraska law, staff reporters may not be required to show a completed story to the source for the source's approval. If a question comes up about a story, the source will be contacted to verify information and direct quotes.

The **Hi-Spot** will not reveal a minor's name in a story (a Nebraska minor being any person under the age of 19 years old) who attends Waverly High School and is involved in a felony crime. But the **Hi-Spot** may include the name of students involved in misdemeanors serious enough to stimulate permanent expulsion from Waverly High School.
Hi-Spot
Waverly High School
Waverly, Neb.

While we have spoken primarily about the editorial page and opinion function of the newspaper, you can draw parallels for editorial opinions on radio and television. The writing style is usually more concise, and the writer must remember at all times the limitations and advantages of the medium he or she is using.

Wrap-up

Editorial opinions play an important role in today's media. Along with the opportunity journalists have to express opinions comes the obligation to do the needed research. You must understand the major points of view and background on an issue before you write the paper's or your personal position.

Editorial page commentaries, in the form of editorials, editorial opinion features, mini-torials, cartoons, and various columns, serve a variety of functions. They may *explain* an issue; try to *persuade* others to support your viewpoint; *answer* positions of others; *warn* or caution readers, viewers, or listeners about events ahead; provide *brief comments* on a current situation; *criticize* or *praise* an action or event; *entertain*; or provide leadership by initiating or encouraging action.

When writing an editorial, begin with an *introduction* to ensure your audience understands the background of your subject. Then, clearly state the *position* you are taking. Following that, provide clear and concise *details*, or background materials, that strongly support your position and address directly or indirectly the possible positions of others. *Conclude* your editorial by restating your position and indicating your recommendations or possible solutions.

Some editorials are signed with the writer's name. This is particularly the case when the editorial policy states that editorials are the opinions of the writer, not the newspaper. An unsigned editorial usually is interpreted by readers to be the position of the paper, not just the writer.

Newspaper editorial pages consist of a number of elements: editorials, editorial columns, editorial cartoons, opinion features, and point-counterpoint features expressing diverse views on a specific subject. Mini-torials, short one- or two-sentence commentaries stating a strong position on a well-known topic, are useful editorial elements in many publications. And, you are probably familiar with the brief opinion sections in some newspapers, such as *USA Today*, which use photos of several individuals giving their opinions on an issue of the day. Elements like this, along with letters to the editor and guest editorials and columns, help open the opinion pages of the newspaper to the readers.

Student publications should develop and communicate their editorial policies to their readers, and should provide ways for those with differing positions to respond to editorials and other opinion features. The editorial pages should stimulate thought and discussion and help resolve important issues facing your readership.

To ensure that they serve the important functions for which they were intended, editorials require as much homework and research as news, sports, or any other form of journalism.

On Assignment

Teamwork

1. Your team is to be an editorial board setting editorial policy. After careful discussion, write out an editorial policy for your school newspaper on a major issue, such as raising or lowering

the legal age for drinking alcoholic beverages; endorsing political candidates in the next election; endorsing candidates for student offices; requiring that no student activities, such as pep rallies or athletic events, be allowed to interrupt the academic schedule. Be sure you include the reasons for your decision. Compare your policy to those of other groups. Discuss and resolve differences on similar topics. Now, write an editorial that expresses the position of your editorial board.

2. Working as a team, develop a new look for the editorial page of your school newspaper. Prepare a mock-up, cutting similar elements from your newspaper and exchange or local newspapers to show the visual image you are after. Write a brief essay on your team's approach, explaining why you chose your design.

Practice

1. To test your critical thinking, write an essay on each of these questions:

   How appropriate is it for a school publication that is partially financed by public funds to endorse candidates for public office? To endorse candidates for the board of education? Should all editorials express the position of the newspaper, or only of the writer? Should they be signed?

2. Research the most recent elections in your community. Many people feel that the candidates the media endorse have an edge over their opponents. Find out who was endorsed by the newspaper. Find out who, if anyone, was endorsed by your local radio or television stations. Did those individuals win? Interview the candidates who won, the candidates who lost, and the editorial writers to determine how important they believe the endorsement was. Now write an editorial that expresses your personal position on this subject.

3. Using the following information, write an editorial:

   A citizen's task force has proposed to your board of education that the school year be expanded from 180 to 200 class days beginning next school year. This will require starting the school year August 10 and ending July 1. Teachers would start a week earlier and end their duties July 15, after a short break for the Fourth of July.

   The calendar would allow for eight days off for the Christmas–New Year period, one day each for Memorial Day, Labor Day, Martin Luther King Day, Presidents' Day, and Columbus Day, two days for Thanksgiving, and five days for teacher workshops.

   The task force chair, William G. Thoughtful, president of the chamber of commerce and owner and president of University National Bank, said that the task force was unanimous. "Our major concern is that we are falling behind in all test scores and there is not enough time to teach important science, math, computer, writing, and English skills. Our only other alternative would be to eliminate all nonacademic programs in order to provide more instruction."

The board president, Sharon Chandler, said: "This will increase local taxes by over 20 percent in order to cover increased salaries and operating expenses. We will also need to initiate an immediate bond election for $20 million to air-condition the rest of the schools."

Employee representatives all welcomed the proposal but expressed concern over how teachers would be allowed time to take classes for their own advancement and to keep up-to-date in their subjects.

Membership on the task force included two board of education members, the superintendent, the president of the chamber of commerce, two representatives from each employee group, the local state senator and representatives, and a dozen local residents—including some who have students in school, senior citizens, and non-parents. No students were represented.

A decision will be made at the next board meeting.

4. Using the last issue of your school newspaper, identify all of the elements of the editorial page. Now, examine the news content of the same issue.

Are there background stories to provide information on the topics covered in the editorials? If so, clip and mount them.

What evidence do you find that the writers of the editorials did their homework? Write a paragraph to explain your evidence.

Does the editorial explain, lead, entertain, answer, persuade, warn, criticize, praise, or briefly comment? Write a paragraph explaining your decision.

Mark the four parts of the editorial: introduction, reaction, details, conclusion.

Rewrite one of the editorials, taking a different approach and an opposite position. Mark the four parts of the editorial on your copy.

5. Invite the local newspaper editor to visit your class and explain how editorial decisions are made. Ask him or her to discuss: Does the newspaper use an editorial board? What is the reporter's role in editorial decisions? What is the role of the publisher

or owner? Who actually writes the editorials? What kind of homework does the editorial writer usually do?

6. Compare the editorial pages of your local newspaper, your school newspaper, *The Wall Street Journal*, and *USA Today*. What are the differences in the elements used? Is more than one page used? Are editorials signed? What types of columns appear? Make a chart showing the contents of each one. Analyze the differences you find. Why do they exist? Clip the editorial pages to your essay.

Your Turn

1. Using the last issue of your school newspaper, clip five news, sports, or feature articles and mount them on separate sheets of paper. Now, write one or more mini-torials for each story.

2. Make a list of editorial summary sentences on which you would like to write. Submit the ideas to your teachers who will select one topic. Write the editorial. Mark each key section on your copy. At the top of the page, identify the type of editorial you wrote.

3. Assume you have total freedom to select a type of editorial column you want to write for the school paper. Prepare a list of five topics that fit the category you have selected (for example, fashion, profile, entertainment). Your teacher will select one for you to write.

4. Submit a list of five topics for an inquiring-reporter opinion feature to your teacher who will select one for you to write.

5. Write an editorial on the topic: The student newspaper should not write articles or editorials on non–school-related topics. You may support or oppose the statement.

6. Working in pairs, select a controversial topic of current interest to other students. Each of you should take an opposing point of view. Write editorials expressing your views. Then, ask six non-journalism students to write a one-paragraph summary opinion on the same issue without telling them your positions. Discuss in class how these viewpoints differ, the pros and cons of stimulating discussion through this technique, and how the views of the students compare to those of the editorial writers. Would you change your editorial positions after hearing the discussion? Why or why not?

Richard Cohen

Richard Cohen has no idea how he got interested in newspapering. "That's the honest answer," the *Washington Post* columnist says when you ask him. Then a pause. "Now I'll have to start making stuff up."

Such is the life of the local columnist, always wondering what you'll come up with for your next column: creating something three times a week. No one tells you what to do.

It's not like sitting around the newsroom as a general assignment reporter, Cohen said. "No one turns to you and says, 'Cohen, there's a fire at 14th and U, go cover it.' "

But Cohen has covered his share of fires.

The New York native took college classes for nine and a half years before graduating from New York University. "You name it, I did it," Cohen said. That included sociology, psychology, and journalism.

"I always wanted to write," the columnist said. "It was a question of finding someone who'd pay me to do it."

He free-lanced as an undergraduate, worked as a copy boy for the *New York Herald-Tribune*, worked for United Press International in New York City, got a master's degree in journalism at Columbia University, and, in 1968, landed a job with the *Washington Post*.

Covering politics and education, being an investigative reporter and a general assignment reporter, knowing cops and courts—all those are essential to being a columnist, says Cohen.

"I don't think you could go into it (column writing) thinking this is what I want to be," he said. "You have to have some scar tissue . . . . you have to have some experiences, an understanding of what's going on."

The *Washington Post*'s local column initially was intended as a platform for comment on local and political matters. But Cohen says he frankly didn't think it would work.

The Washington metropolitan area, unlike Mike Royko's Chicago or Jimmy Breslin's New York, is divided into numerous independent political subdivisions and is "full of people who came to Montgomery County (Maryland) from Albany," Cohen said. It lacks a central political figure to tie the area together. It has a basically suburban, highly educated, middle-class population and racial divisions that affect how people perceive things, he says. In short, Cohen saw no sense of community, an essential ingredient of many of the great urban columnists' work.

"You get someone [to be a columnist] and he does what he wants," Cohen said. "I try to focus on what I think concerns people, what people are talking about."

Although he worries less than he once did, Cohen said he still doesn't find writing the column

easy. He added, "It's more successful than anyone imagined . . . ."

To Cohen, the biggest advantage of being a columnist is working for yourself. You set your own hours. You write for your readers, not for an editor.

"I think about my column obsessively, unhealthily," he said.

Although many columnists started out as reporters, not all reporters write well or even enjoy writing. But to be a columnist, Cohen noted, "you have to get a kick out of writing.

"A column is one idea," he said, "sometimes just one line. Your writing has to carry it."

Cohen thinks it's a bad idea for anyone to aspire to become the local newspaper's version of Mike Royko or Jimmy Breslin.

"Royko is Royko. Breslin is Breslin. If you're going to do this, be yourself," Cohen said. "Don't try to do Breslin. Try to do yourself. Find your own style, your own voice. Learn how to relax at the typewriter and be yourself."

"And once you figure it out, let me know how it's done." ∎

Ed Fischer

When Ed Fischer sits down to draw an editorial cartoon each evening, he doesn't stare at a sheet of clean paper and wait for inspiration to strike.

"It's something that's intuitive," the cartoonist for the *Rochester* (Minn.) *Post Bulletin* said. "I don't think anybody can explain how you come up with ideas."

But the ideas come to Fischer because he prepares carefully for that two-hour stint when the idea is transformed into words and pictures.

Fischer wouldn't last long at his job if he didn't prepare carefully, since there are only about ninety jobs for full-time editorial cartoonists at daily newspapers in the United States.

He browses through newspapers, reading national and local news stories. He keeps up with what other cartoonists are doing in those publications, too.

By late in the day, he has picked the general topic he feels is the day's most important news event. Then he watches the evening news shows on television.

Only then can he put his wit and artistic talent to work.

"I think every cartoonist has the urge to sit down and put his or her fantasies in graphic form. But an editorial cartoonist has to make a point," Fischer said.

Although he never earned a degree, Fischer attended classes at three colleges. "I always took things that were related to art and journalism, and that's what cartooning is—a combination of both," he said.

He was also drawing cartoons the whole time, contributing 200 to 300 cartoons at the daily student paper at the University of Minnesota.

With so few cartooning jobs, Fischer began his career in advertising, a field that is "really kind of related," he said. He was coming up with ideas and making drawings to "get through to the common person."

All the while, though, he pursued a cartooning job.

The *Minneapolis Star* began to buy cartoons from him after the paper's cartoonist took an interest in Fischer's work. Soon he was selling the paper three cartoons a week.

His first full-time job was editorial cartoonist for the daily newspaper in Tulsa, Okla. After three years, he moved to an Omaha paper, where he was drawing as many as nine cartoons a week.

"The big things I can offer the paper," he said, "are things that are area-wide, state-wide, or city-wide. I really think those are my best cartoons. Everybody can relate to them. There is a lot happening, really, in your own area. . . ."

Fischer said, "There are some really great cartoonists who are not syndicated. Most jobs today are held by people who are paying attention to what's happening locally. Kids who aren't paying attention locally are in trouble."

He said he once thought the future of cartooning was in the proliferation of weekly newspapers, many of them in suburban areas. He now thinks the future may be in television.

With so few jobs on daily newspapers, Fischer admits prospects aren't all that bright. "It's very difficult to get into this profession, but it's not impossible," he said.

Sometimes just being able to poke fun at someone is its own reward. "Even if they don't go on to be editorial cartoonists, they can have a lot of fun with it," he said, referring to high school and college cartoonists.

Even though he likes to make a point, Fischer said, "I like to make people laugh." So he doesn't always try for biting satire. Once or twice a week, he'll do something a little softer.

But he wouldn't want to do that too often. "Plenty of editorial cartoonists are doing the wish-washy. They don't make a point," he said. ∎

SECTION
FIVE

Producing the School Newspaper

EDITING AND LAYOUT

A publication's goal of getting the news to its readers is only partly achieved when all the reporters have turned in their copy. There remains the editing process, an often unglamorous but extremely important side of news work. The people on the staff involved in this process are copy editors. On small staffs, of course, everybody does everything. Editors edit *and* report; reporters write *and* edit, although never their own work.

It is the copy editor's job to prepare the copy for the typesetter if the publication has not yet adopted desktop publishing technology. If it has, the copy editor edits the story on screen (frequently a Macintosh), codes the copy, writes the headline, and places the story on the page. Once the page has been designed, it can be taken to a printer for platemaking or be zapped to the printer by a modem.

The copy editor's job is vital because if an error has crept into the reporter's copy, it almost certainly will get into the paper unless the copy editor catches it. The copy editor is the last line of defense; what gets past the copy desk gets into the paper.

Copy Editing

The copy editor must be a master of the stylebook. (Do we refer to a man as Mr. Jones or just Jones, after first reference? Do we hyphenate *re-election*?) Reporters certainly should know style rules, too, but their primary job is to get the facts. The copy editor's job is to polish. Copy editors have to know the rules of grammar, spelling, and punctuation. They need to know whether the history instructor's name is Anderson or Andersen. Every scrap of information, no matter how trivial, that the copy editor can jam into his or her head may come in handy at some point. Copy editors must have a good memory and must know how to locate information—in standard reference books, for example.

In addition to making the reporter's copy agree with the stylebook in terms of punctuation, capitalization, abbreviations, spelling, and the use of titles, the copy editor must also catch repetition, dangling modifiers, misplaced pronouns, subject-verb agreement errors, and a whole list of other grammar and sentence structure problems. Very important, too, are matters of organization. The copy editor may change the order of elements in a story to create a more logical style and to make the story read more smoothly.

The traditional tools of the copy editor once included soft pencils, scissors, glue, an up-to-date dictionary, a style manual, a

The copy editor today works with a pencil as well as a computer.

directory of students and teachers, and a community telephone directory. A more modern tool is a computer or a desktop publishing system with visual display terminals on which editors can call up a given story, correct and rearrange it at the touch of a key, then store it for later editing or transmittal to typesetting equipment.

Copy editing is vastly different from reporting; the copy editor has to be content with processing the creative work of others. This is not to say that editing isn't creative. It is, very definitely, but in a much less obvious way than a great lead by a reporter. Copy editors are usually anonymous; they rarely get credit.

Copy editors also need excellent judgment and the ability to make fine distinctions in taste and word usage. They must have an ear for rhythm and an understanding of reporting and writing too, because a copy editor should never change anything in a story except to improve it. Slavish adherence to rules—any rules, whether of style or of structure—can lead to editing that harms the copy rather than helps it. If a reporter writes a story in unconventional fashion, selects sentence fragments for impact, injects acceptable humor—and can defend doing so—the copy editor should not tinker with it.

Copy Editing Symbols

Most school publications now use desktop publishing systems that have greatly simplified the mechanical—though not the intellectual—problems of copy editing. The gluepot, scissors, and paste have, for the most part, gone the way of quill pens and manual typewriters. Few people mourn their passing. The copydesks of commercial newspapers used to be messy places. No more. Editing workplaces today are bright and clean.

Some school publications, however, still find themselves preparing copy with pencil and paper and then handing over the material to a commercial printer. This brief section will be helpful to staffers at such publications.

This section considers the symbols copy editors use as they work—the signals, if you will, that they put on the copy that tell typesetters and printers, or whoever is handling the strictly mechanical phase of publication, what to do. Every time someone forgets to capitalize a proper noun, for instance, the copy editor can't write a long note pointing out that such-and-such a word on such-and-such a page should be capitalized. Instead, the copy editor simply puts three horizontal lines under the first letter of the word, and the typesetter knows to capitalize it.

The basic symbols follow.

Copy Editing Symbols

Indent for paragraph	⌐ or ¶
Insert a letter	. . . she told the crod . . .
Lower case	. . . he Ran with the ball . . .
Capitalize	. . . the student council also . . .
Delete and close up	. . . the studdent council also . . .
Delete and close up	. . . he ran with the the ball . . .
Delete and close up	. . . Tech won it's ninth title . . .
Abbreviate	. . . occurred at 9 No. 10th Street . . .
Delete and close up	. . . the life-saving equipment . . .
Spell out	. . . 7 persons were arrested . . .
Insert a dash	. . . 17 persons all under 21 wore . . .
Set in numerals	. . . thirty-seven fled the scene . . .
Spell out	. . . the gov. Tuesday told . . .
Transpose letters	. . . the footabll coach said . . .
Insert a hyphen	. . . a well dressed person will . . .
Transpose words	. . . was also chosen . . .
Insert a word	. . . something was out . . . left
Separate words	. . . they arrivedon Tuesday . . .
Insert period	. . . he said But Jones . . .
Insert comma	. . . never again she said . . .
Let it stand: ignore copy mark	. . . this is wrong . stet
Center	⌐Copyright 1992⌐
Set flush right	By the Associated Press⌐
Set flush left	⌐By the Associated Press
No paragraph	no ¶ . . but not until then. Later, however, she said . . .
Insert quotation marks	. . "Get out," he said . . .
Insert apostrophe	. . . its always like this . . .

Here is how a piece of copy looks after it has been edited:

A torrential downpour friday forced the forty-seven members of mrs. Smith's Geology class to call off their fieldtrip.

the group has asembled in the North parking lot at dawn but could not make it across the pools of water that had been formed by the tremendous rainfall.

We'll have to hold it next week," said Mrs. Smith. She added the reason for the trip was to locate fossils in an old riverbed sixteen miles from Town.

Senior Tom Johnson received a brake from the rain. He overslpt and would have missed the busy anyway.

The Copy Editor's Work

If all of the millions of words written about the art of copy editing had to be condensed into one short sentence, that sentence would be: *Make sure it's accurate.* Copy editors do many things, but their most essential function is to watch for mistakes.

An interesting thing about mistakes is that to the reader involved, the smallest mistake may appear enormous.

Good editors must know how to spell. Here are the correct spellings of some of the most frequently misspelled words in the English language:

a lot	cemetery	develop
accordion	committee	dormitory
Albuquerque	computer	dilemma
auxiliary	consensus	embarrass
buoy	defendant	embarrassed
calendar	definite	existence
category	dependent	extension

fiery	nickel	restaurant
fluorescent	niece	seize
fulfill	ninety	separate
governor	occurred	sergeant
guerrilla	paraphernalia	sherbet
harass	pavilion	sheriff
hemorrhage	Pittsburgh, Pa.	siege
homicide	plagiarism	silhouette
judgment	questionnaire	subpoena
lieutenant	receive	suppress
missile	recommend	weird
misspell	rescind	wield
mustache	resistance	yield

A relatively harmless error, like identifying someone as a freshman instead of a sophomore, casts doubt, for that sophomore, on every other fact in the paper. Mistakes cost credibility; they make people doubt us. If Fact A is wrong, maybe Fact B is too. The reader wonders, "If they got my address wrong that day I was in court for a traffic violation, how do I know they're not wrong about a million other things?"

For checking spelling, as all computer-wise people know, spell-checking programs are a blessing. But they're dangerous, too. Spell checkers won't alert you to a word that is just wrong. For example, if you want to refer to guerrilla warfare and instead write "gorilla warfare," your spell checker will sail right past it. There's a famous story of a reporter who listened to a speech about euthanasia and then wrote about "youth in Asia." Humans, not spell checkers, have to catch those kinds of mistakes.

Fact Checking

The key to maintaining accuracy in your news columns is having a staff of competent copy editors. One of their secrets is knowing which facts to check. Obviously there is not time to check every detail in every story, because you must meet a deadline. So copy editors develop a sense, a suspicion, about certain kinds of things.

For instance, they pay special attention to stories with numbers. Does the lead say six students won scholarships, but the story lists only five names? Does the story mention four federal grants to the school totaling $3,600 and then provide figures that add up to only $3,000? Does the story say teacher salaries are going up 3 percent and then name a teacher getting a 15 percent pay increase? In all these cases something is wrong, and it is up to the copy editor to find out what it is and to correct it.

Accuracy also involves special attention to names. Copy editors should not assume that the usual spelling is the correct one. They must check: Is it Patti or Patty? Smith or Smyth? Hansen or Hanson? Curtis or Kurtis? It is never safe to guess. The same is true of titles. Is a person assistant superintendent or associate superintendent? Counselor or chief counselor? People are proud of their titles; they usually represent years of hard work, and having them come out wrong can hurt.

Special attention also must be given to stories involving police activity and morals. If you incorrectly involve someone in a crime or in any way suggest that his or her moral standards are less than they should be, you will be in deep trouble very fast. High school newspapers do not usually deal with stories of this nature, but they might. The copy editors who work (process) these stories must be extra careful.

Cutting

Copy editors have other jobs besides catching inaccuracies. They must make sure the story conforms to newspaper style (see the sample stylebook in the Appendix). It makes no sense to spell out a word in one story and abbreviate it in the next. Although style is arbitrary, consistency is everything. The whole staff must observe house style.

The copy editor watches for loose writing and tightens it up by scratching out excess words and by substituting single words for phrases. For example, a sentence like "The field of journalism offers many challenges" should be changed to "journalism is challenging." "At the present time" becomes "now," and "he continued by saying" is changed to "he added." Trivia is edited out.

The copy editor smooths rough passages in the copy, often by cutting long sentences into short, simple ones. For example, this sentence is badly in need of repair:

> Appointments are now being made for students wishing to interview for the positions of managing editor, news editor, sports editor, feature editor, and editorial writer now open on the staff of the *Banner,* according to Mr. Jones, journalism adviser.

That's certainly too much for one bite. So the copy editor makes the repairs:

Students wishing to work on the *Banner,* Central High School's student newspaper, are being asked to make interview appointments, said John Jones, journalism adviser.

Positions open are those of managing editor, news editor, sports editor, feature editor, and editorial writer.

Now the reader can say it and breathe at the same time.

Spelling and Grammar

Grammar, spelling, and punctuation must be checked. Although copy editors need to be good spellers, they must also be habitual users of the dictionary. Don't guess; look it up. And watch those reporters for careless things, such as this common error:

The committee voted to turn over their profits to the council.

Their profits? "Committee" is singular and "their" is plural, so the sentence is not grammatical. Change "their" to "its." An alert copy editor will not let such mistakes get by.

Almost all sentences in the story should be in the active, not passive, voice. If the sentence said, "Suggestions are wanted by the student council," the copy editor changes it to "The student council wants suggestions."

A skilled copy editor relies on her dictionary when in doubt about the spelling of a word.

Organization

Organization should be checked in the editing process. Is the best material at the end of the story instead of near the top, where it belongs? Is something referred to in the lead but not mentioned again until the twelfth paragraph? Does the next-to-last paragraph belong somewhere else? In these situations the copy editor makes the changes.

Typically it works this way, although computer systems vary: First, the editor places the cursor—a flashing rectangle of light—on the paragraph to be moved. Second, he or she taps the appropriate key (marked ''move'' in some systems), and the paragraph disappears into the computer—sort of on hold. Then the editor moves the cursor to the spot where the paragraph belongs and taps the ''move'' button again. Presto! The paragraph reappears, in the correct location.

Attribution

Attribution, providing the source of the facts in the story, is another area that often needs to be checked. Many reporters provide attribution in the lead and then never mention the source again, leaving the reader to believe that the opinions are the writer's—which should not be the case. In such circumstances the copy editor goes through the story and puts in all the necessary ''he saids,'' ''she saids,'' ''he addeds,'' ''she pointed outs,'' and so on. The reader must know at all times whose opinion is being expressed or where the information came from.

When all the corrections have been made, the copy editor goes over the story one more time, reading it for sense, for total effect rather than for mechanical problems. The editor takes the role of the reader and asks, ''Are all the questions answered? Is it clear? Easy to read?'' If the answer in each case is yes, then this phase of the copy editor's job is finished. It is now time to write the headline.

Writing Headlines

Headline writers face what seems a nearly impossible task. From perhaps 500 words of copy in a story, they must select three or four or five that tell the entire story. And they must do it according to a rather strict set of rules. The headline form is by far tougher than, say, a Petrarchan sonnet.

The headline's job is to lure the reader into the story. But it must do it honestly; the headline can't promise something that isn't in the story. It should be lively and interesting, with sparkling verbs. It must cram as much information into those words as possible, since readers tend to scan headlines looking for something of interest. When they do, they should be able to pick up some information they would not have otherwise.

Type Size

So let us begin at the beginning. Glance at a newspaper and the first thing you are apt to notice about headlines is that they vary widely in size. Headlines, or heads, are measured by *points*. A point is $1/72$ of an inch high. Thus, a 72-point head is 1 inch high, a 36-point head is $1/2$ inch high, an 18-point head is $1/4$ inch high. This measurement system is transferable to any newspaper anywhere. Body type, the type the story itself is set in, is usually 8-point or 9-point. The really small type you see on market pages and in baseball box scores is called agate, and is usually $5^1/2$- or 6-point type. The copy you are reading now is 10-point type.

The smallest headline usually is 12 points high. From there it goes in specified gradations: 14, 18, 24, 30, 36, 42, 48, 54, 60, 72, 84, 96, and on into the really large type saved for truly fantastic events.

Width

Headlines vary in width and number of lines as well as in type size. A headline may be anywhere from one to six columns wide if you have a six-column paper. If it's a four-column paper, then obviously that is the maximum width. Most headlines are one, two, or three lines long. Occasionally they may be four or five lines long, but only for special effect.

Editors have a definite system of referring to these dimensions. A busy editor cannot constantly be telling copy editors to write, for example, a 3-column, 36-point, 2-line head. Instead the editor uses shorthand and asks for a 3-36-2. The first digit specifies the width (3 columns), the second the size (36 point), and the third the number of lines (2). Thus, a 6-84-1 would call for a very large, six-column streamer, or banner, all in one line.

Headlines are typeset in various ways. Some are centered.

This Is a Centered Head

A few are "stepped," or given a kind of stairstep effect.

This Head
Is Shaped
That Way

Most newspapers these days use the flush-left system. A flush-left headline rests squarely against the left-hand side of the column.

This Represents
Flush Left

Other less common variations exist, but students may seek them out themselves. There is also an infinite number of typefaces, that is, the style of type a newspaper uses. These range from Gothic—the medieval-looking, elaborate type many newspapers use on their nameplates—to script, type that resembles handwriting. The typeface used in your newspaper is determined by what your typesetter offers or—if you have desktop publishing—what font is available with your software.

Making It Fit

The next step is making the headline fit. An editor who says he or she wants a 3-column headline means it, because headlines cannot go beyond their allotted space. You can't have headlines breaking through the right-hand margins, poking into another area; they must fit. On most systems, the process is simple. The editor writes a headline and then taps a button that commands the computer to decide if the headline fits. If it doesn't, the offending line may break apart on the screen, or the part that is too long may change color. Either way, the editor knows and can start over.

Before this technology was developed, starting over meant finding different words so the headline would fit. Today, the journalist has the option of *slightly altering* the size of the type. When type was really type—pieces of metal—a 36-point head had to be 36 points. You can't squeeze or stretch metal. But computer-generated type can be altered. Thus, depending on the system you're using, if your 36-point head won't fit, you can make it 35.9 or 35.8. Some commercial newspapers permit individual editors to make a decision to squeeze the type. At others, that decision has to be made by a desk chief. And no one permits anyone to squeeze a head more than two points. That 36-point head can't go below 34 points because large changes in point sizes, done by copy editors, can spoil the careful work of page designers.

At newspapers with less sophisticated equipment, a system once used at virtually every newspaper in the land is still effective. Journalists have assigned a numerical value to each letter of the alphabet, based on the letter's width. Notice how much fatter a capital M is than a small i; or how much fatter a capital W is than a small t. These variations in width complicate headline writing.

Newspaper Headline Schedule

Headline writers refer to this schedule to determine headline unit counts. For example, a 3-column, 36-point headline has a maximum unit count of 28 under this schedule.

18 pt.	Roman/Italic 1 col/18	The Quick Brown Fox Jumped Over *The Quick Brown Fox Jumped Over*
24 pt.	Roman/Italic 1 col/14	The Quick Brown Fox Jun *The Quick Brown Fox Jun*
30 pt.	Roman/Italic 1 col/11 2 col/22	The Quick Brown Fo *The Quick Brown Fo*
36 pt.	Roman/Italic 1 col/9 2 col/18 3 col/28	The Quick Brown *The Quick Brown*
48 pt.	Roman/Italic 2 col/14 3 col/21 4 col/29 5 col/36	The Quick B *The Quick B*
60 pt.	Roman/Italic 2 col/11 3 col/17 4 col/23 5 col/29 6 col/35	The Quick *The Quick*

Two words, both with, say, five letters, can vary a great deal in width. For example, in headline type, the word "mommy" is a great deal wider than the word "title." To compensate for these variations, headline writers use the numerical system. It is called the unit count system.

Unit Count System

Letter	Count	Letter	Count
Capital I	1	Spaces	1/2
Capital M, W, O	2	Numerals	1
All other capitals	1 1/2	The numeral 1	1/2
Lowercase j, l, f, t, and i	1/2	Question mark, dash	1
Lowercase w and m	1 1/2	All other punctuation	1/2
All other lowercase letters	1		

Capital Letter	Count	Capital Letter	Count	Lowercase Letter	Count	Lowercase Letter	Count
A	1 1/2	N	1 1/2	a	1	n	1
B	1 1/2	O	2	b	1	o	1
C	1 1/2	P	1 1/2	c	1	p	1
D	1 1/2	Q	1 1/2	d	1	q	1
E	1 1/2	R	1 1/2	e	1	r	1
F	1 1/2	S	1 1/2	f	1/2	s	1
G	1 1/2	T	1 1/2	g	1	t	1/2
H	1 1/2	U	1 1/2	h	1	u	1
I	1	V	1 1/2	i	1/2	v	1
J	1 1/2	W	2	j	1/2	w	1 1/2
K	1 1/2	X	1 1/2	k	1	x	1
L	1 1/2	Y	1 1/2	l	1/2	y	1
M	2	Z	1 1/2	m	1 1/2	z	1

Suppose you have been asked to write a 2-36-2, with a maximum count of 16. First you write:

Fifteen Seniors Win
University Scholarships

Under the unit count system, the top line counts 17½ and the bottom line 21—too long. So you try something else:

University Cites
15 AHS Seniors

The top line is 14, the bottom 14—and that is close enough. You may not violate the maximum count, of course, and you should be no more than two counts short.

Style

Those are the mechanics. Now let's turn to the writing itself.

First of all, headlines are written in a telegraphic style. All extra words are trimmed. The articles *a, an,* and *the* usually are left out.

Wrong: **The School Has Won**
            a High Rating from State
Right: **School Wins High State Rating**

Headlines are also written in present tense to give readers a feeling of immediacy.

Wrong: **Tigers Defeated Tech, 7–0**
Right: **Tigers Defeat Tech, 7–0**

Occasionally a story about something historic will crop up, and then the past tense is acceptable. For example: Vikings, Not Columbus, Discovered America. Headlines about future events are written with infinitives to indicate future tense: 360 Seniors to Graduate Saturday.

Punctuation in headlines usually involves just three marks: the comma, the quote sign, and the semicolon. When part of a headline is enclosed in quotes, a single quote (') is used, not a double quote(''). Thus, it is: Coach Calls Tech 'Best Team We've Faced' rather than: Coach Calls Tech ''Best Team We've Faced.'' The reason is that single quotes save space. The semicolon is used whenever a period seems appropriate:

Bush Announces Freeze;
Congress to Discuss It

A comma is used in place of the word ''and.'' It is, Smith, Jones Win Scholarships, not Smith and Jones Win Scholarships. The period is never used except in abbreviations, such as U.S. Exclamation points are used only rarely, and then for good reason; their value is debased if they are used very often.

There are other considerations. Most newspapers prefer not to use headlines that split infinitives, like this:

Smith to
Go Abroad

The verb is "will go," and it is best not to split from one line to the next. The same is true of names:

Jim Williams, Jane
North Win Elections

Try to get "Jane North" all on the same line. It is also not acceptable for a line to end in a preposition, like this:

Smith Critical of
America's Journalists

Each line should be a coherent unit by itself, and such splits do not help.

Parts of the verb "to be" also are to be avoided generally. It is, 15 Seniors Chosen; not, 15 Seniors Are Chosen. Lively, active verbs attract more attention than the dull "are."

Headline writers should also avoid repeating a word in a headline. Avoid this, for example:

Student Council to Discuss Student Rights

As for capitalization, most newspapers use "down style." That is, all letters except proper nouns and the first letter of the first word are lowercase, or down. Such a headline looks like this:

Library offers amnesty
on all overdue books

If you decide to use a style with capital letters, you may either capitalize prepositions and articles or leave them uncapitalized. Both ways are acceptable, though the latter is preferable.

Aside from all these considerations, the headline writer must cultivate a special vocabulary of short words, such as "panel" for "committee," "kin" for "relative," "blast" for "explosion," "cuts" for "reductions," "quits" for "resigns," and "named" for "selected."

The headline writer should also cultivate a sense of humor. For reasons that are not exactly clear, many newspapers like headlines with a certain wry twist. For example, when the Los Angeles Dodgers lost out in the National League division title competition, the *Los Angeles Times* headlined it in Porky Pig fashion:

Th-Th-Tha-Tha-That's All Folks!
Dodgers Miss

The Omaha (Neb.) *World-Herald* published a story about the tongue-in-cheek annual contest for people who think they can imitate Ernest Hemingway's writing style. The headline recalled Hemingway's novel *The Sun Also Rises:*

The Fun Also Rises

When the governor of Illinois verbally attacked one of his opponents, the *Chicago Sun-Times* told it this way:

Says the Governor: & + ?(!

The *New York York Times* had this headline:

Harvard Crew Not Resting on Its Oars

Puns are considered particularly appropriate. The play on words often is a handy way to tell a story:

Phone Users Have No Hangups
New Spray Bugs Farmers
Three Booked in Library Dispute
Hikers Can't See the Forest
for the Wheeze

Finally, these words of caution: use alliteration sparingly. A little of this—Tigers Tame Tech Team; Teachers' Tests Trigger Trauma; Bartered Books Bring Big Bundle—goes a long way. The same is true of verse. Unless it's really good, toss it out. The job is, as always, to convey information, and cuteness can get in the way.

Newspaper Layout

Newspapers today look a lot different from those published just four or five years ago. Nearly all daily newspapers (except those more traditional ones like *The Wall Street Journal* and the *New York Times*) are using large and dramatic color photos, spot color, colorful weather maps, strong art, and graphics. Much of this change came about through the pioneering of *USA Today*. Many doubted that this paper would last or that the experiment to make a national newspaper would be accepted by the public. But it has. And its dramatic use of graphics, photos, art, and color have had an impact on all aspects of print media.

Even more dramatic is the impact of desktop publishing. Computers are changing the way newspapers are written, edited, designed, and laid out. Nearly all aspects of *USA Today*, for example, are completed on Macintosh computers. More and more high school and college publications are now prepared for printing on some form of computer. Whether the system is sophisticated enough to handle complete page design and graphics, or merely is used to prepare copy in camera-ready galleys for pasteup, there is little question that technology is changing the way newspapers look. In fact, these days anyone with a computer can be a publisher.

Desktop publishing not only saves money but also allows you the opportunity to experiment. Try it. We will provide some guidelines for page design, but, like all rules, they are meant to be stretched. Who says a newspaper has to have six column—or four—or two? Who says it has to be rectangular? Has anyone tried a round newspaper? Why not design your newspaper to follow a magazine format?

Remember, you need to learn to walk before you run. Once you do that, you can determine which design rules to stretch or break and which to follow. In chapter 20 on new publishing technology, you'll read more about desktop publishing.

Making the Dummy

The traditional process of page design is known as "dummying." This is because the editor lays out the page on a dummy, which is nothing more than a blueprint or map for the printer to follow. (In the case of desktop publishing, of course, layout is done on the display screen.) In regard to the traditional layout or dummy on page 256, notice the dummy is smaller, proportionally, than the actual newspaper page. The true size of each item is indicated using picas for photos or art and using the shorthand method of noting column width, point size and number of lines of the headline for news stories. Promotional items and the flag are indicated by the word "promos," as you can see.

The principles upon which layout decisions are based are our concern here. These are the generally agreed-upon guidelines:

1. Simple, uncluttered design is better than complicated design.
2. Consistency from issue to issue is an aid to the reader.
3. Headline faces should be harmonious and headline style consistent.
4. Large pictures look better than small ones.
5. Headlines of equal or near-equal size should not be placed beside each other. (This is called "tombstoning.")
6. White space aids the reader, so provide plenty of it, perhaps by eliminating the column rule or using a flush-left head style with flexible minimum counts.
7. Page design should indicate to the reader which story or stories the editor considers most important. Put the biggest headline on the most important story, and put that story on the most important part of the page.
8. Pages should be neither top-heavy nor bottom-heavy. Place "heavy" elements, pictures and stories with large headlines, strategically around the page to create a pleasing effect. Strive for balance—or a relaxed unbalance.
9. Ornamentation should be kept to a minimum. Fancy or cluttered column headings and the like distract the reader.
10. A lot of long lists or tabular material (box scores, for example) can ruin a page.

Position of Stories

The reader looks first at the upper left-hand corner of a front page, yet many newspapers continue to place their most important story in the upper right. There is no reason for this except tradition,

Laying out or dummying pages should be guided by the basic guidelines of newspaper design.

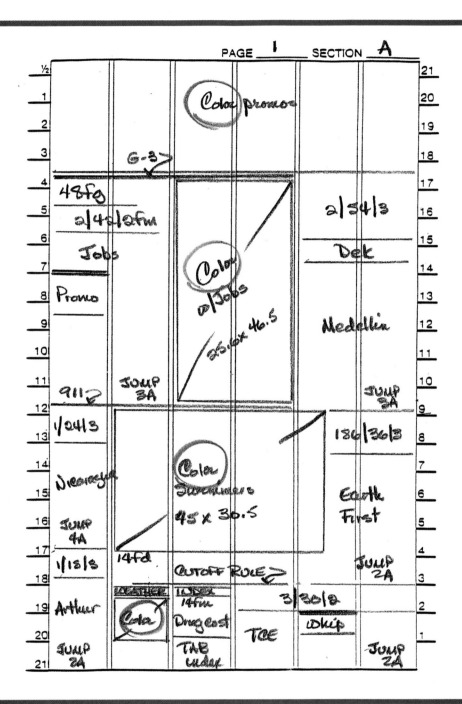

Traditionally, editors design pages on a dummy, or ''blue-print,'' for the pasteup person to follow. In the dummy above for the *Arizona Daily Star* shown on the right, observe how photos and jumps are indicated and how the various page elements are labeled.

THURSDAY

'Goatwalking'
Jim Corbett turns author
—Accent, Page 1C

High-tech bed
Patient can take control
—Health & Science, Page 9A

He has a dream
Toro owner wants to build
— Sports, Page 1D

The Arizona Daily Star

©1991 The Arizona Daily Star

Vol. 150   No. 171 ★   Final Edition, Tucson, Thursday, June 20, 1991   35¢   46 Pages

Working

County unemployment reaches 34-year low

By Richard Ducote
The Arizona Daily Star

Pima County's unemployment rate last month hit a 34-year-low of 3 percent, down one-tenth of a percentage point from the April level, state economists reported.

Not since layoffs were coming out of Detroit has the Tucson area seen a lower jobless rate.

The Pima County jobless rate has not been lower since July 1957 when

Coming Monday in Moneyplus

A jobless rate of 3 percent does not necessarily indicate a vigorous local economy, experts say. In Monday's Moneyplus section, the Star will take a look behind the statistics.

It stood at 2.8 percent, according to analysts for the state Department of Economic Security.

And the latest figures available show that of 271 metropolitan areas around the country, only 12 had unemployment rates lower than those in Pima County, DES reported.

State analysts said it was not job growth last month, but rather a sharp decline in the number of unemployed people, that accounted for Pima County's unusually low May jobless rate.

There were 800 fewer unemployed people counted by DES in the county last month, down 8.1 percent from the previous month.

People can fall off the jobless rolls several ways, DES economists say, including finding a job, leaving the area, or simply quitting a formal job search.

Since January, the number of unemployed people tracked by DES in Pima County has declined from 12,100 to 9,000.

The unusually low jobless rate reported for May was greeted by one economist as another sign of an improving economy in the Tucson area.

University of Arizona economic forecaster Marshall Vest said the jobless figures confirm that "the worst is clearly behind us" for the Tucson economy.

Pima County has had "decent" job growth in the last year, Vest said, which has helped keep jobless rates low.

"Unemployment rates have been consistently low here (in recent years) even though we think our economy is somewhat sluggish. But you clearly can't look at only one statistic to give you a full picture of the economy."

DES reported yesterday that although jobs actually decreased by 200 in Pima County between April and May, over-the-year job growth was 6,660 jobs, or a relatively healthy 3.7 percent. That was nearly double the statewide average of 1.4 percent for the same period.

In the state's job and population center, Maricopa County, the unemployment rate also fell last month to

See Working, Page 3A

Unemployment
May 1990 - May 1991

Arizona 4.6%

Pima County 3.0%

M J J A S O N D J F M A M   M J J A S O N D J F M A M

Elsewhere in Arizona

County	Rate	Previous month	County	Rate	Previous month
Apache	12.1%	13.4%	Maricopa	3.8%	4.0%
Cochise	8.9	8.1	Mohave	5.2	6.4
Coconino	6.3	8.3	Navajo	9.2	8.9
Gila	7.6	7.3	Pinal	6.5	6.7
Graham	6.2	5.7	Santa Cruz	10.3	12.8
Greenlee	4.4	4.4	Yavapai	4.7	5.0
La Paz	7.7	6.4	Yuma	15.5	14.1

Total employment statewide

1.64 million

In millions

1.70
1.65
1.60
1.55

M J J A S O N D J F M A

Source: Arizona Department of Economic Security; previous months figures are revised amounts

Judy Margolis, The Arizona Daily Star

Medellin head gives up; era of peace seen

Alleged drug lord in custody hours after extradition ban

By Joseph B. Treaster
© 1991 The New York Times

Pablo Escobar Gaviria, one of the world's most violent drug traffickers, surrendered to authorities in Colombia yesterday hours after an assembly writing a new constitution voted to ban extraditions of Colombian criminals.

Colombian officials said Escobar, 41, a multibillionaire, was picked up by helicopter at an undisclosed location and flown to a luxurious prison that had been especially prepared for him in his home town of Envigado, near Medellin.

Escobar, a leader of one of the biggest cocaine smuggling organizations, is believed to have ordered the killing of hundreds of Colombians, and Colombian officials said they hoped his surrender would usher in an era of calm.

But U.S. officials and many Colombian drug specialists said they doubted that the jailing of Escobar would significantly reduce the flow of cocaine to the United States and the rest of the world.

The officials said they expected he will either continue doing business from jail or be replaced by others in the enormously lucrative trade.

Escobar, who issued no statement

yesterday, said in late May that he was preparing to give up in exchange for a promise from President Cesar Gaviria Trujillo of lenient punishment and no extradition to the United States, where he is facing 10 indictments for drug trafficking and murder.

His surrender came hours after the constitutional assembly voted to ban extradition entirely. Some Colombians had speculated that, as insurance against a change of heart by the president, Escobar had been delaying giving up until the edited 74-member assembly took its long-expected action, which was opposed by U.S. officials. The vote was 51-13, with the rest abstaining.

Escobar, who was reportedly wearing camouflage military fatigues and dark glasses, was accompanied on the helicopter by the Rev. Rafael Garcia Herreros, 82, a Roman Catholic priest who mediated the surrender in a series of meetings and shortwave radio conversations beginning in late May.

"I'm so happy for Colombia," Herreros told radio reporters. "I think the country will now enter a new era of peace."

At least three other members of Escobar's organization, widely

See SURRENDER, Page 3A

Ortega talks of war again in Nicaragua

MANAGUA, Nicaragua (AP) — Former President Daniel Ortega warned yesterday that war could return if the legislature repeals a giveaway that enriched thousands of his Sandinista followers.

Sandinista sympathizers held at least six city halls and three radio stations in a protest against the proposed repeal.

The occupations continued after a night of bombings that rocked a Sandinista radio station and the headquarters of several pro-government parties. No injuries were reported and damage was minor.

Ortega, a major benefactor from the Sandinista giveaway, warned a repeal would bring retribution against deputies in the National Assembly.

"The (Sandinistas) and all honest Nicaraguans have the unavoidable

See ORTEGA, Page 4A

Jean Arthur dies; film star of '30s, '40s

CARMEL, Calif. (AP) — Actress Jean Arthur, who began her career with small parts in silent western films and went on to starring roles as an urbane, witty comedian in Hollywood hits of the 1930s and '40s, died yesterday. She was 90, a friend said.

Arthur, who had lived in the Carmel area about 35 years, died at Carmel Convalescent Hospital, said Ronald Stein of the Paul Mortuary of Pacific Grove. She was 90, according to Peter Wright, a retired banker who was a friend and financial adviser. Some reference books put her age at 82 or 85.

Arthur and Jimmy Stewart starred in Frank Capra's 1939 classic "Mr. Smith Goes to Washington," with Arthur playing the savvy political

See ACTRESS, Page 2A

Evaporative cooling
It may have hit 105 degrees yesterday, but it was still breezy enough to send a chill through these wet swimmers

at Archer Pool. It will be breezy and hot once again today, with an identical high near a sizzling 105.

Ron Medvescek, The Arizona Daily Star

'Ecoterrorism' charged, denied at Earth First! trial

By Douglas Kreutz
The Arizona Daily Star

PRESCOTT — Five radical environmentalists, acting as self-appointed defenders of the planet, engaged in "ecoterrorism" and had fun doing it, a prosecutor contended.

But defense attorneys maintained that FBI undercover agents were the real terrorists because they tried to coax the environmentalists into wrongdoing.

Those sharply opposed views of reality emerged yesterday in opening statements by attorneys at the Earth First! sabotage and conspiracy trial in U.S. District Court in Prescott.

Defendants in the case are Tucsonan Dave Foreman, a co-founder of the militant Earth First! group, and Prescott residents Peg Millett, Ilse Asplund, Mark Davis and Marc Baker. Foreman severed his ties with Earth First! last year, citing philosophical differences with West Coast members.

The five defendants are charged with conspiring to sabotage nuclear power and weapons plants in Arizona, California and Colorado.

A federal indictment also accuses them of cutting bolts on a ski-lift line at Fairfield Snow Bowl near Flagstaff, sawing down power poles at the Canyon Uranium Mine south of the Grand Canyon, and trying to topple Central Arizona Project power lines.

The government's case is based heavily on information gathered by an FBI undercover agent, who infil-

See TRIAL, Page 2A

WEATHER

Continued hot. Today is expected to be sunny and breezy with southwest winds of 10 to 20 mph. Look for the high near 105, and an overnight low in the upper 60s. Yesterday's high was 105, and the low 68. Details on Page 11A.

INDEX
What the users spent

Accent	1-4C	Horoscope	3C
Bridge	8C	Money	8-9B
Classified	3-10D	News summary	2A
Comics	2C	Obituaries	9D
Comment	12-13A	Public records	4B
Crossword	9D	Sports	1-7D
Dear Abby	3C	Tucson today	1C
Dr. Gott	2C	TV	3C

Southside residents come out in force to support reopening of TCE lawsuit

Illegal-drug cost. The office of the nation's drug czar estimates that Americans spent roughly $40 billion last year on illegal drugs. That reflects a decline from the estimated $49.8 billion spent in 1989 and $51.6 billion the year before, a report says. Page 4A.

By Keith Bagwell
The Arizona Daily Star

Thousands of southsiders hoping to reopen a federal lawsuit over TCE pollution of their water packed the El Pueblo Neighborhood Center last night.

A lawsuit filed in 1985 was settled out of court earlier this month for $84.5 million. Lawyers distributed checks to nearly 2,000 plaintiffs on June 8.

But Rose Marie Augustine, presi-

dent of Tucsonans for a Clean Environment, sponsor of last night's meeting, said possibly thousands of others were left out of the suit.

"A lot of people with illnesses, some who speak little or no English, and many children were left out of the suit," Augustine said. "A lot of people didn't know about it or how it worked."

She said her group has found Tucson attorneys who are interested in trying to reopen the case. "Nobody will be turned away this time, although we'll have to screen the forms after they come in," she said.

Augustine said her group passed 2,000 to 3,000 one-page forms for the potential new plaintiffs to fill out, giving their names and addresses and brief descriptions of their illnesses.

All the forms were handed out last

See TCE, Page 2A

now that reader eye movement has been so well established. Put the main story in the upper left. The reader's glance will go from there to the upper right, then to the lower right, then to the lower left, and then in a circle to the middle of the page.

Note that the reader's glance stops at each of the corners, so place something particularly interesting in each corner. Have a picture or a spread head (a head of two or more columns) in each such spot to "anchor the corners." Anchor the bottom, too. Too often editors let their front page trickle into nothingness at the bottom, with lots of little stories but nothing to keep the reader's attention there.

Headlines and Photos

Headlines should reflect in their size the length or importance of the stories they are over. Stories of one, two, or three paragraphs rarely take a headline larger than 18-point. Middle-sized stories, from about four paragraphs to nine or ten, take headlines no larger than 30 or 36 point. Longer stories take larger heads.

Photographs should be used to break up masses of type that otherwise become gray and unappealing to the reader. The photos should be linked to the story they illustrate. Don't let the subject of the photograph look away from the story, because the reader's glance will follow the direction of the subject's eyes. Tie the elements together. Photo captions, or cutlines, should be short and to the point, and should avoid duplicating material that appears in an accompanying story.

Stories should always be directly under their headline. Don't let them run from under the head, because this is especially difficult for the reader to follow, and the job of page design is to make it easier for the reader to get information.

Placing the Flag

The name of the paper and the information included around it (date, edition number, and so on) is called the flag. There is no reason why the flag has to be at the top of the page. It can go anywhere above the fold, which is an imaginary horizontal line across the middle of the page—in other words, where it's folded. Moving the flag around on the page from edition to edition is known as "floating the flag." Commercial newspapers sometimes use this technique. Floating works best if the flag is smaller than the width of the paper. If you have a six-column paper, the flag ought to be four or five columns wide; you don't want to stretch from side to side unless it's at the top of the page.

School newspapers today are visually appealing, with more use of color, magazine design technique, and design variation, due in large part to the advances of desktop publishing.

Page Design

Most modern newspapers prefer horizontal makeup, which means that they use lots of headlines wider than one column so that the general "movement" on the page is from side to side, not up and down. Before 1900 most newspapers used vertical make-up; some modern newspapers still do, such as *The Wall Street Journal.*

Horizontal makeup has the advantage of guiding the reader's glance in a natural left-to-right movement. It also makes stories seem shorter (and, therefore, easier to read) than they really are.

When handling page make-up, the editor must compile a list, called a schedule, of everything planned for each page. The editor must know how long each story will be and the size of each picture. Copy can be converted to inches in type this way: Seven lines of typewritten, double-spaced copy equal two inches of type, provided you are using a traditional newspaper column of just under two inches wide and the copy is prepared in the usual fashion.

Sometimes the occasion arises to do something really different with page design, such as a special edition or feature section. Today magazine style layout has become an option for newspaper design. One of the latest trends is the centerspread, such as the one below from *The Journal,* the newspaper of Parkersburg (W. Va.) High School.

Wrap-up

The editing process at a newspaper is unglamorous but extremely important. Copy editors prepare the copy for the typesetter or edit it on-screen, doing the coding and headlining before placing the story on a page.

If an error is in a reporter's copy, it almost certainly will get into the paper unless the copy editor catches it. The copy editor is the last line of defense.

Copy editors must master the stylebook and check stories for proper punctuation, capitalization, abbreviations, and spelling. Stories sometimes are reorganized by editors. Copy editors need good news judgment and must make fine distinctions in taste and word usage. They are anonymous, however. Few newspapers give bylines to copy editors.

Copy editors use traditional editing symbols at schools that have not converted to desktop publishing.

The biggest task facing copy editors is watching for mistakes. There is no such thing as a small mistake; all mistakes undermine a publication's credibility. Copy editors pay special attention to stories with numbers, often re-checking reporters' arithmetic. Names, which must be correct, also receive extra attention.

Stories are trimmed, attribution smoothed, grammar repaired. Then editors write headlines. Some schools continue to use the traditional headline unit count system, although most headline writing today is on-screen. In either system, headlines have to fit their allotted space and writing them can be difficult.

Most school publications use desktop publishing systems that greatly simplify the mechanical—though not the intellectual—elements. Editing workplaces today are bright and clean.

Much change has occurred in newspaper design and there is room, especially with modern equipment, for great creativity and inventiveness. Some principles remain. Design should be simple, uncluttered, and consistent. Pages need to be balanced, pictures played large, and white space emphasized.

Placement of stories indicates to readers which stories are most important. The upper left-hand corner of a page attracts the reader first. Corners cannot be neglected.

Headlines and photographs break up the type and reduce unappealing gray masses. Today most newspapers use horizontal makeup.

On Assignment

Teamwork

Take the stories your team wrote for your in-depth reporting project and minor sports coverage project. Brainstorm ideas to illustrate them. What photos or drawings would be effective? Prepare a layout for one page in your school paper. Block the spaces for art or photos. Write the headlines. Edit all the copy and measure it. When the teacher returns it, keep it handy. You'll soon take and prepare the photos!

Practice

1. Edit unnecessary words from the following expressions:

assembled crowd of people	during the winter months
brown colored cloth	was completely destroyed
set a new record	played a small, cameo role
hot water heater	a small-sized child
soothing balm	made advance reservations
personal friendship	was of circular shape
in the city of Chicago	his future plans
the present incumbent	her future prospects
an actual fact	told his listeners
spoke on the topic of football	unsolved problem
for a period of three weeks	specific example
every single year	official government document
was completely decapitated	past history

2. Edit the following sentences to conform to the stylebook in the back of this book. Use correct editing marks.

They decided to move to Fla.

Beautiful weather is forecasted for the rodeo.

The soldiers were trained at Ft. Bliss.

She was an employee of the Federal Bureau of Investigation.

This quiz will effect your grade.

His salary was upwards of $35,000 a year.

They lived at 1010 Sycamore Avenue.

She was sixteen years old on her last birthday.

She has written 9 books and 22 songs.

Lt. Governor John Smith poured over his books.

The Sierra Nevada Mountains attract good skiers.

The boy, nine, ran across the St.

Soon this quiz will be past history.

They were from Saint Louis, Missouri.

I'm from the federal govt., and I'm hear to help you.

The troops often employed gorilla warfare tactics.

The group will review their decision January 2.

The cars collided headon.

Future planning helps you pass quizzes.

The principle, Mr. Smith, addressed the assembly.

3. Provide the correct abbreviation (if any) for each of the fifty states, according to the AP-UPI Stylebook.

Alabama	California	Florida
Alaska	Colorado	Georgia
Arizona	Connecticut	Hawaii
Arkansas	Delaware	Idaho

Illinois	Montana	Rhode Island
Indiana	Nebraska	South Carolina
Iowa	Nevada	South Dakota
Kansas	New Hampshire	Tennessee
Kentucky	New Jersey	Texas
Louisiana	New Mexico	Utah
Maine	New York	Vermont
Maryland	North Carolina	Virginia
Massachusetts	North Dakota	Washington
Michigan	Ohio	West Virginia
Minnesota	Oklahoma	Wisconsin
Mississippi	Oregon	Wyoming
Missouri	Pennsylvania	

Your Turn

1. Find shorter (headline) words for the following:

Agreement	Inform	Defeat
Prevent	Argument	British subject
Schedule	Question	Small child
Decline	Decision	Tornado
Former	Resign	Bridge
Criticize	Examine	Capture
Charge	Consider	Injure
Commission	Victory	Relative
Promise	Prejudice	Sister
Advocate	Demonstration	Brother
Increase	Destroy	Quarrel
Attempt	Silent	Fight
Vicinity	Robbery	Movie

2. Brainstorm this question: If you had no concept of what a newspaper was, and someone told you to design one, how would you go about it?
3. Rewrite five headlines from the latest issue of your school paper. Make each one a column narrower and then a column larger than it originally appeared in your paper.
4. Examine sports headlines and headlines over feature stories and on the editorial page. How do they differ from the spot-news or front-page headlines? Why? Write a short essay on your findings.
5. Carefully clip apart all of the elements from the front page of a local newspaper. Rearrange these elements in a different format. Discuss layout variations as a class.

6. Go to the library and look up the microfilm of old issues of your local newspaper or some national newspaper with which you are familiar. What changes have taken place in the design of those pages? Write about your findings.

7. Look at three newspapers from across the country on a given day, and notice the different treatment given each story. Note also the amount of local news on the front page. What does this say about the newspapers' definition of their audience? What about the news elements? Write about your findings, attaching the newspapers.

CHAPTER FOURTEEN

Using Photographs Effectively

Good photographs can enhance your publications in numerous ways. They are the means by which a newspaper, magazine, or yearbook can *show* readers what is happening as well as tell them. Photographs "humanize" a publication. They enable readers to see how people involved in news and sports events felt and reacted. Pictures also enable a publication to establish its own "look," or identity.

Functions of Photographs

Before you begin taking pictures, you should be aware of the six major functions photographs fulfill. They are

1. **Capturing attention**

    This is extremely important for newspapers and magazines, which rely on photographs to attract readers. Newsstand sales depend to a great extent on the impact of the photographs on the front page or cover.

A good photograph compels potential readers to look at it. Once people have examined the picture and read the cutline, they usually look at the rest of the page, then flip through the remainder of the publication. A newspaper or magazine that consistently runs good photos can build readership based on pictures alone.

2. **Providing information**

   Pictures that stand alone give readers the essence of a situation at a glance. They show readers what is happening, where it is taking place, and who is involved. Pictures that accompany stories offer readers additional information about major points in those stories.

3. **Providing entertainment**

   Photographs that are humorous or lighthearted give readers a lift. They provide a break from the straightforward, serious content that dominates most publications. Editors know that readers need such a break. This is why so many newspapers and magazines devote space to pictures that will make people smile.

4. **Establishing links with readers**

   Establishing emotional and psychological links with readers is important because readers identify strongly with publications that appeal to their hearts and minds. Photographs help publications do this in three ways. *First*, pictures give readers the sense of being there. They make readers feel as if they are watching or taking part in what is occurring. This lends a sense of immediacy to the publication.

   Second, because pictures show readers the feelings and reactions of the people involved in events, they appeal to the basic part of human nature. People are interested in how other people feel. In recording the range of emotion—joy, sorrow, fear, anger, pity—photographs frequently communicate feelings more effectively than words can.

   Third, photographs appeal to readers' emotions by evoking memories of past and expectations of future experiences. A picture of graduation can make people wistful. A picture of children playing can make them happy.

5. **Acting as a layout device**

   Photographs break up large gray areas of type. They make a publication more attractive and easier to read. Photographs also help lead readers' eyes from one part of the page to another. Promoting this kind of eye movement helps ensure that readers will look at the entire page. This is a principal function of page layout.

6. **Helping establish an identity**

   Newspapers and magazines develop a certain look through their use of photographs. Publications that use large, dramatic pictures tend to look streamlined and modern. Those that use smaller, less dynamic pictures look more staid and traditional.

Discussing the photo assignment and planning carefully result in an effective photograph for a news story.

Photo Assignments

Many publications have a photo department. The photo editor makes assignments after consulting with other editors, and supervises the work of the photographers. The photo editor also participates in layout decisions and oversees photo selection.

Some school publications do not have sufficient staff to have a separate photo assignment editor. Photo assignments are usually handled by the editor-in-chief or managing editor, and the reporters also may work as photographers.

Regardless of how your paper is staffed, photo assignments usually are developed the same way. They are discussed at the same time as story assignments. Editors decide which stories require photos because of their importance, and which lend themselves to photographs simply because they are visually interesting.

For example, a story about an arts and crafts fair may not be worth a major article, but the editors may want a photographer to cover the event simply because it offers numerous possibilities for good pictures. The published piece may be the photos with cutlines only. This is often referred to as a photo-cutline story.

Editors also discuss ideas for "wild art," pictures that run without stories. These photos are usually feature-oriented. They are published principally because they are entertaining and catch the readers' attention. The first snowfall on campus or an unusual-looking car owned by a student are possible subjects for wild art.

After the list of story and photo ideas is prepared, photographers are assigned. The editor gives each photographer background on his or her assignment and discusses how it might be photographed.

If the assignment is not for wild art or a photo-cutline story, the photographer should discuss it with the reporter. The more they work together, the stronger the story and photo ''package'' will be. The photographer needs to know what story angle the reporter is going to take and what points he or she expects to emphasize. The photographer can then take pictures that illustrate these points.

The photographer can give the reporter another point of view about how the story might develop. He or she may also know something about the story that the reporter doesn't.

Photographers should research background before going on assignment. By reading previous articles about the subject in both school and local publications, they will take better pictures and write better cutlines.

Preparing cutlines is almost always the photographer's responsibility. The photographer must keep track of who is in each picture, how subjects' names are spelled, and to what organizations they belong.

Pictures with Impact

From one perspective, photographs can be divided into two groups: those that look professional and those that look amateurish. The difference is impact. You don't have to be a paid professional to create pictures with impact. To get dynamic, effective photographs, follow these basic guidelines.

Get Close

Get as close as you can to the subject. There's a saying in photojournalism: ''If your pictures are not good enough, you were not close enough.''

The people or objects you are photographing should fill the entire frame. Most pictures should be taken within seven to ten feet of the subject; some should be even closer. You generally should not have more than three people in the picture. If you try to include more, you will have to get too far away. Readers will not be able to see what's going on in the picture.

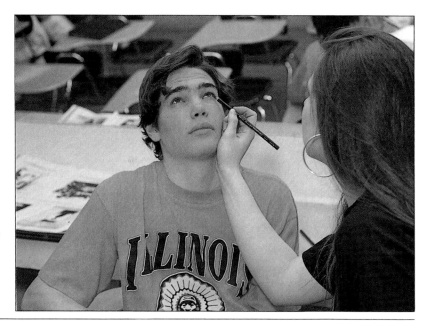

Photographs like this one capture the attention of readers. Good photos help sell the paper and encourage buyers to read through it.

Getting close to your subjects also helps keep the picture simple and the composition balanced. The photos with the most impact are those that concentrate on showing the essence of an action or event.

For example, if you are taking pictures of a school play, try photographing a climactic scene during rehearsals. Include two or three of the principal characters. Get the actions and facial expressions that will show readers the characters' emotions and conflicts. Make sure that nothing else is in the frame. Exclude minor characters, scenery, and lights; they simply draw readers' eyes away from the important aspects of the picture.

Moving close to your subjects eliminates two major problems: clutter and wasted space. Your pictures won't have extra people at the sides of the frame. Your outdoor photos won't be dominated by empty sky. Your sports pictures won't be ruined because the playing field or gym floor has taken over the foreground.

Sometimes you cannot get as close to the action as you would like. When this happens, use a telephoto or zoom lens to bring the action closer to you. Remember to be very careful about focusing. Telephoto and zoom lenses have little depth of field, so there is not much margin for error. However, this sometimes can work to your advantage. Because telephoto lenses keep so little in focus, they are excellent when you have a cluttered background. Focus on the people, and the background will automatically fall out of focus.

Get Action

Get action into your pictures. Pictures in which nothing is happening are dull. Avoid posed pictures that involve people shaking hands and smiling, or holding up something and looking straight at the camera. (Photojournalists call these ''grip-and-grin'' shots.)

Every type of event, even the most routine, has its own characteristic actions. For example, meetings are characterized by hand gestures and facial expressions. The next time you cover the student council, try taking close-ups of animated speakers. Concentrate on getting good hand movements and expressions. These pictures are much more dynamic than the usual shot showing everyone sitting and listening.

Getting action shots is particularly important for stories about future events. Too often photographs that accompany these stories show people sitting at a table looking at papers. Such pictures are boring. They also provide readers with very little information; the people at the table could be discussing anything.

Instead, get pictures of the physical preparations for the event. If you're taking an advance picture for graduation, get photos of students renting caps and gowns, or workers setting up bleachers, or the orchestra rehearsing. For student elections, you could photograph people preparing or distributing ballots.

Use Appropriate Lighting

Many potentially good pictures are ruined because the photographer didn't think about how the lighting would make the subject look. People in such pictures may be squinting ferociously because the sun is so bright. Or they may have heavy shadows under their eyes, noses, and mouths. Buildings may look washed out and uninteresting.

If you are taking pictures of people outdoors, try photographing them in the shade. The light on their faces will be even, so you won't have to contend with deep shadows. The people won't be squinting, either.

If you must take your photos in the sun, try to do so between 9 and 11 A.M. or 1 and 3 P.M. During these times, the sun is shining at about a 45-degree angle. The light is not too harsh, and the shadows it creates are relatively minor. Also, consider using flash outdoors to ''fill'' the shadows.

Don't forget that pictures taken at night can be very dramatic. Photographs of buildings, statues, and other inanimate objects are particularly striking. Be sure to use a tripod, and attach a cable

Many beginning photographers try to show too much in their photos and lose the feeling and emotion essential to a good picture. Get close; capture emotion through expressions; communicate the feeling of the event in your picture.

When you cannot get close to your subject, use a telephoto or zoom lens. Focus on the person or object. Your photo will not show much background detail when printed, but will help you capture an event that otherwise might be lost.

Too much flash tends to wash out objects that are close to the camera. Controlling the flash intensity and direction results in a more pleasing photograph.

release to your shutter. Many light meters cannot take accurate exposure readings at night. To compensate, take numerous exposures, using varied combinations of f-stops and shutter speeds.

If you are taking pictures indoors, remember that natural light almost always provides more pleasing results than flash. See if nearby windows provide enough illumination for your pictures. If not, use a flash unit that you can detach from the camera. This will enable you to hold the light above your head and aim down at the faces of the people in the scene. Because the light won't be hitting their faces directly, they won't have that washed-out look.

If you must use a flash unit that remains attached to the camera, try to get one that has a swivel head. Then you can aim the flash at the ceiling and "bounce" the light onto your subjects. This also produces pleasing, natural-looking pictures.

Photo Selection and Layout

Once you have finished shooting your pictures, process the film and make contact sheets. Then meet with the photo editor or assignment editor to select the pictures that should be enlarged. Other editors and the reporter frequently participate in these discussions.

By the time photo selection starts, the page dummies or layouts usually are ready. These blueprints for each page show you the exact size of each photo. Sometimes editors change the dummies after seeing the final photos. If the pictures are especially good, editors may make more space for them. If the pictures are weak, editors may reduce their size or eliminate them.

After editors have looked at the contact sheets, they will probably ask you to enlarge several negatives. Final photo selection is frequently made from enlargements because the details are easier to see. Also, the editor can get an idea of how the photo actually will look when it's published.

Criteria for Selection

Editors follow several criteria when selecting photos for publication. These include:

Content

Editors use the same principles when choosing pictures that photographers use when taking them. Editors look for medium-shots and close-ups that have a lot of action and good lighting.

Relevance to story

It is vital that the picture and the copy work together as a unit. A picture that does not tie in with the major points of the story will jar the reader. Editors go to great lengths to avoid using such a picture.

Shape

Photographs must have the basic shape indicated on the dummy. It is almost impossible to crop a vertical photograph to fit a horizontal space, and vice versa.

For this reason, it is important that you shoot both horizontal and vertical pictures on all assignments. Sometimes, you will have preliminary dummies before you go out to shoot. Even if these dummies show a vertical picture for a story, be sure to shoot both types. You can never be sure when an ad or another story or photo assignment will fall through. Dummies can be changed at the last minute, and editors may need to use your additional pictures as replacements.

Position on page

One of the functions of photographs is to lead readers' eyes around the page. A photograph that makes readers look off the top or sides of the page is counterproductive. For example, if a photograph is dummied for the right side of the page, and the subjects are looking to the right, an editor will not use that picture. If possible, check preliminary dummies before you go out on assignment so you know where the picture is scheduled to run.

Special Photo Techniques

There are several special techniques that can make photos work even more effectively in layouts. For a change of format, try the occasional photo sequence or photo essay. Printing techniques that make a photo stand out include duotones, screens, and four-color.

Photo sequences

These are series of photos that show how something changed or developed over time. For example, you may have a sequence of two to five photos showing the motion of the baseball team's best pitcher. Or you may have a sequence showing how facial expressions of one official changed during the course of a meeting. Sequences usually involve one action or one person, and the photos are usually published side by side.

Photo essays

These are stories told in pictures. They usually involve three to seven photographs and a short copy block. Because photo essays take time and space, subjects must be chosen carefully. Brainstorm possible ideas; then give the photographer plenty of time to work on the project.

Duotones

These are photographs that are printed in two colors. One is always black. The other may be any other color. Duotones are expensive to produce because they require two press runs—one for the regular black ink, and another for the second color.

Publications frequently use duotones for special issues, such as those published around Christmas or graduation. But the photograph must be selected carefully. It should be very simple, with sharp images, and should not contain any people. The second color must also be chosen carefully. Red, green, and blue are used most frequently, but blue seems to work best. Green tends to look "muddy," especially next to black type. Red often looks too dark or too harsh.

Too often publications decide to use a duotone simply because an advertiser buys an ad and is willing to pay for a second color. A duotone should never be used only because it won't cost the publication anything extra. An appropriate photograph must be available.

Screens

Halftone screens are devices that the printer uses when preparing photographs for reproduction. Any photograph has to be screened or quality reproduction is not possible on the printed material. Printing processes cannot reproduce a photograph with its varying tones without the use of a halftone screen that converts the continuous tone image into a pattern of very small dots. See the next page for an illustration of some screen processes used in printing photographs. Note that newspapers usually use 65-line, 85-line, or 100-line halftone screens for photographic reproduction.

For special effects, straight line, mezzo tint, etch tone, or other "arty" or surreal looking screens can superimpose a textured pattern over photographs. Such special effects are usually reserved for advertisements or feature sections of a publication. A photo to be treated with a special effect screen must have balanced composition, excellent contrast, and no clutter.

Color photographs

Color photographs are often called "four-color" photos because four press runs are required to reproduce them on printed material. Most newspaper photography is done in black and white because the printing process for 4-color photography is not only more time-consuming and technically complicated, but also more expensive. The original photograph must be taken with color film, processing has to be done by a professional photo lab, and four separations must be made for color reproduction, involving direct screening or electronic scanning.

Today, many commercial newspapers have started to use more color photography, usually on a selective basis, such as on the front page of the Sunday edition or in special feature sections. Some school publications have the funds for color photographs, at least for selective use in the yearbook. In any case, be advised not to use color for its own sake. Instead, use it judiciously, such as for special events, because participants are frequently in colorful clothing, or the setting or background is colorful and dramatic.

In order to reproduce the varying tone of a picture, photos are screened (shot as halftones) for use in printed material. Without a screen (above left), reproduction is poor. A 65-line halftone treatment (above right) is often used for newspaper reproduction.

For reproduction in books such as this one, photos are often treated as 133-line halftones (above left). For special effects, treatments such as a mezzo tint screen (above right) can be used.

Preparing Photos

After the photos have been selected, any necessary changes in the dummies are made. Then the photos are prepared for publication. This involves three steps: cropping, sizing, and writing cutlines.

Cropping

Cropping a picture means getting rid of any clutter at the top, bottom, and sides of the frame. If the photographer followed the rules for taking effective photographs, then he or she did a lot of cropping with the camera. However, cropping gives you a chance to make your pictures even better. You can eliminate the student

You can see how cropping this photo increases its impact. Uncropped, the fans distract attention from the central action.

who walked into the edge of the picture just as you snapped the shutter, or the roof of the gym that dominates the top of your basketball picture.

Crop either contact sheets or enlargements. Find exactly where you want the top of the finished picture to be. Mark this area on the contact sheet or print with a grease pencil by drawing a line across the top or making a tic mark just outside the image area. Repeat this procedure at the bottom of the frame. Then do the same thing on both sides.

Remember that the finished picture must still match the basic shape indicated on the layout. For example, don't crop a picture so much that it becomes a square and won't fit into a rectangular hole dummied on the page.

Also, a photograph that has been drastically cropped may look very grainy when published. This is because you are taking a small portion of the picture and magnifying it. The more you magnify a photograph, the grainier the enlargement becomes.

The most important thing to remember about cropping is that most of it should be done in the camera. Cropping a picture after it has been taken can eliminate minor defects but cannot remedy major problems.

Sizing

When the layout is finished and the photograph has been cropped, the picture can be sized. This means you have to figure out how much the picture must be reduced or enlarged to fit exactly into the space indicated on the dummy.

The easiest way to size a picture is to use a proportion wheel. First, make tic marks in the margin of the print to indicate the part of the picture you want to use. Measure the new size in width and depth to the nearest eighth of an inch. Measure the width of the space it will occupy in the publication.

To figure out how deep the picture will be when it is reproduced, use the proportion wheel. Find the figure for the width of the original picture on the inside wheel. Then turn the inside wheel until this figure lines up with the figure for the reproduction width, on the outside wheel.

Hold the wheels firmly so they don't move. Then find the figure for the original picture's depth on the inside wheel. Right above it, on the outside wheel, you'll find the unknown figure, the depth of the reproduction.

When you have determined what size the picture should be when reproduced, give this width and depth, along with your enlargement, to the printer. Write these figures in grease pencil

The proportion wheel is an inexpensive but highly useful tool for sizing photos.

on the back of your print. Don't use ballpoint pens or pencils. They crack the print and may show up in the final photo.

After you have sized the pictures, final changes can be made in dummies. Sometimes this is necessary because a picture ends up being "deeper" than the editors expected.

Cutlines

The third step in preparing photos for publication is writing cutlines. This is usually the photographer's responsibility.

There are several basic guides for writing good cutlines. First, cutlines must be able to stand alone. The reader should not have to read the story in order to understand what is going on in the picture.

Second, cutlines always identify who is in the picture and where it was taken. Sports cutlines also always give the final score. However, cutlines should not repeat word-for-word information in the story.

Good cutlines often include details that may not have been worked into the story. Keep track of any interesting or humorous "bits" that can make your cutline brighter.

All cutlines except those for sports photos about games that have been played should be written in the present tense. This lends a feeling of immediacy to the publication and makes readers feel as if they are watching the action as it occurs.

Wrap-up

Good photographs are the means by which publications show readers what is happening as well as tell them.

Photographs fulfill six major functions. They capture attention, provide information, provide entertainment, establish links with readers, act as a layout device, and help establish an identity.

Photo editors make picture assignments after consulting with other editors and supervise the work of photographers. If there is no photo editor, this job usually is done by the editor-in-chief.

Photographers are sent for specific pictures about events or for feature-oriented "wild art." Reporters and photographers should discuss their assignments and share ideas. Cutline information is gathered by the photographer.

In one sense, photos can be divided into two groups: those that look professional and those that look amateurish. Professional, dynamic photos can be attained by following certain guidelines.

Photographers should work as close to their subjects as possible, probably within seven to ten feet. If this is not possible, a telephoto or zoom lens can be used.

News photos need to have action and should not look posed.

Photographers pay special attention to lighting. If people are photographed outside, they should be in the shade. If photos must be taken in sunlight, try to shoot between 9 and 11 A.M. or 1 and 3 P.M. for the best sun angle. Night photos can be dramatic but require a tripod and a cable release. Natural light, too, is very effective.

After fulfilling a photo assignment, the photographer makes contact sheets of all the negatives and assists in selecting which shots to publish.

The criteria for publication include content, relevance to story, shape, and position on the page.

Several special techniques are available to make photos work even more effectively. These include photo sequences, photo essays, duotones, screens, and color pictures.

After photos are selected, three steps remain. The photos must be cropped, which means eliminating clutter at the top, bottom, or sides. They must be sized, which means figuring out how much the picture must be reduced or enlarged to fit its allotted space. And a cutline must be written. Cutlines, written in present tense, should be able to stand alone and must identify who is in the picture and where it was taken.

On Assignment

Teamwork

1. Working in teams, brainstorm topics that would make a good full-page photo essay for your school newspaper. Select one and take the photos. If you are not particularly skilled at photography, use an instant camera. Keep in mind all the guidelines for taking good photos. Select the pictures carefully, crop

and size them, mark them for the printer, prepare the layout for a photo page, and write the copy that will accompany the photos (including all cutlines and appropriate headlines).

If you have access to a photocopier that enlarges and reduces copy, enlarge or reduce the photos and cut them out. Type the copy and do a pasteup of your page if possible.

Exchange your work products with that of other teams. Critique them constructively. How could photos have been used more effectively? Do the cutlines complement the photos? Does the story work well with the overall photo page? Is the layout exciting?

2. Remember the story with substance and the sports feature page you prepared as teamwork for Chapters 9 and 11? Take the pictures needed to complete the projects.

Practice

1. Brainstorm new ways to cover typical school events or classes with photos. For example, how can you illustrate the school play, a concert, or homecoming? How would you cover physics, world history, or vocational or physical education classes?

2. Look at the front pages of several daily newspapers published the same day. Write a critique of the page design. Were photos used effectively? Was the layout well planned to take advantage of the photos? Were the cutlines written well? Are national photos used differently in different locations? Why? How would you have treated stories that have no photos to take advantage of illustrations?

3. Obtain a contact sheet from a photographer for the newspaper, yearbook, or magazine, or from the photography club (or use your own if you are a photographer). Crop two or three photos on the contact sheets. Arrange to have the photos enlarged. (Once again, a photocopier can give you a feel for what happens. Enlarge the copies progressively three or four times.) Look at how you cropped them on the contact sheets. Do the photographs still have unnecessary elements at the top, bottom, or sides of the frame? Did you crop them too severely, making them a strange shape? How might they have been cropped more effectively? Attach your answers to your contact prints and enlargements.

4. Practice sizing photographs with the proportion wheel. Crop the pictures, then proportion them to fit one-column, two-column, and three-column formats. Discuss the problems you encountered and how you solved them. Did you have to change your cropping?

5. Clip an effective photo and its cutline from a magazine. Also clip one that fails to "tell the story." Write a short editorial column critiquing the quality of the photos and comparing them based on what you have learned about the effective use of photography. Suggest ways to improve the inadequate photo.
6. Find one photograph in newspapers or magazines that fulfills each of the six major functions mentioned in this chapter; capturing attention, providing information, providing entertainment, establishing an emotional link, acting as a layout device, and helping establish an identity for the publication. Write a short paragraph on the function(s) each photo performs. Attach the paragraph to the page on which the photo appears.

Your Turn

Using the photo assignment form used by your school newspaper or yearbook, write photo orders for an academic subject, a school activity, a sports event, a personality feature, or something of your choosing. Be creative.

Take the pictures, or work with a photographer to take them. Start with contact sheets if possible. Crop the ones you would use, then enlarge and print them. Next, write the cutlines to go with your photos and mount them. Take turns constructively critiquing each other's work.

Richard Clarkson

The trouble with some young photographers is that they never get over their "silhouette and sunset" phase, says Richard Clarkson, photography director for the *National Geographic* in Washington, D.C.

There's no denying the "certain artistic self-fulfillment" of photojournalism, Clarkson said. "There's something concrete to look at" after a day's work.

But young photographers, Clarkson has found, "have the greatest trouble understanding that this is journalism first and photography second."

"With photojournalism," he said, "you're not making pictures for yourself, you're making them for other people, pictures that say something, have a point of view."

Clarkson grew up in Lawrence, Kan., and wanted to be a photographer from the time he started a newspaper in elementary school. He became a free-lance photographer, supplying pictures for national magazines and working for Kansas newspapers.

He also has acquired a reputation among the photographers he has trained over the years as a taskmaster who demands perfection—or as close to perfection as photographer and camera can come.

Clarkson has supervised the photo staff at the Topeka (Kan.) *Capital Journal* and the *Denver* (Colo.) *Post* newspapers. He has long been active in the National Press Photographers Association. Newspaper photographers usu-

ally do five assignments a day, sometimes consulting with the city editor by two-way radio in their staff cars as they go out to cover the first event of the day. Short, daily deadlines for newspapers mean those assignments sometimes must be handled "in a bit of a scurry," Clarkson says, but to him, that's no excuse for sloppy quality.

Pictures in daily newspapers have enjoyed a renaissance in recent years, Clarkson believes.

"I remember years ago I used to have to use all of my persuasive powers to make even an occasional spectacular use of pictures," he says, adding that today photographers don't have to argue much at all if the photos are good.

He attributes the change to coincidence and accident.

"We're becoming a very visual nation, a very visual world," Clarkson said, largely as a result of television.

"Readers are people who've grown up in front of television." Also, he says, people coming into journalism and a younger generation of newspaper editors are part of the television era and feel pictures are an effective way of grabbing and keeping readers' short attention span and telling an effective story.

The accidental part, according to Clarkson, is the change in newspaper technology. Cold-type production and offset presses mean photographs look good and can be presented well.

To Clarkson, the changes are fascinating. "We're in a changing time in the media," he said, adding that the "more visual orientation" is an international phenomenon.

But what are not changing, in Clarkson's view, are the requirements of being a good photojournalist.

"Certain people have an incredible innate ability, a visual ability" that tells them how the elements of a photograph should fit together into a simple, clean picture that says what the photographer wants it to say.

"Some people really have a flair for journalism," he continued. "They understand how to photograph a person or subject, light it, crop it, size it, use it with a head, and sell it."

Clarkson advises young photographers to get a broad education with experience that goes in many directions.

"Eventually they will master the camera," he said. But there's no substitute for "really living life, meeting people, being well informed about lots of things—those are factors that set apart the top people." ■

CHAPTER FIFTEEN

BUSINESS AND ADVERTISING

In addition to serving a news and editorial function, a student publication has business responsibilities. A newspaper has to be written and edited, and it must have money to pay its bills.

This section will acquaint you with the activities of the business staffs of student publications. The business side is not a competitor with the editorial side; the two must work together for a successful publication.

Too often student editors feel held back because of a shortage of funds. They need to understand that while they have excellent ideas, these ideas take money. Extra pictures, artwork, color at homecoming and Christmas, and extra pages for special features are not gifts from a printer.

In short, just as the staff must exercise editorial and news responsibility, so must it exercise fiscal responsibility.

Staff Organization

Leading the business staff is the business manager. The business manager's role is to see that the three main functions of this department are carried out: advertising sales and preparation, circulation, and record keeping. The student business manager must be personable, aggressive, and able to lead a sales staff. He or she must also work closely with the editor to plan the number of pages of the publication, work out special layout needs, and coordinate production with the printer.

Business assistants, in addition to selling and preparing advertising, generally are assigned other specific duties. One might be in charge of circulation, another of billing or books and records. The specific breakdown naturally will depend on the size of the staff and the publication. In some schools, reporters also help sell advertising. This is not unlike the way some small-town and weekly publications operate. As in any good organization, there must be a spirit of teamwork and a willingness to help one another.

Advertising

Advertising generates income for the publication, provides a means of communicating product or sales information from a business to the publication's readers, and assists the reader in selecting that business's products and services. Advertising also stimulates competition and helps keep prices down and the economy active.

A school newspaper must often operate as a business.

CODE OF PRACTICE
Newspaper Advertising Executives Association

1. No advertising will be published if it is fraudulent, misleading, or otherwise harmful.
2. Rates and conditions published in the rate card will apply to all advertisers.
3. Definitions of retail and general advertising, as endorsed by the Newspaper Advertising Executives Association, will determine whether retail or general rates apply.
4. Any possible action in connection with publicity which may be sent to the advertising department will be limited to submittal to the news department for use or rejection.
5. Newspaper advertising salespeople will be thoroughly instructed in the fundamentals of good advertising and the usefulness of newspapers as a medium to the end that competent service may be provided to every advertiser.
6. Salespeople will be instructed to advise advertisers in the manner that will produce maximum returns and avoid overselling or other unsound methods.
7. Any mention of competing newspapers or other media will be truthful. Derogatory references to the personnel, policies, or advertising value of other newspapers will be avoided to the end that fair competition may be promoted.
8. In order to assure maximum returns to advertisers, every effort will be made to induce them to improve the quality of their copy and artwork and to assure good typography and printing.
9. Adequate and accurate information regarding the market and the newspaper will be provided.
10. The objective in all respects will be the advancement and improvement of the newspaper as an advertising medium.

Advertising is *not* a contribution to the student publication. It is not charity and should never be looked upon as such.

You have a *real* product to sell. Your publications are well read by students, who are today one of the largest single segments of purchasing power in this country. Well-prepared advertising aimed at students will bring many returns to the advertiser.

Unfortunately, some student-produced publications do treat advertising as if it were a contribution by the business. A lot of little boxes that merely say Joe's Beanery, Little Theater, and the like aren't doing anyone much good. It takes little effort to get them ready for the printer, and they probably do not sell products. More than likely, they are not even read. The publication that carries this sort of advertising is cheating itself, the reader, and the advertiser.

On the other hand, a publication containing good display advertising that sells products readers like, want, and use regularly is performing a service to all parties concerned. Such advertising also makes your publications more attractive, and good advertising will help attract more good advertising. You will discover that a successful ad will keep that business using your publication for years to come. In short, you will become a significant vehicle in the communication process between business and consumer.

Who knows better than you what your fellow students do, how they think, and what they want? Maybe we should hedge on that a bit: Who *should* know better than you?

This brings us to the next major point: You must know your student market. This does not mean just being friends with a number of your classmates. It means knowing how much money they have to spend, where they spend it, and when. If you have done your research, you will be able to go to your advertisers and tell them what potential for success their ads have. This research is essential as you prepare to sell advertising, and it is relatively simple to do.

Before starting the advertising process, though, you should consider the practical and concise philosophy of advertising that follows. It was written by a veteran expert in the field, a partner in one of the world's leading advertising agencies. Keep these points in mind while doing your market research, preparing ad copy, and selling space. The well-conceived ad, from start to finish, will benefit both your paper and your advertisers.

The Plain, Short Story of Good Advertising

Advertising is the business, or the art, if you please, of telling someone something that should be important to him. It is a substitute for talking to someone.

It is the primary requirement of advertising to be clear, clear as to exactly what the proposition is.

If it isn't clear, and clear at a glance or a whisper, very few people will take the time or the effort to try to figure it out.

The second essential of advertising is that what must be clear must also be important. The proposition must have value.

Third, the proposition (the promise) that is both clear and important must also have a personal appeal. It should be beamed at its logical prospects; no one else matters.

Fourth, the distinction in good advertising expresses the personality of the advertisers; for a promise is only as good as its maker.

Finally, a good advertisement demands action. It asks for an order or it exacts a mental pledge.

Altogether these things define a desirable advertisement as one that will command attention but never be offensive.

It will be reasonable, but never dull.

It will be original, but never self-conscious.

It will be imaginative, but never misleading.

And because of what it is and what it is not, a properly prepared advertisement will always be convincing and it will make people act.

This incidentally, is all that I know about advertising.

—Fairfax M. Cone
Foote, Cone & Belding, Inc.

Marketing Surveys

Now start your research by preparing a marketing survey. Maybe your school offers classes in marketing whose members could help conduct a survey for your staff. You may have access to a computer that can help process the data you collect. If a computer system is available, talk with the personnel *before* you start writing the survey to make sure you prepare it in the proper format and use the proper forms.

Here's how one newspaper staff put together its marketing study.

1. Staff members held a brainstorming session during which they identified all the things they and other students might do in a week. Where would they spend money? What types of things would they buy? Where might they go for entertainment? Where might they shop (shopping centers, central business areas)? Staff members also examined related questions in their brainstorming. How much influence do students have over family purchases and deciding, for example, where the family will dine out? How much money do they have to spend each week? Do they have credit cards, savings accounts, checking accounts?

2. The next step was to go to the computer center and determine the alternatives available for processing the information and learn the format for preparing the survey form. The computer center provided specially overprinted forms for the final survey instrument. Students would use lead pencils to mark the proper response, and the survey forms (similar to many standardized tests you take) would then be fed directly into the computer.

Interviewing is only one part of doing a marketing survey.

3. A task force of staff members went to work to prepare the first draft of questions. They asked, ''Why do we want to know this?'' about each question before allowing it to remain in the survey.

4. Armed with a draft, each task force member selected five students at random and had them complete the survey (pilot testing). After they answered the questions, the students went back over each question and noted words that bothered them, anything that was not clear, or other problems they felt they had in completing the survey. Then it was back to the drawing board to revise and finalize the instrument for printing.

5. The survey was then administered. In this case, all classes meeting at 9 a.m. took time out to complete the study. Nearly all students participated. (The staff could have prepared a random sample and conducted the study with a smaller group. You may want to ask your mathematics instructor or a local survey research firm about selecting samples randomly and the number you need for your size student population.)

6. The next step was to process the data and analyze the results. That analysis provided important marketing information for advertising sales staff members to use in their sales pitch to current and prospective advertisers.

> This is a marketing survey to aid the OR-
> ACLE in evaluating its advertising efforts.
> Please answer <u>all</u> questions. Select only
> <u>one</u> answer for each question.

<u>Marketing survey</u>

1. Sex
   Male_____   Female_____

2. Age
   under 14_____   15_____   16_____   17_____   18 or over_____

3. Grade
   Freshman_____   Sophomore_____   Junior_____   Senior_____

4. What section of the ORACLE do you read first?
   page 1_____   editorial page_____   sports page_____   inside pages_____

5. Do you take the ORACLE home?
   never_____   always_____   occasionally_____

6. If you take the ORACLE home, do your parents read it?
   yes_____   no_____   does not apply_____

7. Do you receive a monthly allowance?
   $20 or less_____ $21-$25_____ $26-$30_____   over $31_____
   does not apply_____

If you answered yes to 7, which items in questions 8-13 are covered by your allowance?

8. School lunches
   yes_____   no_____   invalid_____

9. Clothing
   yes_____   no_____   invalid_____

10. Entertainment (movies, dances, etc.)
    yes_____   no_____   invalid_____

11. School supplies
    yes_____   no_____   invalid_____

12. Gasoline
    yes_____ no_____ invalid_____

13. Cosmetics, toiletries, etc.
    yes_____ no_____ invalid_____

14. Do you own a stereo?
    yes_____ no_____ invalid_____

15. Do you own a VCR?
    yes_____ no_____ invalid_____

16. Do you own your automobile?
    yes_____ no_____ invalid_____

17. Do you have a part-time job?
    yes_____ no_____ invalid_____

18. If you answered yes to number 17, how much do you earn weekly?
    under $50_____ $50-$99_____ over $100_____ over $200_____

19. Do you have a savings account?
    yes_____ no_____ invalid_____

20. Do you shop for your own clothes?
    yes_____ no_____ invalid_____

21. About how much money did you (or your parents) spend for clothing at the start
    of this school year?
    up to $100_____ $100-$200_____ $200-$250_____ $250-$300_____
    over $300_____

22. Where do you do most of your shopping?
    downtown_____ Gateway_____ other_____

23. Which radio station do you listen to most?
    KFOR_____ KLMS_____ KLIN_____ KFAB_____ KOIL_____ others_____

24. What TV network do you prefer to watch?
    ABC_____ NBC_____ CBS_____ cable networks_____ other_____

25. About how often do you go to movies each month?
    once_____ 2-3 times_____ 4 or more times_____ none_____

26. About how much do you spend on food (away from home and school) each week for things like soft drinks, snacks, etc?

    less than $5_____ $5-$10_____ $10-$15_____   over $15_____

27. Did you order a yearbook this year?

    yes_____   no_____   invalid_____

28. Do you help make decisions about major family purchases?

    yes_____   no_____   invalid_____

29. Do you read ORACLE ads?

    occasionally_____   almost always_____   never_____

30. If there were a classified ad section in the ORACLE would you utilize it (read and/or place an ad)?

    yes_____   no_____

*Adapted from a survey originally created and used by the *Oracle*, East High School (Lincoln, Neb.)

Other Research Studies

If you are not able to do your own research, you can take advantage of market research conducted by others and reported in the local news media.

For example, a company in Northbrook, Illinois—Teenage Research Unlimited—probes teen buying habits. As they noted in a recent news release, the teenage audience—nearly 25 million strong—spent over $71 billion on themselves, their family, and friends in 1989 and projections were made that teens' purchases of big-ticket items would increase into the 1990s.

TRU conducts market research studies and updates projections on a regular basis, issuing news releases periodically. The studies TRU conducts, along with research from other organizations, often are reported in the local news media. You can go to your school library and do a computer search or check the *Readers' Guide* for recent publications. Translate those results into how much buying power teens have in your community.

If you watch television shows or read publications targeted to the younger audience, you will see ads for everything from soap to stereos. Take a look at MTV or *Seventeen* magazine. Companies have become smart. They know students don't buy just sodas, chewing gum, and recordings. They know students influence many decisions at home, and that they often do the shopping for the family. Through market research, companies choose programs and media aimed at teens to tap their buying power and to influence decisions made at home.

This is important information to use in selling advertisers on your student publications, too.

Advertising Sales

Once you have researched your market and analyzed the results, you are ready to sell advertising. You have the proof of your readers' buying power. You know the market. You do not have to look upon buying advertising as a charitable contribution.

Now you need a list of prospects. Ad salespeople should sit down with the business manager and divide the prospects and accounts. If a student has a personal interest in a specific type of product, he or she is a natural to sell ads to stores selling it. For example, if you happen to be an avid record collector, you'll do well at selling advertising to record stores. You will know the language and have things to talk about with the stores' advertising managers. Naturally, not all your accounts will be of special interest to you. But every product or service interests some of your readers, so don't overlook any potential advertiser.

Once you get your list of prospects—the advertising beat—contact them on a regular basis. It is always best to show prospects a sample ad to demonstrate your knowledge of the market and their business. You might also prepare a standard pitch on how your publication operates and how this particular advertising idea will benefit the prospect's business.

Let's use the marketing survey as an example. You could go to the local record store and tell the owner that 81 percent of your school's students have their own stereos and 73 percent shop downtown where this store is located, according to the survey of your readers. Point out that these students spend thousands of dollars each month on entertainment, records, and similar items. Then show the prospect an ad. Mention a couple of entertainers who are currently popular with your readers and point out that an ad like this could really bring in business.

Discuss how little it costs to reach each student. For example, if a column inch in your newspaper costs $2, a 20-column-inch ad will cost $40. Divide that cost by the 1,000 students who read your paper, and you'll find the ad costs four cents per reader—a price that can't be beat. Be pleasant. Answer questions politely. If the answer is no, thank the store owner and leave your name and school phone number and a rate card if you have one. Go back for another visit when the next issue is being prepared. Don't give up.

Your attitude and appearance will have a direct effect on what you sell. Look neat and clean—no sloppy clothes unless, of course, you have time to waste trying to sell ads people won't buy. It cannot be overemphasized that your appearance and attitude reflect the image of your school and your publication.

Ad Contracts

Some schools have advertising contracts that they sell before the year starts or complete as each issue is prepared. Naturally, contracts are helpful. They provide proof that the advertiser has agreed to the type of ad you plan to run, obligating his or her company to pay the bills. They also make for a businesslike relationship between the advertiser and your publication. Develop a contract that will best suit your situation.

Some student publications have sliding rates for advertising, to encourage advertisers to place more ads of a larger size throughout the school year. It is difficult, however, to keep records on such sales, and a standard rate may be more useful. Remember, you have a product for sale. That product has a value. You sell it for what it is worth. With the buying power of today's student, that value to an advertiser is substantial.

How Many Ads?

One question that must be settled before each issue is "How much advertising does it take to pay for the publication?" To answer this, you must consider the number of pages the news staff can fill with quality news, features, sports, and editorial content; the regular income (subscriptions, activity fee subsidy); and the printer's charges for the size of publication desired.

For example, assume you want to print a six-page newspaper. The printer charges $400 for printing 1,800 copies of the issue. You have $150 budgeted from activity or subscription fees for each issue during the year. You have miscellaneous photography costs, phone charges, and other expenses for each issue of approximately $20. After subtracting income from expenses, you need $270 of advertising income.

At $2 per column inch (one column wide and one inch deep), sales reps need to sell 135 inches of advertising to break even based on this budget. If you have a five-column, six-page paper (510 column inches), that represents a small percentage of advertising. Most newspapers today try to sell enough advertising to fill at least 60 percent of their space.

The Arlingtonian

The Upper Arlington High School Student Newsmagazine

The undersigned business hereby agrees to purchase the specified amount of advertising space in *The Arlingtonian* in each of the issues indicated herein. The undersigned also agrees to pay any additional cost which may be incurred by *The Arlingtonian* staff in preparing the advertisement for print. The rate schedule for these prices is listed below. After publication, a tear sheet will be sent to the advertiser along with a bill for services rendered.

An advertisement can be designed by *The Arlingtonian* graphics staff in cooperation with the advertiser. Camera-ready copy is also accepted.

Business _____ Date _____

Address _____ Zip Code _____

Billing Address _____

Phone _____ Contact _____

Account Summary

+	Base Rate	_____
+	Additional	_____
−	% Discount	_____
=	Total (per insertion)	_____
X	# of Insertions	_____
=	SUM TOTAL over length of contract	_____

Rate Schedule

Base Rate

❑	Full Page	$150.00
❑	3/4 Page	$135.00
❑	2/3 Page	$115.00
❑	1/2 Page	$85.00
❑	1/3 Page	$60.00
❑	1/4 Page	$50.00
❑	1/6 Page	$35.00 (horizontal___ or vertical___)
❑	1/12 Page	$20.00
❑	Insert (provided)	$35.00
❑	Insert (produced)	$70.00 (black and white only)

Additional Charges

❑	Spot Color	$40.00
❑	Photo by staff	$2.00

Discount Rates

❑ 10% Prepaid Discount (full payment due with contract)
❑ 5% Series Discount (4 or more insertions)
❑ 10% Full Year Discount (12 insertions)

1990-1991 Insertion Dates

❑ Sept. 20 (Homecoming)
❑ Oct. 11
❑ Nov. 1
❑ Nov. 21
❑ Dec. 13 (Holiday)
❑ Jan. 10
❑ Jan. 31 (Valentine's)
❑ Feb. 21
❑ March 14
❑ April 11 (Prom)
❑ May 2
❑ May 30 (Senior Issue)

Copy

❑ Camera Ready
❑ Copy Designed
❑ Other (Please Specify)

❑ Send Bill (W/Tearsheet)
❑ Pre-paid: CK___ Cash___

OWNER/MANAGER SIGNATURE _____

ACCOUNT REPRESENTATIVE _____

If you have any questions or problems, please contact your account representative:
1650 Ridgeview Road ● Upper Arlington, Ohio 43221 ● 487-5267

Advertising contracts like this one used by Upper Arlington High School help maintain a businesslike relationship with advertisers and offer a clear explanation of rates and policies of the student publication.

In contrast to commercial newspapers, most student newspapers that receive an activity subsidy have an average advertising content of about 25 percent. There is no hard-and-fast rule; your desires as a newspaper staff will determine your goals. Be realistic. Some student papers barely break even from one year to the next. Others earn several hundred dollars each year, which are spent on special issues, darkroom equipment, typewriters, word processing equipment, or supplies.

These same concepts apply to school magazines and yearbooks. After you calculate the subscription or sales income, subtract the costs of production. The amount that remains must be made up through advertising revenue or other fund-raising activities.

Writing Advertising Copy

When you write advertising copy, you draw on many of the same things we discussed in news and editorial writing: You study the product and do the necessary research, interview the store owners, and study fact sheets on products. Look at the advertising of your clients' competitors. You will also want to determine the appropriate five W's and H—*who* needs or will buy this product or service; *what* will make people want to buy it; *why* should they buy it; *when, where,* and *how* can they get it? Then sit down with the answers from your research and interviews and select the important items for your copy.

First you need a lead, a headline—a few ''grabber'' words.

Then expand the lead—facts about the product or supporting materials that strengthen your appeal to the reader to buy the product or service. Just as a news story quotes authoritative sources, so must unusual claims be verified: ''This is the longest-lasting recording tape made.'' Says who?

Follow up by telling people what they should do, and where and when. (Remember the editorial: reactions, conclusions.)

Eat at Kings! 40th and O Streets
open 7 a.m. to midnight daily

The emphasis in writing advertising copy is on brevity and clarity. Avoid misleading words, superlatives, and clichés. Be accurate and truthful; that is a major responsibility in advertising.

A copywriter writes copy to sell as well as to inform, keeping the targeted customers' needs and wants in mind.

Study advertisements. Look through magazines and newspapers. Note the simplicity of some ads. You will soon note that appeals are made to varied interests of readers through the illustrations as well as copy.

Many advertising books discuss the psychology of selling. Some give long lists of people's desires that copywriters often capitalize on. John Caples of Batten, Barton, Durstine and Osborn, one of the leading advertising agencies in the world, has some thoughts on psychological appeals in his book *Making Ads Pay*:

> Psychologists have published lists of human desires and they have put the most powerful desires on top of these lists. The lists usually read something like this: sex appeal; get ahead; health; etc., etc.
>
> At the bottom of the list you will usually find appeals to your public spirit, such as "how to help your town have a better park system."
>
> Now these lists are okay, but they are sometimes misused by ad writers. The writer looks at the list and says to himself, "Sex appeal is tops. Therefore, I'm

going to use it in selling my product.'' And so you have campaigns which say in effect:

This soap will give you sex appeal.

This toothpaste will give you sex appeal.

This necktie will give you sex appeal.

This shoe polish will give you sex appeal.

These eyeglasses will give you sex appeal.

Moral: It is okay to look at a list of appeals in order to find a good one for your product. But use judgment. Select the best one that is also logical and believable. Select an appeal that will really make sales. Don't try to sell everybody and end up selling nobody. In shooting game it is better to use a rifle bullet that will knock one animal dead than to use buckshot that will merely pepper the whole flock.

So be selective in your writing. Determine what will best sell the product to your reader. Think in terms of the reader's needs. You don't buy a drill because you want the drill for its own sake. What you want are holes, and the drill is an easy, convenient way to get them. Avoid double meanings and unsuccessful attempts at humor. Be creative. The best ad still has not been prepared. None of the experts has all the answers.

Illustrating the Advertisement

In advertising you must always keep in mind more than just your copy. You are preparing a visual impact as well, and the two must work together.

In their book *Advertising*, John S. Wright and Daniel S. Warner comment on arranging the layout:

At any stage in the interrelated visualization-layout process, the designer's task is to combine several different elements, units, or masses into a single effective communication—the complete finished advertisement. Each illustration becomes an element in layout design. So does the headline. Subheads, copy blocks, picture captions, trademarks, the price itself, coupons, product packages, and seals of approval are other elements which may be included in the advertisement. Usually the logotype, a distinctive treatment of the brand or firm name which is also known as the signature, slug, or name plate, is an important layout element. Finally, white space, the blank area not occupied by any other layout element, is itself usually considered an element of layout. Few advertisements contain all of these elements.

Keep these elements in mind as you prepare your advertisement:

1. *Balance*. Think of a teeter-totter: When equal weights are on each side, you have formal balance; when a heavier weight is on one of the two sides, you have informal balance. As you know from science, you can change the fulcrum and maintain the balance of two unequal weights. Balance is important to achieve visual impact.

2. *Optical center*. Generally speaking, the optical center of an advertisement is about two-thirds of the way up from the bottom of the ad. It is not the true center of the allocated space, but it is where most readers will perceive the center to be.

3. *White space*. That you have 10 inches of space to fill for an advertisement does not mean that you have to fill every bit of that space with words and art. You have undoubtedly seen ads with only a few words off to one side, or maybe one illustration and a headline. The rest of the space is empty to emphasize the message. White space used effectively will attract the reader's eye.

4. *Appropriate art*. Art—any drawings, photographs, or other illustrative material—should fit your ad's mood. Art for art's sake is not necessarily a good philosophy. Students from photography and art classes may be willing to help illustrate ads. You can also subscribe to professional clip-art services. These services generally offer a number of pieces of well-done art in topical books (for example, Christmas art, gimmicks, announcements). Check with your printer for names of companies that sell such art, or contact a local advertising agency for advice.

Ad Preparation   After you have discussed with your printer how he or she prefers to receive ad copy and layout, you will be ready to prepare ads for publication.

Some printers need only a rough sketch of how the ad is to look when done, accompanied by a copy sheet where you have marked and keyed the style and size of type you want for various elements.

Other printers, especially offset, welcome camera-ready ads. (You may save money, too.) Camera-ready means the type is already set, the headlines ready, and the art in such a condition that the printer can merely photograph it for printing.

You can submit partially camera-ready copy. For instance, you may prepare the art, set your headline using press-on type (available in bookstores or art-supply stores), and do everything you can to make the ad ready for printing. The printer may then have to prepare the photograph or set some copy blocks before the ad is complete.

At any rate, you probably will be required to prepare your ads in the manner prescribed by your printer.

Today, many ads are prepared on computers using desktop publishing.

Managing the Pieces

It is important that you check your ads carefully before sending the copy, art, and layout to the printer. Be sure you have not left out any important element. You may wish to prepare a rubber stamp, which you can use on the top of your copy for each ad, bearing a checklist of "musts" to include in each ad.

For example:

Store Logo (Uniquely designed name)	**Prices**
Store Hours	**Sizes**
Store Address	**Headline**
Strong Lead-in	**Copy Block(s)**
Special Discounts (If any)	**Art**
Effective Close (Stop by Today; Sale Ends_____; Valentine's Day is Friday— so don't delay!)	**Dates**

Below and on the next four pages, you can see the process by which an actual color ad is put together. The advertising agency starts with the original, rough layout; the basic concept is approved.

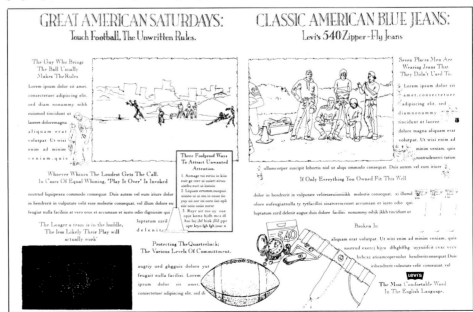

The mechanical is used for positioning of the actual elements; all copy is set and laid out at this time.

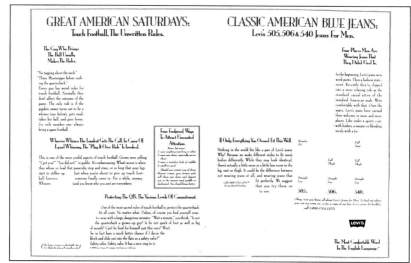

These are color separations. Primary colors are matched to create colors that are true to the original artwork.

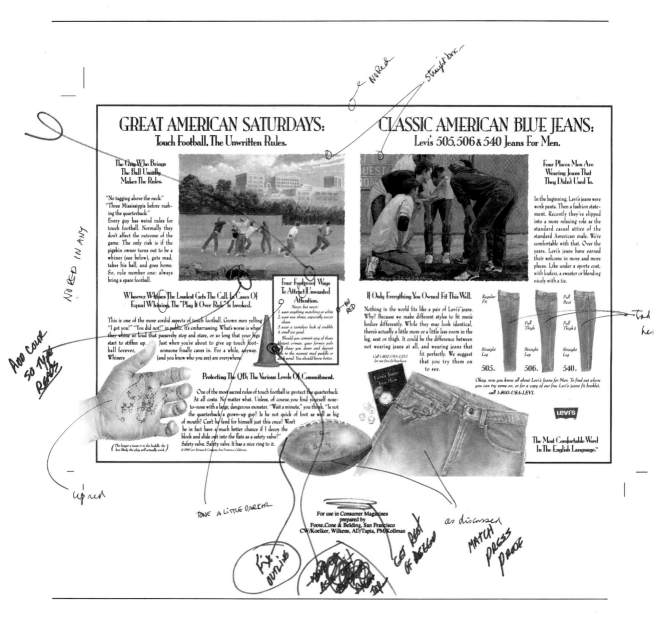

This is the final press proof; approved color proofs and type are laid in together. This is the last chance to make any changes.

This is the final ad as it appeared.

Newspaper Circulation

Just getting your publication printed is not enough; you have to have readers. Circulation is another function usually assigned to the business staff.

Some student newspapers and magazines are sold on a subscription basis. The students purchase a subscription card and take it to a circulation point (usually the cafeteria or student lounge), where it is punched in exchange for the newspaper. People without cards can purchase the issue for a single-copy price. The subscription price should make the per-issue cost low enough to serve as an incentive to the buyer. In some cases, the subscription is sold as part of a total activities ticket.

Maintaining good public relations with the school community includes circulating papers to all faculty members, school personnel, and school officials. It is also important to be sure that each advertiser receives a copy of the paper.

Another circulation method is total or controlled "free" distribution. Under these conditions, the staff publishes sufficient copies for the entire student population. The copies are put in special bins or boxes, placed on counters in the office or building halls, student lounges, cafeteria, or other student gathering places for "free" pickup. The reason we put "free" in quotes is that students usually helped pay for the issue through either an activity supplement or funds made available from general school revenue.

In the case of some strong newspapers with sufficient advertising revenue to be self-supporting, and no subsidy, the paper often is distributed without cost to students. This type of controlled circulation gives your advertisers a known number of readers for each issue. From this the advertising cost per hundred, a figure generally important to advertisers, can be computed.

Many advertisers will test your circulation by running specials only in your publication or by using a coupon.

You also will have mail subscriptions that need to be processed promptly after each issue is published. Some of these may be mailed to alumni, other student publications, students in other schools, and parents. (In some secondary schools and colleges, every parent is mailed each edition the day it comes out.) Subscription lists need to be maintained carefully and purged periodically to make sure you are not mailing to people who have not renewed.

Every publication maintains a list of free subscriptions. These include possible new advertisers, local news media, school board members, key college or school administrators, and leaders in the community. Assuming your product is good, this is effective public relations for your publication and your school.

Evaluate your circulation system often during the year to ensure that it is the best and most cost-effective method for you to use.

Exchange Papers

Naturally, you'll want to receive copies of publications from other schools. Some student staffs mail several hundred newspapers to other schools and receive copies of hundreds of papers in exchange. This is costly. Staff members should evaluate the papers they receive and choose only those they want to receive.

Be sure you have a reason for exchanging with a particular school. Papers from schools that are your athletic rivals are very useful, for example. Once you start the exchange process, be sure your staff is taking advantage of the papers you receive by reading them regularly for ideas. It is a waste of money to receive a pile of newspapers and merely hang them on the bulletin board.

Newspaper staff members can evaluate the quality of their paper by studying newspapers from other schools. Such evaluation helps to generate new ideas for features, layouts, and treatment of advertising.

Many schools put prospective advertisers on their mailing list. This helps the advertiser see what the competition is doing and demonstrates the quality of your product. A prospective advertiser who is familiar with your publication may be more receptive when your sales rep makes that important sales call.

Keeping Records

Every business or organization must maintain records of all business transactions. The business manager will keep accurate books for all income and expense items. Regular monthly financial statements should be typed and distributed to the editor, the adviser, and probably the school business office. All staff members should realize that you cannot spend money that you do not have or that you need for some other purpose.

Also, like any other sound business, a newspaper needs a procedure for approving expenditures of funds by staff members *before* they spend the money. A small authorization slip works well. Or your school may have a purchase order form you can adapt. Staff members must understand that the school and the newspaper are not responsible for items purchased that did not receive prior approval by the business manager, the adviser, or both.

Every school district has developed procedures for spending and collecting money. Some states have laws that also will affect your activities. Be sure you know the rules.

It is important that the business manager keep all records readily available and up-to-date for the adviser. Should a business representative call to check on billing or an account, answers must be easily accessible.

Wrap-up

Without money, there would be no media. Advertising and subscription revenues are essential if a publication is to exist. The more advertising, the more pages you can print; the more photos and quality graphics and color you can use. The more readers who subscribe, the more you can charge for advertising, too, since advertising rates are based on the number of people you reach with your publication.

But advertising is more than revenue to the media. It serves an important function, allowing businesses to communicate directly with potential consumers. Advertising also helps stimulate competition among businesses, keeping prices competitive. Advertisers evaluate their use of media on the basis of cost per reader, viewer, or listener. In the case of student media, you have a valuable audience to market to advertisers— an audience you have the best ability to reach.

But reaching your advertisers, like most other activities in journalism, requires that you really know your readers. You need to be able to support the value of advertising in your publications with facts. Well-conducted market research on buying habits of the age group you serve will give you valuable information for advertisers and will help convince them that an investment in your publication is cost-effective and potentially profitable.

No one wants to read a publication that is packed full of advertising. You will want to compute your minimum need for advertising based on the costs for each issue. Then, determine the extras you want to provide and determine what percentage of your publication will be devoted to advertising. Next, compute your cost per column inch with the assumption that X percent will need to be sold to pay the full costs.

Do some research on the potential advertiser. What products will appeal to your audience? What sales messages would be effective? You might even prepare some sample ads to show how seriously interested you are in the advertiser's business. Then, armed with the benefits of advertising in your publication, a well-developed advertising cost schedule, and knowledge of how that advertising will help your advertiser's business, go sell the ads.

Once ads are sold, they need to be written and illustrated. This requires that you answer the same five W's and H that your leads and news stories require. Although some very effective ads contain only written text, most will include quality graphics, photographs, or both. All ads have *balance*, use the *optical center* of the advertising space effectively (two-thirds of the way up from the bottom of the ad), use *white space* to help enhance the message, and incorporate appropriate *art*, graphics, or photographs.

There are other business functions in addition to selling and preparing advertising. The newspaper needs to be sold and distributed. Businesses don't buy advertising unless they feel assured that the publication will actually reach the intended audience. You also need to make sure that advertisers and subscribers are billed and that bills are paid. Control of expenditures is another critical activity of the business staff, usually composed of the business manager and staff members who will sell and prepare advertising, manage circulation, and handle billing and payment records.

Advertising is a rewarding career with many diverse opportunities. It also plays critical roles for our media and for our society and economy.

On Assignment

Teamwork

As a team, develop a marketing survey for your school publications. Write the questions and responses. Determine how you would conduct the survey (random sample or all students). Compare your survey plan and questionnaire with those of the other teams. Develop a combined survey instrument.

Invite a local opinion researcher to class to discuss research techniques and to critique your combined questionnaire and your planned approach to securing the opinions of the students. (If no one is available, determine if your school or nearby college has a teacher on staff who has had experience in public opinion or marketing surveys, or contact your school's central office to identify someone in evaluation or testing.) Meet with the head of data processing for your school if you plan to have your results tabulated by computer.

Now, make your final revisions in the instrument and conduct your study. When the results are tabulated, each team should conduct its own analysis of the data. Write a report (four pages at most) on the survey. What are the implications for attracting new advertisers? How can the data be used to hold on to current advertisers? As a team, prepare a report to show prospects the benefits of advertising in your publications and to educate them about the student market. Compare your interpretations and marketing report with those of the other teams. Now, write one or two news stories on the study results for your newspaper. Student opinions are news!

Practice

1. To test your critical thinking, write an editorial, column, or opinion feature on one or more of the following statements. You may take any position and use any type of editorial approach. Provide evidence that you did your homework before writing.
   a. Advertising makes people vote for candidates they should not.
   b. Advertising makes people buy products they don't need.
   c. Advertising has been a leading factor in improving our standard of living.
   d. Advertising should be banned from television.
   e. Without advertising, the economy of our nation would suffer greatly.
2. Mount two ads from the local newspaper on a piece of paper (folding large ads to fit the page). Using the same size for an ad, prepare a layout and write new copy aimed at the students in your school. Write the headline and indicate what art you would use from the ad or what new art you would develop. Exchange your ads with those of two other students in your class. Have them write a one-page critique while you do the same for their ads. Use the checklist in this chapter as your guide (see p. 299).
3. Develop an advertisement based on the following information:

   A computer store near your school allows students to rent microcomputers to use at home. The cost is $25 monthly. The microcomputers have built-in modems that can connect to various databases, including games, publications, research libraries, and other records. A printer is also provided.

   All rental payments will apply to purchase of the microcomputer should the student decide to buy it later.

   Rental agreements are for three-month intervals.

Students who bring in the ad from your paper will be given free software, worth $250 that will allow them to access databases for use in doing research.

The equipment is easy to use and comes with an instruction manual. A class is held at the store each Saturday for $10.

You have a photo of two students in your school using the equipment, and a photo of the store.

The store name is ComputeRents & Sales, Ltd.

The size is to be 4 columns by 12 inches.

Supply any information needed to complete the ad.

Your Turn

1. Select a company that does not currently advertise in your school newspaper and develop a two-page sales letter to the potential client. If you have research on your student population's buying habits, use it in your letter. Tell the advertiser about your school, your newspaper, and it's potential as an advertising tool for the company. What would you suggest that the company advertise? Exchange your letter with others in your class. Critique their letters as if you were the potential advertiser. When you get your letter back, rewrite it.
   (Depending on your class situation, you may want to go ahead and send the letter. Then arrange to see the potential advertiser, taking ad layouts, suggested copy, and sales information. If you are successful, you will have a new advertiser!)

2. Do the same thing for the school yearbook or school magazine. Exchange letters with classmates. What are the differences in approach? Why? Discuss these questions in class. Next, prepare advertising ideas and sell the ad for your yearbook or magazine.

3. Visit a local advertising agency, or bring in representatives from local agencies or from the advertising sales departments of local media. Discuss how they go about selling ads. Discuss the issues raised in the critical thinking section. What are the reps' positions on those questions? Compare the ad agencies' approaches to those of the media advertising reps.

4. Interview the business managers for your newspaper, yearbook, or magazine. How are they organized to handle business functions? How do they handle circulation? Determine their budgets? How do they respond to the critical thinking issues raised earlier?

5. Invite the business manager from your local newspaper, radio, or television station to meet with your class. Discuss how he or she prepares to sell advertising to a new prospect. What research is done? Why should anyone want to buy space or time in this medium? How does the business manager "work" the prospect before attempting to make the sale—letters sent in advance, promotional activities?

6. In your library, find articles that discuss research on the buying habits of today's teen and youth markets. In addition to surveys from Teenage Research Unlimited, you might find results from large polling companies like Roper and Gallup, or useful information in *American Demographics and Lifestyles* magazine. Write a sales letter to the businesses currently advertising in your student newspaper. Tell them how important the market is, and how the school media are valuable in helping them tap it. The letter will reinforce their "good judgment" to advertise in your publications. Now, write one to those not using your publication. Make it convincing!

7. Using the research you conducted for activity 6, prepare an article for your school newspaper on the teen and youth markets. And, if you can do so, why not call and do a class interview with one of the researchers? He or she may have even more current information for you.

Mike Quon

There's more to being a graphic artist than drawing.

"If somebody just likes painting pictures of ducks, they might want to be a fine artist, not a graphic designer," says New York's Mike Quon.

Quon has owned and operated the Mike Quon Design Office in lower Manhattan since 1972.

While drawing skills and creativity are key elements in becoming a successful graphic designer, Quon said one must also be able to understand business. "You're there to serve a company. It really is to sell." Out of necessity, Quon realized he had the ability to sell himself and his work.

Quon originally was "nudged into an attempt at a medical career," despite a natural talent for design that he picked up from his father, who worked in design and advertising. "Twenty-five years ago I was geared toward chemistry and science, preparing to be a dentist or a doctor," Quon said.

Then he flunked chemistry. "It was obvious I didn't belong in the UCLA medical school, so I immediately transferred to the art department."

Quon was fired from his second job after graduation for being what he calls a "rabble rouser." "I had to survive," Quon said, explaining that the struggle to make a dollar made him realize he could run his own business. "The less-than-wonderful circumstances of being fired can be turned into something

good." For Quon that led to his eight-person design office, an office that has been recognized with several national awards. The office's big-name clients include American Express, Coca-Cola, AT&T, and the 1988 Presidential Debate.

"It's a fairly easy access business. There are no bars or boards to pass," Quon said. "[But] a lot of people in the business are semi-talented. Computers are making it very easy for people to get into the business." He predicted that the graphic design industry will continue to grow and competition will get tougher.

"People get a lot of information from just looking at something. Businesses take advantage of the visual world. It's tried and proven." But there is a limited amount of work out there, and firms soon will compete for clients, he said. That is why potential graphic artists must practice their skills and hone their craft. "High school students need to be conscious of their seeing and drawing ability. You have to work hard and practice. And don't get discouraged," Quon said.

"Everywhere I look there is feedback and information. It's hard to tell where your inspiration comes from," he admitted. "Part of the job is to be inspired with the right inspiration at the right time." Graphic designers must reach into the "vast library" in their minds of everything they've encountered in

their lifetime. "Watch movies, go to animation festivals," Quon suggested. Read lots of books, such as Phillip Megg's *History of Graphic Design* and the American Institute of Graphic Arts' *Graphic Arts*, a compilation of award-winning designs. "It's very inspirational."

The business can be frustrating for designers who are unclear about what a client wants. "Clients may not know what they are doing. Part of the designer's job is to tell them what they need." For Quon, this line of work is a lot of fun. "It's natural for me. It's effortless." But for some, it's just another job. "They're efficient, that's all."

Because the field is going to grow more competitive, Quon said students cannot become discouraged. "Don't compare yourself with someone who's been in the business for ten years. Things that seem impossible now come in due time. You just get better each year." ■

Kent Matlock

"Practical experience is the lifeline to a position in this industry," says Kent Matlock, president and CEO of Matlock & Associates, Inc., an Atlanta advertising and public rela- tions firm. "I guess it's like the old phrase in politics, which says to vote early and vote often."

Matlock got involved in advertis- ing early. He was a college repre- sentative for a major marketing promotion while attending More- house College in Atlanta.

That stint in promotion, plus a liberal arts education, helped pre- pare him to open his own advertis- ing agency. After working for a cou- ple of small agencies, Matlock moved to a *Fortune* 500 company and then formed his own seven- person firm in 1985.

From his college studies, Mat- lock gained a general idea of adver- tising and public relations. But he believes that the hardcore realities of the business happen on the job. What is more, he believes that tim- ing is the key to success, whether that means developing expertise about a particular market, winning the business of a client or product that is hot, or landing in a geo- graphical area that is on the up- swing. "Pick a growing market, and the opportunities start un- folding professionally and person- ally," he said.

Matlock said that if you find the right firm, don't worry about start- ing at the bottom, because there is enough turnover in most firms to allow you to move up.

Matlock's company is a minor- ity firm and naturally does some specialty work in that area. But he urges recent graduates to begin their careers in larger and more generalized corporate environ- ments. "The smaller the agency," he said, "the more likely you are to acquire bad habits," adding that large firms are good places to learn to manage the pitfalls. "It's im- portant to get a neutral orientation in the business," he noted. "Learning the fundamentals are of great value long term." Matlock enjoys the freedom and responsi- bility of running his own firm, but he believes that the experience of working for a large "blue chip" firm was extremely valuable.

"Working for a larger firm en- hances your appreciation for the business," he said. And what you learn there can be applied in a small firm which, by virtue of its size and the number of diverse tasks to be performed, gives you a broader scope of opportunities.

Besides pursuing paying clients, Matlock believes there is an oasis of fulfillment in *pro bono publico* work—that is, work done free, "for the public good."

"My greatest joy is *pro bono* work, perhaps because they [these projects] tend to be the things we do out of kindness," he explained. He added that part of the satisfac- tion comes from the opportunity to express creativity and not be "po- liced," as when a client is paying the bill.

Through the years, Matlock has given professional service to the United Way; the American Cancer Society; the Atlanta Chamber of Commerce; the Martin Luther King, Jr., Center; Southern Christian Leadership Council; the United Ne- gro College Fund; and his alma mater, Morehouse College. "The community loves the insight, guid- ance, and support," he said, add- ing that such work often "opens doors" to paying clients. "The most powerful things we cultivate are our relationships," Matlock said.

Practical experience leads to the honing of those skills necessary for success in advertising and public relations. "Good writing is a must," Matlock says, "and the next most powerful asset is initia- tive, with the ability to think on your feet. You must also be a problem solver and possess analytical skills."

Matlock believes that learning never ends. Even when you think you've paid your dues, a real pro continues "to learn something ev- ery day to be the best craftsman he or she can be." ∎

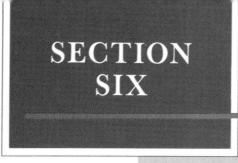

SECTION
SIX

Beyond the Newspaper

CHAPTER SIXTEEN

THE YEARBOOK

Yearbooks have gone through a number of transformations over the years. In fact, writing a chapter on this subject is difficult, since hard-and-fast rules and even trends in this field become obsolete so quickly.

The yearbook is the verbal and visual history of your school year. Yearbooks once were filled with detailed accounts of the entire year; a lot of words, photographs of students and faculty, and a few photographs of school athletics and activities. They contained wills ("I, Susan Smith, will my locker to Bill William") and prophesies ("Susan Smith is destined to become a leading society editor for the *New York Times*"). As photographic techniques became more flexible and easier to use, and as printing methods changed to make it more economical to run photographs, yearbooks changed in style and content.

During the past several years, yearbooks have taken on a more open visual appearance, with dynamic, effective pictures accompanied by crisp, quality writing.

Yearbooks are continually changing. So, as we give you some general advice on yearbooks, we stress that the emphasis is toward creativity and away from rules. Probably the single best bit of advice we can offer is that you become a student of the magazine and the photo essay.

Planning the Yearbook

Yearbooks don't just happen. Like anything else that is done well, they take considerable planning. First, you need to determine the size of your book and how the pages are to be allocated. Some standard book divisions are the introduction, classes, academics, clubs, activities, sports, government and leadership, and advertising. Calculate how many pages are required for each section.

The planning ladder is a useful tool for the yearbook staff.

SIGNATURE #1

1 Page Title 4-Color page 1st deadline	
2 Page Table of Contents — 1st deadline	3 Opening 1st deadline
4 Opening 4-color 1st deadline	5 Opening 4-color 1st deadline
6 Opening 1st deadline	7 Opening 1st deadline
8 Opening 4-color 1st deadline	9 Opening 4-color 1st deadline
10	11
12 4-color	13 4-color
14	15
16 4-color	

Natural Double Page Spread

After you have a general idea of total needs, use a planning ladder provided by your yearbook publishing company or create your own to track page assignments.

In short, you assign every page in the book. Note that the plan starts numbering with the right side in the book. This way you can tell facing pages. Treat your pages in pairs—facing pages—so that they blend attractively as a unit. Never plan layout for single pages even if the two pages of a spread cover different subjects (except for the first and last pages in the book).

Finances

Once you know how many pages you have in the book and how you will allocate them, you need to determine if you can afford it. Because financing the yearbook is a major area of concern, we discuss it separately in a section toward the end of this chapter. After you check your costs for the book, including the type of cover and amount of photography you want, you might have to revise the plan and reduce the size of the book to meet the budget. Or, if your budget is a rich one, you may be able to add some frills—special color sections or cover features.

Theme

After you have planned the content design, you need to meet as a staff to decide on the theme, if you have one (no one says you have to). Do this by brainstorming. Let the ideas sink in for a few days and then discuss the top ones your staff selects. Keep in mind how you can relate the theme to your school situation and how it can be carried out in the division pages of your book (those pages that separate two areas of content and introduce the next section). Ask yourself if the theme is faddish; you wouldn't want to pick something in September that would be old by June. You also need to decide how the theme will be used in the book. Will it be confined to only the title page, general introduction section, and division pages? Or will you try to carry the theme throughout the book in headlines, with a symbol or a color, or through some other device?

Style

Other decisions to be made before work can begin are the type of writing style you will use in the book and the typefaces and sizes to be used. For example, will you use block paragraphs or indent paragraphs? Will you use Mr., Ms., and Mrs. with names? Will you use full first names for students or common names (for example, Ronald or Ron)? Will you write in full sentences or allow thought phrases (a peaceful calm . . . a quiet hall . . . alone before the day begins again . . .)?

Will photo captions for groups read "Row One" or "Front Row"? Will you use J. Smith or John Smith? Middle initials? What will be in boldface? In all capital letters?

A consistent style is important to the total image of your book. After you have determined your style, be sure every staff member knows it and uses the sheet faithfully. And *always* make one final style and typo check before sending your copy to the publisher/printer. Don't rely totally on the spell-check system on your computer. "There" and "their" could be confused, for instance.

For type sizes, similar questions apply. What size and style will you use for captions under group pictures, under informal photographs, for copy blocks, for introduction pages, for advertisements? What will be in italics, boldface, medium type?

The range of your publishing company's type styles will determine your choices. Your company's representative will explain your options.

Planning is also needed in determining the cover design. Again, you will be limited in some ways by your printer, who should spell out completely your options and their costs. Sometimes the simplest design is the most effective. Often, staffs try to do too much with the cover, then are disappointed when they see it in final form.

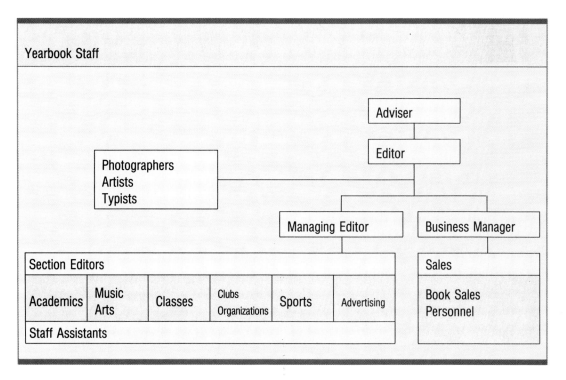

Careful planning and
preparation for a year-
book require the co-
operation of all members
of the staff.

Organizing the Staff

Generally, a yearbook staff is organized as follows: Editor, copy
editor, layout editor, section editors (sports, senior class, activities,
academics) and assistants, business manager, and photographers.
The types of job assignments you make will depend on the size
of your staff and your book.

Editor

The editor directs the staff and sees that deadlines, once established, are kept. He or she also prepares the ladder for the book,
with help from the adviser and the business manager. The editor
is responsible for preparing the opening introduction pages and
usually for the division-introduction pages for each section of the
book. This helps assure consistency in carrying out the theme and
visual concept of the book. The editor also makes the final check
for each page of the book—one final examination as to the style,
content, photo and printer requirements—before it goes to the
adviser and then to the printer.

Copy Editor

In some situations, copy editors write all major copy blocks for the
book. In others they review, edit, make suggestions, and assist
section editors and their assistants in writing copy. We prefer the
latter, since it spreads the work and brings greater involvement.
The copy editor is a checkpoint for quality and coordination. He
or she makes sure that the same copy content does not appear in

more than one place and that the copy follows the required style. The copy editor checks to see that the copy is complete and accurate, free of clichés, and hidden or double meanings—and in good taste.

Layout Editor

A layout editor (a function often tied to the copy editor and in some cases to the editor) is responsible for approving the layout design for the entire yearbook. In some instances, the layout editor designs all pages for each section, and section editors merely fill in the boxes with quality photos and copy. On some staffs the layout editor is the person who checks for layout style. (How far apart are photos? How much space should there be at the top of the page? Can you bleed a picture—carry it into the margin or gutters of the page?) The layout editor can suggest how to crop pictures for maximum effectiveness. Some yearbook staffs may not have this position and may place the responsibility for all layout on individual section editors, with the editor as the final arbiter, style monitor, and coordinator.

Section Editors

Section editors and their assistants prepare the copy, arrange for the photos, and prepare page layouts, if that is part of their responsibility, for all pages in their section. Sections generally cover the areas of school life mentioned earlier—academic, for example,

Students use a planning ladder to organize the page-by-page contents of their yearbook. After this general planning comes the layout and design of each page.

and seniors. Creative photo ideas, interesting copy blocks, and imaginative layout design are the general areas of the section editor's responsibility.

Business Manager

The business manager handles the sale and distribution of books, maintains records, coordinates the sale of all advertising (if you have advertising), and is the editor for the advertising section of the book.

Photographers

Some yearbook staffs assign all photography responsibilities to a photo editor. On other staffs, all members discuss their photo ideas with the editor, who determines the assignments, schedules and manages the photographers, receives and checks all photos, and makes the final crop marks on photos for the printer. It is probably better for each student to handle photo selection, cropping, and other tasks, working with the staff photographer to arrange the schedule. It is also useful for the section editor on major photography assignments to work closely with the photographer.

Photographers receive assignments from staff members and use their own ingenuity and creativity to find pictures that can be used in the book. Some yearbook staffs use local photography studios to take group pictures. Nearly all yearbook staffs contract for the individual ''mug'' shots of students, or students themselves arrange to have them taken by local photographers and brought to the staff before the deadline. Many yearbook staffs announce that any snapshots students may have are welcome and may be included in the book. Planning is important for yearbook photographic content. Know ahead of time what events merit attention and arrange to be there—with a camera.

Writing the Copy

Writing copy for yearbooks is like writing a news feature story. Select the most significant details—covering the entire year—for the copy you write.

Again, be a responsible writer. Be careful of editorializing, unless that is the style you have agreed upon. More opinion, analysis, and reflection can be seen in yearbook copy today, but that does not necessarily make it good. We prefer quality feature writing style based on an objective viewpoint.

When you write for any journalistic publication, you start by gathering the facts and opinions needed to make the story complete. The same is true for the yearbook.

Selecting yearbook photos requires an eye for the composition of each photo and layout of each page.

If you are writing about a student organization, you will want to attend a meeting, interview the members, and review their accomplishments. Talk with the adviser. Interview others who may not be in the group but are knowledgeable about its activities. Start early in the year, looking ahead. Get ideas for photo coverage of real events and avoid having to pose or stage photography.

Write a copy block with substance. Be selective with the information you learned, the same as you would for a newspaper article. Just because this is the "year" book does not mean that you have to record every event of the entire year.

When you write yearbook copy, use quotes. Use names. Use the same crisp, short paragraphs you use in writing news stories. Use active verbs and short sentences. Capture the spirit and feeling of the year. Make your copy live. After all, who said history has to be dull?

Cutlines should be brief and should add to the picture. Don't waste space describing the picture. The reader can see what the picture is saying (unless you have chosen a poor photo). Be sure to identify all people properly.

Yearbook Layout

Two general terms are often used to identify types of yearbook layout: *liberal* and *conservative*. A liberal layout may leave considerable white space on the page for emphasis. It may feature one

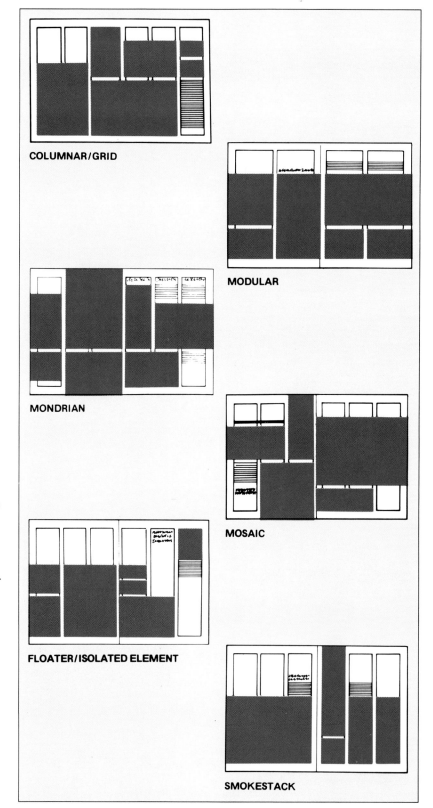

COLUMNAR/GRID

MODULAR

MONDRIAN

MOSAIC

FLOATER/ISOLATED ELEMENT

SMOKESTACK

Here are a number of layout possibilities for two-page spreads. Blue areas indicate photos; lined areas, copy; blank areas, white space. Study each spread carefully. Note that some are predominantly horizontal in design, and others are vertical. Some combine both. Some create a block; others break up space. Some bleed into or across the gutter, or off the page. Examples are reprinted with permission from the National Scholastic Press Association, Minneapolis, MN 55455.

Leading the crowd in a cheer, senior Renee Besanson, junior Rene Felkoff, senior Alesa Shelton, and seniors Michelle Eadie, Lisa Norris, Carrie Burns, and Debbie Corno, lean to the beat. These cheerleaders are essential to every football game. Photo by Kirk Vashaw

Breaking through the line, number 44 senior Adam Klein struggles to gain yardage. This extra effort set the tone for the game and an eventual victory over Paint Branch 14-0. Photo by Gene Orndorff

Going to a football game is a common social activity. Sophomore Kristen Ohlhaber and senior Malissa Stroup meet at a game to share their spirit in supporting the team. Photo by Gene Orndorff

Hunger overwhelms senior David Penn as he munches on a tinfoil hamburger, while senior Jenny Towle dutifully pays for her lunch. Lunches went from $.85 to $1.00 this year. Photo by Pat Owen

Mike Kim of Paint Branch and Terri Speight of Magruder perform one of the common tasks of taking blood pressure.

In Constant Motion

Involvement: symbolic of a positive attitude toward the things which are important. Pupils donated their time to the development or improvement of programs such as HOST and Key Club. Students could be spotted moving to the pulsating rhythms at the ever-popular Cuckoo's Nest, or showing their spirit by cheering on the Warriors during their two Friday night games. This energy and movement created future-thinking and future-seeking students, never static, but always charismatic and ON THE MOVE.
by Marci Feldman

Trying to talk his way out of another predicament, sophomore Larry Hill talks with Mr. Jerry Lea. Lea is not only an assistant principal, but a friend to many students. Photo by Gene Orndorff

4 Opening
►—move—►

Opening
►—move—► 5

This center spread layout in the *Leaves* yearbook of Sherwood High School (Sandy Spring, Md.) reflects two current trends in yearbook design—the magazine-style spread with photos bleeding in the gutter and the use of 4 colors in photography and design.

large, dominant photograph on every pair of facing pages around which other photos and page elements are placed. It will probably have a light, clean look. A conservative layout tries to use as much of the available space as possible. It may be heavy in appearance, with little white space. Some conservative layouts use long copy blocks and a few well-chosen, well-displayed photos for a magazine-like appearance. As a rule, short, well-written copy will not only make your layout more dramatic but will also be read more.

We hesitate to tell you much more about layout than this. Why? Because, as you know, there are no hard-and-fast rules. Again, study quality magazines to see what they are doing with the basic elements of page layout: white space, headlines, copy blocks, cutlines, photographs, and all types of artwork.

The layout artist blends these elements into a pleasing combination that brings the reader-viewer into the pages of the book with great empathy and interest.

Financing the Yearbook

You cannot begin planning the yearbook without a budget. Estimate all sources of income: sales of books, any subsidy you receive, sale of ads, any fees for individual student mug shots in the classes sections, and fund-raising projects. Brainstorm ways to stretch or add to your budget. Here are a few fund-raising ideas:

1. Sell clubs their space in the book. You can charge by the page or portion of a page, or you can charge a certain amount for each person in the club's group photograph.
2. Order and sell T-shirts, buttons, bumper stickers, book covers, and pens and pencils with the name of your school or your yearbook imprinted on them.
3. Show popular movies for an admission fee after school.
4. Arrange to have names stamped on individual books to personalize them, charging a profitable fee for the service (some yearbook companies will do this for you for a modest charge).
5. Sponsor a student-faculty basketball game or other competition.
6. See if you can receive a subsidy from the athletic fund to pay for athletic section pages.
7. Consider using profits from newspaper accounts or a straight subsidy from school authorities or the activity fund.
8. Sell advertising—photo ads prepared in an attractive layout—to local merchants. The size of the student body and the number of yearbooks sold will help determine the rate you charge per page.

Use the ideas about brainstorming in Chapter 3 to identify other ways of raising funds to supplement your yearbook budget.

Despite the almost endless possibilities of fund-raising, the sale of yearbooks is your major source of income. It provides the budget for you to work with. Be realistic and base your sales projections on the number of yearbooks actually sold last year. A budget based on what you hope to sell is not practical.

If you sell ads, we suggest you start several weeks before school begins. All staff members can help sell ads; then the business manager can prepare the section after school starts. The value in early sales is that you know your advertising income and the size of the section at the start of the year. This helps you in budget planning. Also, the advertising section can go to the printer early.

The same holds true for sale of yearbooks. Have all staff members sell books. We recommend one period of concentrated sales— try October only. If students do not order a book during that time, they will have to go without it.

You cannot plan a budget unless you know how many books you will be able to sell. If you spread sales over the entire year, you must operate without knowing how many books you need to order or what you can afford by way of "extras." You can always make exceptions for new students to your school. You can also develop a payment plan to help students spread the cost of the book over several months.

It is essential for the yearbook business manager to keep accurate records and receipts. Without them you could end up in financial chaos at the end of the school year, as well as find yourself with too many or too few books.

Working with the Yearbook Company

Yearbook companies are usually selected through a formal bidding process by the school system business office. Writing specifications for your book is an important task usually done by the adviser. Once selected, a good yearbook company will provide you with a wide range of tools necessary to the success of your book.

When you sign your contract, you will receive your production kit. These kits usually include planning guides and notebooks, clip art you can use in developing ads, lots of "how-to" idea books, ideas and materials to help you raise funds, sales receipt books, ad contracts, photo order forms to use with your photographers, ladder and scheduling charts, layout planning sheets, cropping tools, pencils for marking pictures, a rubber stamp to identify your pages in the printing plant (and probably an ink pad, too), sales posters, and envelopes for shipping your material.

Each company has its own way of working with you and its own array of services. Some may be limited in type styles. Some may limit the number of times or the ways you can bleed pictures.

Getting off to a good start with your publisher/printer is essential. Keep in regular contact with your publisher's representative. Ask questions if you have any doubts at all about how to perform a particular task.

The most important advice we can offer the yearbook staff is to plan carefully and set realistic deadlines. Missed deadlines *add* to the cost of your book or delay its delivery, creating student disappointment.

Remember that the yearbook is for all of the students and for the whole school. Be careful that it does not become a book for a select few or for the staff alone. Balance its content carefully.

Keep in mind that quality doesn't just happen. Good staff members make it happen. Teamwork and cooperation are essential ingredients for your staff. And remember: Your adviser has the final word.

Text-editing operators at a yearbook publishing company must rekey all copy from copyfitting forms sent in by yearbook staffs. Copy is stored on magnetic tape and combined with the layout and output is generated on a high-speed laser image setter.

Photographs are shot on a halftone camera and negatives are made.

The page layout is also taken to the camera department, where a line-shot negative is created. Page negatives and photo negatives meet up in the masking department to be registered as one unit.

Technology is now making it possible to scan all elements at once and produce a single negative.

Color pages require additional work, adding to the cost of the book. Color separations are made of photos using a laser scanner. All color photos can be separated into four colors: magenta, cyan, yellow, and black.

In the pressroom, pages are printed by offset lithography, which means the printing plate created by the masked negatives never touches the paper. The aluminum plate is created using the photographic process, converting the negative image onto the plate, and is then wrapped around a cylinder; ink adheres to the developed areas. The ink transfers to a rubber-coated cylinder and is transferred again to the paper.

While book contents are being prepared, the cover is being processed in another area of the plant. Covers are printed on material or paper and binders' board is attached to create a hard and long-lasting cover.

Different processes can be combined on the cover to produce varied effects. Embossing, seen here, uses a metal die to press or stamp the design into the cover material, giving it a raised effect.

Photos courtesy of the Taylor Publishing Company, Dallas, Texas.

Wrap-up

Yearbooks have changed dramatically over the years. They are quality books covering the school year in photos, artwork, and illustrations, with well-written, feature-style articles. Layout trends often follow such leading magazines as *Life* or *People*, or some of the more popular entertainment magazines.

A quality yearbook begins with effective planning. And, as with other publications, you can only publish what you can afford. Set a realistic budget, develop a plan to meet your projected costs, and be sure that the business staff manages your money carefully. The budget will determine the number of pages, the use of color, the style and design of the covers, and the use of art or other "upgrades." The budget also tells you how many books will need to be sold and how much advertising is needed—and at what rates—to pay for what you plan to publish.

A plan determines the theme for the book (if you have one), the book's style, and the staffing structure appropriate for your needs. It also projects how the book will look, page by page. In developing the plan, staff members need to think through the events of the year ahead and determine how to include them in the book. Standard sections, such as the class pictures, need to be scheduled early in the year to assure effective production scheduling.

All yearbook printing companies have exten-sive materials available to assist staff members in planning and scheduling. These materials are also designed to help you ensure that the important "end-of-the-year" events will be included.

But any plan is only as good as its execution. Planning and taking quality photographs, collecting accurate information on the events of the year, writing crisp and exciting copy, and meeting deadlines are important.

Layout and design of the pages require thoughtful attention. Although there are a number of typical layouts, the emphasis should be on doing what is right and creative for your book. Careful blending of copy blocks and photos produces a dynamic and exciting look that captures your school year. Develop your style sheet and then follow it consistently.

Some school journalists have created video supplements to accompany the yearbook. The same concepts of budgeting, planning, editing, and writing apply to videos. The important challenges are to keep the material brief and to write concisely for viewers rather than readers (see Chapter 17).

Remember, the yearbook is for all students in the school, not just those who are the most active or well known. Your challenge is to make the book a record for all students—you are their journalist-historian!

On Assignment

Teamwork

1. Brainstorm a list of possible yearbook themes. As a class, select the five that seem best for your school this year. As teams, answer the following:

How would you carry out the theme on the cover?
What would you title the book?
How do you relate the theme to your school and students?
How would you carry the theme throughout the book, including the advertising section?

Exchange your ideas during a class reporting session. As a class, select the best ideas for each of the five top themes. You may want to bring together ideas from other groups to develop the best overall way to carry out each theme.

When you have refined and further developed the five best themes as a class, each group is assigned one to implement. Your team will

refine the idea for the cover art and division pages (write your plan in two pages);
sketch the art or describe cover photos you would use;
prepare the division pages;
write a short explanation of how the theme relates to the school and its students;
prepare a layout for an eight-page introduction section;
write photo orders for each picture you plan to use, keyed by page and number;
write the necessary copy and headlines;
take the photos (or find similar ones in files or magazines), crop and size them, and write the cutlines.

2. Develop a marketing plan for your school yearbook or magazine. You have two objectives: Sell the publication to the required number of subscribers, and sell advertising to reach your target budget. If you conducted the marketing survey suggested in Chapter 15, use it to identify advertising pros and cons and target audiences. Plan the ads you would run in your school newspaper or on the school newscast or daily announcements. What special events would you conduct? Design a poster, an eight-week time schedule, and staff assignments for your marketing effort.

Practice

1. Photocopy five sets of facing pages from last year's yearbook. Take them from different sections, but not from the introductory section. Redesign the elements on those pages. You may enlarge, reduce, or crop the photos differently. Rewrite the headlines. You may also rewrite the copy to improve the content or fit your layout style more effectively. Exchange your

layouts with others in class. Critique each other's work, suggesting further improvements. Write your critiques in the form of a letter to the editor of the school newspaper, with a maximum length of two pages.

2. Financing the yearbook is an important staff responsibility. Invite the yearbook business manager to explain how the current budget was prepared and what the sources of revenue are. How does the budget compare with last year's budget? If you have a school magazine, do the same thing with the business manager of that publication.

Your Turn

1. In the school or local library, find copies of your yearbook from five, ten, or more years ago. Write a short paper on the changes you can identify over the years. What did you like about the older books? What did you dislike?

2. If your city has a local magazine or your newspaper publishes a magazine section, invite the local editor or other staff members to a news conference with your class. Learn about the magazine's editorial policy, layout concept and approach, overall target audience, marketing studies, and other details that will help you expand your knowledge about publication planning, design, and execution. Write a news story about the interview. Also, write a critique of the latest issue of the magazine in editorial column style. If you do not have a local magazine editor, consider arranging a telephone interview using a speaker phone.

Marion Elmquist

Marion Elmquist never dreamed of a journalism career in the health care field or even a career in the magazine world.

"That was the last thing I would have thought of . . . maybe skiing or tennis . . . but not health care," said the Iowa native who is managing editor of *Modern Healthcare.*

Modern Healthcare, a biweekly, four-color magazine published by Crain Communications, Inc. of Chicago, deals with issues and concerns in the health care field.

The publication is read mainly by hospital and health care administrators and legislators in Washington, D.C., said Elmquist.

Getting to this point in her career was a somewhat uneven journey, but nonetheless, she feels that it prepared her for a myriad of media tasks.

Raised in a "business" family and being business manager of her high school newspaper stirred her curiosity enough to pursue a journalism/advertising curriculum at the University of Iowa.

Elmquist participated in "an experimental program" at the university that included a bit of television, radio, writing, photography, advertising—"lots of different media"— a program that fits well with her appreciation for a broad-based education.

While in college, she became co-editor of a dental school paper, "which I suppose gave me my first contact with something real." She wrote, took photos, did layouts, set type by hand, and even carried the result to a nearby printer.

It is experiences like these that Elmquist feels best prepare budding journalists for actual jobs as well as for the job market.

Experience pays, she said, whether it be an internship, work on a school newspaper, or free-lance writing or editing.

After graduation, Elmquist got her feet wet for one and one-half years in a Chicago advertising agency before a six-month stint in Colorado. She then returned to Chicago to pick up a master's degree in advertising at the prestigious Medill School of Journalism at Northwestern University.

Then she returned to Colorado for a couple of years, which included odd jobs, "a lot of skiing," and various journalism assignments. In 1977 she decided to return to Chicago where she joined *Advertising Age,* also a Crain publication.

Elmquist is a strong believer in real-life journalism experience and hires people with experience, she said.

"I look for a good journalist with solid reporting and editing skills," she added.

Although all journalism school graduates cannot obtain those few plum positions at major daily newspapers, she said there are a number of publishing companies with an array of specialty publications.

"And these can make for satisfying careers," she said, adding

she has become more and more intrigued by the journalistic possibilities in the health care area.

As managing editor of *Modern Healthcare,* she shoulders the "day-to-day responsibility" and is "deeply involved in hiring." While she answers to an editor, Elmquist handles the 15 staff members and acts "as the hub of the wheel."

Advice?

"Demonstrating your skills, not your degree, is important," she said, again emphasizing a broad-based educational background.

"Once you land that first job, even though it might be entry level, be willing to pitch in and do anything," said Elmquist.

She urges beginning journalists to ask questions and, possibly more important, be reliable.

"Have a good sense of curiosity," noted Elmquist. "You have to have a whole lot of interests . . . have a sponge for a brain." ∎

CHAPTER SEVENTEEN

BROADCASTING

Radio is everywhere—at home, in the car, on street corners, strapped onto joggers' waists, and as background in elevators, stores, and offices. Television sets are in nearly every home and are found in cars, boats, campers, and pockets and onto desks and beaches.

Students should be aware of the important role broadcast journalism plays in their lives today. Millions of people can watch the Olympic games, a state party for the Queen of England, a national political convention, or the coverage of a disaster or an assassination. They can hear instantaneous reports from the site of the news. Broadcasting provides hundreds of careers for journalists as well as for actors, disc jockeys, advertising professionals, technicians, sales representatives, and office personnel.

School Broadcasting

Not every high school today has a radio or television facility directly available to students. But that need not prevent you from gaining broadcasting experience. Contact local radio stations, network television affiliates, or cable TV systems to offer to prepare special student programs for them to air. You might investigate securing a special license for limited radio broadcasting, like KIOS-FM, located at Omaha Central High School.

Some schools use the intercom system as a laboratory facility for broadcast journalism. Instead of the traditional daily bulletin being read by an office staffer, each day student journalists compile the bulletin information, rewrite it in journalistic style, gather other school news and interviews, and prepare special advertising spot announcements for upcoming school events. They tape a tightly written five-minute newscast and play it over the intercom every day at noon. This not only improves the quality of the traditional bulletin and increases its usefulness, but also gives students a practical laboratory. Their equipment consists of nothing more than a good tape recorder, a tape splicer, a cassette or disc player (for the musical introduction and advertising sound effects), a few sound-effect records, and an adapter to play into the intercom system.

Some colleges have established closed-circuit systems to broad-

A student broadcasts from the studio of a school radio station, WONC-FM. Courtesy of North Central College, Naperville, Illinois.

cast news, music and interview shows to all residence halls and campus facilities.

If you don't have a live audience, you can still prepare and tape radio shows in the classroom. More and more schools have television cameras and recording equipment available for the classroom. These can be used to provide a television broadcasting experience. In some newer school buildings, every classroom is wired for television transmission from a central studio, so the student journalism class can televise special programs throughout the campus, or do a daily TV news/interview program.

In addition to preparing newscasts, try your hand at documentaries about major school concerns, such as the issues in a student election or curriculum changes planned for next year.

Combining interviews with quality reporting can provide excellent experience in broadcasting and editing.

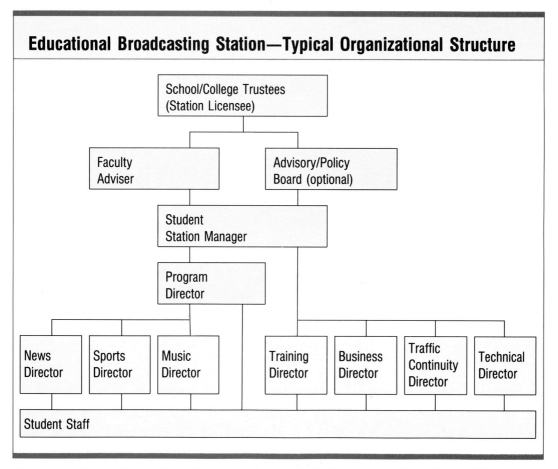

Educational Broadcasting Station—Typical Organizational Structure

*The organization chart was provided by Jeff Tillis, President, Intercollegiate Broadcasting System, P.O. Box 592, Vails Gate, NY 12584.

The Staff

The school radio or television station needs a staff and a clear organizational structure just as the school newspaper does. The chart on the previous page shows how a staff might be organized.

At the top is the board of trustees, board of education, or similar entity in whose name the FCC station license is issued. As licensee, this board is ultimately responsible for the station's operations and programming. In practical terms, day-to-day operations and programming supervision are delegated to a faculty adviser, often someone in the communications, journalism, or a related academic department. The adviser may also be a staff member, such as the director of student activities. The adviser oversees the station and serves as liaison between the licensee board and the station itself.

An optional advisory/policy board may consist of representatives from various groups within the school or college, including students, faculty, and administrators. It may also include representatives of the community served by the station. Its role is generally to act in an advisory capacity or to help set overall policy.

From this point, the remainder of the positions shown are normally held by students. Most serve on a voluntary basis, but some might receive a stipend, academic credit, scholarship, or other appropriate recognition of the enormous amounts of time required of them by the station.

A student production director monitors a television program in the control room.

Station Manager

The Student Station Manager is the highest-ranking student on the staff. The station manager supervises the department directors and the student staff while also serving as principal liaison with the faculty adviser and advisory/policy board. It is the station manager who makes sure the department directors are carrying out their duties. He or she balances the individual department interests for the common good.

Program Director

The program director is in charge of all on-air programming. This includes the design of the program schedule, music format, the selection and assignment of announcers, and the mixture of news, sports, and music to be presented by the station. The program director might supervise those department heads who deal with on-air matters, including the news, sports, production, and music directors.

News Director

The news director works with the program director to select and schedule news programming, news announcers, reporters, writers, and editors. The news director will set the format to be followed for newscasts and other news and public affairs programming. This includes story selection, assignment of reporters, writing style, and integration of audio. The news director selects (within the realistic limitations of the station's budget) equipment and news services to be used by the news department.

Sports Director

The sports director works with the program director to select and schedule sports programming and sports announcers. The news director will set the format to be followed for sportscasts, and decide (along with the program director) which sports events the station will broadcast play-by-play. The sports director selects (within the realistic limitations of the station's budget) portable and remote equipment to be used by the sports department.

Music Director

The music director works with the program director to assist announcers with music selection within the format(s) decided upon by the program director. The music director is responsible for the acquisition of records for the station and for maintaining continuing contact with record companies. Such contact may take the form of periodic playlists to let the companies (and the station's listeners) know what the station is playing. The music director may also be responsible for cataloging new records received by the station, unless there is a record librarian handling that duty. Even in such cases, the record librarian is usually supervised by the music director.

Training Director
The training director is responsible for the recruitment and training of new station personnel as well as ongoing training for existing staff.

Business Director
The business director keeps the station's financial records of income and expenditures, works with appropriate financial authorities within the school or college, prepares annual operating and capital budgets, and works with the station manager to keep the station's spending within its approved budgetary limits.

Traffic/Continuity Director
The traffic continuity director prepares and schedules all public service announcements and program promotional announcements, and prepares and oversees correction of station logs, including the scheduling of all programs and special programs.

Technical Director
The technical director (sometimes called chief engineer) is responsible for the installation, operation, maintenance, and repair of all studio and transmitting equipment, compliance with all FCC technical requirements, and the recommendation of new studio and transmitting equipment.

Development Director
The development director seeks underwriting grants and contributions from businesses, foundations, individuals, and other sources. For closed-circuit stations, this position may be called sales director, in which case it involves the sales of advertising time.

Public Relations Director
The public relations director coordinates all promotion and publicity for the station. This includes writing program promotional announcements, news releases, and contests.

Production Director

The production director is in charge of all production and editing and works with the program director and all other departments using studio editing/production.

Writing for Broadcast

You don't hear things the same way you read them. Everything you write for broadcasting should be read aloud before it is used on the air. The most important thing to keep in mind is that your listener (or viewer) will hear your words only once. This is in contrast to the print media, where the reader can go back over the sentence if it is not clear.

Generally speaking, writing for broadcasting is similar to writing for newspapers. All the basic principles we discussed early in this book apply. Dig into the news. Be a good reporter. You have to write well, clearly, and concisely. Edit your work carefully, remove excessive words, and always check for accuracy. And be objective. Keep these tips in mind:

Copy Preparation

1. Prepare your copy in caps and lowercase, the same as for newspapers. Many people think they should write in all caps. But there is nothing harder to read than all-cap writing.
2. Be concise. Write short, simple sentences.
3. Listen to radio and TV newscasters. Notice how they construct their stories. Listen to the pivot words (the same as transitions). Note their ''headlines'' (often used as a summary—''a car wreck today killed two students'').
4. Remember, words are time. In radio and television, the clock is your enemy because it tells you when you must quit. Use adverbs, adjectives, and descriptive phrases sparingly. There is not much time in a broadcast to go into detail.
5. Spell out all numbers to make them easier to read. (The amount $4,000,225 is fine for a newspaper, but it is hard to read aloud. Write ''four million, two hundred twenty-five dollars.'') This is especially important with large numbers.
6. Use present tense if at all possible. Keep in mind that dates generally are not needed. Broadcast news is immediate; you are there as the news happens.
7. Use phonetic spellings of confusing words or names. Place the emphasis for ease in reading and hearing. Verify identifications.

8. Place the speaker's name at the beginning in all cases, not at the end. Tying a quote with the source is much harder for a listener than for a reader. The names of groups or newsmakers also should appear early in your copy to attract attention. Just as people read selectively, they listen or view selectively. If you are announcing a student meeting with Congressman John Smith as your speaker for Government Club, start with the club name to attract the members' interest: "Government Club members will hear Congressman John Smith discuss his voting record tonight." Always think of the listener.

9. Double or triple space news copy and keep it free of errors and too many pencil corrections. Remember that you can cram only about 180 words into a minute of broadcast news. Depending on your delivery rate, that figure could go up or down—probably down. If you use any music or sound effects in radio, you have to take off words. In television, you have to account for the use of slides, videotapes, or film as well.

On the job in professional TV news broadcasting, Chicago's WGN-TV Nine O'Clock News Team prepares to go on the air. From left are Dan Roan (Sports Anchor), Allison Payne and Rick Rosenthal (Co-Anchors), and Tom Skilling (Meteorologist).

Broadcasting Careers

Even if your school cannot provide for actually broadcasting to the students or the community, you can experience broadcast journalism using a tape recorder or videotape player. It is unlikely that television and radio will ever replace the newspaper, magazine, or other printed materials (the electronic media complement the print media). But they are important vehicles for communications and provide many careers. Many well-trained journalists find it easy to move horizontally from one medium into another.

Wrap-up

It is difficult to go anywhere today and not be within reach of the broadcast media. Cable television news, for example, can be viewed around the clock in nearly every major city in the world as well as in rural communities and on the farm. Radio news summaries reach us in our homes or cars, while jogging, on boats or on the beach. Specialty TV networks meet unique interests, such as religion, education, and sports.

Many schools have developed broadcast journalism experiences for students through internal television facilities or local access cable television. Students can use the school intercom system for radio news programs. In some schools, video-tape provides a television journalism opportunity as students produce—and in some cases sell—quarterly video reports on school activities or a video yearbook.

Regardless of the medium, there is no substitute for the basics of good reporting and quality writing. For broadcast media as for print media, you need to dig into every story to provide the important news for your listener or viewer. There is a difference in how you write and prepare the stories, however. While a reader can go back and read a sentence again for clarification, a listener or viewer cannot hear the information a second time. You have to be conscious of how the listener will hear what you write. Active voice is essential—broadcast news is happening now. Headlines and summaries are important.

There are a myriad of important careers available in broadcasting. Only a few people may ever appear on the television screen or radio, but it takes a lot of people to put them there—people who gather the news, write, edit, film or tape, and produce the program. Support personnel, such as secretaries and librarians, are also important.

On Assignment

Teamwork

As a class, brainstorm topics for documentaries about some facet of your school. Select the top ideas, enough for each team to work on one. As a team, determine your approach to the story. Who are your sources? What research is needed? Do your homework. Prepare for your interviews. Outline a possible scenario for your story so that you have some established direction. Ask yourself, "Who cares?" How can you truly make this story flow and interest your audience? Next, conduct interviews. Use your tape recorder or camcorder. Take good notes to guide your use of the tapes. Prepare your documentary, and play it for your class to critique. How could it have been improved? What were its strong points? Is it of value to the student audience? Ask a local broadcaster to critique it with you.

Practice

1. Clip three news stories from your school newspaper and rewrite them into broadcast style. Then rewrite them for television, indicating what visuals you would use to illustrate the story. Attach the original stories to your work.
2. Invite a local broadcaster to speak to your class. Ask him or her how the station approaches news and how the station works. How do broadcasters cover school news? How is their style unique? Who are their listeners or viewers? Write an interview story as if it were for broadcast.
3. Watch the local television news tonight. List the stories in the order presented. How many minutes were allocated to each? Note the visuals. Then read the local newspaper. How were those same stories treated? Write an editorial feature on the differences in how news is treated by different media on the same day. Include your opinion of how they should have handled it.

Your Turn

1. Write and record a five-minute newscast on the activities in your school for a single day. Plan two commercials to promote school events. Compare your choice of topics to those of the other students.
2. Record an interview with a teacher, a student leader, or someone in the community. Before the interview, arrange your questions in logical sequence. Be sure your meaning is clear (for the interview subject and for a listener who may not know anything about the subject). Be prepared for quick thinking, changes in direction, or following up on new leads as the interview evolves. Have three non-journalism students critique your interview. Were the questions good? Did you follow up? What angles did you miss that would have interested them?

Now, ask two classmates to critique your interview. Write a self-critique—what would you change if you could do it over?

3. The key word for television news today is *change*. If you have been a critical observer of TV news over the past few years, you have seen the local news programs expand their coverage to include national news previously left to the networks. Advances in technology and the ease of setting up local correspondents anywhere in the world have almost made national newscasts a thing of the past. There are those who believe that eventually there will be no ABC, NBC, or CBS national nightly news programs, and that we will begin to see the familiar faces of the anchors reporting for the local news programs. Interview local television news people about this trend. Visit the station and see for yourself the vast number of satellite tools available. Learn about video news releases. See how the local station can prepare stories on major scientific advances, making them look local even though the newsmakers are in some other part of the world. Is this trend good? What might be the benefits? What might be the negative results? What about the 24-hour news programs—CNN or CNBC, for example? As cable expands, will it make the local news change again? Prepare a short editorial on what you find, and give your perspective on television news tomorrow.

Kathy Adams

"The biggest advantage of being a journalist is being a witness to history," says WJBK-TV anchor Kathy Adams.

"A journalist is often given a front row seat to events that impact the lives . . . of people." A journalist, she says, has a great responsibility.

Adams takes her responsibility seriously.

Her interest in broadcasting was sparked when she watched classmates at Kent State University prepare for a television program.

"They were putting together a half-hour talk show," Adams recalled. "I was fascinated by the technology, the immediacy, and the creativity displayed. It was then that I decided to major in telecommunications."

Adams studied broadcast journalism and received her bachelor's degree at Kent State.

After graduation, she joined Storer Broadcasting Company. She started out as a copy aide and eventually became a production assistant.

This experience in television taught her a few things. "I realize how much knowledge, intensity . . . were needed to make headway in this field," Adams said. So she concentrated on her skills.

Soon she showed such promise that she was enrolled in a training program to develop her talents as a reporter.

In 1976, Adams moved to Cleveland and joined the staff at WJKW-TV as a weekend anchor and reporter. After a short time, she was promoted to the weekday anchor position and host of a public affairs program.

She gained five years of experience at WJKW-TV before joining WJBK-TV in Detroit. Within one year, she became a co-anchor of the six and eleven o'clock newscasts.

The path to her present success was not always easy. But Adams pushed on, trying her best.

"Every experience—whether good or bad—is an experience I've learned from," she said. Her success is based on her willingness to look for experiences and grow from them.

So it was not surprising that Adams was nominated twice as Outstanding Woman Newscaster by the American Women in Radio and Television in Detroit.

The National American Women in Radio and Television recognized Adams and WJBK-TV for excellence in programming and presentation of a positive and realistic portrayal of women.

She was also a recipient of the Woman of the Year in Journalism and Communication for 1986 from the Hartford Memorial Baptist Church of Detroit.

When asked what advice she would give to aspiring journalists,

Adams listed three.

"Strive for perfection in your writing and delivery. Use your heritage and do not deny it. Finally, accept the great responsibility of being a role model and conduct your life . . . in such a way that it will be an inspiration to others, no matter what their race, creed or color." ■

CHAPTER EIGHTEEN

STUDENT NEWS BUREAU

The play, operetta, orchestra, or band concert . . . .

Honor Day, Regents winners, National Merit Scholars . . . .

The start of football practice, sports recognition dinner, class reunions, homecoming . . . .

New courses, new teachers, a teacher named best in the state . . . . You could probably compile a list of news stories from your newspaper that would go on for pages.

If a story is good enough for your school newspaper, it is often good enough for the newspaper, radio, and television in your community. Educational institutions belong to those who finance and support them. The general public, for example, elects school boards and sends its children to be educated in the public schools— yet it generally knows the least about what is really going on in the schools.

There is no such thing as a monopoly on news. Since you are learning to be a good journalist, you will want to get the news to *all* of the people who need or want it. Since you are on top of the school news beat, where the action is, why not consider forming a student news bureau? Student news bureaus are easy to operate. In fact, they generally come as a byproduct of a job already done well.

What Is the Student News Bureau?

Essentially, a student news bureau provides information concerning the students, faculty, administration, activities, and programs to the local news media for general dissemination to the community at large. However, it should not infringe on your right as a newspaper to keep a secret and get an occasional scoop. Here is how it might operate.

You know what is coming up. If you are going to be announcing all of the finalists for the local Kiwanis scholarship, make a copy of the news story you have written for your school paper. Copy edit it, put a release date on it—the day your school paper comes out—and mail or deliver it to the local newspaper and radio and TV stations. Since they are journalists, too, they will respect your release date just as you would respect theirs. If you are concerned

A student news bureau member informs community media of important stories.

about "leaks," talk with the editor or news director about handling the story so that he or she does not scoop you. When you publish the story in the school paper for the students, the other citizens in your community will learn of the news at the same time through the local media.

If you have a number of lesser items of general interest, you may want to circle them in red on the printed page and send the marked copies of your student paper to the local media. Do so the very day your paper is distributed—the media are much more likely to use your school's news if it is current.

From time to time you may have really important stories that you want to share with the community media. In such cases, call the local editor or youth editor of the paper and the radio and television news directors in advance. This will help them plan their own coverage of the event and may even result in good photographic coverage or an interview. The result is the same: The public is better informed about education in the community. The better informed people are, the more support they can give to your education.

Using the Local Media

Many radio stations have students who call in weekly five-minute news summaries, and some have on-the-air interviews. A good student news bureau makes sure the student doing the calling or being interviewed has full access to the important news. If the journalism department in your school gathers and presents this news, you will have an excellent broadcast news experience. The same is true for the local newspaper with an education or youth page: it often selects correspondents from the schools to send in regular news items. This is another means of broadening your journalism training.

The Publicity Angle

There can also be an advertising or public relations dimension to the student news bureau. You share the pride of your school when it has a good attendance at a musical or dramatic event, or when the fun night or carnival crowd brings in a great profit for an important school improvement. To help attract those crowds, you,

This is the first page of a sample news release that could be issued by the student news bureau. It includes important information to local editors. Note the embargo—time and date. This shows that the news release is timed to an event or the release of your newspaper. Always write a suggested headline to go with your release. You may want to print news release letterhead for use by the news bureau. Personally delivering releases also allows you the opportunity to emphasize the release time.

YOURTOWN SENIOR HIGH NEWS RELEASE

FOR RELEASE FRIDAY, MAY 10
Embargoed until after 12 noon

Five YHS Seniors Named
Merit Scholar Finalists

Yourtown, USA—Three Yourtown High School seniors were named finalists today in the National Merit Scholarship program, according to Susan Learned, principal.

The seniors are:

•Donna Bean, daughter of Mr. William Bean, 425 South Garfield;

•Carolyn Butler, daughter of Mr. and Mrs. George M. Butler, 825 West Ontario Street; and

•Brad Woods, Jr., son of Mr. and Mrs. Bradley Woods, Sr.

"It is an honor not only for the students but for their parents and all of us at YHS," Learned said. "We have been fortunate to have finalists each year in the Merit Scholarship program who have gone on to become winners. It speaks well for the school's academic program and the quality of our students."

(more)

as a trained journalist, can help the drama department, or any other school department or activity, publicize its programs. You can write, and occasionally record, good radio spot announcements. You can help create good television spot announcements and send news releases to the local media concerning upcoming events. Your photographer could even take a few good shots to send (quickly) to the television stations and newspapers in your area.

A student news bureau can be a worthwhile by-product of your regular journalism program. The benefits are increased public awareness of school programs and activities, wider recognition for deserving students, more information for local news media, and greater experience for you.

A Student News Bureau at Work

Here is an example of an effective student news bureau at work.

> You have been given information, in total confidence, about winners of several scholarships. The scholarships are to be announced on Friday morning at an assembly. The school newspaper is distributed after lunch on Friday, so your newspaper coverage will be very timely.
>
> Since you have an exclusive and the timing is in your favor, this story is ideal for your news bureau. After you have prepared the copy, retype it on your news bureau or publication letterhead. Make duplicate photos, if possible. The morning of the announcement, before school starts, have copies delivered to the local newspaper and local radio and television stations.
>
> At the top of your release, type the words "EMBARGOED: Hold for release until after assembly announcement at 10 A.M. Friday, Date."

You have performed a news service for your school, increased the community's awareness of the students' achievements, maintained your exclusive publication of the story, and acted in what many people call a public relations role.

Develop a list of similar opportunities you have during the course of the school year to provide such a service.

Code of Professional Standards
for the Practice Of Public Relations

This Code was adopted by the PRSA (Public Relations Society of America) Assembly in 1988. It replaces a Code of Ethics in force since 1950 and revised in 1954, 1959, 1963, 1977, and 1983.

Declaration of Principles

Members of the Public Relations Society of America base their professional principles on the fundamental value and dignity of the individual, holding that the free exercise of human rights, especially freedom of speech, freedom of assembly, and freedom of the press, is essential to the practice of public relations.

In serving the interests of clients and employers, we dedicate ourselves to the goals of better communication, understanding, and cooperation among the diverse individuals, groups, and institutions of society, and of equal opportunity of employment in the public relations profession.

We pledge:

To conduct ourselves professionally, with truth, accuracy, fairness, and responsibility to the public;

To improve our individual competence and advance the knowledge and proficiency of the profession through continuing research and education;

And to adhere to the articles of the Code of Professional Standards for the Practice of Public Relations as adopted by the governing Assembly of the Society.

Code of Professional Standards for the Practice of Public Relations

These articles have been adopted by the Public Relations Society of America to promote and maintain high standards of public service and ethical conduct among its members.

1. A member shall conduct his or her professional life in accord with the **public interest**.

2. A member shall exemplify high standards of **honesty and integrity** while carrying out dual obligations to a client or employer and to the democratic process.

3. A member shall **deal fairly** with the public, with past or present clients or employers, and with fellow practitioners, giving due respect to the ideal of free inquiry and to the opinions of others.

4. A member shall adhere to the highest standards of **accuracy and truth**, avoiding extravagant claims or unfair comparisons and giving credit for ideas and words borrowed from others.

5. A member shall not knowingly disseminate **false or misleading information** and shall act promptly to correct erroneous communications for which he or she is responsible.

6. A member shall not engage in any practice which has the purpose of **corrupting** the integrity of channels of communications or the processes of government.

7. A member shall be prepared to **identify publicly** the name of the client or employer on whose behalf any public communication is made.

8. A member shall not use any individual or organization professing to serve or represent an announced cause, or professing to be independent or unbiased, but actually serving another or **undisclosed interest**.

9. A member shall not **guarantee the achievement** of specified results beyond the member's direct control.

10. A member shall **not represent conflicting** or competing interests without the express consent of those concerned, given after a full disclosure of the facts.

11. A member shall not place himself or herself in a position where the member's **personal interest is or may be in conflict** with an obligation to an employer or client, or others, without full disclosure of such interests to all involved.

12. A member shall **not accept fees, commissions, gifts or any other consideration** from anyone except clients or employers for whom services are performed without their express consent, given after full disclosure of the facts.

13. A member shall scrupulously safeguard the **confidences and privacy rights** of present, former, and prospective clients or employers.

14. A member shall not intentionally **damage the professional reputation** or practice of another practitioner.

15. If a member has evidence that another member has been guilty of unethical, illegal, or unfair practices, including those in violation of this Code, the member is obligated to present the information promptly to the proper authorities of the Society for action in accordance with the procedure set forth in Article XII of the Bylaws.

16. A member called as a witness in a proceeding for enforcement of this Code is obligated to appear, unless excused for sufficient reason by the judicial panel.

17. A member shall, as soon as possible, sever relations with any organization or individual if such relationship requires conduct contrary to the articles of this Code.

Wrap-up

Many journalists find their future in some form of public relations. It is a career that allows you to combine your interest in journalism with other interests or hobbies.

A news bureau service at your school can provide important opportunities for you, as well as a valuable public relations service to the school. Most people in our communities have no direct link with education—other than paying the tax bill to provide it! Having access to information about school programs and student successes can help them better understand the educational activities they pay for, and can enhance their support. This information also can help bring people into the school for plays and musical and sports activities, thus expanding audiences for students.

The only way the non-student population can learn about the activities of your school and the successes of its students is if someone takes that information to the local news media. Student journalists can provide that link, writing and delivering news releases, photos, and broadcast information for use in local daily, weekly, and suburban newspapers, radio, and television.

It's easy. It's a by-product of your work in producing the student newspaper or broadcast. It can be done by providing the same story you will use for school media or rewriting the story for external media. Either way, it gives you the opportunity to experience a part of the public relations business—media relations—while promoting good news about your school.

On Assignment

Teamwork

As a class, list all of the media in your town that might be interested in school news. Each team will take one of these media. Watch, listen to, or read the medium over the weekend, specifically paying attention to the main newscasts if it is radio or television. You can get news times by calling the station.

Determine what types of news are covered. Does the station or paper have local reporters? Does it cover your school now? Does it cover only sports events? Major and minor sports? Check out the *Standard Rate and Data* books at your local library to learn about the broadcast stations, local magazines, and newspapers. Who are their audiences? You can also contact the station or newspaper for marketing information.

As a team, write an analysis of the medium. How would you approach the station or paper to interest it in school news? If you did the student survey in Chapter 15, what does it tell you about the number of students who listen to the station or read the newspaper?

Discuss your findings with the rest of the class. After you have exchanged ideas, write a letter to the editor or news director about covering your school activities. Remember to convince these people that there is something in it for them—for instance, better coverage of an important segment of their audience.

Practice

From the last issue of your school newspaper, identify which stories could have been covered by the local newspaper. Use the news elements as one guide. Write a one-sentence reason why each story you chose would have been of interest to the newspaper's readers. Attach the school newspaper to your list. Next, find copies of the local newspaper during the week before and the week after your publication date. Did it use any of those stories? Attach copies. Did the local paper take a different approach from the school newspaper?

Your Turn

1. If your school district employs a media consultant, invite him or her for an interview with your class about working with the media and securing effective coverage. Write an interview-news conference story. You may also write to the National

School Public Relations Association for information about school communications to your community (NSPRA, 1501 Lee Highway, Arlington, VA, 22209).

2. Clip a feature story and a straight news story from your last school newspaper. Rewrite them to interest a broader community audience.

3. Examine the last three issues of your school newspaper. Identify five photos that could have been used in the local newspaper or a local magazine. Mount them to a sheet of paper and write a short statement addressing why they could have been used. Write an appropriate cutline for the local newspaper's use. (Remember that its readers may not know much about your school.)

4. As an exercise in critical thinking, reread the Society of Professional Journalists' Code of Ethics in Chapter 1. Compare it with the ideas expressed in the code of the Public Relations Society of America. What conflicts do you see between the two codes? How can an ethical journalist function as an ethical publicist? Invite local public relations people to class to discuss this. Ask local editors to discuss their policies. Write a short editorial column on this subject, taking any viewpoint you choose. Create a mini-torial, too.

Don Flores

A love of sports sparked Don Flores's interest in journalism and helped him score big in a profession that attracts very few minorities.

From his first bylines as a young reporter covering Little League in his hometown of Goliad, Texas, to his current position as editor of the *New Mexican* in Santa Fe, New Mexico, Flores has followed a specific career path.

He graduated from writing Little League stories to writing for his junior high and high school newspapers. Then, when he entered Southwest Texas State University in San Marcos, Flores joined the student newspaper as its sports editor.

In 1973, Flores graduated, moved to northern Texas, and began working for the *Abilene Reporter-News*. He was first assigned to "doing cops and obits just like everyone else" but quickly advanced, within three years, to the position of city editor.

His career path took him to the *Dallas Times Herald* in 1978.

In less than a year, Flores was promoted to wire editor. By 1981, he was the night metropolitan editor. Then, in 1983, the *Herald* lost him to its competitor—the *Dallas Morning News*.

During his various moves in the newsrooms of Texas, Flores also was becoming active in organizations and programs designed to bring more minorities into journalism. One program in particular was the summer journalism program for minority high school students that was run by Texas Christian University in Fort Worth.

"That's how we get them [minority journalists] in the newsroom," Flores said. "We track them from high school to college and then snap them up as soon as they are ready."

At age 34, Flores left Texas and joined the *Tucson Citizen* in Arizona as assistant managing editor, a job that allowed him to be directly involved in recruiting.

Flores says he is not a joiner, but his activities contradict that statement.

He has been an active member of the National Association of Hispanic Journalists and the National Association of Black Journalists for many years. He regularly attends the conventions of both organizations where he "scouts" for talented minority journalists.

In December 1986, Flores moved to the next level in his accomplished career—editor of the *New Mexican*.

Although this position places a greater demand on his time, Flores is determined to continue his efforts to recruit more minorities into the newsroom.

"I hope I can continue what I am doing. I expect to be out in the community a lot," he said.

Reflecting on his early years as a journalist, Flores said, "As hard as it is to imagine, I was the first Hispanic to edit at the *Record* in San Marcos, Texas."

Today minorities are being encouraged more and more to pursue career opportunities in the newsroom. Flores fully acknowledges the importance of his position as a Hispanic journalist in Texas. "I am concerned about being the role model a lot of us didn't have." ■

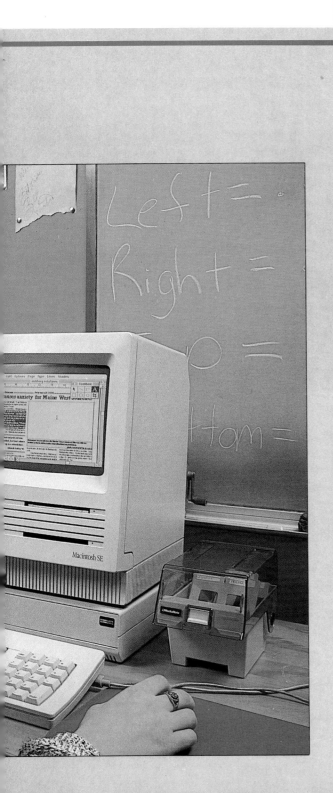

Under-standing the Technology

Chapter 19 Taking, Developing, and Printing Photographs

Chapter 20 The New Technology of Publishing

CHAPTER NINETEEN

Taking, Developing, and Printing Photographs

Words are great tools for storytelling. But sometimes they can't describe or set the mood and scene well enough. Sometimes they don't provide the necessary movement. They may need help from pictures. In fact, pictures sometimes tell stories better than words. Seasoned writers know that pictures can be the central device for explaining and clarifying, in part because audiences have learned to depend on pictures to help them understand.

If you're interested in journalism, don't ignore photography; it can do more for you today than ever before. It may seem technical and mysterious at this point, but don't let it frighten you away. Young journalists probably have more success in this area if they avoid becoming deadly serious about it. Sure, the world's great photographs may result from doing everything just right; but the best photographers are often proudest of pictures taken when they were in a relaxed, receptive mood.

Get the help that's available to you at every turn—in advice, in getting good pictures, or in processing them. It's best if you have a camera, of course, but usually your equipment is limited to what your family owns, what you can afford, or what is provided in class. Don't jump in over your head. If you need to buy a camera, pick one that's easy to operate until you learn more about photography. Reasonably priced cameras for general use are available everywhere. You can get free basic instruction booklets and exposure guides at any film shop, and ask your local photo dealer for advice when you need it.

If you don't have a camera and don't want to invest in one, remember that millions of pictures have already been taken. There may be some of the scene, event, or person you have in mind. You'll be surprised at how easy it is to borrow them.

Parts of a Camera

Cameras in principle are much alike but may differ in three basic parts: the lens, the shutter, and the viewfinder. Variations in these parts usually are adaptations for whatever job the photographer wants to do. A camera is precision made, so take care of it.

Lenses vary from single pieces of ground and polished glass to complex and expensive groupings of several glass elements. They are designed to admit as much light as you need for a picture and to control it. All you need to know now is whether your lens has a fixed focus or an automatic focus, or needs to be focused manually.

The shutter is like a door. You open the door when you squeeze the shutter release to take a picture. It may be a flap that covers an opening near the lens, or it may be a sort of window blind in front of the film in the rear of the camera. With an adjustable-speed shutter, you can determine how long the door is open and how much light passes through the lens to the film.

The opening, or aperture, that the light passes through can't be adjusted on a simple camera, but if yours has an adjustable-speed shutter, it probably has an adjustable aperture also, measured in f-stops. Think of the shutter as a door and of the aperture as the size of the opening that the door covers. Varying the amount of time the door is open or varying the size of the opening, or both, will allow you to control light, the key element in photography. The amount of light you put to work in taking any picture is called exposure.

Viewfinders allow you to plan, or compose, your picture. Whether your viewfinder is an ordinary sighting frame or a complicated device with lenses, the idea is to let you see the whole picture before you take it. If you have a reflex camera, the viewfinder allows you to view the scene through a lens and mirror. If it is a double-lens reflex camera, you see the picture through a second lens much like the one that admits the light to the film. With a single-lens reflex, you actually view the scene through the lens that takes the picture. Studio cameras and view cameras usually allow you to focus the scene directly onto a ground glass so you can compose and adjust the picture before it is taken.

Understanding Film

The "mystery" of photography and the resulting fear many students have toward getting involved in it are usually traced to film. There are many kinds of film, and they vary like cameras in the job they do. The most ordinary film has a base of flexible, transparent material with a smooth, creamy-yellow coating. The working principle in film is that the creamy coating contains millions of tiny silver bromide crystals, which are changed when exposed to light. Each tiny crystal records its individual exposure to light by turning black later on during development.

Some films for black-and-white pictures allow better reproduction of the darkness of some colors than others. Some films are made to react "faster" to light; that is, they require less light than other films. A few films are made for more "contrast"; this means they produce great differences in brightness between the light and dark areas of the picture. Advances in manufacturing film have resulted in some films of finer grain to avoid mottled effects. It's best to remember, though, that films with special qualities are made for special purposes; to get one quality in film may mean giving up another quality you want more.

Using Light Effectively

Light is the key word in photography—the light that reflects off your subject or scene and passes through your lens to the film. Each kind of film works best when exposed to a given amount of light. Your job is to adjust the speed of your shutter and the size of your lens opening to produce the right amount, the correct exposure.

Of course, if your camera is a simple one without shutter or aperture adjustment, it's made to produce usable pictures under maximum sunlight conditions. If it does have shutter and aperture controls, you still have no problem, as long as you follow a few rules of exposure.

There are two ways to measure the amount of light reflecting off a subject. One is to get a printed exposure guide from your film shop, then follow its directions in estimating the amount of light as you prepare to take a picture. Using the guide, find the scale for the kind of film you are using. Then find the right combinations of aperture setting and shutter speed. Remember that the aperture setting will be in *f*-stops, which are marked on the lens. The shutter speed will be in fractions of a second, which are marked on the shutter adjustment. The guide will give you the shutter speed for each aperture setting.

The other way to measure light for proper exposure is with a light meter. There are all kinds of meters in a range of prices, but even the cheapest will probably work better than guessing at the light. If you're lucky enough to have a light meter, either as part of your camera or as a separate device, much of the exposure job is done for you. When you aim the meter at your scene, it will give you reliable settings for both shutter speed and lens opening. Some meters are built into cameras and make these adjustments automatically.

Sometimes the subject of your picture will force you to use an extreme setting of either the shutter speed or the lens opening. You can still admit the proper amount of light in many cases by adjusting the other setting to allow for it; it's trading off one value for another. For example, the subject of your picture is moving rapidly. To "stop" it and prevent blurring of the image on the film, you might decide to use a shutter speed of 1/500 second. Because you will open and close the shutter "door" so swiftly, you must make the opening larger for the correct amount of light to enter. Your exposure guide or light meter will give you the proper aperture setting.

Focusing

The lens in a simple camera can't be moved in relation to the film. It's small and designed so that objects varying considerably in distance from the camera will be acceptably clear, or "in focus," on the film. If your camera has a focusing lens, however, you must adjust it closer to or farther from the film so that your subject will appear sharp on the developed film.

Focusing the lens may vary from camera to camera. You may turn a ring that surrounds the lens, or you may turn a device at the side of the camera with your thumb and forefinger. Reflex cameras and studio or view cameras are focused by simply adjusting the lens until the image in the viewer or ground glass is sharp. With other cameras, measure the distance to your subject by estimating or by reading the distance with a range finder. Like a light meter, a range finder may be built into the camera or separate from it.

However you measure the distance in feet, turn the camera's focus adjustment to that distance. A basic rule: If the distance to the subject is less than 25 feet, the focus setting must be accurate. If it's less than 6 feet, use a range finder or a tape measure. If the subject is 50 to 75 feet away, an estimate is usually good enough. If it is 100 feet or more, set the lens at infinity.

A recent technological development is the automatic-focusing camera. A touch of the button brings the subject into focus automatically.

F-stops

Focusing is closely related to lens size or lens opening. Those *f*-numbers you see on lenses aren't complicated or mysterious. The *f*-number of a lens simply explains its size, when it is fully open, in relation to the distance from the lens to the film. So, an *f*/4 lens has a diameter of one-fourth the distance from the lens to the film; an *f*/8 lens has a diameter one-eighth as large as the distance from lens to film, and so on.

An *f*/4 lens, obviously, has twice the diameter of an *f*/8 lens and its area is four times that of the latter. Because it has four times the area, it will allow four times as much light to pass as will an *f*/8 lens. In photography language, it is four times as "fast."

When you adjust the size of the opening, or aperture, you are really adjusting the size of the lens. These lens opening adjustments are marked in stages to give you a standard measure of how much light each setting will admit. For example, a lens that is rated *f*/4 when wide open usually is adjustable in progressive settings to *f*/5.6, *f*/8, *f*/11, *f*/16, and *f*/22. Because these adjustments to reduce the size of the opening "stop" part of the light, the adjusting process is called "stopping down," and the positions are called *f*-stops. Closing the opening and moving from one *f*-stop to the next larger *f*-stop number reduces the light by one-half.

This photograph illustrates a common depth-of-field problem. Notice that the girl's right hand and forearm are out of focus. Because of the low-light situation, the *f*-stop was kept wide open, thus reducing the depth of field. To get the whole picture in focus, the photographer could have (1) used faster film, or (2) used a slower shutter speed and "stopped down" the lens.

Depth of Field

You don't always use all of your lens sizes, or "speeds," simply because you don't always need them or want them. As you have already seen, a wide-open "door," or lens opening, will allow you to use a fast shutter speed and thus "stop" a moving subject. But a wide-open, or fast, lens won't give you much of what photographers call "depth of field." That's the distance between the points nearest to and farthest from the camera that appear in sharp focus when seen through the lens.

Think of it this way. If you want to get a picture of a lumberjack ten feet from the camera and still get a clear image of the mountain in the background, you'll need to think about depth of field. This means that when converging light rays pass through a small aperture, their angles are small, and nearly all objects in the field of view appear to be in focus.

If the lumberjack in front of you is standing still, you can use a fairly slow shutter speed under normal light conditions. Then you can stop down to a small aperture setting to bring the mountain background into focus as well as the foreground. But if the lumberjack is swinging an ax, you'll have to use a fast shutter speed in order to stop the action. Now, to admit the proper amount of light, you'll have to open up the lens aperture setting. This will cut down the depth of field, and the mountain will disappear in a blur. Face it: You can't always have both lumberjacks and mountains. As you experiment, you'll find that depth of field decreases the closer you get to the subject. It also decreases in indoor photography, when you may have to use a wide lens opening for proper exposure.

Preparing
for Pictures

After you have decided which lens opening and shutter speed to use, frame your picture carefully. Be sure people and objects are exactly where you want them. Check the focus again. Then hold the camera steady with two hands and nine fingers. Use one finger to gently squeeze the shutter release. It's best to stand with your feet shoulder-width apart, your weight evenly balanced on both feet. This will help you support the camera with your body as well as your hands.

Many pictures happen only once, and you may ask how you have time to prepare when your chance for the picture may last only seconds. The answer is in planning for the pictures you're pretty sure will happen. Plan your actions to mesh with predictable actions of the sun, the pole vaulter, or the blooming rosebush. Often you can focus and adjust speed and aperture settings in advance, perhaps by aiming at a dummy scene before the picture subject arrives.

Developing
the Film

You've squeezed the shutter release and exposed the film. Once you've exposed the entire roll, you must develop or have someone else develop that long strip of images that are still invisible. Until you arrange for your own darkroom and equipment, consider having a commercial photographer do it. The developed film becomes negatives, one negative for every picture you've taken. Have your film shop develop the film and make a contact print of each negative. From these contact prints, printed on one large sheet of positive paper, you can easily decide which of your pictures are good enough to have enlarged prints made of them. You can order the prints to be made the exact size they will appear in the publication.

One way to get into picture processing slowly and easily is to have your film developed by a commercial photographer and then make your own positive prints from the negatives. Sooner or later, however, if your interest in photography grows, you're going to want to develop your own film and then your own prints. You'll need several pieces of equipment and some chemicals, but with a little ingenuity, you'll be able to perform basic developing and printing at a reasonable cost. Then, as you get better and want to do more with film, you can add to your equipment.

The Darkroom

First, you need a room in which you can block out all outside light. Kitchens, bathrooms, closets, or basement rooms have started many photographers on their way. A sheet of plain white paper shouldn't be visible to you after the lights have been out several minutes. It's great if your room has running water, and better yet if the water is both hot and cold to mix for the right temperatures in your solutions.

You'll also need four enamel or glass trays about nine by twelve inches, a thermometer, a liquid measure, bottles for storing solutions, a safelight, and a square sheet of glass for printing. Many films are not sensitive to red light and can be developed under a ruby-colored safelight. Panchromatic films are sensitive to all colors, however, and must be developed in full darkness.

Go to your local photographic dealer for developing chemicals, packets, cans, and bottles of chemicals already mixed in just about

Hypo, or fixing solution, hardens the film emulsion and helps protect the surface of the print. After washing the print, the next step is drying.

any amount you want. You need only mix them with water as the instructions tell you. The labels will also give you information on proper temperatures and development times. These aren't merely tips; they come from years of experimenting and practical testing.

Your film must be agitated while it's being developed to keep fresh developer in constant contact with the film emulsion, or coating. You can agitate a single piece of sheet film simply by rocking the tray of developer. If you have roll film, grasp it at both ends and loop it in a U shape. First rinse it in water to keep it from curling. Then dip the bottom of the U in the developer, emulsion side up, pulling the film upward first on one side of the U, then on the other. Make sure the looping action gets both ends in the developer in turn for the proper development time.

Now lift the loop of film to the rinse bath tray and pull the loop through clear water, which will remove the developing chemicals from the film's surface.

To make the film image permanent, loop it through a fixing bath, called fixer in the third tray. The film coating not blackened during the development will be dissolved away in this solution. Also, the fixer will harden the film emulsion enough to prevent any scratching of the finished negatives during ordinary handling. The fixer should clear your film of its yellowish coating in about five minutes. If you're developing panchromatic film and have been working in total darkness, you can now turn on your safelight and see if your pictures are as good as you had hoped. Another ten minutes in the fixer should complete fixation.

Next, wash the film in running water to get rid of all those chemicals. It takes at least thirty minutes of this to prevent chemical stains and fading. Use the fourth tray and keep a flow of fresh water moving into it. That should agitate the film well enough, but you can speed the washing by occasionally running roll film through the U-dipping procedure.

If your camera takes roll film or, especially, 35mm reel film, you'll soon see the advantages of buying a simple developing tank. To use one of these, wind the undeveloped film onto a special reel. Then put the reel and film into the little tank and fasten the cover. Developer, rinse water, and fixer are added and removed through holes in the lid according to regular timing directions. Film and chemicals are agitated by turning the tank over occasionally, or by rocking it. Wash the film with a stream of water directed into the reel.

Your strip of developed film is now all wet. Before you cut individual negatives apart, hang the strip up by one end to dry;

an ordinary cord and clothespins work fine. But drops of water will cause spots when they dry, so remove them by slowly wiping each surface down with a clean, dampened cloth as soon as you hang up the film.

After the film is dry, remove the clothespins and with scissors cut the strip of film into individual negatives, or, for 35mm film, into strips of five or six. At this point your negatives are the most valuable product of your photographic interest. They are fragile and easy to lose, so take care of them. You'll save time and money if you find envelopes and a box to hold your negatives. File them according to the date they were taken, or by subject matter. Listing exposure settings and developing data on the envelopes can be a big help later. Be sure to handle negatives only at the edges.

Making Prints

We can't do much in photography without negatives, but they aren't much good as they are. Look at one. The image of your "shot" is there, but reversed. The dark areas look light and the light areas look dark. The areas that should be dark appear light because they are transparent, or at least more transparent than other areas.

To get a truer image of blacks and whites, you must pass light through the negative onto paper that has a light-sensitive surface. The most transparent parts of the negative will allow the most light to pass through and thus create a dark area on the printing paper when it is developed. Now light and dark areas will appear as they were in the scene you photographed.

You can place the negative directly against the printing paper and expose it to a light source. The image on the paper, once it's developed, will be the same size as the negative. This is called a "contact" print. If your camera takes a large-size film, your negatives will be large, and contact prints may be big enough.

You'll need your makeshift darkroom again, but because most printing papers react only to blue light, you can work under a red safelight. There are four steps in the printing process: exposure of the paper, development, fixing, and washing. For the last three steps you'll need trays big enough to hold printing paper the size you'll be using. Buy prepared printing chemicals in packets or bottles so they can be mixed easily with water. As before, follow the instructions for mixing, temperature, and timing.

You can buy or even make a good printing frame for contact printing. An ordinary clean sheet of glass, about six by eight inches, taped around the edges for protection will do fine for a start. The glass will hold the negative and printing paper in close contact for the exposure.

Working under the safelight in your darkroom, remove one sheet of printing paper from its light-tight container and close the container tightly. Place the paper, emulsion side up, on a clean table surface. Now place the negative, emulsion side down, on top of the paper, and cover both with the clean sheet of glass. You can't tell which are the emulsion sides? Well, printing paper usually curls toward the emulsion side. On a negative, the dull side is the emulsion side.

Check again to see that your container of unused printing paper is closed tightly. Now position an ordinary 40-watt electric light about a foot above your printing glass and turn it on for a few seconds. Turn off the light and remove the exposed sheet of printing paper from under the glass. It's ready to develop.

Probably the most reliable way to find the correct light exposure time is by trial and error—but not with full sheets of printing paper. Cut one sheet into four or five strips. Expose each one against a negative for a measured amount of time, increasing the timing a second or two for each strip. Develop the strips normally and check the results. As your experience grows, you'll need less testing to find the correct exposure.

Slide the exposed sheet of printing paper into the tray of developer quickly so development will be even. Rock the tray, and in seconds you should see the image forming. It may appear to be completely formed in about 45 seconds, but allow another 10 or 15 seconds for sharp blacks and whites; the darkened room can fool you.

Your next step is the stop bath. This second tray contains a chemical to rinse off the developer and thus stop development. Leave the printing paper in the stop bath only about five seconds before shifting it into a third tray, which contains fixing solution. This fixer tray should be rocked every minute or so to provide agitation. If you are processing several prints at a time, they should be rotated inside the tray. It will take about 10 minutes to fix your prints, but you can turn on the room lights and get a look at the results after they have been in the fixer two or three minutes.

Wash your prints thoroughly after they come out of the fixer, just as you washed your film. If the chemicals aren't washed off they can cause fading images or staining of the prints. Leaving prints in a tray under running water for an hour, or changing the water every five minutes for a total of an hour, should do the job. Place your wet prints flat between two blotters to dry them. To get a glossy surface on the prints, you will need to place them on a special highly polished metal surface to dry.

Examine your dry print. It should have good contrast, that is, a complete range of black-to-white tones. If it's too light overall, try a longer exposure in printing; if it's too black, go to a short exposure. Or the problem may be in the negative; your original camera exposure may have been off. If that's the case, don't give up. You can still do some correcting while you're printing.

Most printing paper is made in contrast grades from 0 to 5. Numbers 4 and 5 are high-contrast papers; use them with low-contrast negatives to produce usable prints. Numbers 2 and 3 are normal-contrast papers to use with normal-contrast negatives. Numbers 1 and 0 are low-contrast, or "soft," papers; use them with high-contrast negatives to produce usable prints.

Making Enlargements

If your camera takes small roll film or 35mm film, use contact prints as "proofs" to help you decide what to enlarge. Make contact prints of several negatives on one sheet of printing paper.

This person is carefully adjusting a photo enlarger to get a sharp print. It is a good idea to edit your photograph before enlarging it; that is, crop and size the picture for the exact look and dimensions the layout requires.

After you have decided which negatives you are going to work with, use an enlarger to project the image onto the printing paper. The enlarger lens must be focused exactly so the resulting enlarged print, or "blow-up," will be sharp and not blurred.

The Value of Photographs

You've come a long way since you sighted through the viewfinder to take your first picture. You may have wondered at times whether picture taking was worth all that remembering of exposure settings and the development timing. But the day your publication is distributed all the fussing and care is forgotten. That picture on page one was taken by you. It may not qualify for photographic awards or stir the journalistic world, but it's yours. You feel the pride of achievement and also the knowledge that you have contributed to your publication's efforts to communicate and inform.

Wrap-up

Pictures sometimes tell stories better than words. Audiences rely on pictures to help them understand.

Students with an interest in photography might find their futures in journalism. Although photography is technical, it is not intimidating. Some of the best photos come when the photographer is in a relaxed, receptive mood.

Help is available for the novice. Until you learn more about photography, avoid buying a lot of expensive equipment.

Cameras in principle are much alike but may differ in three parts: the lens, the shutter, and the viewfinder. Lenses vary from single pieces of ground and polished glass to complex groupings of several glass elements. The shutter is like a door. Light enters when the door is opened. Adjustable-speed shutters let the photographer determine how long the door is open and how much light gets in. Viewfinders permit the photographer to plan, or compose, a picture. The viewfinder lets the photographer see the whole picture before taking it.

Much of the mystery attached to photography is about film. There are many kinds of film. Films vary in "speed," meaning how long they must be exposed to light to create a picture.

Light is the key word in photography. Each kind of film works best when exposed to a given amount of light, and the photographer adjusts the speed of the shutter and the size of the lens opening to control the amount of light. Light can be measured with an exposure guide from the filmshop or with a light meter.

Focusing involves moving the lens in relation to the film. Focusing may be done by turning a ring around the lens or a device at the side of the camera. Focusing is closely related to lens size or lens opening. The *f*-number of a lens explains its size, when it is fully open, in relation to the distance from the lens to the film.

Careful planning is required to take good photos. Your actions should be planned to mesh with those of your subject. Often you can focus and make necessary adjustments in advance.

Sooner or later, anyone seriously interested in photography will want his or her own darkroom to develop film and print pictures. A room is required in which you can block out all outside light. Various sizes of trays, a thermometer, a liquid measure, bottles, a safelight, and a large sheet of square glass are needed. Hot and cold running water would make the job easier. Film must be agitated, or moved, during development and washed thoroughly afterward.

Prints are made from negatives. In a negative, dark areas look light and light areas look dark. Light is passed through the negative onto printing, or light-sensitive, paper. The paper is then developed, fixed, and washed, much like film. Test strips to judge correct exposure save expensive paper.

The rewards of photography come on the day the publication is distributed and the photographer's work is prominently displayed.

On Assignment

Teamwork

Arrange for a special minicourse on the basics of photography for a group of interested students. You might be able to interest a local newspaper photographer in organizing a series of short seminars for your team, or a local photographic studio might be willing to assist you. If you have a darkroom available, each student could take a particular step in the process and study it carefully, then instruct the rest of the team. The more you study and share ideas with others, the better the photographs in your paper and yearbook will look.

Practice

Experiment with your camera. Whether or not you actually process your film and print your own pictures, you can learn to take more effective photos. Keep a small notebook in which you write the shutter speed setting and light for each photograph you take. Was the day cloudy or sunny? How far were you from your subject? Try taking the same picture with different settings. Start, for example, by setting the light and speed where you think they should be—without using a meter. Use your own sense of the physical factors that will affect the photograph. Next, leave the speed constant—say, at 500. Change the light from the lowest possible setting to the highest. Be sure to keep a record of your settings for each picture. Have your film processed and prints made. (You may have to tell the processor that you are experimenting—they may not want to print what they call ''bad'' photos.) Study your prints. What have you learned about the relationships between light and speed? Many photographers develop a special sense about settings for their cameras. However, most good photographers learn to use light meters, understand film types, and know their cameras. Write a short essay on what you learned by experimenting.

Your Turn
Spend time with a photographer for your school newspaper, local newspaper, or commercial studio. Try to get permission to go on assignment with that person. Take your camera. Parallel what the photographer does. Process your photos and make contact prints; select the best; print them. How do your photos compare with what the photographer took? Mount copies of them together and write a short commentary on what you see. What have you learned?

José Galvez

Photojournalism can no longer be taught the way it has been for the past ten years. That's what *Los Angeles Times* photographer José Galvez believes.

Technological advances are quickly changing photojournalism, and schools need to change how and what they teach, he said.

Galvez, who joined the *Times* in 1980, predicted that within the next five to ten years, darkroom work will be eliminated at major newspapers and every assignment will be shot in color negatives. In simplest terms, he said news photographers will become image framers and button pushers.

Negative transmitters and digital cameras and darkrooms are making it possible to transfer the image of a picture directly from camera to production room without ever printing the photo. Students need to learn how to use the new technology, Galvez said.

Regardless of new technology, Galvez said students also need to learn how to anticipate a picture, how to conduct themselves, and how to be aware of everything around them.

Students interested in journalism should pick a mentor, such as a local professional, he said. "Find somebody you respect." Then contact that person and ask him or her if you can tag along on assignments. "Most journalists are flattered. But you have to show a commitment. We tend to give up on flakes," Galvez said. "I like to take

students on assignments with me," he added. "There's a lot that they can learn."

Galvez knows this from experience.

He received his first taste of photography from carrying the equipment of a Tucson, Ariz., contract photographer who owned a studio across the street from where Galvez used to set up a shoeshining station.

"In the evenings, he used to take me with him on assignments. I carried his camera bag," Galvez said. Going on sports shoots was most exciting for 11-year-old Galvez.

"I used to look into the stands and think, 'Wow, this is the neatest. You're up there and I'm down here.'"

That "neatness" hooked Galvez on journalism. In school, he directed his energy toward newspapers, but not necessarily photography. "I leaned more toward reporting. It seemed more intellectual to be a reporter."

He worked at Tucson's *Arizona Daily Star* as a copy clerk, writing stories, taking pictures, and observing other reporters. But "reporting was very boring" at the time, Galvez said. It was the late 1960s and early 1970s when Galvez took to reporting and writing. The 1972 Watergate scandal hadn't influenced journalism yet. "It was before investigative writing, before features. It was boring." So Galvez decided he'd rather be a photogra-

pher. That way, "I'd get a variety of the boredom."

Galvez worked on the *Star*'s photography staff until 1980 when he got a break from the *Times*. "The level of assignment [at the *Times*] is much bigger. It is of more national significance," Galvez said. At the *Star* he would shoot three to five assignments a day. At the *Times*, he averages 1.6 assignments a day. "Generally I shoot two assignments a day. Sometimes, I shoot only one. Some, none."

The competition is tough. "A lot more is expected of you just because you're an *L.A. Times* photographer. You can't miss a shot." That means being aware of what is going on and what others are going to view as newsworthy photos. "You may think [Soviet leader] Mikhail Gorbachev taking his hat off or putting it on isn't much, but the AP [Associated Press] guy got the shot. When the editors see the AP's print, they ask if you got the shot."

There is little guarantee that the *Times* will print his photos, Galvez said, adding that this can be frustrating. ''You've got to have the proper attitude.''

The pay is good—very good, Galvez said. Making money is important because ''photography becomes an expensive endeavor.'' (Any student serious about photojournalism should have at least one camera body with two lenses—a wide angle, such as a 28mm, and a mild telephoto, such as a 135mm or a 185mm.)

Excellent travel benefits at the *Times* complement the good pay, Galvez said. For example, the *Times* sent a photographer to Germany when the Berlin Wall came down. The editors used about four or five of the staff photographer's prints and ten or more of the AP's, he said. You have to accept and enjoy the benefits, but don't be upset if they don't use your pictures, he advised. ''You'll just go crazy and start pulling your hair out.'' ■

Career Profile/Photo Editor

Olga Camacho

Some people are writers. Some are photographers. A few, like Olga Camacho, are both. ''I could never quite decide. When I was reporting, I wanted to be shooting. When I was a photographer, I wanted to be writing,'' says the *New York Times* photo editor. It was Camacho's writing that got her in the door at the *Times*. She started in 1986 in the paper's writing program for journalistic newcomers. ''I worked as a clerk and a news assistant. You do odds and ends and freelance for the different sections,'' she said.

After the year-and-a-half program, Camacho left to travel through Europe and Mexico. ''It was the best time of my life,'' she said. But when she returned, she knew she had to find a job.

''I was trying to figure out what I was going to do. I had decided that I wanted to get into photography again.''

Having maintained good relations with editors at the *Times*, Camacho called them and asked what was available in photography. ''I wanted to know what was—what made—a good photograph. I figured the *Times* was a good place to start,'' she said. ''They sort of invented a position for me.'' Camacho trained on the photo desk in that makeshift position. She ''bounced around the entire building'' for one year, learning picture editing for the paper's various sections. ''It was sort of rigorous,'' she said. The rigor paid off. Today, Camacho is one of three photo editors at the *Times*.

Although she attributed much of her success to ''confidence, ability, and luck,'' Camacho gave credit to her journalism education, which began when she was a child. ''It goes so far back I can hardly remember,'' Camacho said. One day in grade school, she recalled, she went to a teacher and told him the school needed a newspaper. The teacher suggested that Camacho start one.

''It was just a couple of Xerox sheets, but it was neat,'' she said.

From then on she knew she would pursue a journalism career. After working on her high school paper, Camacho took a double major in photojournalism and journalism at the University of Texas in El Paso.

Students interested in journalism should work on their college newspaper, she said. ''That's the best place to make all of your mistakes.''

But the key to getting good jobs is making contacts with editors, Camacho said, adding that internships are best for this. ''That's how you get jobs,'' she said. ''You call them up and send them clips all the time.'' ■

CHAPTER TWENTY

THE NEW TECHNOLOGY OF PUBLISHING

The way words and images are brought together for readers has changed a lot in the last few years. No longer does producing a newspaper mean working with several people in several locations. Setting type, designing pages, and processing illustrations can now be done fairly quickly in a single location. Desktop publishing has made this possible. With desktop publishing, the newspaper staff does not have to depend upon outsiders to translate their ideas into finished pages.

What Is Desktop Publishing?

Desktop publishing has become the most popular way to prepare material for printing. It is pretty much what it sounds like. Desktop publishing involves using equipment that fits on top of a desk to prepare copy and illustrations electronically.

Desktop publishing consists of a microcomputer with a keyboard, a display monitor, and a laser printer. The microcomputer drives the whole operation. The display monitor is simply a screen like a TV screen that shows you what you are doing. The laser printer prints the copy that is displayed on the screen. The laser printer comes close in quality to old-fashioned typesetting done with metal type, but it is much quicker. That's the hardware.

In addition, you need a software package, like the popular PageMaker designed by the Aldus Corporation or Ventura designed by Xerox. These are the basics of desktop publishing.

The list of available equipment is not complete. Many options (*peripherals* they are called) exist for expanding the basic system and making it more flexible.

For example, you would probably want to have a mouse. This is a hand-held device, attached to the microcomputer by a cable, that allows you to easily manipulate what you see on the display monitor. With it you can move or delete copy or illustrations.

Another useful peripheral is a scanner, a device that can transfer graphics—photographs and line drawings—from paper directly into the computer. Still another useful peripheral is a modem. A modem connects the microcomputer to a telephone line so that material can be sent, even at great distances, to another computer. Last, but still not exhausting the list of peripherals, is the local area network (LAN). A LAN is used to link several computers to a laser printer so that a number of people can work at the same time without having to wait turns at the printer.

Desktop publishing has made it possible for anyone with a relatively modest investment to produce professional-looking publications.

Advantages of Desktop Publishing

Desktop publishing is not printing. It will give you only single pages with illustrations. For multiple copies, you still need to have someone do the printing. That being so, what are the advantages of this equipment?

Using a microcomputer, the mouse, and a laser printer, student journalists see a newspaper page go from a display on the monitor to camera-ready copy at the laser printer in a matter of minutes.

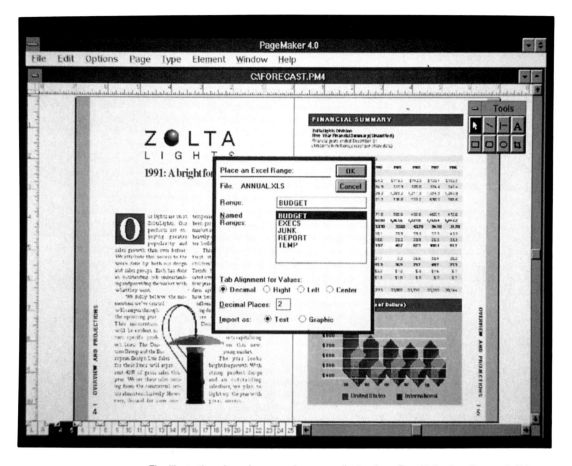

The illustration above is a sample screen display from PageMaker® software: © Aldus Corporation 1990. Used with the express permission of Aldus Corporation. Aldus® and PageMaker® are registered trademarks of Aldus Corporation. All rights reserved. Desktop publishing, using software such as PageMaker®, gives newspaper and magazine staffs, along with other organizations and businesses, the ability to create attractive publications right in the office.

Desktop publishing, first of all, eliminates the expense of outside typesetting. And in addition to saving money, it also saves time. No longer does copy have to be marked up, shipped off to a typesetter, and then, days later when it comes back, proofread and returned for corrections. Instead the whole process takes place right there on top of your desk.

Equally important, desktop publishing gives the user great control over what is produced. A term has been coined to describe the process: WYSIWYG. Pronounced *wiz-e-wig*, it means "what you see is what you get." On a monitor screen, you can now prepare whole pages of news, move blocks of type around, change type faces and sizes, shift from one column width to another, alter the shapes of pictures, create new art, or transfer art from various software programs directly onto your pages. What is more, you will see exactly what you will get before you press the print command on the computer. This technology is so powerful that you are limited only by your imagination.

Before 1984 these functions could be performed only by expensive and bulky equipment. But in that year Apple Computers, Inc. produced the Macintosh microcomputer, capable of producing text and graphic design and of integrating the two. After that, other computer makers, including IBM, began offering models of their own, designed specifically for desktop publishing. Today, estimates are that over half the desktop publishing equipment is Macintosh, with IBM a close second.

A final, important advantage of having a microcomputer is its ability to assist in other areas of student publications. For instance, with the proper software, the computer can keep track of circulation and expenses, advertising and promotions, assignments and deadlines.

Meeting Your Needs

Three factors go into deciding what desktop publishing equipment to buy and when—cost, technology, and complexity. Even though you may have no direct say in purchase decisions, you should understand the factors that influence them.

Cost

How much money do you have to spend? This is always a factor. But in figuring your costs, you should take into consideration how much money you will save by not having type set by an outside supplier. Desktop publishing has enabled some schools to save enough on typesetting in a very few years to pay for the equipment.

But if initial outlay is an overriding concern, consider buying a "clone," a computer that conforms to the operating system of a brand-name computer. Often, the savings are considerable. Some manufacturers of clones even take advantage of hindsight and correct minor design flaws that exist in the name-brand equipment.

At the same time, you should know that less expensive equipment may mean you will have to change the appearance of your publication. Some schools, for instance, have changed to a smaller, magazine-size page to accommodate their computer equipment. This may seem like letting "the tail wag the dog," but the smaller format has a pleasing, open appearance.

Technology

Should you hold off on your purchase until the hardware and the software are fully perfected? If you do this, you will probably never buy desktop publishing equipment. There will always be something better just around the corner, a new computer with "all the bells and whistles."

The fact is that new software usually works on the original hardware and your original hardware may do the job for years to come.

Complexity

How difficult will it be to learn to operate the new equipment? A hidden cost of desktop publishing is training. And lack of training is one of the basic reasons many desktop publishing projects fail. You should be aware that desktop publishing is more complicated than word processing, which produces only a printed text.

However, many stores that sell computer software and hardware also offer, at reasonable fees, courses of instruction. You may find, too, that someone in your class is a computer whiz and is willing to share his or her knowledge with the publications staff. In fact, it would be wise if such a person could be recruited for the staff.

Variety of Uses

More and more student newspapers and yearbooks are prepared—at least in part—on computers. At the most basic level, students set their stories in type in columns, ready for the printer to lay out and paste up. This is word processing. At a deeper level, the staff prepares their own pasteups, including placing headlines and leaving windows, or empty spaces, for art and photographs. Still other publications produce complete pages directly through desktop publishing equipment. This edition of *Journalism Today!* was designed using desktop publishing.

Desktop publishing, in addition to saving time and money, gives a news staff great flexibility. For example, if an important news event breaks, the staff can shift material to make room for a new story in a matter of minutes. Having all the pages in the computer, the staff can cut or trim stories, relocate ads, and change art to remake pages quickly.

A Word of Caution

It's easy to get carried away with desktop publishing. You have so many resources available—a wide range of type faces, sizes, and styles, for example—that it's tempting to use them all. You might find yourself sticking in pie charts simply because you can. That's why it's imperative to keep your readers in mind. Remember, your purpose is to communicate with them, not to dazzle them with a crazy quilt of design.

The emphasis of this book is on learning to be a journalist. We have stressed the importance of quality writing, ethics, journalistic judgment, and responsibility. It was not our intention to teach you to become a printer or designer. In this regard, it was instructive to hear one of the editors of *USA Today*, a fully computerized newspaper, say, ''Regardless of the technology, we want and need journalists, not techies.''

Printing

Perhaps you prepare your newspaper the old-fashioned way—typing the copy, doing a dummy, specifying headlines, and sending it all off to a printer. If that's how you do it, fine. You can still get good results. But even if you prepare finished pages on a desktop system, you need to have your paper printed. At one time all newspapers were printed by letterpress. Letterpress printing is done from cast metal type or plates on which the image or printing areas are raised above the non-printing areas. The raised areas are inked and, during the printing process, the inked image is transferred directly to paper. Some publications are still printed using letterpress; however, most newspapers today are printed by offset presses, also referred to as lithography.

Offset

Offset printing has helped to create thousands of small printshops across the country that handle everything from brochures, booklets, letterheads, and business cards to newsletters and publications like your school newspaper. It is far less expensive than letterpress, which is now almost a thing of the past.

To understand the difference between letterpress and offset, place your finger on an ink pad and then on a sheet of paper. That is how letterpress works. An inked image is transferred directly from your finger to paper, much as printing is transferred from the raised letters on metal type. Now, while the ink is still wet on the paper, lay another sheet on top of it. Rub gently, so as not to smear the image of your fingerprint. This is how offset works. Offset printing transfers an image from one flat surface to another.

To print by offset, you need to prepare camera-ready pasteups of the pages of the newspaper. The printer then photographs these pasteups and uses the film to transfer the images of your pages onto specially coated, lightweight metal plates. These plates, when put onto a roller on the press, become coated with ink. The ink adheres only to the specially treated parts of the plates, those parts that carry the images of your pages. The ink-covered images are then transferred to sheets or rolls of paper that move through the press, and you get the pages of your newspaper.

Some schools have an offset press on their premises, usually in the industrial arts department, on which the school newspaper is printed. However, most schools have their publications printed at a commercial printing plant or at a quick-print shop.

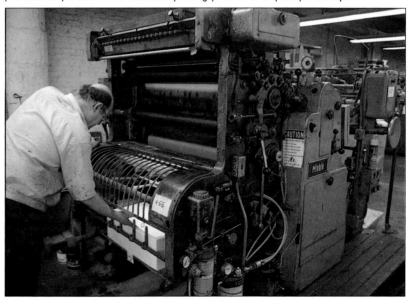

USA TODAY is produced using sophisticated computer pagination techniques and is printed at offset printing plants around the country via satellite.

Reprinted by permission of USA TODAY, © 1989.

A student operator prepares computer-generated copy for a school newspaper.

Type-proof needs to be carefully checked.

Final adjustment of negatives is done before the plates are shot.

A modern offset press is shown here as it prints the *Wall Street Journal*. Photo courtesy of Dow Jones.

Technology and the Future

As computers become more powerful, more compact, and less expensive, the production of publications will continue to change dramatically. The technological changes in just the past thirty to forty years give some idea of the kinds of changes we can expect in the future.

Back when letterpress was the only game in town, a journalism teacher used to start his class in typography by giving each student a piece of type. He urged them to squeeze the type tightly and see if it could be made smaller. Naturally, it could not. That was his point: Metal type was only the size it was made to be.

Today, however, advances in computer typesetting and in desktop publishing enable you to squeeze type or stretch it, to make it taller or shorter, fatter or slimmer. If you don't like your type 14 points, you can make it 15 points or even 13, allowing you to fit the headline you want without having to rewrite it.

Until recently, writing copy and setting type was a lengthy, multi-step process, involving many rounds of proofreading and marking changes and requiring extra time for delivering copy to the typesetter and getting typeset galleys back. Page makeup was a hands-on, cut-and-paste process that also required many steps and a significant amount of time.

Today, the same machines can be used to write the story, set the type, make up the pages, and generate the printer-ready pages. Even newspaper staffs that don't have full desktop publishing capabilities can use computers to streamline their editing processes. Stories can be sent via the phone lines from the publication staff's computer to the typesetter. The typesetter can fax copies over telephone lines of laser-printed galleys back for proofreading, incorporate any changes, and generate repro galleys only once, thus saving everyone time and money.

Changes like these only hint at what is to come. News in the twenty-first century may come in formats we are only beginning to imagine. Today we have fax machines that have speeded up the transmission of information. We have huge data bases that allow us to search for information directly on a computer. With modems, thousands of computer users communicate with computer "bulletin boards," receiving updates of specialized news and information. Computer "clip" services allow individuals to automatically receive information on any topic published in one or more of hundreds of publications.

All of this suggests that readers of the future may be able to receive customized news reports. People who like their news heavy on the sports, light on the lifestyle or tempo sections, could receive a customized paper tailored to them. The news might come via the fax machine or as a special computer file delivered via modem. News could be updated hourly, through the day and night. Schools and offices might even develop their own news delivery services. When you arrived at school, for instance, you could punch in your code on the computer and receive a personalized printout of messages from friends and teachers. You might even get your scores on last week's exam. And you could even get a summary of the day's world, local, or other news—all printed out on high-speed laser printers, complete with pictures. There might even be an ad or two.

Regardless of the delivery system, there will always be a need for those who seek out, report, and write the news. Technology is no substitute for the skilled journalist. It only helps the journalist do the job more efficiently and effectively.

Wrap-Up

Technology has dramatically changed the way information is processed and prepared for publication. Probably the most revolutionary change has been in preparing material for printing. With desktop publishing, anyone who has access to a microcomputer, the right software package, and a laser printer can be in the publishing business. Although school journalists used to send their copy to a typesetter, wait for it to be sent back in galleys, proof the galleys, send them back again, and then check the copy on page proofs, publication staffs now go to the computer, call up the copy on the screen, make instant changes, and move into production.

Desktop publishing saves money and time, gives you more control over the final product, and allows for changes up to the last minute before production starts. To determine whether desktop publishing is the best method for pro-

ducing your publication, you will need to consider the costs, quality needed, type of technology that will meet your needs, and whether or not you have the capabilities to use the technology. Training is an important part of making a shift to desktop publishing.

With computers handling more and more of the pre-press stages of newspaper publication, the only outside supplier you may still have to work with is the printer. While many printers still offer page pasteup services, with desktop publishing you can submit camera-ready laser-printed pages or a disk that the printer can download directly to the offset press. Offset printing is the most common way to print newspapers today. However, with the speed of changing technology, only one thing is certain: No matter how things are done today, there is likely to be a faster, more efficient way of getting out the news tomorrow.

On Assignment

Teamwork

1. Whether or not your journalism class uses desktop publishing, it would be very helpful to visit another school that does. Your teacher may arrange such a visit. Be prepared with some good questions. What problems have you had with your equipment? What software do you recommend? How long did it take to train the staff?

2. Prepare a written report or an oral presentation to the class on the future of published newspapers. Think about questions like these:

   Will there be printed newspapers in 2010?

   What delivery system will be used to get the news to readers?

   Will there be only national newspapers?

   What expanded role will satellites and lasers play in producing the newspaper or getting news to readers?

   Will the growth in telecommunications through home computers play a role in delivering the news?

   Will you someday be able to program your home computer to bring you a newspaper with only the news you want on the topics you like?

   Brainstorm with your team ideas on how answers to these questions will affect our society. Be creative. It is tomorrow's journalism that you are helping conceptualize today.

Practice

1. Examine the exchange papers you receive from other schools. Can you tell which are prepared using desktop publishing and which were professionally pasted up by the printer? How can you tell? Select an exchange paper and write a short editorial column titled: ''Your image is showing,'' commenting on the printing and physical characteristics of the paper. Be sure to discuss how, using the same printing process, you think the image could be improved. How does that newspaper compare with your school's newspaper?

2. Tour local printing facilities. Be sure to include an instant print shop and your local newspaper printing plant. Learn about the method used by each printer. What do they feel are the benefits and problems of each method? Write a short article on the tour and what you learned.

Your Turn

Prepare an editorial column on the subject: ''It is not what a newspaper looks like; it is what it says that is important.'' Take any position you want.

Glossary

Advance: A story about a coming event.

Anchoring the corners: The placing of a heavy element in each corner of a newspaper page.

Attribution: Telling the reader exactly where or from whom information was obtained.

Beat reporter: Reporter assigned to check the same news source for each issue of the paper (for example, art, music, theater, police administration).

Bleed: To carry a picture into the margin or gutters of a page.

Brainstorming: The art of obtaining many ideas in a short time.

''By authority:'' Most early American newspapers were published with this statement, which meant they had the government's approval.

Byline: The name and often the title of the writer of a story.

Chronological style: After a summary lead, the story is written in the order in which it occurred.

Civil libel: Written defamation of an identified individual, group, or corporation.

Cliché: Overused, overworked, old, and trite expression (for example, busy bees, blushing bride, dull thud).

Color sidebar: See **Sidebar.**

Conflict: One of the elements of news. Involves tension, surprise, and suspense, and arises with any good story topic—sports, war, elections.

Consequence: Element of news that refers to the importance of an event. The greater the consequence, the greater the news value.

Conservative layout: A layout that tries to use most of the space available. It may be heavy in appearance, with little use of white space. (*The Wall Street Journal* is an example.)

Contact sheet: A sheet of photographs, printed negative size, from which photo selection is made.

Copy: Typed, manuscript version of stories, cutlines, and the like, from which type is set.

Criminal libel: Defamatory statements that might bring about public anger, revolt, or disturbance of the peace.

Cropping: The cutting or marking of a photograph to eliminate unnecessary material and highlight important elements.

Cub reporter: A novice reporter assigned to pick up brief items or do weekly checks with sources for news.

Cutline: Copy used under or with a photograph. It identifies what or who is in the picture and where it was taken.

Depth of field: The distance between the points nearest to and farthest from the camera that appear in sharp focus when seen through the lens.

Desktop publishing: Using a desktop computer to set and design type, edit, produce graphics, and determine page layout.

Down style: A headline style in which all letters, except the first letter of the first word and proper nouns, are set lowercase.

Dummying: The process of setting up the newspaper or printed page design for space and placement of copy, headlines, artwork, photos, and other elements.

Duotones: Photographs printed in two colors. One is almost always black; the other may be any color.

Editorial page editor: Works closely with the managing editor to plan the editorial page. Writes or directs staff to write the editorials that express the newspaper's opinions, the editorial columns, or editorial features.

Elements of news or news values: The basic elements of news are timeliness, human interest, proximity, prominence, consequence, and conflict. These elements make the information more interesting and useful to the reader or listener.

End sign: 30 or pound sign #. Either symbol placed at the end of copy signifies "the end" of the copy.

Evergreen: A term applied to material acceptable for publication at any time. Timeliness is not a factor in the material.

***F*-stop:** The focusing on a camera is closely related to lens size or lens opening. The *f*-number of a lens explains its size, when fully open, in relation to the distance from the lens to the film.

Fair comment and criticism: A complete libel defense protecting a journalist's opinion of public figures or review of books or records, movies, theatrical events, public entertainments, or the public part of a performance or creative art.

Five W's and the H: Who, What, When, Where, Why, and How. These elements belong in nearly every newspaper story.

Fixer: Fixing bath which makes a film image permanent. The film coating not blackened during the development is dissolved away in this solution and the film emulsion is hardened to prevent scratching of the finished negatives.

Flag: The name of the newspaper and the information included with it (date, edition number, city, state). May be placed anywhere above the fold (upper half) of the front page.

Floating the flag: Moving the flag to different locations on the front page from edition to edition.

Flush-left head: A headline that rests squarely against the left-hand side of the column.

Focus: Adjustment of the camera focusing lens closer to or farther from the film so that the subject will appear sharp (in focus) on the developed film.

Fold: The imaginary horizontal line across the middle of the page, or where the newspaper could be folded in half.

Future book: A chronological listing of events coming up that you might want to cover. A long-range calendar of events and ideas.

General assignment reporter: Writes articles or does the work on any subject assigned as the editor sees fit.

Gutters: The space between columns or between facing pages.

Headline: A brief description of the contents of a news story printed in larger type, usually above the story.

Heavy elements: Large headlines or pictures, strategically placed around a page to create a pleasing visual effect.

Horizontal makeup: Newspaper design technique in which the general movement on the page is from side to side (across the page), not up and down (vertical).

Human interest stories: Stories that cause the reader to feel such emotions as sorrow, pity, or amazement.

Inverted pyramid: A style of newswriting in which the main facts go at the top of the article (the lead). The facts become less significant until, toward the bottom, they may be dispensable. This gives the reader the essential facts first and permits expansion or contraction in editing and page layout.

Ladder: A planning device for printing specific pages (as in a yearbook). Specific information or material is planned for each page, and the ladder shows which pages are on the right side of the book and which are on facing pages.

Laser printer: A printer that uses a laser beam to form characters and graphic images onto paper, similar to a photocopier.

Layout editor: A person responsible for preparing or approving the layout design for a project. In some instances the layout editor designs all pages.

Lead: The first paragraph of a news story. It usually, but not always, consists of just one sentence.

Lens: The eye of the camera, designed to control the amount of light admitted. Lenses vary from single pieces of ground and polished glass to complex and expensive groupings of several glass elements.

Letterpress: A printing method used by many large newspapers. The ink is applied to the type (or page plate). Paper is placed on the type or plate, pressure applied, and an impression made.

Libel: Written defamation; damaging false statements against another person or institution that appear in writing or are spoken (broadcast) from a written script.

Liberal layout: Designing the page to leave areas of white space for emphasis. It may feature one large, dominant photograph on each pair of facing pages. This layout may have a light, clean look.

Localization: Writing a regional, national, or even international story to bring out the local angle.

Logotype: A distinctive treatment of the brand or company name. Also known as the signature, slug, or nameplate. An important layout element in every advertisement.

Managing editor (Editor-in-chief): Has overall responsibility for the news operation or publication.

Microcomputer: A computer, small enough to be set on a desktop, that has a central processing unit built on one or more silicon chips.

Mini-torial: A very, very brief editorial, usually one or two sentences.

Monologophobia: A term coined by Theodore Bernstein to describe the fear of repeating a word. Also called the ''elongated yellow fruit'' school of writing.

Muckrakers: A term still used today to refer to journalists who develop significant social consciousness and through their writing crusade for social justice or expose wrongdoing.

News editor: The chief copy editor and headline writer.

Newsfeature: A feature story related to a breaking or developing news story.

News judgment: The knowledge and instinct a reporter or editor calls on to determine whether an event is news.

Newspaper style: Guidelines to follow that include standardized forms for capitalization, abbreviation, and spelling. They are set forth in a publication's stylebook and establish consistency for the reader.

Offset printing: A printing process in which the page is photographed and then a thin, flat metal plate is made for printing. Also known as multilith and lithograph, among other names.

Opinion feature: A feature story in which the writer expresses his or her personal opinions, makes interpretations, and draws conclusions.

Optical center: In an advertisement, about two-thirds of the way up from the bottom of the ad. (This is not the physical center of the space.)

Paraphrase: To put the speaker's words into the reporter's own words without changing the meaning or inserting opinion. Used to clarify lengthy, fuzzy, or complicated thoughts. Paraphrased material is not enclosed in quotation marks.

Partisan press: Early American newspapers that allied themselves with one political party. This was commonplace during the Revolutionary period.

Pasteup: Pasting type to a grid sheet in preparation for photo-engraving and printing. The pasteup shows what the page will look like when printed.

Penny Press: In the mid-nineteenth century, Benjamin Day founded the *New York Sun* and sold it for a penny. Others soon imitated this new type of paper, which was filled with news, achieved a mass audience, and carried advertising.

Photo essay: A story told in pictures. It usually involves three to seven photographs, a short copy block, and cutlines.

Photo sequence: A series of photos that shows how something changed or developed over time.

Plagiarism: Taking and using as one's own the writings or inventions of another person.

Points: A measurement of type sizes. There are 12 points in a pica and 72 points in an inch.

Post-game story: A sports feature written after the event. It may be a sideline story, background story, sports interview, or locker-room story.

Pre-game story: An advance story on a sports event. It may include background and information on both teams.

Press: A word used to refer to the print and electronic news media—radio, television, newspapers, magazines, and all other news gathering and disseminating agencies.

Primary source: A person whose business it is to have the best and most reliable information about the topic. Especially important in interviewing.

Prior restraint: The halting or forbidding of publication. This is illegal in the United States except in the rarest of circumstances, usually pertaining to national security in wartime.

Profile: A column or story that centers on a certain individual—a student, instructor, or person in the community—who has done something unique, outstanding, or unusual.

Prominence: An element of news that refers to how well known an individual is in the community, school, or nation.

Proximity: An element of news that refers to the geographic nearness of a given event to your place of publication or your readers.

Publick Occurrences: The first newspaper in the American colonies, published in Boston in 1690 by Benjamin Harris. It lasted only one issue before the British authorities stopped it.

Publisher: Person or body that owns, runs, or controls a publication. Sets broad guidelines and general policies but is rarely concerned with day-to-day operations.

Redundancy: Using words or phrases together so that they say the same thing twice (for example, 2 A.M. in the morning, a spherical globe).

Reporters: The people who carry out the assignments that have been determined by the news editor (editor in chief) in conference with the managing editor and the publication's adviser.

Right of reply or **Simultaneous rebuttal:** Permitting a person criticized in a story to respond to that criticism in the same story.

Scanner: Digitizing equipment that scans and transfers visual material, such as illustration or type, to a computer.

Schedule: A list compiled by the editor of everything on each page, including lengths of stories and sizes of pictures.

Screens: Devices the printer uses when preparing pictures for printing. Halftone screens are used to prepare photos for reproduction, as well as textured screens for special effects.

Shutter: The part of a camera that is released to take a picture. The shutter may be a flap that covers an opening near the lens, or it may be made like a window blind in front of the film in the rear of the camera.

Sidebar: A story supplementing, but kept separate from, another story on the same subject in the same issue of the paper.

Simultaneous rebuttal: See **Right of Reply.**

Sizing: Reducing or enlarging a cropped photo to exactly fit the space indicated on the layout.

Slander: A damaging false statement against another person or institution spoken or broadcast extemporaneously.

Slanguage: In sports writing, trite expressions stemming from the jargon of sports (for example, pigskin for football, grapplers for wrestlers).

Slug: Brief identifying name (usually one or two words) for a story. Used on copy, page layouts, and the schedule.

Spread head: A headline of two or more columns.

Stepped head: Headline set so that each line is indented more than the one above, giving a stairstep effect.

Streamer or **Banner:** A headline that stretches across the columns of the page.

Summary lead: A lead that provides the briefest possible summary of the major facts of a story in the first sentence.

Tabular material: Long lists, box scores, stock tables, or statistics, usually set in small type.

Timeliness: An element of news that has to do with how new or current the event is.

Tombstoning: Placing of headlines of equal or similar size beside each other.

Transition: Words, phrases, or even whole paragraphs that hold a story together and smooth the shift from one topic to another. Examples of transitional words are: for example, besides, consequently, furthermore, however, likewise, moreover, nevertheless, therefore, thus, finally, then, later, and, but, or, meanwhile, also, in addition, in general.

Typeface: The style of type a newspaper uses.

Verbatim transcript: A technique, often called the ''Q and A'' system, in which the reporter's exact questions are reproduced, followed by the source's exact answers. A verbatim transcript of an interview requires a tape recorder for accuracy. The term can also refer to printing the exact text of a speech or message.

Video Display Terminal (VDT): A computer device by which keyboarding produces an image on a TV-like screen, used today by virtually all newspaper reporters to compose stories. When a story is finished, the reporter hits the button and the editor edits the copy displayed on his or her VDT. Both writing and editing are done without pencil or paper.

Viewfinder: An ordinary sighting frame or a complicated device with lenses that enables the photographer to compose the desired picture before it is taken.

White space: The empty space in ads or page design that helps emphasize the message. Used effectively, white space attracts the reader's eye.

Wild art: Artwork or photographs run in a newspaper without stories. These pictures (often with cutlines) are usually feature-oriented and are published principally because they are entertaining and catch the reader's attention. They also break up otherwise heavy layouts.

Wire services: Provide news from around the world to publications that subscribe for a fee. Some frequently used wire services are the Associated Press, United Press International, Reuters, and The New York Times Service.

Yellow journalism: A sensational brand of journalism given to hoaxes, altered photographs, screaming headlines, frauds, and endless promotions of the newspapers themselves. The term derives from the name of the Yellow Kid, a cartoon character popular in the late nineteenth century.

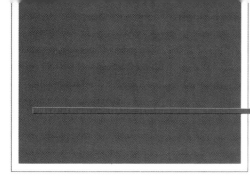

STYLEBOOK

ASSOCIATED PRESS
UNITED PRESS INTERNATIONAL

Learning the style of the profession is essential to any journalist. Both major wire services and nearly all newspapers use a common stylebook for consistency in writing.

Many school journalism staffs have stylebooks of their own. We feel it is important that journalists in the schools use the style agreed upon by the Associated Press and United Press International as the basis for their own publication style, making additions where required.

We are grateful to United Press International for permission to use material from the current stylebook. Reprinted here are only the major segments we feel are important for student journalists. All school newsrooms should have several copies of the complete stylebook for student use and reference.

A

abbreviations and acronyms   A few universally recognized abbreviations are sometimes required. Others are acceptable but, in general, avoid alphabet soup.

Apply the same guidelines to acronyms—pronounceable words formed from the letters in a series of words: *ALCOA, NATO, radar, scuba*, etc.

Guidelines:

1. Use *Dr., Gov., Lt. Gov., Mr., Mrs., Rep., the Rev., Sen.,* and abbreviate certain military titles before a name outside direct quotations. Spell out all except *Mr., Mrs.,* and *Dr.* before a name in direct quotations.

2. Abbreviate *junior* or *senior* after a person's name. Abbreviate *company, corporation, incorporated* and *limited* after a company name.

3. Use *A.D., B.C., a.m., p.m., No.* and abbreviate certain months when used with the day of the month.
   Right: *In 450 B.C.; at 9:30 a.m.; in room No. 6; on Sept. 16.*
   Wrong: *Early this a.m. he asked for the No. of your room.* The abbreviations are correct only with the figures.
   Right: *Early this morning he asked for the number of your room.*

4. Abbreviate *avenue, boulevard* and *street* in numbered addresses: *He lives on Pennsylvania Avenue. He lives at 1600 Pennsylvania Ave.*

5. Certain states, the *United States* and the *Union of Soviet Socialist Republics* (but not other nations) are sometimes abbreviated.

6. Some organizations are widely recognized by their initials: *CIA, FBI, GOP, TVA,* which are acceptable. Even then, an abbreviation is not always necessary. If it fits the occasion, use *Federal Bureau of Investigation*, for example, rather than *FBI*.

Do not use an abbreviation or acronym in parentheses after a full name. If the abbreviation would not be clear without this arrangement, do not use it. Do not reduce names to unfamiliar acronyms solely to save a few words.

academic degrees   If it is necessary to establish credentials, avoid an abbreviation. Make it: *a bachelor's degree, a master's* (note the apostrophe), *a doctorate in psychology.*

Use *B.A., M.A., LL.D., Ph.D.,* etc., only when many listings would make the preferred form cumbersome. Use the abbreviation only after a full name—never after just a last name.

Set an abbreviation off by commas: *Mary Smith, Ph.D., spoke.* But don't use both *Dr.* and an abbreviation in the same reference.

Wrong: *Dr. Jane Jones, Ph.D.*
Right: *Dr. Jane Jones, a chemist.*

For spelling and abbreviations, follow the first listing in Webster's New World Dictionary.

academic departments   Lowercase except for proper nouns or adjectives: *the department of history, the history department, the department of English, the English department.*

academic titles   Capitalize and spell out such formal titles as *professor, dean, president, chancellor, chairman,* etc., before a name. Lowercase elsewhere.

Lowercase such modifiers as *history* in *history Professor Oscar Handlin* or *department* in *department Chairman Jerome Wiesner.*

addresses   Use *Ave., Blvd.* and *St.* with a numbered address: *1600 Pennsylvania Ave.* Spell out without a number: *Pennsylvania Avenue.*

Lowercase standing alone or in plural uses: *the avenue, Massachusetts and Pennsylvania avenues.*

Do not abbreviate similar words, such as *alley, drive, road* and *terrace.* Capitalize as part of a formal name: *Printers Alley.* Lowercase standing alone or in plural uses: *the alley, Broadway and Tin Pan alleys.*

Use figures for an address number: *9 Morningside Circle.*

Spell out and capitalize *First* through *Ninth* as street names; use figures with two letters for *10th* and above: *7 Fifth Ave., 100 21st St.*

Abbreviate compass points that indicate directional ends of a street or quadrants of a city in a numbered address: *220 E. 42nd St., 600 K St. N.W.*

Do not abbreviate if the number is omitted: *East 42nd Street, K Street Northwest.*

adviser   Not *advisor.*

allege   The word must be used with great care. Guidelines:

Avoid any suggestion that the writer is making an allegation.

Specify the source of an allegation. It should be an arrest record, an indictment or the statement of a public official connected with the case.

Use *alleged bribe,* etc., to make it clear that an unproved action is not being treated as fact.

Avoid redundant uses of *alleged.* It is proper to say: *The district attorney alleged that she took the bribe.* Or: *The district attorney accused her of taking a bribe.* But not: *The district attorney accused her of allegedly taking a bribe.*

Do not use *alleged* before an event known to have occurred when the dispute is over who participated in it. Do not say: *He attended the alleged meeting,* when what you mean is: *He allegedly attended the meeting.*

Do not use *alleged* as a routine qualifier. Instead, use *apparent, ostensible, reputed,* etc.

ampersand (&)   Use an ampersand if it is part of a company's proper name: *Baltimore & Ohio Railroad, Newport News Shipbuilding & Dry Dock Co.* Do not otherwise use the ampersand in place of *and.*

ante-   Hyphenate with a capitalized word or to avoid a double *e: ante-Victorian.* Elsewhere, follow Webster's New World, hyphenating words not listed there.

anti-   Hyphenate all except the following words:

antibiotic	antiknock	antiseptic
antibody	antimatter	antiserum
anticlimax	antiparticle	antithesis
antidote	antipasto	antitoxin
antifreeze	antipathy	antitrust
antigen	antiperspirant	antitussive
antihistamine	antiphon	

Hyphenated words, many of them exceptions to Webster's New World, include: anti-aircraft, anti-bias, anti-inflation, anti-intellectual, anti-labor, anti-slavery, anti-social, anti-war.

apostrophe (')   Use an apostrophe to show possessives. Elsewhere:

1. Use the apostrophe to show omitted letters or figures: *I've, it's, don't, rock'n' roll. 'Tis the season to be jolly. He is a ne'er-do-well. The class of '62. The Spirit of '76. The '20s.*

2. Use the apostrophe to show the plurals of single letters, but not multiple letters: *Mind your p's and q's. He learned the three R's and brought home a report card with four A's and two B's.* But: *She learned her ABCs.*

Arabic numerals   The numerical figures *1, 2, 3, 4, 5, 6, 7, 8, 9,* and *0.* In general, use Arabic forms except for wars and for personal sequence for people or animals.

arrest   To avoid any suggestion that someone is being judged before a trial, do not use *arrested for killing,* etc. make it: *arrested on a charge of killing.*

average   *Average* refers to the result obtained by dividing a sum by the number of quantities added together: the average of 7, 9, 17 is 33 divided by 3, or 11.

Mean commonly designates a figure intermediate between two extremes: the mean temperature of the day with a high of 56 and a low of 34 is 45.

Median is the middle number of points in a series arranged in order of size: the median grade in the group of 50, 55, 85, 88, 92 is 85; the average is 74.

Norm implies a standard of average performance for a given group: *The child was below the norm for his age in reading comprehension.*

B

baseball   The spelling of some frequently used words and phrases:

backstop	outfielder
ballclub	passed ball
ballpark	pinch hit (v.)
ballplayer	pinch-hit (n., adj.)
baseline	pinch hitter
bullpen	pitchout
center field	play off (v.)
center fielder	playoff (n., adj.)
designated hitter	put out (v.)
double-header	RBI (s. pl.)
double play	rundown

fair ball	sacrifice
fastball	sacrifice hit
first baseman	sacrifice fly catch
foul ball	shoestring (n.)
foul tip	shortstop
foul line	shut out (v.)
ground-rule double	shutout (n., adj.)
home plate	slugger
home run	squeeze play
left-hander	strike
line drive	strike zone
line up (v.)	Texas leaguer
lineup (n.)	triple play
major league(s)	twi-night double header
major-league (adj.)	wild pitch
major-leaguer (n.)	

Some sample uses of numbers: *First inning, seventh-inning stretch, 10th inning, first base, second base, third base; first home run, 10th home run; first place, last place; one RBI, 10 RBI. The pitcher's record is now 6-5. The final score was 1-0.*

Use *American League, National League, American League West, National League East, the league, the pennant in the West, the league's West Division,* etc.

In box scores:

The visiting team is always listed on the left, the home team on the right.

Only one position, the last he played in the game, is listed for any player.

Figures in parentheses are the player's total in that category for the season.

Use the *First Game* line shown here only if the game was the first in a double-header.

Two lines in this example—*None out when winning run scored*—and; *Alcala pitched to 2 batters in ninth*—could not have occurred in this game as played. They are included here to show their placement when needed.

FIRST GAME

Cincinnati					San Diego				
	ab	r	h	bi		ab	r	h	bi
Rose 3b	5	0	1	0	Almon ss	4	0	1	0
Griffey rf	5	2	2	0	Grubb cf	2	0	2	0
Morgan 2b	2	1	1	0	Melendez rf	0	1	0	0
T Perez 1b	5	0	1	2	Rttmund lf	2	1	1	0
Driessen lf	3	0	0	1	Valentine lf	2	1	0	0
Armbrstr lf	0	0	0	0	MChmpn 2b	0	1	0	0
Geronimo cf	4	0	0	0	Ivie 1b	3	1	2	2
Plummer c	3	0	1	0	Fuentes 2b	2	0	1	0
Flynn ss	3	0	0	0	Turner ph	1	0	0	0
Gullet p	3	0	1	0	WDavis cf	0	0	0	0
Alcala p	0	0	0	0	DoRader 3b	3	0	1	2
Lum ph	0	0	0	0	Kendall c	4	0	0	1
					TGriffin p	3	0	0	0
					Metzger p	0	0	0	0
Totals	33	3	7	3	**Totals**	26	5	8	5

Cincinnati	002	010	000—3
San Diego	000	200	03x—5

None out when winning run scored.

E—Fuentes. DP—Cincinnati 2. LOB—Cincinnati 10, San Diego 6. 2B—Fuentes, T. Perez, Rettenmund. 3B—DoRader. HR—Ivie (3). SB—Griffey, Morgan, Geronimo. S—Grubb, Fuentes, Rettenmund. SF—Driessen.

	IP	H	R	ER	BB	SO
Gullett	7	5	2	2	4	2
Alcala (L 11-4)	1	3	3	3	1	1
T. Griffin (W 8-6-)	8	7	3	3	6	4
Metzger	1	0	0	0	0	0

Alcala pitched to 2 batters in ninth.

Save—Metzger (4). HBP—by Gullet (Grubb). WP—Gullet. Balk—Alcala. PB—Kendall. T—2:19. A—8,230.

When a bare linescore summary is required, use this form:

Los Angeles	100	020	000—3 8 3
San Francisco	002	311	t00x—7 7 0

Sutton, Downing (6) and Yeager; Halicki and Rader. W—Halicki, 9-11. L—Sutton, 16-12. HRs—Los Angeles, Cey (3). San Francisco, Joshua 2 (6), Montanez (10).

The form for league standings:

NATIONAL LEAGUE
(Night games not Included)
East

	W	L	Pct.	GB
Pittsburgh	92	69	.571	—
Philadelphia	85	.75	.531	6½
etc.				

West

	W	L	Pct.	GB
Cincinnati	108	54	.667	—
Los Angeles	88	74	.543	20
etc.				

Monday's Results
Chicago 7, St. Louis 5
Atlanta at New York, rain
Tuesday's Games
(All Times EDT)
Cincinnati (Gullet 14-2 and Nolan 4-4) at New York (Seaver 12-3) and Matlack 6-1) 2, 6 p.m.
Wednesday's Games
Cincinnati at New York
Chicago at St. Louis, night
Only games scheduled

In subheads for results and future games, spell out day of week as: *Tuesday's Games,* instead of *Today's Games.*

basic summary Summarize sports winners in the order of finish. A figure shows place, followed by an athlete's full name, affiliation or hometown, and time, distance, points, or whatever performance factor is applicable to the sport.

If a contest involves several types of events, begin the paragraph with the name of the event.

A typical example:

60-yard dash—1, Steve Williams, Florida TC, 6.0. 2, Hasley Crawford, Philadelphia Pioneer, 6.1. 3, Mike McFarland, Chicago TC, 6.2. 4, etc.

See individual entries for each sport.

Most basic summaries are a single paragraph per event, as shown. In some competitions with large fields, however, the basic summary lists each winner in a single paragraph.

For international events in which U.S. or Canadian competitors are not among the leaders, add them in a separate paragraph as follows:

Also: 14, Dick Green, New York, 6.8. 17, George Bensen, Canada, 6.9. 19, etc.

In events where points, rather than time or distances, are the standard, mention points on the first usage only:

1, Jim Benson, Springfield, N.J., 150 points. 2, Jerry Green, Canada, 149.3, etc.

basketball   The spelling of some frequently used words and phrases:

backboard	half-court press
backcourt	halftime
backcourtman	hook shot
baseline	jump ball
field goal	jump shot
foul line	layup
foul shot	man-to-man
free throw	midcourt
free-throw line	pivotman
frontcourt	play off (v.)
full-court press	playoff (n., adj.)
goaltending	zone

Some sample uses of numbers: *in the first quarter, a second-quarter lead, nine field goals, 10 field goals, the 6-foot-5 forward, the 6-10 center. He is 6 feet 10 inches tall.*

NBA is acceptable in all references for National Basketball Association.

For subdivisions: *NBA East, the division, the conference,* etc.

A box score sample:

The visiting team is always listed first.

In listing the players, begin with the five starters—two forwards, center, two guards—and follow with all substitutes who played.

Figures after each player's last name denote field goals, free throws, free throws attempted and total points.

ATLANTA (85)

Brown 2 2-3 6, Hawkins 1 1-2 3, Jones 3 2-2 8, Henderson 6 0-0 12, Hudson 7 0-0 14, Etc. Totals 36 13-19 85.

LOS ANGELES (107)

Calhoun 4 1-1 9, Warner 4 3-3 11, Abdul-Jabbar 10 3-4 23, Allen 5 2-3 12, Goodrich 6 2-2 14, Etc. Totals 45 17-24 107.

Atlanta 21 27 17 20—85

Los Angeles 29 22 30 26—107

Fouled   out—Goodrich,   Henderson.   Total fouls—Atlanta 24, Los Angeles 24. Technical Brown, Los Angeles bench. A—10,969.

In college boxes, the score by periods is omitted because games are divided only into halves. The bottom of the box would look like this:

Halftime—UCLA 45, Minnesota 36. Fouled out—Jones, Smith. Total fouls—UCLA 22, Minnesota 19. Technical—Smith, UCLA coach Bartow, Minnesota bench 2, UCLA fans. A—19,450.

The format for professional standings:

Eastern Conference
Atlantic Division

	W	L	Pct.	GB
Boston	43	22	.662	—
Philadelphia	40	30	.571	5½
etc.				

The format for college conference standings:

	Conference			All Games		
	W	L	Pct.	W	L	Pct.
Missouri	12	2	.857	24	4	.857
etc.						

bi-   Hyphenate with a capitalized word or to avoid a double *i: bi-iliac.* Elsewhere, follow Webster's New World Dictionary, hyphenating words not listed there.

biannual, biennial   *Biannual* means twice a year and is a synonym for *semiannual. Biennial* means every two years.

Bible   Capitalize the book or its parts without quotation marks: *the Bible, a Bible verse, the Old Testament, the New Testament, the Gospels.*

Lowercase as a non-religious term: *My dictionary is my bible.*

Do not abbreviate individual books of the Bible.

To cite chapter and verse: *Matthew 3:16, Luke 21:1-13, 1 Peter 2:1.*

The books of the Old Testament, in order, are: Genesis, Exodus, Leviticus, Numbers, Deuteronomy, Joshua, Judges, Ruth, 1 Samuel, 2 Samuel, 1 Kings, 2 Kings, 1 Chronicles, 2 Chronicles, Ezra, Nehemiah, Esther, Job, Psalms, Proverbs, Ecclesiastes, Song of Solomon, Isaiah, Jeremiah, Lamentations, Ezekial, Daniel, Hosea, Joel, Amos, Obadiah, Jonah, Micah, Nahum, Habakkuk, Zephaniah, Haggai, Zechariah, Malachi.

The books of the New Testament, in order: Matthew, Mark, Luke, John, Acts, Romans, 1 Corinthians, 2 Corinthians, Galatians, Ephesians, Philippians, Colossians, 1 Thessalonians, 2 Thessalonians, 1 Timothy, 2 Timothy, Titus, Philemon, Hebrews, Epistles of James, 1 Peter, 2 Peter, 1 John, 2 John, 3 John, Jude, Revelation.

biweekly Means every other week. *Semiweekly* means twice a week.

C

call letters Use all caps. Hyphens separate the type of station from the basic call letters: WSB-AM, WSB-FM, WSB-TV.

Until summer 1976 the format for citizens band operators was three letters and four figures: KTE9136. Licenses issued since then use four letters and four figures: KTEM1234.

Amateur radio stations, which transmit on different frequencies than citizens band stations and may use greater power, are assigned a combination of letters and figures: WA2UUR.

Canada *Montreal, Ottawa, Quebec* and *Toronto* stand alone in datelines. For all other datelines, use the city name and the name of the province or territory spelled out.

The 10 provinces of Canada are Alberta, British Columbia, Manitoba, New Brunswick, Newfoundland (includes Labrador), Nova Scotia, Ontario, Prince Edward Island, Quebec and Saskatchewan.

The two territories are the Yukon and the Northwest Territories.

capital The city where a seat of government is located. Do not capitalize.

In a financial sense, capital describes money, equipment or property used in a business by a person or corporation.

capitalization Avoid unnecessary capitals. Use a capital letter only if you can justify it by one of these guidelines:

1. Capitalize proper names of a specific person, place or thing: *John, Mary, America, Boston, England.*
2. Capitalize common nouns such as *party, river, street* and *west* as an integral part of a proper name: *Democratic Party, Mississippi River, Fleet Street, West Virginia.* Lowercase common nouns that stand alone: *the party, the river, the street.* Lowercase common noun elements in all plural uses: *the Democratic and Republican parties, the Hudson and Mississippi rivers; Main and State streets.*

   Capitalize popular, unofficial names that serve as a proper name: *the Combat Zone* (a section of Boston), *the Badlands* (of South Dakota).
3. Capitalize words derived from a proper noun and still dependent on it for their meaning: *American, Christianity, English, French, Marxism, Shakespearean.*

   Lowercase words derived from a proper noun but no longer dependent on it for their meaning: *french fries, herculean, manhattan* (cocktail), *malapropism, pasteurize, quixotic, venetian blind.*
4. Capitalize the first word in every sentence. See **sentences.**

   In poetry, capital letters are used for the first words of some phrases that would not be capitalized in prose.
5. Capitalize the principal words in the names of books, movies, plays, poems, etc. See **composition titles.**
6. Capitalize formal titles before a name. Lowercase mere job descriptions and formal titles standing alone or set off by commas. See **titles.**

7. Capitalize some abbreviations and acronyms. See **abbreviations and acronyms.**

8. Capitalize the interjection *O* and the pronoun *I.*

capitol   Capitalize references to the national or state buildings and their sites: *The meeting was on Capitol Hill in the west wing of the Capitol. Thomas Jefferson designed the Capitol of Virginia.*

Celsius   Use this metric term rather than centigrade. Named for Swedish astronomer Anders Celsius, who designed it. Zero is the freezing point of water and 100 the boiling point at sea level.

To convert to Fahrenheit, multiply a Celsius temperature by 9, divide by 5 and add 32 (25 × 9 equals 225, divided by 5 equals 45, plus 32 equals 77 degrees Fahrenheit).

The forms: *40 degrees Celsius,* or *40 C* (note the space and no period after the capital C). See **temperatures.**

cents   Spell out *cents* and lowercase, using figures for amounts less than a dollar: *5 cents, 12 cents.* Use the $ sign and decimals for larger amounts: *$1.01, $2.50*

chairman, chairwoman   Capitalize as a formal title before a name: *company Chairman Henry Ford, committee Chairwoman Margaret Chase Smith.*

Lowercase a casual, temporary position: *meeting chairman Robert Jones.*

Use *chairperson* in quoted matter or if it is an organization's formal title for an office.

chauvinism, chauvinist   Unreasoning devotion to one's sex, country, etc. The terms are derived from Nicolas Chauvin, a soldier of Napoleon I, who was famous for his devotion to the lost cause.

chess   In stories, spell out the pieces and related terms, and lowercase: *king, queen, bishop, pawn, knight, rook, kingside, queenside, white, black.*

Examples:

White was unable to defend his kingside bishop. The black pieces were cramped. Black brought pressure on the queenside knight file. White took black's kingside bishop's pawn.

The news services use the descriptive notation in providing tabular summaries. Capital letters represent the pieces and files: B for bishop, K for king, N for knight, Q for queen, R for rook, P for pawn. Each file is given the name of the piece originally posted on it, and the ranks are numbered from 1 to 8 away from the player. Each rank thus has a dual designation, depending on which player makes the move.

The initial of the moving piece comes first, followed by a hyphen, followed by the designation of the square moved to. Thus, moving a pawn to the fourth rank of the queen's bishop file would be noted: P-QB4.

The *castle,* a move involving two pieces, is noted by lowercase *o*'s separated by a hyphen. The kingside castle: *o-o;* the queenside castle: *o-o-o.*

To note a capture, a lowercase *x* is substituted for the hyphen. Thus, if a pawn takes another pawn it would be noted: P*x*P.

The initials *ch* are used to indicate a check. The word *mate* is used for checkmate.

Indication of queenside Q or kingside K are omitted when no ambiguity would result. The form, taken from the first modern international tournament in London in 1851:

White Anderssen	Black Kieseritzkl
1. P-K4	P-K4
2. P-KB4	PxP
3. B-B4	P-QN4
4. BxNP	Q-R5ch
5. K-B1	N-KB3
6. N-KB3	Q-R3
7. P-Q3	N-R4
8. N-R4	P-QB3
9. N-B5	Q-N4
10. P-KN4	N-B3
11. R-N1	PxB

White Anderssen	Black Kieseritzkl
12. P-KR4	Q-N3
13. P-R5	Q-N4
14. Q-B3	N-N1
15. BxP	Q-B3

16.	N-B3	B-B4
17.	N-Q5	QxP
18.	B-Q6	BxR
19.	P-K5	QxRch
20.	K-K2	N-QR3
21.	N-Pch	K-Q1
22.	Q-B6ch	NxQ
23.	B-K7, mate	

Christmas   Dec. 25. The federal legal holiday is observed on Friday if Dec. 25 falls on a Saturday, on Monday if it falls on a Sunday.

Never abbreviate to *Xmas* or any other form.

church   Capitalize as part of the formal name of a building, a congregation or a denomination; lowercase in other uses: *St. Mary's Church, the Roman Catholic Church, the Catholic and Episcopal churches, a Roman Catholic church, a church.*

Lowercase *church* in an institutional sense: *He believes in separation of church and state. The pope said the church opposes abortion.*

city   Capitalize city (and town, village, etc.) as an integral part of a proper name: *Kansas City, New York City, Greenwich Village.*

Lowercase elsewhere: *a Texas city, the city government, the city Board of Education* and all *city of* phrases: *the city of Boston.*

Capitalize as part of a formal title before a name: *City Manager Francis McGrath.* Lowercase when not part of the formal title: *city Health Commissioner Frank Smith.*

The preferred form for the section of a city is lowercase: *the west end, northern Los Angeles.* But capitalize widely recognized popular names: *Southside* (Chicago), *Lower East Side* (New York), *the Combat Zone* (Boston). If in doubt, use lowercase.

Spell out the names of cities unless in direct quotes: *A trip to Los Angeles.* But: *"We're going to LA."*

city council   Capitalize as part of a proper name: *the Boston City Council.*

If the meaning is clear the city may be dropped and capitalization is retained: BOSTON (UPI)— *The City Council met.*

Lowercase other uses: *the council, the Boston and New York City councils,* any *city council.*

Use the proper name if the body is not known as a city council: *the Miami City Commission, the Louisville Board of Aldermen.* Use *city council* to refer to more than one: *the Boston, Louisville and Miami city councils.*

coach   Capitalize only when it is used without a qualifying term before the name of the person who directs an athletic team: *General Manager Red Auerbach signed coach Tom Heinsohn to a new contract.*

If coach is preceded by a qualifying word, lowercase it: *third-base coach Frank Crosetti, defensive coach George Perles, swimming coach Mark Spitz.*

collective nouns   Nouns that denote a unit take singular verbs and pronouns: *class, committee, crowd, family, group, herd, jury, orchestra, team. The committee is meeting to set its agenda. A herd of cattle was sold.*

Words plural in form become collective nouns and take singular verbs when the group or quantity is regarded as a unit.

A thousand bushels were created. (Individual bushels.)

A thousand bushels is a good yield. (A unit.)

The data have been carefully collected. (Individual items.)

The data is sound. (A unit.)

Meat and potatoes are the two items we sell most. (Individual items.)

Meat and potatoes is a tasty dish. (A unit.)

colloquialisms   The words and phrases characteristic of informal speech and writing: *bum, giveaway, phone, talk a blue streak, easy on the eyes,* etc. They are neither substandard nor illiterate and are acceptable in news stories if they fit the occasion.

Webster's New World Dictionary uses *colloq.* to label colloquialisms. If the dictionary also notes, as it does with *ain't,* that the word or phrase is substandard, avoid the usage. See **dialect.**

colon(:)   The most frequent use of a colon is at the end of a sentence to introduce lists, tabulations and texts. Capitalize the first word after a colon only if it is a proper name or the start of a complete sentence:

There were three considerations: expense, time and feasibility.

He promised this: The company will make good all the losses.

Elsewhere, use a colon:

1. To give emphasis. *He had only one hobby: eating.*
2. To give elapsed time *(1:31:07.2)*, time of day *(8:31 p.m.)*, and biblical and legal citations *(2 Kings 2:14, Missouri Code 3:245-260).*
3. In dialogue, in coverage of a trial, for example (no quotation marks around the quoted matter):
   Bailey: What were you doing the night of the 19th?
   Mason: I refuse to answer that.
4. For question-and-answer interviews:
   Q: Did you strike him?
   A: Indeed I did.
5. To introduce a direct quotation of more than one sentence. Use a comma for shorter quotations.
   Colons go outside quotation marks unless they are part of the quotation.

comma(,)   As demanded by the structure of the sentence, use a comma:

1. After an introductory clause: *When he had tired of the mad pace of New York, he moved to Dubuque.* Omit the comma if no ambiguity would result unless it would slow comprehension: *During the night he heard many noises. On the street below, the curious gathered.*
2. To set off an element not essential to the meaning: *We saw the 1977 winner in the Academy Award competition for best movie, "Rocky."* (Only one movie won the award. The name is informative, but even without the name no other movie could be meant.)
   Omit commas if the element is essential to the meaning. *We saw the award-winning movie "Rocky."* (No comma, because many movies have won awards, and without the name the reader would not know which movie was meant.)
3. To separate parts of a series. Omit the final comma in a simple series: *The flag is red, white and blue.* Use a final comma in a complex series: *I had orange juice, toast, and ham and eggs for breakfast.*
4. To separate equal adjectives. If the commas could be replaced by *and* without changing the sense, the adjectives are equal; *a thoughtful,*

precise manner. a dark, dangerous street. Omit the comma for unequal adjectives: *a cheap fur coat; the old oaken bucket; a new, blue spring bonnet.*

5. To separate main clauses joined by *and, but, or, nor* or *for: She was glad she looked, for a man was approaching the house.* Omit the comma if no confusion would result: *Jack went up the hill and Jill went down.*
6. To set off a complete, one-sentence quotation, but not a partial quotation: *"Rub my shoulders," Miss Cawley suggested. Wallace said, "She spent six months in Argentina and came back speaking English with a Spanish accent." He said his victory put him "firmly on the road to a first-ballot nomination."* Use a colon to introduce quotations of more than one sentence.
7. To separate a city from a state or nation: *His journey will take him from Dublin, Ireland, to Fargo, N.D., and back. The Selma, Ala., group saw the governor.* Use parentheses to insert a location within a proper name: *The Knoxville (Tenn.) News-Sentinel.*
8. To replace *of* between a name and home-town: *Mary Richards, Minneapolis, and Maude Findlay, Tuckahoe, N.Y., were there.* The *of* is preferred: *Mary Richards of Minneapolis and Maude Findlay of Tuckahoe, N.Y., were there.* If an age is used, set it off with commas: *Maude Findlay, 48, Tuckahoe, N.Y., was present.* Or: *Mary Richards, 36, of Minneapolis and Maude Findlay, 48, of Tuckahoe, N.Y., participated.*
9. To set off direct address or an introductory *yes* or *no. Yes, I will be there. Mother, I will be late. No, sir, I did not do it.*
10. To separate duplicated words that might be confusing: *What the problem is, is not clear.*
    Commas always go inside quotation marks. Commas also are used in most numerals above 999: *654,321.* The major exceptions are addresses *(1234 Main St.)*, broadcast frequencies *(1460 kilohertz)*, serial numbers *(A02205689)*, Social Security numbers *(123-45-6789)* and years *(1984).*

composition titles   In titles of books, movies, plays, poems, programs, songs, works of art, etc., capitalize the first word and all succeeding words except articles and short (four letters or less) conjunctions or prepositions. Use quotation marks for most:

"The Star-Spangled Banner," "The Rise and Fall of the Third Reich," "Gone with the Wind," "Of Mice and Men," "For Whom the Bell Tolls," "Time After Time," the NBC-TV "Today" show, the "CBS Evening News."

Use no quotation marks for the titles of:

—A sacred book or its parts: *the Bible, the New Testament, the Koran, the Apocrypha, the Torah, the Talmud.*

—Reference works: *Jane's All the World's Aircraft, Encyclopaedia Britannica, Webster's New World Dictionary, the World Almanac, the UPI Stylebook.*

Translate a foreign title into English unless it is known to Americans by its foreign name: *Rousseau's "War."* Not: *Rousseau's "La Guerre."* Also: *Leonardo da Vinci's "Mona Lisa." Mozart's "The Marriage of Figaro"* and *"The Magic Flute."* But: *"Die Walkure"* and *"Götterdämmerung"* from Wagner's *"The Ring of the Nibelungen."*

congress   Capitalize Congress in references to the U.S. Senate and House. Although it sometimes is substituted for *the House*, it properly applies to both. Lowercase to mean any assembly.

copyright   *(n., v., adj.) The disclosure was made in a copyright story.* Use *copyrighted* only as the past tense of the verb: *He copyrighted the article.*

counsel   also: *counseled, counseling, counselor, counselor-at-law.* To *counsel* is to advise. A *counselor* is one who conducts a case in court, usually, but not always, a lawyer. A *counselor-at-law* is a lawyer.

county   Capitalize as an integral part of a proper name: *Dade County, the Dade County Commission.* But: *the county Board of Health, the county.* Lowercase all *county of* and generic and plural uses: *Westchester and Rockland counties, the county of Westchester, any county.*

Capitalize as part of a formal title before a name: *County Manager John Smith.* Lowercase when it is not part of the formal title: *county Health Commissioner Frank Jones.*

courtesy titles   In general, do not use *Miss, Mr., Mrs.* or *Ms.* in the first reference: *Betty Ford, Jimmy Carter, Susan Smith.*

Use *Mrs.* on first reference only if a woman requests that her husband's first name be used or her own first name cannot be determined: *Mrs. James Smith.*

Do not use *Mr.* in any reference unless it is combined with *Mrs.: Mr. and Mrs. John Smith, Mr. and Mrs. Smith.*

On sports wires, do not use courtesy titles in any reference unless needed to distinguish among people of the same last name.

On news wires, use courtesy titles for women on second reference, following the woman's preference. Guidelines:

1. If a married woman is known by her maiden name, use *Miss* on second reference unless she prefers *Ms.*

   If known by her married name, use *Mrs.* on second reference unless she prefers *Ms.: Carla Hills, Mrs. Hills.*

2. For women who have never been married, use *Miss* on second reference unless a woman prefers *Ms.* For divorced women or those whose husband are dead, use *Mrs.* on second reference unless a woman prefers *Ms.*

3. If a woman prefers *Ms.*, do not include her marital status in a story unless it is clearly pertinent.

court names   Capitalize the full proper names of courts at all levels, with or without the name of the jurisdiction: *the U.S. Supreme Court, the Supreme Court; the Massachusetts Superior Court, the state Superior Court, the court.*

For courts identified by a numeral: *2nd District Court, a district court, 8th U.S. Circuit Court of Appeals, the appeals court, the court.*

cross country   No hyphen, an exception to Webster's New World Dictionary based on the practices of U.S. and international governing bodies for the sport. Scoring is in minutes, seconds and tenths of a second. Extend to hundredths if available.

Use a basic summary. Example:

National AAU Championship
(Cross Country)

1, Frank Shorter, Miami, 5:25.67. 2, Tom Coster, Los Angeles, 5:30.72., 3, etc.

Adapt the basic summary to paragraph form for a field of more than 10.

D

dangling modifiers   Avoid modifiers that do not refer clearly and logically to some word in the sentence.

Dangling: *Taking our seats, the game started.* (*Taking* does not refer to the subject *game,* nor to any other word in the sentence.)

Correct: *Taking our seats, we watched the opening of the game.* (*Taking* refers to *we,* the subject of the sentence.)

dash   Indicate the dash on video display terminals by striking the separate key provided for it. On typewriters, indicate a dash by striking the hyphen key twice.

Put a space on both sides of a dash in all uses except the start of a paragraph and in sports agate summaries.

Guidelines:

1. Use dashes to denote an abrupt change in thought in a sentence or an emphatic pause: *We will fly to Paris in June—if I get a raise. Smith offered a plan—it was unprecedented—to raise revenues.*

    But be wary of the damage this does to the flow of a sentence.

2. When a phrase that would otherwise be set off with commas contains a series of words that must be separated by commas, use dashes to set off the full phrase: *He listed the qualities—intelligence, charm, beauty, independence—that he liked in women.*

3. Use a dash before an author's name at the end of a quotation: *"Who steals my purse steals trash."—Shakespeare.*

4. Use a dash in datelines: *NEW YORK (UPI)— The city is broke.*

5. Use dashes to introduce individual sections of a list. Capitalize the first word following the dash.

Jones gave the following reasons:
—He never ordered the package.
—If he did, it didn't come.
—If it did, he sent it back.

dates   Use figures without letters: *April 1.* Not: *April 1st.*

When a month is used with a specific date, use the abbreviations *Jan., Feb., Aug., Sept., Oct., Nov.* and *Dec.* Spell out other months.

When a phrase lists only a month and a year, do not separate with commas. When a phrase refers to a month, day and year, set off the year with commas.

January 1972 was a cold month. Jan. 2 was the coldest day of the month. Feb. 14, 1976, was the target date. His birthday is May 15.

days   Capitalize them: *Monday, Tuesday,* etc. Other guidelines:

1. Spell out days of the week in stories for morning newspapers. Use *today, tonight,* etc., but not *yesterday* or *tomorrow,* for afternoon editions. Avoid an awkward placement: *The police jailed Tuesday,* etc.

2. Avoid an unnecessary use of *last* or *next.* Past, present or future tense are an adequate indication of which day is meant.

    Wordy: It happened *last* Tuesday.

    Better: It happened Tuesday.

3. Do not abbreviate, except in tabular format (three letters, without periods): *Sun, Mon, Tues, Wed, Thu, Fri, Sat.*

decathlon   Summaries include time or distance performances, points earned in that event and cumulative total of points earned in previous events.

Contestants are listed in the order of their overall point totals. First name and hometown (or nation) are included only on the first and last events on the first day of competition; on the last day, first names are included only in the first event and in the summary denoting final placings.

Use the basic summary format. Include all entrants in summaries of each of the 10 events. An example of individual events:

Decathlon (Group A)

100-meter dash—1, Fred Dixon, Los Angeles, 10.8 seconds, 854 points. 2, Bruce Jenner, San Jose State, 11.09, 783.3, etc.

Long jump—1, Dixon 24-1 (7.34m), 889, 1,743.2, Jenner 23-6¼ (7.17m), 855, 1,638. 3, etc.

Example, final result:

Decathlon final—1, Bruce Jenner, San Jose State, 8,524 points. 2, Fred Dixon, Los Angeles, 8,277. 3, etc.

decimal units   Use a period and figures to indicate decimal amounts. Carry decimals to two places. See **fractions.**

dialect   There are some words and phrases in everyone's vocabulary that are typical of a particular region or group. Quoting dialect, unless used carefully, implies substandard or illiterate usage. Avoid dialect, even in quoted matter, unless it is clearly pertinent.

When there is a compelling reason to use dialect, use phonetic spellings. Apostrophes show missing letters and sounds: *"Din't ya yoosta live at Toidy-Toid Street and Sekun Amya? Across from da moom pitchers?"*

dictionaries   For spelling, style and usage questions not covered in this stylebook, consult Webster's New World Dictionary of the American Language, Second College Edition.

Use the first spelling listed. If spellings differ in separate entries (*tee shirt* and *T-shirt*, for example), use the spelling that has a full definition (*T-shirt*). If each entry has a full definition (*although* or *though*, for example), either is acceptable.

For spelling and usage not covered in this book or in Webster's New World Dictionary, consult Webster's Third New International Dictionary, which has more entries.

directions   Always lowercase compass points (*north, south, northeast, northern,* etc.) that indicate direction: *He drove west. The cold front is moving east.* Elsewhere:

1. Capitalize compass points that designate regions of the world or United States: *The North was victorious. The South will rise again. Settlers from the East went west in search of new lives.*

    Also: *the Far East, the Eastern establishment, the Eastern Hemisphere, the Middle East, the*

Mideast, the Midwest, the Northeast, a Northerner, the North Woods, a Northern liberal, Southeast Asia, a Southern strategy, the South Pacific, the West, a Western businessman, Western Europe, the Western Hemisphere, the Western United States, the West Coast (the region; lowercase *west coast* for the physical coastline itself).

2. Capitalize compass points as part of a proper name: *North America, the South Pole, North Dakota, Northern Ireland, West Virginia, the Eastern Shore.*

3. Lowercase compass points with other nations except to designate a politically divided nation: *northern France, eastern Canada.* But: *East Germany.*

4. In general, lowercase compass points to describe a section of a state or city: *western Texas, southern Atlanta.* But they may be capitalized if a particular section has a widely known popular name: *Southern California, South Side* (Chicago), *Lower East Side* (New York). If in doubt, use lowercase.

dollars   Always lowercase. Use figures and the $ sign in all except casual references or amounts without a figure: *The book cost $4. Dad, please give me a dollar. Dollars are flowing overseas.*

For specified amounts, it takes a singular verb: *He said $500,000 is what they want.*

For amounts of more than $1 million, use the $ and figures up to two decimal places. Do not use hyphens: *He is worth $4.35 million. He is worth exactly $4,351,242. He proposed a $300 billion budget.*

The form for amounts less than $1 million: *$4 $6.35, $25, $500, $1,000, $650,000.*

E

ellipsis   (. . .) Treat an ellipsis as a three-letter word, constructed with three periods, with spaces before and after it.

1. Use an ellipsis to indicate an omission of one or more words within a quoted passage in texts or transcripts.

    "No man is an island . . . every man is a piece of

the continent, a part of the main.''—John Donne.

''. . . to be honest, as this world goes, is to be one man picked out of ten thousand.''—Shakespeare.

''Poetry lifts the veil from the hidden beauty of the world. . . .''—Shelley.

''A foolish consistency is the hobgoblin of little minds. . . . With consistency a great soul simply has nothing to do.''—Emerson.

''Forbid it, almighty God! . . . Give me liberty or give me death.''—Patrick Henry.

2. In most news stories, an ellipsis is not necessary before and after quotations:

''A foolish consistency is the hobgoblin of little minds,'' Emerson said.

3. An ellipsis may be used to separate small items in a gossip column.

4. Do not use an ellipsis to indicate a pause or hesitation in speech, or a thought that the speaker or writer does not complete. Use a dash instead.

equal, equaled, equaling   *Equal* has no comparative forms. When people speak of a *more equal distribution of wealth,* what is meant is more *equitable* or *more nearly equal.*

equally as   Do not use the words together. One is sufficient.

Omit *equally* in: *She was (equally) as pretty as Marilyn.*

Omit *as* in: *She and Marilyn were equally (as) pretty.*

ex-   No hyphen unless it means former: *excommunicate, expropriate, ex-convict, ex-president.* It modifies the entire term: *ex-New York Gov. Nelson Rockefeller.* Not: *New York ex-Gov.,* etc. Better: *former* Gov. Nelson Rockefeller.

exclamation point(!)   Use it sparingly, only in very exceptional cases to express a high degree of surprise, incredulity or other strong emotion.

Do not use the exclamation mark with mild interjections, mildly exclamatory sentences or to indicate irony or humor.

Place the exclamation mark inside quotation marks if it is part of the quoted material; outside if it isn't.

''Never!'' she shouted.

''I hated reading 'The Carpetbaggers'!'' he said.

F

fact   All facts are true. A *false fact* is impossible; *actual fact, real fact* and *true fact* are redundant.

Fahrenheit   The temperature scale commonly used in the United States, after Gabriel Daniel Fahrenheit, a German physicist who designed it. In it, the freezing point of water is 32 degrees and the boiling point is 212 degrees at sea level.

The forms, if needed: *86 degrees Fahrenheit* or *86 F* (note the space and no period after the F).

To convert to Celsius, subtract 32 from the Fahrenheit figure, multiply by 5 and divide by 9 (77 minus 32 equals 45 × 5 equals 225 divided by 9 equals 25).

felony, misdemeanor   A *felony* is a serious crime. A *misdemeanor* is a minor offense. Further distinctions vary from jurisdiction to jurisdiction.

At the federal level a misdemeanor carries a potential penalty of no more than a year in jail. A felony carries a potential penalty of more than a year in prison. Anyone convicted of a felony is a felon even if no time is actually spent in confinement.

fencing   Identify epee, foil and saber classes as: *men's individual foil, women's team foil,* etc. Use a match summary for early rounds in major events, lesser dual meets and tournaments.

For major events, where competitors meet in a round-robin and are divided into pools, use this form:

Epee, first round (four qualify for semifinals) Pool 1— Joe Smith, Springfield, Mass., 4-1. Enrique Lopez, Chile, 3-2. etc.

football   The spelling of some frequently used words and phrases:

ball carrier	end zone	fullback
ballclub	fair catch	goal-line
blitz (n., v.)	field goal	goal-line stand
end line	fourth-and-one	halfback

halftime	out of bounds	quarterback
handoff	(adv.)	runback
kick off (v.)	out-of-bounds	running back
kickoff (n.)	(adj.)	split end
left guard	pitchout (n.)	tailback
linebacker	place kick	tight end
lineman	place-kicker	touchback
line of scrim-	play off (v.)	touchdown
mage	playoff (n., adj.)	wide receiver

Use figures for yardage: *the 5-yard line, the 10-yard line, a 5-yard pass play, a 7-yard gain.* But: *a fourth-and-two play.* Elsewhere: *The Texas 11 won the championship. The score was 21-14. The team record is 4-5-1.*

NFL is acceptable in all references for National Football League. Also: *the Eastern Division, AFC West,* etc.

The summary style:

Always list the visiting team first.

Field goals are measured from where the ball was kicked—not the line of scrimmage—to the goal posts, including the end zone.

Abbreviate team names to four or fewer letters on scoring and statistical lines.

The passing line shows, in order: completions—attempts—had intercepted.

Example of scoring summary:

Stanford   16   7   3   2-28
Army   8   6   15 6-35
Army-John 6 run (Chambers run)
Stan-Temple 2 run (Central pass from Temple)
Stan-Powers 26 run (Powers run)
Army-Tennyson 11 run (kick failed)
Stan-Lutz 22 pass from Chambers (Chambers kick)
Stan-FG Lutz 23
Army-Tennyson 34 pass interception (Jones kick)
Army-Brandt 22 punt return (Jones pass from Tennyson)
Stan-Safety Doakes tackled in end zone
Army-Hallmark 16 pass from Tennyson (run failed)
A-26,571

Fourth Estate   Journalism or journalists. The term is attributed to Edmund Burke, who is reported to have called the reporters' gallery in Parliament "a Fourth Estate." The other three were the clergy, the nobility and the bourgeoisie.

fractions   Whenever practical, convert fractions to decimals. Fractions are preferred, however, in stories about stocks and in recipes.

When using fractional characters, remember that most newspaper type fonts can set only $\frac{1}{8}$, $\frac{1}{4}$,

$\frac{3}{8}$, $\frac{1}{2}$, $\frac{5}{8}$, $\frac{3}{4}$ and $\frac{7}{8}$ as one unit. For mixed numbers, use $1\frac{1}{2}$, $2\frac{5}{8}$, etc. with a space between the whole number and the fraction. Other fractions require a hyphen and individual figures, with a space between the whole number and the fraction: 1 3-16, 2 1-3, 5 9-10.

If fractions must be spelled out, hyphenate them: *two-thirds, three-fourths, twenty-seven-hundredths.*

G

geographic names   The authority for spelling place names in the U.S. states and territories is the U.S. Postal Service Directory of Post Offices. But do not use the postal abbreviations for state names (see separate entries), and abbreviate *saint* as *St.* and Sainte as *Ste.* in U.S. names.

The first source for the spelling of all foreign place names is Webster's New World Dictionary. Use the first-listed spelling if an entry gives more than one. If the dictionary provides different spellings in separate entries, use the spelling that is followed by a full description of the location. Also:

1. Use Cameroon, not Cameroons or Cameroun.
2. Use Maldives, not Maldive Islands.
3. Use Sri Lanka, not Ceylon.

These three exceptions conform with the practices of the United Nations and the U.S. Board of Geographic Names.

If the dictionary does not have an entry, use the first-listed spelling in the Columbia Lippincott Gazetteer of the World.

Follow the styles adopted by the United Nations and the U.S. Board of Geographic Names on new cities, new independent nations and nations that change their names. If the two do not agree, the news services will announce a common policy.

Capitalize common nouns as an integral part of a proper name, but lowercase them standing alone: *Pennsylvania Avenue, the avenue; the Philippine Islands, the islands; the Mississippi River, the river; the Gulf of Mexico, the gulf.*

Lowercase all common nouns that are not part of a specific proper name: *the Pacific islands, the Swiss mountains, Chekiang province.*

golf   Some frequently used terms:

Americas Cup No apostrophe.

birdie *(s.)*, **birdies** *(pl.)* One stroke under par.

bogey *(s.)*, **bogeys** *(pl.)* One stroke more than par. Past tense: *bogeyed.*

eagle Two strokes under par.

fairway

Masters Tournament No apostrophe. On second reference: *the Masters.*

tee, tee off

U.S. Open Championship On second reference: *the U.S. Open, the Open.*

Use figures for handicaps: *He has a 3 handicap; a 3-handicap golfer; a handicap of 3 strokes; a 3-stroke handicap.*

Use figures for par listings: *He had a par 5 to finish 2-up for the round; a par 4 hole, a 7-under-par 64, the par-3 seventh hole.*

Use figures for club ratings: *a No. 5 iron, a 5-iron, a 7-iron shot, a 4-wood.*

Also: *The first hole, the ninth hole, the 10th hole, the back nine, the final 18, the third round, he won 3 and 2.*

PGA is acceptable in all references for Professional Golfers' Association (note the apostrophe); *LPGA* in all references for Ladies Professional Golf Association (no apostrophe).

Summaries-Stroke Play: Use separate summary style for stroke (medal) play and match play.

In stroke play, use a dash before the final figure on a line. Use hyphens between other figures.

Stroke play, scores in ascending order:

First round:

Jack Nicklaus	35-35—70
Johnny Miller	36-35—71
etc.	

Second round:

Jack Nicklaus	70-70—140
Johnny Miller	71-70—141
etc.	

Final round, professional tournaments, including prize money:

Jack Nicklaus, $30,000	70-70-70-68—278
Johnny Miller, 17,500	71-70-70-69—280
etc.	

Use hometowns, if ordered, only on national championship amateur tournaments. Use home countries, if ordered, only on major international events such as British Open. If used, place the hometown or country on a second line, indented one space:

Arnold Palmer	70-69-68-70—277
United States	
Tony Jacklin	71-70-70-70—281
England	

The form for cards:

Par out	**454**	**343**	**454-36**
Par in	**443**	**545**	**344-36—72**
Nicklaus out	444	333	454-34
Nicklaus in	443	445	344-35—69
Miller out	434	343	444-33

Summaries-Match play: Note the following forms. In the first example, one hole, the 18th, was left but not played because Nicklaus had a 2-hole lead. In the second, the match went 18 holes. In the third, a 19th hole was played because the golfers were tied at the end of 18.

Jack Nicklaus def. Lee Trevino, 2 and 1.

Sam Snead def. Ben Hogan, 2-up.

Arnold Palmer def. Johnny Miller, 1-up (19).

government   Always lowercase. Never abbreviate. A *government* is an established system of political administration: *the U.S. government.*

A *junta* is a group or council that often rules after a coup: A military *junta* controls the country. A junta becomes a government after it establishes a system of political administration.

Regime is a synonym for political system: *a democratic regime, an authoritarian regime.* Do not use it to mean government or junta. For example, use *Franco government* in referring to the government of Spain under Francisco Franco. Not: *Franco regime.* But: *The Franco government was an authoritarian regime.*

An *administration* consists of the officials who make up the executive branch of government: *the Carter administration.*

governmental bodies   Capitalize the full proper names of governmental agencies, departments and offices: *the U.S. Department of State, the Georgia Department of Human Resources, the Boston City Council, the Chicago Fire Department.* Retain capitals if the specific meaning is clear without the jurisdiction: *the Department of State, the Department of Human Resources, the state Department of Human Resources, the City Council, the Fire Department, the city Fire Department.* Elsewhere:

1. Capitalize names flip-flopped to delete *of: the State Department, the Human Resources Department.*

2. Capitalize widely used popular names:

Walpole State Prison (the proper name is Massachusetts Correctional Institution-Walpole).

3. Lowercase when the reference is not specific: *Nebraska has no state senate.*

4. Lowercase generic terms standing alone or in plural uses: *the Boston and Chicago city councils, the department.*

gymnastics   Scoring is by points. Identify events by name—sidehorse, horizontal bars, etc.

Use a basic summary. Example:

Sidehorse—1, John Leaper, Penn State, 8.8 points. 2, Joe Jumper, Ohio State, 7.9. 3, etc.

H

habeas corpus   A petition requiring those detaining someone to justify it. If the term is used, define it.

handball   Games are won by the first player to score 21 points, unless it is necessary to continue until one player has a two-point spread. Most matches go to the first winner of two games.

Use a match summary. Example:

Bob Richards, Yale, def. Pau. Johnson, Dartmouth, 21-18, 21-19.

Tom Brennan, Massachusetts, def. Bill Stevens, Michigan, 21-19, 17-21, 22-20.

Hanukkah   The Jewish Feast of Lights, an eight-day commemoration of the rededication of the Temple by the Maccabees after their victory over the Syrians. It usually occurs in December, but sometimes falls in late November. This spelling is an exception to Webster's New World Dictionary.

heavenly bodies   Capitalize the proper names of planets, stars, etc.: *Mars, Arcturus, the Big Dipper, Aries, Halley's comet.*

Lowercase sun and moon, but if their Greek names are used, capitalize them: *Helios and Luna.* Lowercase nouns and adjectives derived from the proper names of planets and other heavenly bodies: *earthling, jovian, lunar, martian, solar, venusian.*

historical periods   Capitalize proper nouns and adjectives in describing periods of history: *ancient Greece, classical Rome, the Victorian era.*

Elsewhere, some cultural and historical periods and events are capitalized: *the Atomic Age, the Pliocene Epoch, Prohibition, the Reign of Terror, the Stone Age, the Middle Ages, the Boston Tea Party, the Exodus* (of the Israelites from Egypt).

Some are not: *antiquity, the neolithic period, the fall of Rome, the gold rush, the ice age, the industrial revolution, the westward movement.*

Follow the capitalization in Webster's New World Dictionary, using lowercase if it is one of the options listed. If there is no listing in Webster's New World, use lowercase except for proper nouns and adjectives.

hockey   The spelling of some frequently used words:

blue line	goal line	power-play
crease	goaltender	goal
faceoff (n.,	penalty box	red line
adj.)	play off (v.)	short-handed
face off (v.)	playoff (n.,	two-on-one
goalie	adj.)	break
goal post	power play	

A *hat trick* is the scoring of three goals in one game by one player.

NHL is acceptable in all references for National Hockey League; *WHA* for World Hockey Association.

Summaries: The visiting team is always listed first in the score by periods.

Note that each goal is numbered according to its sequence in the game.

The figure after the name of a scoring player is his total number of goals for the season. Provide this only for NHL and WHA games.

Names in parentheses are those of players credited with an assist on the goal.

The final figure in the list of each goal is the number of minutes elapsed in the period when the goal was scored.

Do not use the designation minor after a penalty unless part of a major-minor combination.

Philadelphia	0	0	1—1
NY Islanders	3	0	2—5

First period—1, New York, Trottier 28 (D. Potvin, J. Potvin), 3:39. 2, New York, St. Laurent 8 (Howatt, Nystrom), 6:40. 3, New York, Howatt 21 (unassisted), 9:15. Penalty—Clarke, Phi, 2:32.

Second period—None. Penalties—None.

Third period—4, New York, D. Potvin 30 (Parise, Westfall), 2:10. 5, New York, Trottier 29 (Gillies), 2:55. 6, Philadelphia, Barber 46 (Bladon, Clarke), 5:33. Penalties—Watson, Phi, major-minor (misconduct) 1:09; Parise, NY, major, 4:15; Bladon, Phi, 10:25; Phi, bench (served by King), 13:10.

Shots on goal—Philadelphia 10-10-17—37. New York 16-12-5—33.

Goalies—Philadelphia, Stephenson. New York, Resch. A—14,865.

The form for standings:

Campbell Conference
Patrick Division

	W	L	T	Pts.	GF	GA
Philadelphia	47	10	14	108	314	184
NY Islanders	45	17	9	99	310	192

hyphens   Hyphens are joiners. Use them to join words to express a single idea or to avoid ambiguity. Guidelines:

1. Use a hyphen whenever ambiguity would result if it were omitted: *She will speak to small-business men.* (The normal spelling is *businessmen,* but *small businessmen* is unclear.) Also: *He recovered his health. He re-covered the leaky roof.*

2. If a compound modifier—two or more words that express a single concept—is listed separately as an adjective with hyphens in Webster's New World Dictionary (Example: *well-known*), the compound is always hyphenated: *She is a well-known woman. She is well-known.* Also: *The child is soft-spoken. The censor is self-appointed. The boy is quick-witted.*

3. Compounds not listed separately in the dictionary usually take a hyphen before a noun, no hyphen after it: *A first-quarter touchdown, a touchdown in the first quarter; a bluish-green dress, the dress is bluish-green.*

   But never use a hyphen when the compound includes the word *very* or an adverb

ending in *-ly: a very good time, an easily remembered rule.*

4. Some prefixes and suffixes are hyphenated.

5. Some numerals, odds, ratios, etc., are hyphenated.

6. Suspensive hyphenation: *the 5- and 6-year-olds attend morning sessions.*

I

inter-   Hyphenate with a capitalized word: *inter-American.* Elsewhere, follow Webster's New World, hyphenating words not listed there.

intra-   Hyphenate with a capitalized word or to avoid a double a: *intra-European, intra-atomic.* Elsewhere, follow Webster's New World, hyphenating words not listed there. Also: *Intracoastal Waterway.*

J

judge   Capitalize a formal title before the name of a public official who presides in a court of law. Drop the title on second reference.

Lowercase judge as a job description: *beauty contest judge Bert Parks.*

Do not use *court* as part of a title unless ambiguity would result without it: *U.S. Judge John Sirica, District Judge John Sirica, federal Judge John Sirica, Judge John Sirica.* But: *Juvenile Court Joe Zilch, Criminal Court Judge Joe Zilch, Superior Court Judge Joe Zilch, state Supreme Court Judge Joe Zilch.*

L

lay, lie   To *lie* is to recline. To *lay* is to cause to recline.

Right: *He will lie down on the bed. He lay down the book.*

Wrong: *He will lay down on the bed. He lie down the book.*

Other forms of *lie: He lay down on the bed* (past

tense). *He has lain down on the bed* (past participle). *He is lying down on the bed* (present participle).

Other forms of *lay: He laid down the book* (past tense). *He has laid down the book* (past participle). *He is laying down the book* (present participle).

legislative titles   Capitalize formal titles before names; lowercase elsewhere. Use *Rep., Reps., Sen.* and *Sens.* before names in regular text, but spell them out in direct quotations.

Spell out other legislative titles *(assemblyman, assemblywoman, city councilor, delegate, etc.)* in all uses. Other guidelines:

1. Use *U.S.* or *state* before a title only if necessary to avoid confusion: *U.S. Sen. Herman Talmadge spoke with state Sen. Hugh Carter.*
2. The use of a title such as *Rep.* or *Sen.* in first reference is normal in most stories. It is not mandatory, however, provided the title is given later in the story: *Barry Goldwater endorsed President Ford today. The Arizona senator said he believes the president deserves another term.*
3. Do not use legislative titles before a name on second reference unless they are part of a direct quotation.
4. Use *congressman* and *congresswoman* as capitalized formal titles before a name only in direct quotation.
5. Capitalize formal, organizational titles before a name: *Speaker Thomas P. O'Neill, Majority Leader Robert Byrd, Minority Leader John Rhodes, Democratic Whip James Wright, Chairman John Sparkman of the Senate Foreign Relations Committee, President Pro Tem John Stennis.*

libel   If you are threatened with a libel suit or if someone demands a retraction, take the following steps *immediately*.

—Receive all threats and demands politely and without comment. If someone gets insistent, say the matter is out of your hands.

—Gather all the facts and contact your bureau manager or supervisor immediately.

—Don't admit any fault or error on your own or on anyone's part.

—Don't defend what has been done. There is a very human tendency to be apologetic or defensive when someone is angry, but this may only make things worse.

—Don't release any news or picture copy or audio tapes to anyone.

—Don't discuss what you did with anyone but management or counsel.

—Don't write letters or memos describing what you did unless explicitly requested by counsel.

—Don't wait until you've made a mistake. If you think a story, caption or picture may involve potential libel or invasion of privacy problems, talk to management. Don't be shy about asking questions.

M

magazine names   Capitalize, without quotation marks. Lowercase *magazine* unless it is part of the publication's formal title: *Harper's Magazine, Newsweek magazine, Time magazine.* Check the masthead if in doubt.

majority, plurality   Majority means more than half. To measure a majority, compare the majority figure to the sum of all others. In an election, for example, where candidate A gets 100,000 votes, candidate B gets 200,000, and candidate C, 350,000, then C has a majority of 50,000 votes.

Plurality means more than the next highest number. If candidate A gets 65,000 votes, candidate B gets 40,000 and candidate C gets 35,000 then A has a plurality of 25,000, but does not have a majority.

When majority and plurality are used alone, they take singular verbs and pronouns: *The majority has made its decision.*

With an "of" construction they take either a singular or plural verb, whichever fits the occasion: *A majority of two votes is not adequate to control the committee. The majority of the houses on the block were destroyed.*

metric system   A decimal system of weights and measures. The basic units are the gram, the meter and the liter. Larger and smaller units are defined by prefixes, such as "kilo." Thus, a kilogram is 1,000 grams.

Larger units include deka- (10), hecto- (100), kilo- (1,000), mega- (1 million), giga- (1 billion) and tera- (1 trillion).

Smaller units include deci- (one-tenth), centi- (one-hundredth), milli- (one-thousandth), micro- (one-millionth), and pico- (one-trillionth).

Do not abbreviate metric terms in news copy, except for certain cameras, films and weapons: *an 8mm film, a 105mm cannon.*

A conversion table for frequently used terms (approximations):

Into Metric

When you know	multiply by	to find
Length		
inches	2.54	centimeters
feet	30.0	centimeters
yards	0.9	meters
miles	1.6	kilometers
Area		
sq. inches	6.5	sq. centimeters
sq. feet	0.09	sq. meters
sq. yards	0.8	sq. meters
sq. miles	2.6	sq. miles
acres	0.4	hectares
Weight		
ounces	28.0	grams
pounds	0.45	kilograms
tons	0.9	metric tons
Volume		
teaspoons	5.0	milliliters
tablespoons	15.0	milliliters
fluid ounces	30.0	milliliters
cups	0.24	liters
pints	0.47	liters
quarts	0.95	liters
gallons	3.8	liters
cubic feet	0.03	cubic meters
cubic yards	0.76	cubic meters
Temperature		

Fahrenheit minus 32 $\times$ 5 $\div$ 9 = Celsius

Out of Metric

When you know	multiply by	to find
Length		
millimeters	0.04	inches
centimeters	0.4	inches
meters	3.3	feet
meters	1.1	yards
kilometers	0.6	miles
Area		
sq. centimeters	1.16	sq. inches
sq. meters	1.2	sq. yards
sq. kilometers	0.4	sq. miles
hectares	2.5	acres
Weight		
grams	0.035	ounces
kilograms	2.2	pounds
metric tons	1.1	tons
Volume		
milliliters	0.03	fluid ounces
liters	2.1	pints
liters	1.06	quarts
liters	0.26	gallons
cubic meters	35.0	cubic feet
cubic meters	1.3	cubic yards
Temperature		

Celsius $\times$ 9 $\div$ 5 plus 32 Fahrenheit

military titles   Capitalize a military rank as a formal title before a name on first reference. Lowercase elsewhere. Drop the title on subsequent references.

Do not abbreviate any title standing alone or in a direct quotation.

In some cases it is pertinent to explain a title: *Army Sgt. Maj. John Jones, who holds the Army's highest rank for enlisted men, said the attack was unprovoked.*

Do not capitalize or abbreviate job descriptions, such as *machinist, radarman, torpedoman, yeoman,* etc.

To form plurals of the abbreviations, add *s* to the principal element in the title: *Majs., Maj. Gens., Sgts. Maj., Specs. 4, Pfcs., Prvts.*

The first-reference usage before a name:

Rank	Usage Before A Name
Army	
Commissioned Officers	
general	Gen.
lieutenant general	Lt. Gen.
major general	Maj. Gen.
brigadier general	Brig. Gen.
colonel	Col.
lieutenant colonel	Lt. Col.
major	Maj.
captain	Capt.
first lieutenant	1st Lt.
second lieutenant	2nd Lt.
Warrant Officers	
chief warrant officer	Chief Warrant Officer
warrant officer	Warrant Officer

Enlisted Personnel

sergeant major of the Army	Army Sgt. Maj.
command sergeant major	Command Sgt. Maj.
staff sergeant major	Staff Sgt. Maj.
first sergeant	1st Sgt.
master sergeant	Master Sgt.
platoon sergeant	Platoon Sgt.
sergeant first class	Sgt. 1st Class
specialist seven	Spec. 7
staff sergeant	Staff Sgt.
specialist six	Spec. 6
sergeant	Sgt.
specialist five	Spec. 5
corporal	Cpl.
specialist four	Spec. 4
private first class	Pfc.
private 2	Pvt. 2
private 1	Pvt. 1

Navy, Coast Guard

Commissioned Officers

admiral	Adm.
vice admiral	Vice Adm.
rear admiral	Rear Adm.
commodore	Commodore
captain	Capt.
commander	Cmdr.
lieutenant commander	Lt. Cmdr.
lieutenant	Lt.
lieutenant junior grade	Lt. j.g.
ensign	Ensign
commissioned warrant officer	Commissioned Warrant Officer

Warrant Officers

warrant officer	Warrant Officer

Enlisted Personnel

master chief petty officer	Master Chief Petty Officer
senior chief petty officer	Senior Chief Petty Officer
chief petty officer	Chief Petty Officer
petty officer first class	Petty Officer 1st Class
petty officer second class	Petty Officer 2nd Class
petty officer third class	Petty Officer 3rd Class
seaman	Seaman
seaman apprentice	Seaman Apprentice
seaman recruit	Seaman Recruit

Marine Corps

Ranks and abbreviations for commissioned officers are the same as those in the Army. Warrant officers are abbreviated the same as the Navy. There are no specialist ratings.

Others

sergeant major	Sgt. Maj.
master gunnery sergeant	Master Gunnery Sgt.
master sergeant	Master Sgt.
first sergeant	1st Sgt.
gunnery sergeant	Gunnery Sgt.
staff sergeant	Staff Sgt.
sergeant	Sgt.
corporal	Cpl.
lance corporal	Lance Cpl.
private first class	Pfc.
private	Pvt.

Air Force

Ranks and abbreviations for commissioned officers are the same as those in the Army.

Enlisted designations

chief master sergeant	Chief Master Sgt.
senior master sergeant	Senior Master Sgt.
master sergeant	Master Sgt.
technical sergeant	Tech. Sgt.
staff sergeant	Staff Sgt.
sergeant	Sgt.
airman first class	Airman 1st Class
airman	Airman
airman basic	Airman

Retired Officers

A military rank may be used in first reference before the name of an officer who has retired if it is relevant to a story. Do not, however, use the military abbreviation *Ret.*

Instead, use *retired* just as *former* would be used before the title of a civilian: *They invited retired Army Gen. Joseph Zilch.*

Firefighters—Police Officers

Use the abbreviations listed here when a military-style title appears before the name of a police officer or firefighter outside a direct quotation. Add police or fire before the title if necessary in context: *police Sgt. William Smith, fire Capt. David Jones.*

military units Use figures and capitalize the key words when linked with the figures: *1st Infantry Division* (or the 1st Division), *5th Battalion, 395th Field Artillery, 7th Fleet.* But: *the division, the battalion, the artillery, the fleet.*

monthlong One word.

months Capitalize the names of months in all uses. Use the abbreviations *Jan., Feb., Aug., Sept., Oct., Nov.*

and *Dec.* with a specific date. Do not abbreviate any month standing alone or with a year alone.

In tabular material, use three letters without a period: *Jan, Feb, Mar, Apr, May, Jun, Jul, Aug, Sep, Oct, Nov, Dec.*

movie ratings   The ratings used by the Motion Picture Association of America:

G—General Audiences. All ages admitted.

PG—Parental Guidance. Some material may not be suitable for children less than 13 years old.

PG 13—Parental Guidance. Parents are strongly urged to give special guidance for attendance of children under 13.

R—Restricted. Persons under 17 must be accompanied by a parent or adult guardian.

NC 17—No children under 17 admitted.

Capitalize and hyphenate adjectival forms: *a NC 17-rated film.*

Mr. (s.), **Messrs.** (pl.), **Mrs.** (s.), **Mmes.** (pl.) Do not spell out these courtesy titles, even in direct quotation.

Ms.   A title, not an abbreviation, free of reference to marital status, used before the name of women who prefer it instead of *Miss* or *Mrs.* There is no plural. If several women who prefer *Ms.* are listed in a series, repeat *Ms.* before each name.

N

names   In general, people are entitled to be known however they want to be known, as long as their identities are clear.

When someone changes personal names, such as Cassius Clay's transition to Muhammad Ali, provide both names in stories until the new name is widely known. After that, use only the new name unless there is a specific reason for including the earlier identification.

newspapers   Capitalize *the* in a newspaper's full name if that is the way a publication prefers to be known: *The New York Times.* But lowercase *the* in a shortened name: *the Times.* Lowercase *the* in plural uses: *the New York Times* and *the Washington Post.*

Where location is needed but is not part of the official name, use parentheses: *The Knoxville (Tenn.) News-Sentinel.*

Consult the International Year Book published by Editor & Publisher to determine whether a two-name combination is hyphenated.

nicknames   Use a derivative of a proper name only when it is the way the individual prefers to be known: *Jimmy Carter.*

A descriptive nickname, if used, takes quotation marks, not parentheses: *Sen. Henry "Scoop" Jackson.* Also: *Jackson is known as "Scoop."*

In sports stories and sports columns, widely used nicknames are acceptable without quotation marks: *Woody Hayes, Bear Bryant, Catfish Hunter.* But if the given name is used, and in all news stories: *Paul "Bear" Bryant.*

Capitalize other nicknames without quotation marks: *Sunshine State, the Old Dominion, Motown, the Magic City, Old Hickory, Old Glory.*

non-   Hyphenate all except the following words: nonchalance, nonchalant, nonsense, nondescript, nonsensical

numerals   A numeral is a figure, letter, word or group of words expressing a number.

Roman numerals use the letters I, V, X, L, C, D and M. Use Roman numerals for wars and to show personal sequence for animals and people: *World War II, Native Dancer II, King George VI, Pope John XXIII.*

Arabic numerals use the figures 1, 2, 3, 4, 5, 6, 7, 8, 9 and 0. Use Arabic forms unless Roman numerals are specifically required.

Guidelines:

1. When large numbers must be spelled out, use a hyphen to connect a word ending in "y" to another word; do not use commas between other words that are part of one number: *twenty, thirty, twenty-one, thirty-one, one hundred forty-three, one thousand one hundred fifty-five, one million two hundred seventy-six thousand five hundred eighty-seven.*

2. Spell out any numeral, except a year, that begins a sentence. If necessary, recast the sentence.

    Wrong: *25 boys went. 993 freshmen entered the college last year.*

    Right: *Twenty-five boys went. Last year 993 freshmen entered the college.*

    Right: *1976 was a very good year.*

3. Spell out casual expressions: *A thousand times*

no! Thanks a million. He walked a quarter of a mile.

4. Follow an organization's practice in using words or numerals in proper names: *20th Century-Fox, Twentieth Century Fund, Big Ten.*

Many separate entries provide guidelines on specific uses, and there are separate listings for each major sport.

For uses not covered by these listings, spell out whole numbers below 10, use figures for 10 and above: *The woman has three sons and two daughters. He has a fleet of 10 station wagons and two buses. They had 10 pictures, six smudges and 97 bottles of beer on the wall. They had four four-room houses, 10 three-room houses and 12 10-room houses.*

O

obscenities Do not use obscenities, profanity, vulgarities, etc., in stories unless they are part of direct quotations and there is a compelling reason for them. When they are used, flag the story at the top.

Editors: Note language in 4th graf

Then confine the offending language to a separate paragraph that can be easily deleted by editors who do not want it.

olympics Capitalize all references to the international athletic contests held every four years: *the Olympics, the Winter Olympics, the Olympic Games, the Games.*

An Olympic-sized pool is 50 meters (165 feet) long by 25 meters (82.5 feet) wide. Depths vary according to the event.

Lowercase other uses: *a beer-drinking olympics.*

organizations and institutions Capitalize the full names of organizations and institutions: *the American Medical Association, First Presbyterian Church, General Motors Corp., Harvard University.* Or simply: *General Motors, Harvard.*

Capitalize major divisions: *the Pontiac Motor Division of General Motors.*

Lowercase others with widely used generic names: *the board of directors of General Motors, the board of trustees of Columbia University, the history department*

of Harvard University, the sports department of the Daily Citizen-Leader.

Capitalize those without widely used generic names: *the General Assembly of the World Council of Churches, the House of Delegates of the American Medical Association, the House of Bishops and House of Deputies of the Episcopal Church.*

Capitalize flip-flopped names that delete *of: College of the Holy Cross, Holy Cross College; Harvard School of Dental Medicine, Harvard Dental School.* But do not flip-flop a title unless it is common usage: *Massachusetts Institute of Technology.* Not: *Massachusetts Technology Institute.*

P

parentheses ( ) Parentheses are jarring to the reader. Use them in sentences only if no other arrangement will fit the occasion. There are occasions when parentheses are the only effective means of inserting necessary background or reference information.

Guidelines:

1. If parenthetical information inserted in a direct quotation is at all sensitive, place an editor's note at the bottom of a story alerting copy desks to what has been inserted.

2. Place a period outside a closing parenthesis if the material inside is not a sentence *(such as this fragment).*

   (An independent parenthetical sentence such as this one takes a period before the closing parenthesis.)

   When a phrase placed in parentheses *(this one is an example)* might normally qualify as a complete sentence but is dependent on the surrounding material, do not capitalize the first word or end with a period.

3. Use parentheses if a location is inserted in a proper name: *The Huntsville (Ala.) Times.* But use commas if no proper name is involved: *The Selma, Ala., group saw the governor.*

4. Use quotation marks, not parentheses, around a nickname.

5. Use commas, not parentheses, to set off a political figure's party affiliation.

6. Do not use parentheses to indicate that an unusual spelling or term is correct. Include the confirmation in an editor's note under a dash at the bottom of a story.

Editors: The spelling Jorja is correct.

people, persons Use *people* when speaking of a large or uncounted number of individuals: *Thousands of people attended the fair. Some rich people pay no taxes. What will people say?* Do not use *persons* in this sense.

Persons is usually used for a relatively small number of people who can be counted, but *people* often can be substituted.

Right: *There were 20 persons in the room.*

Right: *There were 20 people in the room.*

People is also a collective noun that requires a plural verb and is used to refer to a single race or nation: *The American people are united.* In this sense, the plural form is *peoples: The peoples of Africa speak many languages.*

period (.) Use a period at the end of a declarative sentence, an indirect question, a polite request phrased as a question and most imperative sentences: *The book is finished. He asked what the score was. Why don't we go. Shut the door.* Elsewhere:

1. Use a period in some abbreviations.
2. Use three periods to construct an ellipsis mark.
3. Use a period in initials in a name: *John F. Kennedy, T.S. Eliot (no space between T. and S.). Use no period if initials are used instead of a name: JFK, LBJ.*
4. Use a period to indicate order of enumeration: *1. Wash the car. 2. Clean the basement.* Or: *A. Punctuate properly. B. Write simply.*
5. Periods always go inside quotation marks.

-persons Do not coin new words such as chairperson or spokesperson in regular text. They may be used in direct quotations or when they are an organization's formal title for an office. Words listed in Webster's New World, however, are acceptable: *salesperson.*

In general, use *chairwoman, spokeswoman,* etc., to refer to a woman; *chairman, spokesman,* etc., to refer to a man. Or use a neuter word, such as *leader* or *representative.*

planets Capitalize the name of planets; *Jupiter, Mars, Mercury, Neptune, Pluto, Saturn, Uranus.*

Capitalize *earth* when used as the proper name of our planet: *The astronauts returned to Earth.* Lowercase elsewhere: *What on earth do you mean?*

Lowercase words derived from the planets and other heavenly bodies: *earthling, martian, jovian, lunar, solar, venusian.*

plants Lowercase, except for proper nouns or adjectives that occur in a name: *tree, fir, white fir, Douglas fir, Dutch elm, Scotch pine; clover, white clover, white Dutch clover.*

If a botanical name is used, capitalize the first word, lowercase others: *Pinus* (pine), *Juniperus virginiana* (red cedar), *Callicarpa americana* (blue azalea), *Gymnocladus dioica* (Kentucky coffee tree).

plurals Separate, alphabetical listings give guidelines on forming and using some troublesome words. Some problem areas:

1. Use *'s* to form the plural of single letters: Mind your *p's* and *q's.*
2. Add *s* to form the plural of multiple letters: She knows her ABCs.
3. Add *s* to form the plural of figures: *The custom began in the 1920s. Temperatures will be in the low 20s. There are five size 7s.* (No apostrophes, an exception to Webster's New World guideline for apostrophes.)
4. Do not use *'s* for words used in a special sense, as a word: His speech had too many *ifs, ands* and *buts.* (Exception to Webster's New World.)
5. Some words are plural in form, singular in meaning. Some take singular verbs: *measles, mumps, news.* Others take plural verbs: *grits, scissors, trousers.*

For questions not covered by this book, follow the first-listed plural in Webster's New World Dictionary. See the guidelines the dictionary provides under its alphabetical entry ''plural.''

p.m., a.m.   Lowercase, with periods. Avoid the redundant *10 p.m. tonight.*

police department   Capitalize a specific reference with or without the name of the community: *the Los Angeles Police Department, the Police Department.*

Lowercase *department* alone or in plural uses: *the Los Angeles and San Francisco police departments.*

political parties   Most political parties have names that also indicate a general philosophy or belief.

A democrat, for instance, is one who believes in and upholds government by the people, an advocate of majority rule. There are similar uses of communist, conservative, liberal, national, republican, socialist and others.

Capitalize such words only if the reference clearly is to the proper name of a political party or to its members. Capitalize also *party* as an integral part of a proper name: *The liberal Republican senator and his Conservative Party colleague said democracy and communism are incompatible.*

Always lowercase a usage such as *communist regime. Regime* designates a type of political system, not a specific name.

Capitalize a philosophy derived from a proper name: *Marxism, Nazism.* But lowercase all philosophies not derived from proper names: *communism, democracy, socialism.*

polls   Consider the following questions, based on guidelines suggested by the National Council on Public Polls, before using a story about a canvass of public opinion.

1. Who paid for the poll?
2. When was the poll taken? (Most pollsters concede that rapid, last-minute changes in voter sentiment can take place.)
3. How were the interviews obtained? (Some pollsters think people are less candid on the telephone than in person.)
4. How were the questions worded? (They can be loaded to achieve a desired result. Even the sequence of questions should be considered.)
5. How were the people chosen? (At random, or by some other procedure?)
6. How many people responded? (The larger the number of responses, the smaller the margin for error in projecting the results.)
7. How big was any smaller group on which conclusions are based? (A nationwide survey of 1,500 people might show one set of figures on overall attitudes about abortion, while also reporting on the attitude of Catholics toward abortion. If the attitude of Catholics is cited, ask how many Catholics were interviewed.)

possessives   Use an apostrophe to indicate possessive, except for personal pronouns.

1. Add an apostrophe and an *s* if the ending, either singular or plural, is not an *s* or *z* sound: *the church's needs, the ship's route, today's problems, death's call, your money's worth, a month's pay, anybody's room, women's rights.*
2. Add only the apostrophe if the plural ends in an *s* or *z* sound: *the churches' needs, the ships' wake, girls' toys, the horses' food, states' rights, the VIPs' entrance, the Joneses' boy.*
3. If the singular ends in an *s* or *z* sound, add the apostrophe and an *s* for words of one syllable. Add only the apostrophe for words of more than one syllable unless you expect the pronunciation of the second *s* or *z* sound: *the bus's schedule, anyone else's attitude, the press's error, the fox's den, the justice's verdict, Marx's theories, the prince's life; for goodness' sake, Jesus' life, Moses' law, Tennessee Williams' play.*
4. Compounds or joint possession show the possessive in the last word only. But if there is separate possession, each noun takes the possessive: *the attorney general's request, my brother-in-law's house, Joe and Susan's apartment* (joint possession), *Joe's and Susan's clothes* (separate possession).
5. Follow the user's practice for proper names: *Actors Equity, Diners Club, the Ladies' Home Journal, the National Governors' Conference.*
6. Do not use the apostrophe for personal pronouns: *his, hers, its, mine, ours, theirs, whose, yours.*

prefixes   Three rules are constant, although they yield some exceptions to listings in Webster's New World Dictionary:

—Hyphenate with a capitalized word: *trans-Atlantic.*

—Hyphenate to avoid a duplicated vowel or tripled consonant: *pre-exist, shell-like.*

—Use a hyphen to join doubled prefixes: *sub-subparagraph.*

In addition, most words beginning with *anti-* and *non-* are hyphenated.

prison, jail   In general, a *prison* is any place of confinement: *His backyard was his prison.*

As a place where criminals are confined:

—A *prison* or *penitentiary* is for those convicted of serious crimes carrying a year or more penalty.

—A *jail* is for those convicted of relatively minor offenses carrying a penalty of less than a year, for civil offenses such as non-payment of alimony, and for those awaiting trial or sentencing.

—A *reformatory* or *reform school* is for young offenders convicted of lesser crimes, sent for training and discipline intended to reform rather than punish.

Several euphemisms—*correctional institution, correctional center, detention center*—are widely used in proper names.

Capitalize a proper name or a widely used popular name: *Massachusetts Correctional Institution-Walpole* (the proper name), *Walpole State Prison* (a widely used popular name).

Lowercase plural or generic uses: *The Colorado and Kansas state penitentiaries, the federal prison, the state prison, the prison, the county jail, a federal detention center.*

punctuation   Think of it as a courtesy to your readers, designed to help them understand a story.

There are many gray areas. For this reason, all the punctuation entries in this book are guidelines rather than rules. But don't disregard them lightly.

Q

question mark (?)   Use a question mark at the end of a direct question.

"Who started the riot?" he asked. (Note that a comma is not used after the question mark.) *Did he ask who started the riot?* Elsewhere:

1. Use a question mark at the end of a full sentence that asks a multiple question. *Did you hear him say, "What right have you to ask about the riot?"*

2. In a series, use a question mark after each item if you wish to emphasize each element. If no emphasis is intended, use a comma.

    Right: *Did he plan the riot? Employ assistants? Give the signal to begin?*

    Right: *Did he plan the riot, employ assistants and give the signal to begin?*

3. Do not use a question mark at the end of an indirect question. *He asked who started the riot.*

4. Do not use a question mark in parentheses to express doubt about a word, fact or number, or to indicate humor or irony.

5. Do not use a question mark for an interpolated question. *You told me—Did I hear you correctly—that you started the riot.*

6. In a Q-and-A format, use question marks but no quotation marks and paragraph each speaker's words.

    Q. *Where did you keep it?*
    A. *In a little tin box.*

7. Place a question mark inside quotation marks if it applies to the quoted material, outside if it applies to the whole sentence.

    Who wrote "Gone with the Wind"?
    He asked, "How long will it take?"

quotation marks   Use quotation marks to set off direct quotations, some titles, nicknames and words used in a special sense. Guidelines:

1. Use quotation marks to surround the exact words of a speaker or writer when reported in a story:

    "I have no intention of staying," he replied.

    "I do not object," he said, *"to the tenor of the report."*

    Franklin said, "A penny saved is a penny earned."

    A speculator said the practice is "too conservative."

2. In direct quotations of two or more paragraphs, the quotation marks come before each paragraph and at the end of the last; they do not come at the end of intermediate

paragraphs, unless the quoted matter is an incomplete sentence.

He said, "I am shocked and horrified by the incident.

"I am so horrified, in fact, that I will ask for the death penalty."

But:

He said he was "shocked and horrified by the incident."

"I am so horrified, in fact, that I will ask for the death penalty," he said.

3. In dialogue or conversation, place each person's words, no matter how brief, in a separate paragraph:

"Will you go?"

"Yes."

"When?"

"Thursday."

4. Quotation marks are not required in a question-and-answer format or in full texts or textual excerpts. See **ellipsis** and **question marks.**

5. Use quotation marks for some nicknames and book titles, movie titles, etc.

6. Put quotation marks around words used in a special sense or being introduced to the reader:

The "debate" soon turned into a free-for-all.

Broadcast frequencies are now measured in units called "kilohertz."

Do not use quotation marks around such words after first reference.

7. Do not use quotation marks to emphasize ordinary words. Omit the quotation marks in: *The senator said he would "go home to Michigan" if he lost the election.*

8. When a partial quote is used, do not put quotation marks around words that the speaker could not have used.

Wrong: *The accused man said he "was not in the habit of setting fires."*

What he must have said was: *"I am not in the habit of setting fires."*

9. For quotes within quotes, alternate between double quotation marks *("or")* and single marks *('or'):*

She said, "I quote from the letter, 'I agree with Kipling that "the female of the species is more deadly than the male," but the phenomenon is not an unchangeable law of nature,' a remark he did not explain."

But note the damage such a structure does to comprehension.

Use three marks together if two quoted elements end at the same time: *she said, "He told me, 'I love you.'"*

10. The period and the comma always go within the quotation marks. The dash, the semicolon, the question mark and the exclamation point go within quotation marks when they apply to the quoted matter only. They go outside when they apply to the whole sentence.

quotations in the news Quotations normally should be corrected to avoid the errors that often occur unnoticed when someone is speaking but are embarrassing in print.

Do not routinely use such phonetic spellings as "gonna" in attempts to convey regional dialects or mispronunciations.

Such phonetic spellings are appropriate, however, when the usage, dialect or mispronunciation is relevant to the facts of the story or helps to convey a desired touch in a feature.

Avoid fragmentary quotes. If a speaker's words are clear and concise, favor the full quote. Paraphrase cumbersome language, reserving quotation marks for particularly sensitive or controversial passages that must be identified specifically as coming from the speaker.

Remember that you can misquote someone by giving a startling remark without its modifying passage or qualifiers. The manner of delivery sometimes is part of the context. Reporting a facial expression or gesture may be as important as the words themselves.

R

race Use a racial identification only if it is clearly pertinent, such as:

—In biographical and announcement stories, particularly when they involve a feat or appointment that has not been routinely associated with members of a particular race.

—When it provides the reader with a substantial insight into conflicting emotions known or likely to be involved in a demonstration or similar event.

—When describing a person sought in a manhunt.

In some stories that involve a conflict, it is equally important to specify that an issue cuts across racial lines. If, for example, a demonstration by supporters of busing to achieve racial balance in schools includes a substantial number of whites, that fact should be noted.

religion　　Lowercase *religion* in all uses: *the Christian religion, humanism as a religion, make a religion of fighting.* Other guidelines:

1. Lowercase all titles that merely describe a job: *minister, pontiff, priest, shaman,* etc.

    Capitalize a formal title before a name on first reference, lowercase standing alone or set off by commas: *Bishop John Jones, the bishop; Deacon Susan Smith, the deacon; Pope Paul VI, Pope Paul, the pope; Rabbi David Small, the rabbi.* Drop the title in subsequent references and use *Miss, Mrs.* or *Ms.,* as appropriate, for women. If a title appears in quoted matter with a name: *Rabbi Small.*

    Use *Sister* or *Mother* in all references before the name of a nun. If a nun uses no surname: *Sister Agnes Rita* in all references. If a nun uses a surname: *Sister Clare Regina Torpy* on the first reference, *Sister Torpy* on second. But lowercase *the sister* or *the mother* without a name.

2. Capitalize references to religious orders or their members: *He is a member of the Society of Jesus. He is a Jesuit.*

3. Capitalize proper nouns referring to a monotheistic deity: *God, Allah, Jehovah, the Father, the Son, Jesus Christ, the Holy Spirit,* etc. Lowercase words derived from God and all pronouns referring to the deity: *god-awful, goddaughter, godfather, godless, godlike, godliness, godsend, godson, godspeed, he, him, his, thee, thou, who, whose, thy, thine,* etc.

4. Lowercase *god* in references to a deity of a polytheistic religion, but capitalize names of gods and goddesses: *Aphrodite, Baal, Bacchus, Janus, Venus.*

5. Capitalize alternate names for Mary, the mother of Jesus: *Holy Mother, Virgin Mary.* But: *virgin birth.*

6. Capitalize *Last Supper* and *Lord's Supper,* but lowercase other rites, celebrations, sacraments or services: *baptism, bar mitzvah, confirmation, eucharist, holy communion, liturgy* (divine liturgy), *mass* (high mass, low mass, requiem mass, etc.), *matrimony, penance, vesper service, worship service.*

7. Lowercase *angel, cherub, devil, heaven, hell, satanic,* etc., but capitalize proper names: *Hades, Satan, Gabriel.*

S

school　　Capitalize as part of a proper name: *Public School 2, Madison Elementary School, Doherty Junior High School.*

scores　　Use numerals exclusively, placing a hyphen between the totals of the winning and losing teams: *The Reds defeated the Red Sox 4-3. The Giants scored a 12-6 football victory over the Cardinals. The golfer had a 5 on the first hole but finished with a 2-under-par score.*

Use a comma in this format: *Boston 6, Baltimore 5.* See separate listings for each sport.

secretary-treasurer　　With a hyphen. Capitalize as a formal title before a name: *Secretary-Treasurer John Hancock.*

semi-　　Hyphenate with a capitalized word or to avoid a double *i; semi-American, semi-intoxicated.* Elsewhere, follow Webster's New World, hyphenating words not listed there.

semiannual　　Twice a year; a synonym for biannual. Do not confuse it with biennial, which means every two years.

semicolon (;)   In general, the semicolon is used to indicate a greater separation of thought and information than a comma can convey but less than the separation that a period implies.
Guidelines:

1. Use semicolons to separate elements of a series when the individual segments contain material that must also be set off by commas:

    The nominees for best actor are: Jack Nicholson, "One Flew Over the Cuckoo's Nest"; Walter Matthau, "The Sunshine Boys"; Al Pacino, "Dog Day Afternoon"; Maximillian Schell, "The Man in the Glass Booth"; and James Whitmore, "Give 'Em Hell, Harry!"

2. Use a semicolon when a coordinating conjunction such as *and, but* or *for* is not present: *The package was due last week; it arrived today.*

    If a coordinating conjunction is present, use a semicolon before it only if extensive punctuation is also required in one or more of the individual clauses: *They pulled their boats from the water, sandbagged the retaining walls and boarded up the windows; but even with these precautions, the island was hard-hit by the hurricane.*

3. Semicolons are placed outside quotation marks as illustrated in the example listing Oscar nominees.

senate   Capitalize in references to a specific governmental legislative body: *the U.S. Senate, the Senate; the Virginia Senate, the state Senate; the Senate.*

Lowercase plural uses: *the Virginia and North Carolina senates.*

Lowercase references to non-governmental bodies: *The student senate at Yale.*

sentences   Capitalize the first letter of every sentence, including quoted statements and direct questions:

Patrick Henry said, "I know not what course others may take, but as for me, give me liberty or give me death."

Capitalize the first word of a quoted statement if it constitutes a sentence, even if it was part of a larger sentence in the original: *Patrick Henry said, "Give me liberty or give me death."*

In direct questions, even without quotation marks: *The story answers the question, Where does true happiness really lie?*

skating, figure   Scoring includes both ordinals and points.

Use a basic summary. Examples:

Men
(After 3 compulsory figures)
1, Sergei Volkov, Soviet Union, 19.5 ordinals, 44.76 points. 2, John Curry, Britain, 21.5, 44.96. 3, etc.

Women's Final
1, Dorothy Hamill, Riverside, Conn., 9.0 ordinals, 215 points. 2, Dianne De Leeuw, Netherlands, 20.0, 236. 3, etc.

skating, speed   Scoring is in minutes, seconds and tenths of a second. Extend to hundredths if available. Use the basic summary format.

skiing   Identify events as: *men's downhill, women's slalom*, etc. In ski jumping, note style where two jumps and points are posted:

Use a basic summary. Example:

90-meter special jumping—1, Karl Schnabel, Austria, 320 and 318 feet, 234.8 points. 2, Toni Innauer, Austria, 377-299, 232.9.3, etc. Also: 27, Bob Smith, Hanover, N.J., 312-280, 201. 29, Jim Jones, etc.

sports stories   They are not exempt from normal style rules, unless specifically permitted in this stylebook. See individual entries for each major sport.

squash   Games are won by the first player to score 15 points, unless it is necessary to continue until one player has a two-point spread. Most matches go to the first winner of two games.

Use a match summary. Example:

Bill Davis, Boston University, def. Larry Elders, Bates, 15-8, 8-15, 17-15.

state(s)   Usually lowercase: *New York state, the state of Washington.* Also: *state Rep. William Smith, the state Transportation Department, state funds, state church, state bank, state of mind, state of the art.*

Capitalize as part of a proper name: *the U.S. Department of State, Washington State University.*

Four states—*Kentucky, Massachusetts, Pennsylvania*

and *Virginia*—are legally known as commonwealths rather than states. Make the distinction only in formal uses: *The commonwealth of Kentucky filed a suit.* Elsewhere: *Tobacco is grown in the state of Kentucky.*

Always spell out the names of the 50 U.S. states standing alone.

With the name of a community, some states are abbreviated in stories, datelines or with party affiliation.

Rule of thumb: Spell out *Alaska* and *Hawaii.* Abbreviate any of the 48 contiguous states with six or more letters, spell out those with five or fewer.' The list:

Ala.	Hawaii	Mass.	N.M.	S.D.
Alaska	Idaho	Mich.	N.Y.	Tenn.
Ariz.	Ill.	Minn.	N.C.	Texas
Ark.	Ind.	Miss.	N.D.	Utah
Calif.	Iowa	Mo.	Ohio	Va.
Colo.	Kan.	Mont.	Okla.	Vt.
Conn.	Ky.	Neb.	Ore.	Wash.
Del.	La.	Nev.	Pa.	W. Va.
Fla.	Md.	N.H.	R.I.	Wis.
Ga.	Maine	N.J.	S.C.	Wyo.

sub-   Hyphenate with a capitalized word: *sub-Mycenaean.* Elsewhere, follow Webster's New World, hyphenating words not listed there.

subcommittee   Lowercase with the name of a full committee: *a Ways and Means subcommittee.* Capitalize a proper name of its own: *the Senate Permanent Subcommittee on Investigations.*

suspensive hyphenation   The form: *The 5- and 6-year-olds attend morning classes.*

swimming   Scoring is in minutes, if applicable, seconds and tenths of a second. Extend to hundredths if available.

Events in the United States are normally measured in yards. Olympic contests and other international events are measured in metric units.

Identify as *men's 100-yard freestyle, women's 100-meter backstroke* in first reference. Condense to *men's 100 freestyle, women's 100 backstroke* in second reference.

See **track and field** for the style on relay teams and events where a record is broken.

Use the basic summary format. Example, where qualifying heats are required:

Men's 200-meter Backstroke Heats (fastest eight qualify for final Saturday night): Heat 1—1, John Nabor, USC, 2:03.25. 2, Zoltan Verraszio, Hungary, 2:03.50. 3, etc.

T

team   A collective noun, it always takes a singular verb: *The team of soldiers is playing war games.* If the intent is to refer to individuals, rather than the unit, use a plural subject: *Members of the team are playing,* etc.

For sports teams with plural names, use a plural verb with the name: *The Chicago Bears are playing.*

Singular forms take singular verbs: *The Utah Jazz is playing.* To refer to individuals, rather than the unit, use a plural subject: *Utah Jazz players are tall.*

teen, teen-ager *(n.),* **teen-age** *(adj.)* Do not use teen-aged. *Teenage,* without a hyphen, is a shrub.

temperatures   Use figures for all except zero. In stories, use a word, not a minus sign, to indicate temperatures below zero. Not: *The day's low was − 10.*

Right: *The low was minus 10. The low was 10 below zero. The temperature rose to zero by noon. The high was expected to be 9 or 10.*

Also: *5-degree temperatures, temperatures fell 5 degrees, temperatures in the 30s* (no apostrophe).

The minus sign is acceptable for below-zero temperatures in tabular material.

Temperatures get higher or lower, not warmer or cooler.

Wrong: *Temperatures are expected to warm up in the area Friday.*
Right: *Temperatures are expected to rise in the area Friday.* See **Fahrenheit** and **Celsius.**

To convert Fahrenheit to Celsius subtract 32 degrees and multiply by 5, divide by 9; to convert Celsius to Fahrenheit, multiply by 9, divide by 5 and add 32 degrees.

F	C	F	C	F	C
– 40	– 40.0	34	1.0	86	30.0
– 30	– 34.4	40	4.4	90	32.2
– 20	– 28.9	50	10.0	95	35.0
– 10	– 23.3	60	15.6	98	36.7
0	– 17.8	68	20.0	100	37.8
10	– 12.2	70	21.1	104	40.0
20	– 6.7	75	23.9	110	43.3
30	– 1.1	80	26.7	120	49.0
32	0.0	85	29.4		

titles   Capitalize only formal titles when used before a name. Some specifics:

1. Lowercase and spell out all titles not used with a name: *The president spoke. The pope gave his blessing. The duchess of Windsor smiled.*

2. Lowercase and spell out all titles set off from a name by commas: *The vice president, Nelson Rockefeller, declined to run again. John Paul II, the current pope, does not plan to retire.*

3. Capitalize *Mr., Mrs., Miss, Ms.,* etc., when used.

4. Capitalize formal titles with names: *Pope Paul, President Washington, Vice Presidents John Jones and William Smith.*

5. Lowercase titles that are primarily job descriptions: *astronaut John Glenn, movie star John Wayne, peanut farmer Jimmy Carter.* If in doubt about whether a title is formal or merely a job description, set it off by commas and use lowercase.

6. Capitalize *duke, king, queen, shah,* etc. only when used directly before a name.

7. Set long titles off with a comma and use lowercase: *Charles Robinson, undersecretary for economic affairs.* Or: *the undersecretary for economic affairs, Charles Robinson.*

8. If a title applies to only one person in an organization, insert *the: John Jones, the deputy vice president, spoke.*

track and field   Scoring is in distance or time, depending on the event.

Distance events in the United States are normally in feet and yards. Olympic contests and other international events are measured in metric units.

Do not use colon before times given in seconds and tenths of a second. Use *6.0, 9.4, 10.1,* etc. Extend times to hundredths if available.

For longer distances, such as the mile run, it is *3:36.1* for three minutes, 36.1 seconds.

In running events, the first event should be spelled out as: *60-yard dash.* Others may be *100, 220, mile, 120-hurdles*, etc., except where metric distances are included in a meet otherwise run in yards. Then: *100-meters.*

For field events—those that do not involve running—use these forms: *26-¹⁄₂ for 26 feet, one half inch; 25-10-¹⁄₂ for 25 feet, 10-¹⁄₂ inches.*

In general, use a basic summary. For the style when a record is broken, note the example for the mile event. For the style on listing relay teams, note 1,600-meter relay. Examples:

60-yard dash—1, Steve Williams, Florida TC, 6.0. 2, Hasley Crawford, Philadelphia Pioneer, 6.2. 3, Mike McFarland, Chicago TC, 6.2. 4, etc.

100—1, Steve Williams, Florida TC, 10.1. 2, etc.

Mile—1, Filbert Bayi, Tanzania, 3:35. 1, meet record; old record 3:59, Jim Beatty, Los Angeles TC, Feb. 27, 1963. 2, Paul Cummings, Beverly Hills, TC, 3:36.1. 3, etc.

Women's 880—1, Johanna Forman, Falmouth, T.C., 2:07.9. 2, etc.

1,600-meter relay—1, St. John's, Jon Kennedy, Doug Johnson, Gary Gordon, Ordner Emanuel, 3:21.9. 2, Brown, 3:23.5. 3, Fordham, 3:24.1. 4, etc.

Team scoring—Chicago TC 32, Philadelphia Pioneer 29, etc.

Where qualifying heats are required:

Men's 100-meter heats (first two in each heat qualify for Friday's semifinals) Heat 1—1, Steve Williams, Florida T.C., 10.1. 2, etc.

On major meets where both metric and feet and inches are available, use this form:

Long jump—1, Larry Myricks, Mississippi College, 26-¹⁄₂ (7.94m). 2, Arnie Robinson, Maccabi Union TC, 25-10¹⁄₂ (7.88m). 3, etc.

U

ultra-   Hyphenate with a capitalized word or to avoid a double *a: ultra-English, ultra-ambitious.* Elsewhere, follow Webster's New World, hyphenating words not listed there.

un-   Hyphenate with a capitalized word: *un-American*. Elsewhere, follow *Webster's New World*, hyphenating words not listed there.

V

verbs   The splitting of compound verb forms, including infinitives, is not necessarily an error, but often is awkward.

An infinitive is a verb form containing the word *to: to go*. It is split when something separates the word *to* from its partner: *to quickly go*.

Avoid awkward constructions that would damage the rhythm or meaning of a sentence.

Awkward: *She was ordered to immediately leave on an assignment.*

Better: *She was ordered to leave immediately on an assignment.*

Awkward: *There stood the wagon that we had early last autumn left by the barn.*

Better: *There stood the wagon that we had left by the barn early last autumn.*

The sense often requires that a compound verb be split. Examples:

The budget was tentatively approved.

How has your health been?

He wanted to really help his mother.

vice-   Two words in all uses: *vice admiral, vice chairman, vice chancellor, vice consul, vice president, vice principal, vice regent, vice secretary, a vice presidential candidate.* (Several are exceptions to *Webster's New World*.)

vice president   No hyphen. Capitalize as a formal title before a name: *Vice President Walter Mondale.* Lowercase standing alone or set off by commas: *the vice president, Walter Mondale.* Do not drop the first name when used with the title. Drop the title on second reference. Also: *a vice presidential candidate.*

W

water skiing   Scoring is in points. Use a basic summary example:

World Water Skiing Championships
Men

Overall—1, George Jones, Canada, 1,987.2, Phil Brown, Britain, 1,756.3, etc.

Slalom—1, George Jones, Canada, 73 buoys (two rounds). 2, etc.

weightlifting   Identify events by weight classes. Where both pounds and kilograms are available, use both figures with kilograms in parentheses, as shown in the examples.

Use a basic summary. Example:

Flyweight (114.5 lbs.)—1, Zygmont Smalcerz, Poland, 744 pounds (337.5 kg). 2, Lajos Szuecs, Hungary, 728 (330 kg). 3, etc.

who, whom   Use *who* or *whom*, not *that* or *which*, to refer to humans or to animals with names.

Whom is required in certain idiomatic expressions: *to whom it may concern, for whom the bell tolls.*

Elsewhere, *who* is acceptable in all references: *Who did you vote for? The man who came to dinner. He asked who I thought would be elected. Who shall I say is calling?*

Whom is also acceptable as the object of a verb or preposition, and many writers prefer to use it. But it may be awkward and often should be recast.

Awkward: *The boy to whom I threw the ball cast it to the ground.*

Better: *I threw the ball to the boy but he cast it to the ground.*

-wise   Use no hyphen if you mean *in the manner of* or *with regard to: clockwise, lengthwise, otherwise, slantwise.* Use no hyphen also in words coined and used for a single or particular occasion: *moneywise, religionwise,* etc. Such contrived words are usually best avoided.

Use a hyphen if you mean skilled, smart or prudent: *penny-wise, street-wise.*

For example, *weatherwise,* no hyphen, means in regard to the weather: *Weatherwise, it may rain. Weather-wise,* hyphenated, means skilled in predicting weather: *She is a weather-wise young woman.*

women   Women should receive the same treatment as men in all areas of coverage. Physical descriptions, sexist references, demeaning stereotypes and condescending phrases should not be used.

To cite some examples, this means that:

—Copy should not assume maleness when both sexes are involved, as in: *Jackson told newsmen . . .* or in *the taxpayer . . . he* when it can easily be said *taxpayers . . . they,* etc.

—Copy should not express surprise that an attractive woman can also be professionally accomplished, as in: *Mary Smith doesn't look the part but she's an authority on . . .*

—Copy should not gratuitously mention family relationships when there is no relevance to the subject, as in: *Golda Meir, a doughty grandmother, told the Egyptians today . . .*

—Use the same standards for men as for women in deciding whether to include specific mention of personal appearance or marital and family situation.

In other words, treatment of the sexes should be evenhanded and free of assumptions and stereotypes. This does not mean that valid and acceptable words such as *mankind* or *humanity* cannot be used. They are appropriate if they fit the occasion.

INDEX